3/55

BYZANTINE STUDIES
AND OTHER ESSAYS

Byzantine Studies and Other Essays

By Norman H. Baynes

Hon. D.D. (St. Andrews); Hon. D.Litt.
(Oxford and Durham); Hon. Litt.D.
(Cambridge); Hon. D.Lit. (London)
Fellow of the British Academy

UNIVERSITY OF LONDON
THE ATHLONE PRESS
1955

Published by
THE ATHLONE PRESS
at the Senate House, London W.C.I

Distributed by Constable & Co. Ltd.
12 Orange Street, London W.C.2

U.S.A.
John de Graff Inc.
64 West 23rd Street
New York 10

Printed in Great Britain by
ROBERT MACLEHOSE & CO. LTD
THE UNIVERSITY PRESS
Glasgow W.3

Preface

THE purpose of this book is to make more readily available some of those lectures and articles of Professor Baynes which are of more general interest to students of the ancient and medieval world. The task of selection was difficult and imposed the sacrifice of papers that were either too long or too specialised for the scope of the volume which we had in mind.[1] We are sorry to leave out 'The Military Operations of the Emperor Heraclius' (*The United Services Magazine*, xlvi and xlvii, 1913)—which was one of the first of Professor Baynes' notable contributions to Byzantine studies —and 'Constantine the Great and the Christian Church' (*Proceedings of the British Academy*, xv, 1929). We hope that it will be possible to republish these two papers in another volume.

The papers here reprinted have been selected with the help of Professor Baynes himself, and it is with his consent, also, that three unpublished papers are included. He had hoped to revise them all. Prolonged illness has made this task impossible. But the notes enclosed in square brackets call attention to such modifications as he has made in the text or represent the incorporation of fresh material. These notes, therefore, with one exception, are those of the author, not of the editors.

For nearly 30 years Professor Baynes was associated with the teaching staff of University College, London. His learning, breadth of vision, sense of duty and kindness made him a true custodian of the traditions of the College. We feel that this book would not be complete without his address 'The Custody of a Tradition' delivered to the University College Union on March 13th, 1942, when the College was in war-time residence at Bangor. We like to think that reprinted here it will make a particular appeal to present and future students of our College.

[1] A bibliography of Professor Baynes' writings (1904-1942) by Professor Hussey is contained in *An Address presented to Norman Hepburn Baynes*, printed privately at the University Press, Oxford, 1942. It was reprinted and supplemented in *The Journal of Roman Studies*, xxxvii (1947), p. 7.

It remains for us to thank all those who have helped us to see the book through the Press. The Principal of Brasenose, Dr H. M. Last, gave us encouragement and advice from the beginning and found the time to read a set of proofs. Another of Professor Baynes' friends, Mr H. St. L. B. Moss, consented to prepare the Index. We also received much help in proof-reading from Professor Joan Hussey, Miss M. S. Drower, Mr R. Browning and Dr J. Morris. Finally we are greatly indebted to the personal interest in this book shown by the secretary to the Athlone Press, Mr W. D. Hogarth.

Department of History,   R. A. HUMPHREYS
University College, London   A. D. MOMIGLIANO
July 1954

ACKNOWLEDGMENTS

For permission to include in this volume material which has previously appeared elsewhere grateful acknowledgments are made to the Society of Antiquaries, the Société des Bolland-istes, the Egypt Exploration Society, the Historical Association, the Institut de Philologie et d'Histoire Orientales, the Pontificio Istituto Orientale, the Society for the Promotion of Roman Studies; to the Council of Westfield College, University of London; to the Editors of the *Classical Quarterly*, and of the *Harvard Theological Review*; and to Messrs. Longmans Green & Co., and the Oxford University Press. Full particulars of the original place and date of publication are given in the head-notes to the several lectures, articles and reviews.

Contents

LECTURES

ARTICLES

I

The Hellenistic Civilization
and East Rome

[The James Bryce Memorial Lecture delivered at Somerville College, Oxford, on 17 November 1945. Oxford University Press, 1946.]

BEFORE we can have any adequate account of modern historiography we shall need monographic studies of outstanding historians, of their literary methods and characteristics. And it may be found that the most fruitful starting-point for such inquiries will be works which have been reconsidered, revised, and published in successive editions by their authors. For Lord Bryce it would thus be natural to take as starting-point that remarkable Arnold Essay 'The Holy Roman Empire'. There can be but few Oxford Prize Essays which have become historical classics. Over a period of precisely forty years Bryce sought to improve and refashion his first book. The Essay was presented to the examiners in 1863: in 1864 Shrimpton in Oxford issued the *editio princeps* in such an uninviting form that it seems to anticipate the worst excesses of war-time economy in printing. In this edition, however, the original essay was so greatly changed and enlarged that Freeman said of it: 'Mr Bryce's book has been written since it gained the historical prize at Oxford.' And still, if you would convince yourself of the calibre of Bryce's mind, turn to that edition of 1864 and re-read his treatment of the Empire as an International Power. Why did men preserve this Holy Roman Empire when its force was spent, when it had become the shadow of itself? Because, Bryce replies, it was felt that the Empire was the only institution which could control the emergent national states: the Imperator Pacificus was the sole sovran power which could make and maintain peace in a world of conflicting rivalries. That chapter might easily have been written to-day after the experience of our time, but written by a young man, still in his twenties, in 1864 it is surely a triumph of insight and sympathetic understanding. There followed the editions of 1866, 1871, 1873, 1875, 1887, and 1904. In the final edition of 1904 the text was revised with scrupulous care, and now not only did he add three maps, a Chronological Table of Important Events in the History of the Empire which ran to twenty-eight pages, a new Epilogue, and twenty-four long Additional Notes, but having read the works of Krumbacher, Gelzer, and Bury, as he tells us, he felt that for his book to be complete there must be inserted a chapter on the East Roman Empire. For a student of Byzantine history it is pleasant to think that Bryce thus widened his horizon to include in his survey that other Holy Roman Empire of the East which had its capital in the city of Constantine. My remarks this afternoon are conceived simply as a marginal note on the seventeenth chapter of this last edition of Bryce's classic book.

It is unfortunate that the Greeks thought that they were justified in allowing the Hellenistic age to fall into oblivion. In their eyes it was a regrettable interlude in Greek history: they took no pains to preserve its literature and resolutely returned to the masterpieces of the Great Age. And thus it is that the three centuries after the death of Alexander, so far as the East Mediterranean lands are concerned, however much intensive study modern scholars may give to them, will always remain an obscure period beset with doubts and problems while the works which might have given to us the thought of the age are represented only by such fragments as those collected by Stobaeus in his *Florilegium*. The loss of the literature of the Hellenistic Age we can never cease to deplore, for it leaves a gap in the story of the intellectual development of the Greek world which cannot be filled by arguing back from the better-known history of the Principate. Man cannot be trusted to estimate the significance of his own past achievement: he must at least seek to preserve the record for the judgement of posterity. The British Museum Library, the Bodleian Library, they are our tribute of *pietas* to the departed.

As I see it, the Byzantines are the intellectual heirs of the Hellenistic Age: that age acquired the habit of looking backwards to a past which in retrospect became only the more wonderful. So the Byzantines, their gaze fixed on the distant glories of the classical period, had no eyes for the more recent past: they ignored the nearer landscape and thus let the original works produced during the Hellenistic period sink into oblivion while they appropriated—made intimately their own —the Hellenistic outlook. That outlook determines the essential character of the thought-world of East Rome. For here, I would suggest, is a surprising continuity: this Hellenistic civilization as it arose in the Near Eastern lands during the centuries which followed the death of Alexander the Great remained unaltered after the Roman conquest of the Greek kingdoms: it determined the character of civilization in the Eastern Mediterranean under the early Caesars of Rome and it played the same historic role under the Christian emperors ruling from Constantinople.[1] And the paradoxical fact about this influence is that, though it persists with unabated vigour, it remains so much the same, it suffers so little development or essential alteration in the course of the centuries. One might expect in an influence which underwent so little development a slow but sure decline: instead of that, while continuing so largely unchanged, it yet obviously possesses an inherent energy which can ever and again reassert its power with a new intensity. Never perhaps in the history of a culture has so static and traditional a past exercised so masterful a supremacy over the minds of men.

To characterize the thought-world with which in the Near East the Roman of the Republican period came in contact is, I would repeat, a matter of great difficulty. One can *feel* the gulf which divides the Greece of the fifth century from the Greece of the third, but one can hardly hope to trace the process by which that gulf was formed. Would you agree with me that in the Athens of Pericles man is securely entrenched in *this* world? The city-state supplies his needs: he feels himself at home and can afford to be on terms of easy intimacy even with his Gods: it is to Athena—who is precisely the personification

[1] On the Hellenistic Age see: J. B. Bury, E. A. Barber, Edwyn Bevan, and W. W. Tarn, *The Hellenistic Age: Aspects of Hellenistic Civilization* (Cambridge University Press, 1923); Julius Kaerst, *Geschichte des Hellenismus*, 2nd edn., vol. ii, *Das Wesen des Hellenismus* (Teubner, Leipzig, 1926); M. Rostovtzeff, *The Social and Economic History of the Hellenistic World*, vol. ii, *Summary and Epilogue*, pp. 1026 sqq. (Clarendon Press, Oxford, 1941).

of the city which bears her name—that his loyalty is pledged. In an early novel by Benjamin Swift the Roman Catholic remarked that Protestantism was too coldly logical: it seemed to walk round its God in complete comprehension. Do you not feel that in large measure that is true of the Athenian of the fifth century? He was 'at home in the body' (2 Cor. v. 6).

And in the fourth century that proud confidence in the democracy of the city-state is clouded over with doubt: it gives place to the disillusionment of Plato. The appeals of Demosthenes to the spirit which, he was assured, had inspired the age of Pericles fail to awaken any enduring response. In the West the tyrant Dionysius of Syracuse is a portent: he is the pioneer who points the way to the new monarchy which in Greece will reach its full development in Philip of Macedonia and in Alexander the Great. And before the might of the territorial kingdoms of the Hellenistic Age the city-state is a very little thing. The animosities of faction strife may live on, but political questions are of less significance under the autocracy of the Hellenistic monarchies. The city-state is overshadowed: it no longer inspires the conviction that it can satisfy the needs of its citizens: the gods of the city-state pale before those human Saviours and Benefactors, the rulers of the Greek kingdoms, who can undoubtedly rescue and help their friends. But suppose that you have incurred the autocrat's displeasure, what then? In a world of unleashed egoism, where that egoism has at its service the overwhelming force of the new scientifically organized armies, what can your city-state avail you?—even Tyre fell at last to Alexander the Great—your city fortifications sink out of your thought: the individual cowers defenceless before the rivalries of these Hellenistic *Gewaltmenschen*: no comfortable embrace of his city's walls surrounds him: nothing stands between him and the utmost limits of the inhabited world: he is face to face with the οἰκουμένη: and thus the two poles of Hellenistic thinking are the individual—and the universe: it is now, as Bury used to say, that the oecumenical idea is born. Man is alone in the cosmos—alone and afraid.[2]

It is thus the concern for the individual and the individual's

[2] Cf. Edwyn Bevan, *Stoics and Sceptics* (Clarendon Press, Oxford, 1913), ch. i.

problems which determines one of those queer shifts of human interest which are for the historical student of such primary significance and are yet so baffling. One is at times tempted to say that the more significant a movement is the less adequately can we as students of history explain it. Alexander the Great had been accompanied on his campaigns by scientists, and their researches in the new lands which Alexander's conquests had opened up to the Greek gave to others that wealth of comparative material which Aristotle had lacked. In Alexandria, the city which under the Ptolemies made full use of this scientific capital, new sciences were born, comparative botany (ecology) and climatology, for example. But the vigorous pursuit of natural science which marked the third century did not maintain itself in the second. It was on life's casuistry—on the moral problems of the individual in a dangerous world— that attention was concentrated: Metaphysics gives place to Ethics.

Thus in the centre of the picture stands the individual: defenceless, alone, and afraid. At the same time scepticism is triumphant and doubt challenges all accepted views. With the ground of certainty giving way beneath his feet, faced with forces which he cannot control, man seeks security. That search is answered by Stoicism: amidst the quicksands of doubt and questioning Zeno taught that some conceptions and ideas have so immediate, so gripping a sense of their inherent truth that man can trust them—there is *some* firm standing ground—and further there is in man something which nothing external can touch—his own inmost self: the fortress of Mansoul can despite everything remain inviolate—its peace serene, untroubled. Stoicism, as Dr Bevan has pointed out, is essentially an answer to a great doubt and a great fear: Stoic scientific discussion is intended only to justify and support this assurance: here lies the heart of its message to the men of this Hellenistic world.[3] Only it was not easy always in the midst of trials—the trials of others as well as your own—to maintain this untroubled calm: the Stoic could not admit sympathy with the sufferer, for *sumpathein* would of necessity introduce

[3] This has been well stated by Bevan in *Stoics and Sceptics* (see n. 2), pp. 13–76.

disturbance into the soul of the sympathizer.[4] It is an austere
demand which the Stoic teacher makes upon you if you would
gain his peace. There is in Stoicism no place for Gethsemane,
no room for vicarious suffering. And thus it is that others
sought the answer to their need in the mystery cults: of these
much has been written, though very little is really known. But
here at least man was brought into direct contact with the
divine and received a personal and individual blessing—as, for
instance, the promise of survival after death. Here was something more intimate than were the remote deities of an out-
worn mythology, here was a salvation of a kind which the
Olympians were powerless to give to their worshippers. But
whichever way it was—through a philosophy which to many
must have come with the force of an answer to prayer or
through the mystery cults—men were no longer content with
the religion of the city-state: they were seeking a response to
a question which the city-gods had never considered; δεισιδαιμονία, the need for divine help, the petition for salvation,
these must have been in large measure the mark of the age:
St Paul at Athens could say: 'I see that in all things you are
extremely religious'—ὡς δεισιδαιμονεστέρους ὑμᾶς θεωρῶ (Acts
xvii. 22). 'The God to whom you in your ignorance are appealing, Him declare I unto you.' The Byzantine world is filled
with the spirit of δεισιδαιμονία—religion, superstition, translate
the word how you will.

And part of man's daily, hourly fear is the demon world
which besets him on every side.[5] Whence came these myriad

[4] 'Pity in the sense of a painful emotion caused by the sight of other men's
sufferings is actually a vice. The most that can be allowed when the Wise Man
goes to console a mourner is that he should feign sympathy as a means of attaining his object, but he must take care not to feel it. He may sigh, Epictetus says,
provided the sigh does not come from his heart. In the service of his fellow men
he must be prepared to sacrifice his health, to sacrifice his possessions, to sacrifice his life; but there is one thing he must never sacrifice, his own eternal calm.'
Bevan, op. cit., p. 67. But on this cf. Gilbert Murray, *The Stoic Philosophy*
(Conway Memorial Lecture; Watts, London, 1915), pp. 44–7.

[5] There is still room for further study of demon possession, cf. Julius Tam-
borino, *De antiquorum daemonismo* [= *Religionsgeschichtliche Versuche und
Vorarbeiten*, vol. vii, part 3] (Töpelmann, Giessen, 1909); F. J. Dölger, *Der
Exorzismus im altchristlichen Taufritual* [= *Studien zur Geschichte und Kultur
des Altertums*, edd. E. Drerup, H. Grimme, and J. P. Kirsch, vol. iii, parts 1–2]
(Schöningh, Paderborn, 1909); G. G. Dawson, *Healing, Pagan and Christian*
(S.P.C.K., 1935); T. K. Oesterreich, *Possession demoniacal and other* (Kegan
Paul, London, 1930).

foes of man? Are they invaders of Greece from Iran, a legacy
of the Persian world which Alexander had planned to take into
partnership?—or were they always there in the Greek countryside, banished only from the city-state where rationalism had
rendered men immune from supernatural terrors—are they
the Keres which in the earliest days of Greece filled land and
sea[6]—have they merely changed their name? When you once
begin to ask awkward questions like that you realize afresh
how little we know of the history of the ordinary folk of classical Greece. Time has preserved the thoughts of the master
minds: do you not as you follow panting in the wake of that
thought sigh at times for something less mountainous—a little
more of thought's foot-hills? Xenophon's essays are just so
attractive because one can go for a hare-hunt and never leave
the foot-hills. But whether these unseen powers were always
denizens of the Greek country-side or were later Iranian
invaders, the Hellenistic world is a demonic hunting-ground
—and they are even more terrifying than the bacilli of our
modern world, for they are inspired by a maleficent will
and that will is directed against man. Hence amulets, charms,
adjurations, magic—of all this the Hellenistic world is full.
You remember that conversation when Gilbert Murray and
J. B. Bury were discussing the change that took place between
say, Plato and the Neo-Platonists: Gilbert Murray had been
calling it a rise of asceticism, or mysticism, or religious passion.
'It is not a rise,' said Bury, 'it is . . . a sort of failure of nerve.'[7]
Is that, do you think, an adequate description of the transformation of the thought-world of the Greek? Or is it not in
the last analysis something more positive—is it not that man
has set his confidence elsewhere? At least this world is not
enough: man is no longer 'at home in the body'.

And it is to this demon-haunted world that Christianity
came as a great liberation. You remember that excited scene
when the seventy returned to their Master: Lord, Lord, they
said in their joy—καὶ τὰ δαιμόνια ὑποτάσσεται ἡμῖν ἐν τῷ ὀνόματί
σου (Luke x. 17). 'Even the demons are subject to us in thy

[6] The 'Kēres of death' in *Iliad*, XII. 326-7, are μυρίαι—ten thousand of
them.
[7] For the 'failure of nerve': Gilbert Murray, *Five Stages of Greek Religion*
(Watts, London, 1935), pp. 123 sqq.; and for the origin of the phrase, ibid., p. xiii.

name!' The atmosphere of the Hellenistic Age will continue to be the atmosphere of the Byzantine world, but that world has added to the Hellenistic pharmacopoeia the most powerful wonder-working charm—the Sign of the Cross. Armed with this the East Roman can venture to face those principalities and powers, those cosmic rulers of this dark world with whom the Christian's wrestling-bout is waged (Ephesians vi. 12). Here too, I would repeat, is continuity.

I have spoken of the monarchy which became the universal form of government in the states built on the ruins of the single empire of Alexander. Ptolemies in Egypt, Seleucids in Asia, Antigonids in the Macedonian homeland—kings everywhere. Greek thinkers of the classical period had taken the city-state as the necessary basis of their political philosophy: now they were faced with monarchy as a *fait accompli* and, as always, the Greek must endeavour λόγον διδόναι, to rationalize pheno-mena, he seeks to explain and justify accomplished fact: he gives to monarchy a more philosophic foundation than that of military supremacy. The duty of the king is to imitate, to copy God: the well-ordered kingdom is a μίμησις, a copy of the order of the universe—the cosmos: the Logos which is the immanent principle of order which pervades the cosmos is the counsellor of the true king. The king is thus the agent of the supreme power whose is the government of the universe. That theory, formulated by the pagan philosophers of the Hellenistic Age, will be ready to the hand of Eusebius when he for the first time sets forth the theory of the Christian Empire: the very wording of the pagan ideal can be taken over in the Christian restatement.[8] Here, too, is continuity.

In this Hellenistic world so many sundering barriers fell: it is a period of widespread intercommunication. And to the uni-versalism of the lands round the Mediterranean Sea both Greece and Rome made their own characteristic contribution. Alexander the Great had with difficulty held together a single empire, but the single empire did not outlive its founder, and the Greek kingdoms which emerged from the rivalries of Alex-

---

[8] Cf. 'Eusebius and the Christian Empire', *Annuaire de l'institut de philologie et d'histoire orientales*, Université Libre de Bruxelles, ii (1934), pp. 13–18 [= *Mélanges Bidez*]. See pp. 168–72 *infra*.

ander's successors wore down their strength in continuous hostilities and thus opened the way for the intervention of Rome.
The ceaseless strife of Seleucid, Lagid, and Antigonid had kept
the Near East in turmoil: it was left to Rome to restore the
single empire which had been buried with Alexander the Great.
And within the immense majesty of the Roman peace the
Roman roads bound city to city and province to province,
linking the Roman world in a common life of intercourse. Such
is Rome's contribution to Mediterranean universalism: a single
empire and those material highways which were the symbol of
a realm at peace. And the contribution of the Greek to that
Mediterranean universalism is equally characteristic: frequency
of intercourse creates the common Greek dialect in which
much-travelled folk can readily make themselves understood.
The κοινή spreads from East to West: the Western Mediterranean becomes a bilingual world. Paul writes to the Romans
in Greek; until early in the third century the language of the
Christian liturgy in the Church of Rome was Greek. And in
Hellenistic Alexandria it was into this Greek κοινή that the
Hebrew scriptures were translated: that translation was ready
for the Christian missionary when he began to carry his Good
News through the world which Rome had unified. In the syna-
gogues which had sprung up during this Hellenistic Age
throughout the cities of the Greek East this translation was
read and studied. Without the Septuagint and the synagogue
what would the early Church have done?—how would Paul
have accomplished his missionary work? It was this translation of the Old Testament that Byzantium received, along with
that New Testament which was from the first written in the
κοινή of the Hellenistic world. This conquest of Rome, and the
consequent unification of the Mediterranean world, this creation of a common speech for this unified world: they are both
part of the Praeparatio Evangelica—the making of the high-
way for the victorious advance of the Christian faith. Of the
conquest of all the nations who were under the rule of Augustus
Eusebius writes (*Dem. Evang.* iii. 7, 140): 'And no one could
deny that the synchronizing of this with the beginning of the
teaching about our Saviour is of God's arrangement if he considered the difficulty of the disciples taking their journey, had

B

the nations been at variance one with another and not mixing together because of varieties of government. But when these were abolished they could accomplish their projects quite fearlessly and safely, since the Supreme God had smoothed the way before them.' On the text, 'And he shall speak peace to the Gentiles,' Eusebius comments: 'This stands specially and literally fulfilled from the reign of Augustus, since from that date varieties of government ceased and peace enwrapped most of the nations of the world' (ibid. viii. 4, 410).

But there is a debit as well as a credit side to that account which was the legacy of the Hellenistic Age to the Byzantine world, and that too has its significance. When the interest of the scholars of Alexandria in natural science declined towards the close of the third century they turned to the texts of the Greek classics: they sought by the study of manuscripts to restore to their original form the masterpieces of the Great Age. In editions and commentaries they paid their tribute of respect to the past. And these masterpieces were now recognized as standing beyond rivalry, unsurpassed and unapproachable. At the most they may be imitated. Real originality in Hellenistic literature is limited to a narrow field: to the love romance, to the pastoral poem, and, one ought perhaps to add, to historical biography.[9] The love romance is the natural product of a sophisticated age enjoying a story of peril and adventure—a 'thriller' where the scene is set in strange lands among unfamiliar peoples—while the pastoral poem is proverbially the outcome of city life. The real countryman does not picture Watteau shepherdesses when he writes of the life on the farm.

[9] Hellenistic biography has been so completely lost that there has been much disagreement concerning its character and there has also been much discussion concerning the relation of Plutarch's 'Lives' to his Hellenistic sources. 'The origin of Plutarch's biographical method as a literary form is a riddle, and a riddle it will remain until we gain some fundamentally new knowledge of the historiographical and biographical literature of the early Hellenistic period'— so Adolf Weizsäcker, *Untersuchungen über Plutarchs biographische Technik* [= *Problemata*, edd. P. Friedländer, G. Jachmann, and F. Jacoby, part 2] (Weidmann, Berlin, 1931), p. 82. See F. Leo, *Die griechisch-römische Biographie nach ihrer literarischen Form* (Teubner, Leipzig, 1901); Uxkull Gyllenband, *Plutarch und die griechische Biographie* (Stuttgart, 1927) (at the moment this work is for me inaccessible). The views of Leo and Gyllenband are fully discussed in Nicolaie I. Barbu, *Les Procédés de la peinture des caractères et la vérité historique dans les biographies de Plutarque*, (Nizet and Bastard, Paris, 1934); see in particular the Introduction and ch. 1 on 'L'Historiographie et la biographie politique à l'époque alexandrine', pp. 1–35, and cf. pp. 235–42.

Hesiod knew better than that as he wrestled with Nature on his exasperating land in Askra: his father came to mainland Greece fleeing from evil penury and 'he made his dwelling near Helikon in a sorry township, even Askra, bad in winter, hard in summer, never good'. It is an austere education that man is given in the school of Nature: the idealization of Nature is the townsman's picture.

And those editors and commentators of Alexandria in the Hellenistic Age are already beginning to experience the danger of possessing a too great literature: such a literature is a daunting thing: it may lamentably depress the reader with a sense of his own inferiority. It may stifle initiative and put to silence the poet. The Byzantine, like the folk of Alexandria, is overweighted by his literary inheritance. Blessed is the country which is not haunted by the splendours of its own past!

But perhaps the most fatal legacy which the Greek kingdoms left to the Roman Empire was an education which was based upon the study of rhetoric. It is true that rhetoric may reasonably claim a legitimate place for itself: it is indeed piteous that in general we modern folk in England make so poor an exhibition when we are called upon to speak in public. But it is another matter when *what* you say becomes far less important than *how* you say it. And verbal elaboration is a slippery plane, and when you are once launched on the perilous slope there is little chance that you will be able to cry a halt. Rhetorical euphuism is an infectious disease, and very certainly the pagan infected the Christian with the horrid virus. The excesses of the Christian are hardly less incredible than those of the pagan. Here indeed the continuity of Byzantine practice with that of the Hellenistic Age is as undoubted as it is regrettable.

We can never know fully how much this Hellenistic civilization accomplished, but in any attempt to estimate its achievement its failures must not be ignored: for those failures had a great influence upon the later history of the Near East. The Greek had been moulded by his own creation, the city-state, and it was by means of the city-state that he sought to hellenize the non-Greek East. But the land beyond the Asiatic coast-line belonged essentially, as Dr Tarn has recently pointed out, to those who worked the land: 'Conquerors might come and go over their heads, but at the end the children of the soil remained. To make a really permanent settlement the Greeks would have had to go on the land, as did the Angles and Saxons in Britain; that they never did.' 'Considered broadly, what the Asiatic took from the Greek was usually externals only, matters of form; he rarely took substance . . . and never spirit.'[10] There is always that limitation to be remembered in any consideration of Hellenistic culture: Antioch in Syria may have been later the capital of the Greco-Roman East and essentially a Greek city: but beyond its walls, even in the time of Chrysostom, folk used a Semitic language, and Greek civilization, sea-borne, tended always to hug the coast and not to attempt the difficult task of hellenizing the hinterland. That was indeed one of the outstanding differences between the Greek and the Roman, for the influence of Rome was carried inland along the Roman roads and thus Latin spread through the country-side. In Anatolia after a millenium of Greek occupation of the coast-line it would seem that it was the Christian missionary in the fifth and sixth centuries of our era who carried the Greek language victoriously into the interior and caused the native tongues to give way before this late wave of Christian Hellenism.[11] Thus the range of the intensive influence of Hellenistic civilization was often very narrowly restricted, and Greek cities in Syria, and elsewhere in Asia, must have stood as islands surrounded by a Semitic sea. When this Near Eastern world is ruled by Greeks from a Greek city—Constantinople—the population of the country-side, grown conscious of its 'otherness', will present to the emperors of East Rome an insoluble problem.

When Rome had come as conqueror to this Hellenistic East she was true to her traditional method of *laissez-faire*; she had come into a Greek-speaking land of Greek city-states and she was content to leave both the Greek language and the Greek city-states: she did not seek to Latinize and Romanize the Near East. Thus, though the Greek kingdoms had fallen, Greek

[10] W. W. Tarn, *The Greeks in Bactria and India* (Cambridge University Press, 1938), p. 67.

[11] See Karl Holl, 'Das Fortleben der Volkssprachen in Kleinasien in nachchristlicher Zeit', Hermes, xliii (1908), 240–54; reprinted in *Gesammelte Aufsatze zur Kirchengeschichte*, vol. ii (Mohr, Tübingen, 1928), pp. 238–48.

thought was free to develop naturally. And the last original creation of Greek pagan thought was Neo-Platonism, a philosophy which to many was essentially a religion. The third century of our era is the period which is marked in the realm of culture by two movements of outstanding significance: one is the appropriation of the best of pagan thought by Clement and Origen as teachers in the Christian school of Alexandria: the other is the growing consciousness amongst pagan thinkers of the danger of Christianity; this resulted in the serious study by pagans of the Christian scriptures and a ruthless attack upon the rival faith. Neo-Platonism, as Augustine learned later, had so much in common with Christianity that the conflict was bound to be embittered. It is this double movement of attraction and repulsion which distinguishes the development of Greek thought in the third century of our era: the attraction of the Christian thinkers for Greek philosophy: even after Origen's death it was impossible to escape from Origen's influence; the repulsion from Christianity of the pagans—a repulsion which is perhaps implicit in Plotinus,[12] but receives

[12] The attitude of Plotinus towards Christianity has been much discussed; he wrote against the tenets of the 'Gnostics', and in this attack upon the Gnostics Carl Schmidt thought that one could discern an attack upon Christianity. Carl Schmidt, *Plotins Stellung zum Gnosticismus und kirchlichen Christentum* [= *Texte und Untersuchungen zur Geschichte der altchristlichen Literatur*, edd. Oscar von Gebhardt and Adolf von Harnack N.F. 5, part 4], (Hinrichs, Leipzig, 1901), pp. 82 sqq. 'Plotinus inaugurated the literary attack of the Neoplatonists against Christianity', ibid., p. 84. Similarly, Wundt argued that Plotinus shared the concern of Celsus: Christians were withdrawing from political life and refusing to serve in the Roman army. Thus the desire of Plotinus to support Gallienus in his attempt to effect a moral reformation in the Empire led him to lay stress upon the qualities of a good soldier: Max Wundt, *Plotin: Studien zur Geschichte des Neuplatonismus*, part 1 (Kröner, Leipzig, 1919), at pp. 54–5; while Enneads 3, 2, 8–9 (Volkmann's edition, Leipzig, 1883, vol. i, pp. 236–8) are, Wundt thinks, levelled against the Christians, especially the passage κακοὺς δὲ γενομένους ἀξιοῦν ἄλλους αὐτῶν σωτῆρας εἶναι ἑαυτοὺς προεμένους οὐ θεμιτὸν εὐχὴν ποιουμένων. οὐ τοίνυν οὐδὲ θεοὺς αὐτῶν ἄρχειν τὰ καθέκαστα ἀφέντας τὸν ἑαυτῶν βίον. In McKenna's translation: 'But the law does not warrant the wicked in expecting that their prayers should bring others to sacrifice themselves for their sakes [this rendering hardly does justice to σωτῆρας εἶναι—"to be their saviours"], or that the gods should lay aside the divine life in order to direct their daily concerns' (cf. the sentence in 3, 2, 8, 'Not even a god would have the right to deal a blow for the unwarlike; the law decrees that to come safe out of battle is for fighting men, not for those that pray' (Stephen McKenna, *Plotinus*, vol. ii (Lee Warner, London, 1921), pp. 22–3). Heinemann considered that in the third period of Plotinus' thought his insistence on the natural goodness of the soul is directed against the Christian view that man is born in sin and is by nature evil: Fritz Heinemann, *Plotin, Forschungen über die plotinische Frage, Plotins Entwicklung und sein System* (Meiner, Leipzig,

full and avowed expression in Porphyry's work *Against the Christians*.[13] That work is preserved for us only in fragments which do not enable us to form any adequate conception of the whole, but it was doubtless the arsenal from which other critics of Christianity, such as Julian the Apostate, drew their most effective arguments.

Thus the battle between the pagan and the Christian apologist was engaged: but this conflict had a result to which sufficient attention has not always been paid. Porphyry was no

1921), pp. 234–6. Alföldi, it would appear, adopts in general the standpoint of Wundt and Heinemann: Gallienus in staying the persecution of the Christians did not mean to end the struggle against Christianity, but only to change the tactics. Plotinus, supporting Gallienus, in his writings against the Gnostics was not merely attacking a sect, but in his defence of 'the religion of the fathers' was attacking 'the whole Christian-Gnostic movement'. The project for the foundation of Platonopolis had as its aim 'the formation of an organization which would conduct the fight against the spread of the Christian sects': Andreas Alföldi, *Die Vorherrschaft der Pannonier im Römerreiche und die Reaktion des Hellenentums* in *Fünfundzwanzig Jahre Römisch-Germanische Kommission*, Archäologisches Institut des Deutschen Reiches (De Gruyter, Berlin and Leipzig, 1930), pp. 11–51, at pp. 22 sqq. These conclusions may be plausible, but are they anything more than that? If Plotinus' attack was in fact directed against orthodox Christianity what was there to prevent him from saying so openly? And surely his attack upon the 'Gnostics' is concerned with specific Gnostic tenets and not with 'the whole Christian-Gnostic movement' or with the distinctive beliefs of the orthodox Christian church. Indeed Geffcken's considered judgement was that the 'Gnostics' attacked by Plotinus belonged to a pagan movement allied to Hermetism; Johannes Geffcken, *Der Ausgang des griechisch-römischen Heidentums* (Winter, Heidelberg, 1920), pp. 43–4, 55, 265, and especially *Nachträge*, ibid., 1929, p. 354. And Reitzenstein was of the same opinion: R. Reitzenstein, *Poimandres* (Teubner, Leipzig, 1904), p. 307. Cf., further, J. Cochez, *La réligion de l'empire dans la philosophie de Plotin*, in *Mélanges d'histoire offerts à Charles Moeller* [= *Recueil de travaux publiés par les membres des conférences d'histoire et de philologie*, Université de Louvain, Fasc. 40] (Louvain, 1914), i, 85–101, especially n. 4, p. 86, for a criticism of Carl Schmidt. For Plotinus cf. J. Bidez, in *Cambridge Ancient History*, vol. xii (1939), pp. 629–35.

[13] For a collection of the fragments of Porphyry's work against the Christians see Adolf von Harnack, *Porphyrius 'Gegen die Christen', 15 Bücher. Zeugnisse, Fragmente und Referate*. Abhandlungen d. königl. preuss. Akademie der Wissenschaften, Jahrgang 1916, phil.-hist. Klasse, No. 1 (Berlin, 1916), and the supplement to this, *Neue Fragmente des Werks des Porphyrius gegen die Christen*, Sitzungsberichte of the Academy, 1921, no. 14. On Porphyry see J. Bidez, *Vie de Porphyre* [= *Recueil de travaux publiés par la faculté de philosophie et lettres* Université de Gand, Fasc. 43] (Goethem, Gand, 1913); *Cambridge Ancient History*, vol. xii (1939), pp. 629–35; Pierre de Labriolle, *La réaction païenne*, (L'Artisan du Livre, Paris, 1934), pp. 223–96 (or as an article in *Revue d'Histoire de la Philosophie*, année 3, part 4, 1929); Amos B. Hulen, *Porphyry's Work against the Christians: an Interpretation* [= *Yale Studies in Religion*, no. 1, 1933]. Augustus Nauck's edition of *Opuscula selecta* of Porphyry (Teubner, Leipzig, 1886) is convenient; Alice Zimmern has issued separately a translation of Porphyry's letter to his wife Marcella (new and revised edition, The Priory Press, London, 1910).

mere controversialist, he was deeply concerned with religion, and it may well have been his study of Christianity which opened his eyes to the weakness of the pagan worship of his day. He sought to awake his pagan fellow-believers to a fresh examination of their faith by propounding ἀπορίαι, doubts, and questions, which demanded a considered answer: from these doubts he advanced to the rejection of the cults of the cities with their animal sacrifices, while in his Letter to his wife Marcella paganism is so much a matter of the spirit and not of any popular cult that the approximation to contemporary Christianity is striking. But this pagan Modernism had its dangers: Christian apologists quoted Porphyry in their attacks on paganism and thus the defence of the older faith was weakened. The pagans closed their ranks: the Modernist was condemned and a strict pagan Fundamentalism takes the place of free criticism and inquiry. The whole of the pagan inheritance from the past is reaffirmed—oracles, bloody sacrifices, miracles, theurgy: it is dangerous to surrender any part of the traditional deposit of the faith lest such a sacrifice be exploited by the Christian critic of paganism. Iamblichus is the representative of this pagan conservative reaction. But this reaffirmation made the pagan faith less easily defensible: while Lactantius can contend that reason is on the side of the Christians, he complains that the pagans will not attempt to give a reasoned defence of their religion: they consistently avoid the challenge of the Christian controversialist. When modern scholars object that Christian apologists of the early fourth century were wasting their energy and time in attacking a paganism which was long dead—its place taken by a pagan philosophic monotheism—they forget this reactionary movement within the body of the defenders of the gods.[14] Julian the Apostate is preeminently a child of this reaction, sacrificing hecatombs of animals to the gods, believing in the ambiguous wonders wrought by Maximus the Neo-Platonist, in his indiscriminate acceptance of the whole tradition an object of surprise, amusement, ridicule even to the pagans themselves.[15]

[14] On Lactantius and Christian apologetic cf. *Cambridge Ancient History*, vol. xii (1939), pp. 649 sqq.

[15] For Julian's religious development, see J. Bidez, *La vie de l'empereur Julien* (Les Belles Lettres, Paris, 1930).

And thus, I would suggest, this pagan Fundamentalist movement helped on the solution of the problem which in the fourth century faced the cultured world of the Near East. Culture was based upon the classical literature of the great period: that literature had from the beginning been intimately associated with the pagan religion; there was no alternative culture for Greek-speaking folk in the lands round the Eastern Mediterranean, and Christianity claimed its share in the classical inheritance as a possession which could be held in common by pagan and by Christian. That claim a religious enthusiast like the Emperor Julian the Apostate could not admit: these masterpieces of the past were not just literature: they were scriptures, sacred books, and to them the pagans had an exclusive right. But Julian the Apostate died on his return march from Persia and his successor on the throne was a Christian. As we see from the regrets of Libanius the movement which Julian had championed died with him, and though officially and formally Christian writers might repeat the prejudices against the pagan literature—prejudices which represented a traditional sentiment in the Church—their practice belied their words. The education of pagan and Christian is based on a study of the same authors, the rhetoric of pagan and of Christian is to the modern reader equally wearisome: both pagan and Christian share a single culture, and the literature of the ancient world has been cut loose from its attachments to a dying faith. The pagan embracing Christianity is not forced to relinquish the treasures of antiquity: the way of the convert is not into barbarism: and another bridge has been thrown across the gulf which separated the faiths: it is thus that the great transition was mediated which led from the ancient world to the Europe of the Middle Age.

For the Christian of the fourth century the acceptance of the pagan inheritance was beset with doubts and scruples: profane letters, as Boulenger has said, were at once his torment and his joy. Jerome was a humanist in his own despite: 'I could not altogether', he writes, 'give up my library which I had collected at Rome with much zeal and much labour. And so, poor wretch, I used to fast when I was on the point of reading Cicero. After the long vigils of the night, after the tears which the remembrance of past sins drew from the depths of my heart, I would take up Plautus. If ever I recovered my senses and tried to read the prophets, their uncouth style rubbed me the wrong way.'

But in the end scruples were laid to rest and victory remained with the heritage from the ancient world. In the fifth century Socrates wrote his Church History, and in the sixteenth chapter of his third book he inserted a reasoned defence of the use by Christians of the pagan literature; that defence is too lengthy for me to quote here, but it is well worth careful study: it closes with the exhortation to reject the evil, but to retain what is beautiful and true, for the beautiful wherever it be found is part and parcel of the truth: τὸ γὰρ καλόν, ἔνθα ἂν ᾖ, ἴδιον τῆς ἀληθείας ἐστίν. Will you look up and read iii, c. 16 of Socrates' *Historia Ecclesiastica?*—it marks the clear recognition of the principle which carried over the legacy of paganism and united it with the Christian tradition. Thus was the continuity with the Greek past, with the Hellenistic culture, preserved for the folk of East Rome.[16]

And it was not merely that pagan and Christian shared the treasure of the past in common: the Church used this treasure for the formulation of its own faith: the theory of Christian sovranty, of the basis of East Roman autocracy, as it was framed by Eusebius is simply an adaptation of the view of

---

[16] E. K. Rand, *Founders of the Middle Ages* (Harvard University Press, 1928). On this 'coming to keep house together' of the classical literature and Christianity there is a large literature: e.g., Joseph Stiglmayr, *Kirchenväter und Klassizismus*, 114th Ergänzungsheft to Stimmen aus Maria-Laach (Herder, Freiburg im Breisgau, 1913); Henri Pinault, *Le Platonisme de Saint Grégoire de Nazianze* (Romain, La Roche-sur-Yon, 1925); E. Fleury, *Hellénisme et christianisme: Saint-Grégoire de Nazianze et son temps* (Beauchesne, Paris, 1930); Yves Courtonne, *Saint Basile et l'hellénisme*, (Firmin-Didot, Paris, 1934); Leo V. Jacks, *St. Basil and Greek Literature* (the Catholic University of America, *Patristic Studies*, vol. i, Washington, 1922). For a study of literary forms in Christian literature: Hermann Jordan, *Geschichte der altchristlichen Literatur* (Quelle and Meyer, Leipzig, 1911), and cf. Aimé Puech, *Histoire de la littérature grecque chrétienne* (Les Belles Lettres, Paris, vol. iii, 1930). For the mediation to the Arabs of Greek classical works by the Christians through Syriac translations see R. Walzer, *Arabic Transmission of Greek Thought to Medieval Europe*, reprint from the *Bulletin of the John Rylands Library*, vol. xxi, no. 1, July 1945. —It was because of this conscious continuity in culture, Heisenberg contended, that there was no such Renaissance in the East Roman Empire as there was in Western Europe. Even for romances of chivalry East Rome could provide her own native materials: 'the romantic literature of the West did not come as a new revelation': J. B. Bury, *Romances of Chivalry on Greek Soil*, Romanes Lecture, 1911 (Clarendon Press, Oxford), p. 23.

Hellenistic philosophers: the ruler no longer himself a god but God's vicegerent, his duty to copy the God of the Christians, his task to establish on earth a μίμησις of the Christian Heaven, himself sustained by the Divine Word—the Logos.

And from this reconciliation between Greek culture and the Christian Church came the great Christian creeds expressed in the terminology of contemporary philosophical thought. Here is the last great original achievement of the Greek genius. You may not like the Chalcedonian creed: you may consider that for you it is incomprehensible, since for its understanding it demands the knowledge of a thought-world which belongs to a past age. You may hold that that creed only restates a problem and does not solve it, but Chalcedon is still with us: it cannot be simply ignored. Hellenists at times would seem to regard the conversion of the Greeks to Christianity as a regrettable incident: the less attention paid to it the better: Εὐφη-μεῖτε. But has any other part of the Greek achievement exercised a greater influence upon European history and thought than this late flowering of the Greek intellect in the Christian creeds? What would your answer be?

But for us perhaps the most vital element in the civilization of the later empire is its art, and here too East Rome met and defeated the challenge which threatened to deprive it of its Greek inheritance. Modern historians have explained the Iconoclast revolution on economic grounds: the monasteries were absorbing wide lands and enjoying immunity from taxation; or on the ground of the needs of military defence: men were deserting the State and escaping into asceticism. But the essential thing to remember is that this was a religious revolution which had its source in the protest of Anatolian bishops against idolatry:[17] the struggle centred in the question whether the God-Man Christ could be represented in an image. Within the Church was a representational art—an art of *Darstellung*—to give place to a symbolic and decorative art? Should the Church abandon its Greek iconography? We have been told with great insistence that East Rome was essentially an oriental empire, that through the centuries it became increasingly oriental, that

[17] G. Ostrogorsky, *Les débuts de la querelle des images* in *Mélanges Charles Diehl* (Leroux, Paris, 1930), i, 235–55.

by the eighth century it had become 'étroitement orientalisé'. Yet when this oriental empire was given the opportunity of adopting an Eastern art of symbolism and decoration and of abandoning its icons, it preferred to suffer persecution under the Iconoclast sovrans and rejected with resolute determination their religious revolution. The icon and the Greek iconography triumphed. The iconoclast held, it would seem,[18] that an icon must be of the same substance, the same essence—*homoousios*—as that which is imaged, and thus the only admissible representation of Christ is the eucharistic elements after the prayer of consecration, for then these are clearly the body and blood of Christ: to the defender of the images this conception of an image appeared ridiculous: the icon would cease to be an image if it were identical with that of which it was an image: rather the single icon is related to its prototype as are objects to the Platonic idea: the honour shown to the icon passes over to the Prototype. A Platonic argument in support of a Greek iconography carried the day.[19] It is a striking illustration of the continuity which meets us throughout East Roman history.

The history of ancient Hellas is dominated by the contrast between the Greek and the Barbarian: barbarism was so near: to the world of the Greek city-states it presented a constant menace. The life-lines of Hellas were so vulnerable—think of the link with the granary of the Black Sea which was so vital to fifth-century Athens—how easily it could be cut. The Persian wars and the miracle of the Greek victory were not forgotten. The task of keeping barbarism at arm's length was the condi-

---

[18] G. Ostrogorsky, *Studien zur Geschichte des byzantinischen Bilderstreites* [=*Historische Studien*, edd. E. Kornemann and S. Kaehler, Heft 5], (Marcus, Breslau, 1929). It may be doubted whether Ostrogorsky's view has been disproved by Hans Barion, 'Quellenkritisches zum byzantinischen Bilderstreit', *Römische Quartalschrift*, xxxviii (1930), pp. 78–90, and Gerhard Ladner, 'Der Bilderstreit und die Kunstlehren der byzantinischen und abendländischen Theologie', *Zeitschrift für Kirchengeschichte*, l (1931), pp. 1–23, st p. 6, n. 20.—An interesting link between the fourth-century objections to an art of *Darstellung* (Eusebius and Epiphanius) and those of the Iconoclasts is to be found in a recently published document of the time of Justinian: see Franz Diekamp, *Analecta Patristica* [=*Orientalia Christiana Analecta*, no. 117] (Rome, Pontif. Institutum Orientalium Studiorum, 1938), pp. 109 sqq. (representations admitted on door-hangings, but not on wood or stone). On this, see pp. 226–39 *infra*.

[19] For the argument in defence of the icons there is an English translation of St John Damascene's work on Holy Images by Mary H. Allies (Baker, London, 1898), and cf. the recent book by Hieronymus Menges, *Die Bilderlehre des hl. Johannes von Damaskus* (Aschendorff, Münster, 1938).

tion of the survival of Greek civilization. And when Rome entered the Eastern Mediterranean she in her turn was forced to assume the same task and that legacy was inherited by the city of Constantine, the imperial power-house of the later Roman world. And through the centuries Constantinople stood as the warden of the Eastern gate, the rear-guard of Europe keeping at bay the hosts of successive Asiatic invaders. It is easy so to concentrate attention on the world of Greek cities as to lose sight of the barbarian fringe which encircled the area where the Greek lived a life which was so consciously 'other' than that of the alien peoples 'without the law'. The maintenance of that 'otherness' was often so precarious: the Greek knew that it was an ἀγὼν περὶ ψυχῆς—a matter of life or death—and so for the Byzantine world it remained.

And after Alexander the Great the contrast between Greek and barbarian was no longer based on an ethnic difference, but rather, as Jüthner has said,[20] on membership of a *Kulturgemeinschaft*, a common civilization which embraced the pagan religion and a pagan *Weltanschauung*. And since neither Jew nor Christian could enter into this pagan world of the Hellenic civilization, 'Hellene', both for Jew and Christian, became identified with idolater and polytheist, and when Christianity had triumphed 'Hellenism' was outlawed, and thereby the Greek was robbed of his national name. But the fullness of content which had been given to the conception of Hellenism after Alexander was not sacrificed: it was but transferred to the new Christian term Rhomaios. In the strange mixture of races which made up the Byzantine Empire it could be no ethnic distinction which marked off the Rhomaios from the barbarian; the distinctive characteristic of the Rhomaios is his membership of the orthodox Greek Church: where a common nationality was impossible religion formed the tie which bound the East Roman to his fellow-believer and to the Emperor, the vicegerent of God. It is, I think, important to realize that though the Greek had lost his Hellenic name he still clung with intransigent loyalty to that interpretation of the difference between the Greek and the Barbarian which the Hellenistic age had established—the membership of a *Kulturgemein-*

[20] Julius Jüthner, *Hellenen und Barbaren* (Dieterich, Leipzig, 1923), p. 92.

schaft which was founded on a *Weltanschauung* and a religion. Thus in the restored empire of the Palaeologi while, to meet the onset of the Turk, Emperor and ecclesiastical diplomat might be prepared to accept union with the Western Church to gain the help of a Western army, the Rhomaioi would have none of such treachery to the faith—better the turban of the Turk than the tiara of a Latin Pope. And the same passionate defence of Greek orthodoxy had been implanted amongst the Slavs by East Roman missionaries. To Russia, for instance, Byzantium brought five gifts, 'her religion, her law, her view of the world, her art and writing',[21] and that view of the world inspired a hatred of any truckling to Latin heresy: in Russia the faith of the Fathers, the faith of the Seven Councils, was secure, without spot or blemish, and when Constantinople fell to the Moslem Moscow was ready to take its place. Santa Sophia, that heaven on earth, that throne of the glory of God, the chariot of the Cherubim, the delight of the whole world, had been desecrated: 'Two Romes had fallen,' wrote Philo-theos of Pskov early in the sixteenth century, 'but the Third Rome stands, and a Fourth Rome there will not be.' The woman clothed with the Sun of the Book of Revelation fled from Old Rome to the New Rome, the City of Constantine: but there she found no rest, for the city had united itself to the Latins; then 'she fled to the Third Rome, that is, the New Great Russia; now she shines, the only apostolic church, brighter than the sun'.[22] The Russian Tsars of Moscow step into the inheritance of the Byzantine Caesars and their theory of sovranty is taken over from East Rome. Still today it is the common liturgy which is the bond between the separate branches of the Orthodox Church—the liturgy in the ver-nacular tongue which was the gift of Byzantium, the liturgy to which the Russian clung with such intensity that the Old Believers preferred to split the Russian Church in two rather than accept the reforms of Nikon, that liturgy which may yet even in the Russia of Stalin see a resurrection and reassert its

[21] B. H. Sumner, *Survey of Russian History* (Duckworth, London, 1944), p. 178.
[22] Hildegard Schaeder, *Moskau des Dritte Rom* [=*Osteuropäische Studien*, University of Hamburg, vol. i] (Friederichsen, De Gruyter and Co., Hamburg, 1929); Nicolas Zernov, *Moscow, The Third Rome* (S.P.C.K., 1937).

claims against the propaganda of a Godless creed. The defence of a way of life through the centuries—it would be a good subject for an essay: Greek democracy and life under law against the arbitrary violence of a barbarian autocrat as mirrored in Herodotus; the widening of Greek horizons with Alexander the Great; the catholicity of a *Kulturgemeinschaft* which would include the barbarian if he would accept the Greek view of life as it should be lived; the Jewish and Christian attack upon the content of that pagan *Weltanschauung* which Julian the Apostate defended in vain; the Christian acceptance of pagan culture divorced from the pagan gods; the Hellene condemned as a pagan but rechristened as the Rhomaios of Constantine's Eastern capital, where the *Kulturgemeinschaft* becomes a *Kultgemeinschaft*—a community based upon a common Christian worship—and under the protection of the city Palladium —the Virgin's robe—maintains its reading of life against the barbarous hordes of Asia while it carries its faith to the Slav peoples, so that when at length Constantinople falls to the Turks its disciples could step into the breach and claim that upon them the mantle of Rome had fallen—that with them the way of life was safe: a fourth Rome would never be. It is a pity that Freeman did not write that essay.

As one studies the later developments of Hellenism one cannot but be struck by the hold which it continued to possess over the minds of the Greeks of East Rome—even in the last phase of the Byzantine Empire there was a renewal of Atticism, a laboured effort to regain the purity of the classical language, as in the work of the historian Chalkokondylas. A Byzantine princess studied the authors of the great period: Anna Comnena, you will remember, read Aristotle and Plato, Homer and Demosthenes, the historians and the poets. Anna you may write down as a bluestocking, but there is a story which is better evidence for the knowledge of the Greek classics among the Rhomaioi: in the eleventh century when the beautiful Caucasian mistress of the Emperor first appeared by his side in a public procession to the hippodrome a courtier expressed his admiration in two words, οὐ νέμεσις: 'it were no shame . . .'. The lady saw the impression created by the quotation, but did not understand: she summoned the courtier to her side and asked for an explanation. But for the court of Byzantium those two words from Homer (*Iliad*, III. 156) had sufficed to conjure up the picture of the old men on the walls of Troy who gazing at Helen in her radiance said, οὐ νέμεσις: 'It were no shame that men should fight for such as she.'[23] So well did the East Romans know their Homer: such was the strength of the continuing Greek tradition.

The defence of a way of life. Yes, really that essay must be written. It would even have its relevance for us today.

[23] For the scene when Constantine IX appeared with Skleraina see Psellos, *Chronographia*, vi. 61, in E. Renauld's edition (with French translation) in the *Collection byzantine* (Les Belles Lettres, Paris, 1926), i, 146.

II

The Thought-World of East Rome

[A Lecture delivered in Westfield College, University of London, on 15 October 1946. Oxford University Press, 1947.]

'THE Thought-World of East Rome.' You may well think that any attempt to squeeze a thought-world into an hour's lecture is an absurdity. So it is, but my title has been chosen deliberately and with a purpose. Last autumn in Oxford I suggested[1] that we sorely needed an essay in the style of Freeman on the Greek defence through two millennia of a way of life which was continually menaced by the barbarian from without. Similarly to-day I would suggest that we need— and again sorely need—an essay on the thought of the Byzantine world. The task of the historian has been defined[2] as a 'continual putting of questions'—a *fortgesetzte Fragestellung*; the successful student of history is not so much he who solves questions, but rather he who asks the right—the suggestive— questions. But how are you going to ask the right questions unless you get—unless you try to get—behind the bare chronicle of events to the thought—the preconceptions—of the actors? Will you ask yourselves the question: Why are histories of the Byzantine Empire as they have been written in the past such heavy going? Why do we weary of them so soon? And I think your answer to that question would probably be: Because they are so exclusively concerned with diplomacy and politics, because these histories are so full of wars and invasions and revolutions: in Professor Collingwood's phrase they give you the outside of an event, the inside of an event being that which can only be described in terms of thought.[3] The historian, Collingwood wrote, is investigating not mere events but actions, and an action is the unity of the outside and the inside

---

[1] *The Hellenistic Civilization and East Rome* (Oxford University Press, 1946) [*Supra*, p. 1, ff.].   [2] Theodor Linner, *Weglgeschichte seit der Völkerwanderudtn* (Cotta, Stuttgart 1901), vol. i, p. x.

[3] R. G. Collingwood, *The Idea of History* (Oxford University Press, 1946), p. 213.

of the event. In the writing of Byzantine history there has been too great a divorce between the inside and the outside.

And in that challenging posthumous book of Professor Collingwood's, which has recently been published under the title *The Idea of History*, he reminds us that the object of historical knowledge must be such that it can revive itself in the historian's mind: the historian's mind must be such as to offer a home for that revival. He must be the right man to study that object. If the historian working against the grain of his own mind tries to master the history of a thought into which he cannot personally enter, instead of writing its history he will merely repeat the statements that record the external facts of its development, the dry bones which may some day become history when someone is able to clothe them with the flesh and blood of a thought which is both his own and theirs.[4] And to-day with the new generation I feel that the auspices should be favourable for a deeper sympathy with the folk of the Byzantine Empire, for a better understanding of the inside of the history of East Rome. As a Victorian I was born into a world which really believed in the inevitability of Progress: only let man be free and human nature could be trusted: it would advance on the path of Progress.[5] This faith in the inevitability of Progress a German writer has said was 'the People's Church of the nineteenth century'.[6] And with that faith as the background of his thought the student of history regarded the Byzantine Empire: here was a State which for more than a millennium continued to vegetate without originality, living on a tradition inherited from the past—a State which could point to no progress, which merely—indecently—refused to die. And to-day that fair dream of the inevitability of human progress is shattered, the faith held only—and that precariously—by some orthodox Marxists. And a State which, though continuously assailed by successive waves of foes, yet maintained itself and guarded civilization through the centuries—

[4] Ibid., pp. 218, 304–5, 327.

[5] Cf. Herbert Spencer, 'Progress is not an accident but a necessity. What we call evil and immorality must disappear. It is certain that man must become perfect.' I owe this citation to Arnold Lunn, *The Third Day* (Burns Oates, 1945), p. xiii.

[6] Ernst Jünger: 'die Volkskirche des neunzehnten Jahrhunderts.'

such a State becomes a portent, and survival itself a proud achievement. The present generation should naturally regard the Byzantine Empire with a new interest; it will raise the question: what was the world of thought which inspired East Rome in its sæcular task of self-defence which was at the same time the defence of Christianity alike from pagan barbarism and from the menace of Islam? The title which I have chosen for this talk is not simply senile presumption, it is an appeal to the students of a younger generation. I would suggest then for another essay the theme of the dualism which runs through the thought of the Byzantine world.

And first in such an essay there would come a consideration of the double ethic which is of primary significance in East Roman life—the two standards: one for the ordinary Christian living his life in the work-a-day world and the other standard for those who were haunted by the words of Christ: 'if thou wouldst be perfect.'[7] That double standard can be traced in the second century in the distinction accorded to the confessor and the martyr. It can already be found in the reign of Trajan in the writing of Ignatius, especially in the letter which he addressed to the Romans[8] imploring them not to attempt to rob him of the prize of martyrdom. He was bishop of Antioch, but with the prospect before him of being devoured by wild beasts in the arena of Rome he feels: 'Now I am beginning to be a disciple.' And then when in the fourth century the per-

[7] The double ethic: cf. Eusebius, *Demonstratio Evangelica*, book I, ch. 8. English translation by W. J. Ferrar, *The Proof of the Gospel* (S.P.C.K., 1920), vol. i, pp. 48–50. For St Basil the life of the monk is a return to the life of the Church of the Apostles, and he goes a long way towards identifying the Christian life as such with the life of the ascete: see the passages cited in Karl Holl, *Enthusiasmus und Bussgewalt beim griechischen Mönchtum* (Leipzig, Hinrichs, 1898), pp. 158–9. Successfully to deny oneself and surrender one's will while in the world outside the monastery is 'extremely difficult, even if I do not say impossible'. But by special grace God, caring for our salvation, divided the course of human life into two—marriage and virginity—so that he who could not endure the latter might marry, and he will be excused—will be granted συγγνώμη—for his lack of self-control (ἀκρασία), ibid., p. 167. Never, so far as I know, did any orthodox champion of asceticism directly condemn marriage as a sin: if nothing else, Christ's presence at the marriage feast in Cana would have prevented that. Has the Protestant reaction against such a double ethic impoverished the Christian life by abolishing institutions devoted to the cultivation of the specifically 'religious' vocation of monks and nuns? So von Hügel: cf. E. A. Payne, *Journal of Theological Studies*, xlvii (1946), at p. 249.

[8] Ignatius, Letter 4; there is an English translation in J. H. Srawley, *The Epistles of St Ignatius Bishop of Antioch* (S.P.C.K., 1919), pp. 70–80.

secution of the Christians ceased the place of the martyr was taken by the ascetic: 'if thou wouldst be perfect'—the words drove Antony the first monk into the desert, and the world was well lost for that divine mystery into which initiation came from that withdrawal. That is it: the holy man is God's initiate[9] and thus a creature of power and wonder. Through complete devotion he has attained to that ἀταραξία—that untroubled calm of spirit—which we in our cares and in our sinning cannot—we know it well—ever reach. He thus acquires a position of the highest significance: he is the realization of the Byzantine ideal. In every emergency the saint is a very present help in time of trouble. The Christian faith becomes a religion of mediation, but not distinctively of priestly mediation; the priest in your village, married, with all the anxieties of wife and children, carrying on a trade, it may be, to secure his livelihood[10]—he is far too near to your condition. It is to the πρεσβεία—the mediation—the παρρησία—the freedom of access to God—of the holy man that you naturally turn. I believe that when we have seriously set ourselves to illustrate this dual ethic in its consequences and its influence we shall really have made some progress in our understanding of East Roman thought.

And in the second place our essayist will consider the duality in the sphere of theology. Unfortunately I have not been trained either as a theologian or a philosopher and consequently I have a natural sympathy with the man in the East Roman street. I know that it is the correct thing to admire the catholicity of mind which enabled a Clement of Alexandria and an Origen to go to school with the later Platonists, which led Dionysius the Areopagite to enthrone Neoplatonist thought in the heart of Christian theology. Of course, that alliance with

[9] God's initiate: see Athanasius, *Life of Antony*, ch. 14. There is an English translation in the Athanasius volume (vol. iv) of the *Library of Nicene and Post-Nicene Fathers* (Oxford, 1892), p. 200. The Greek is προῆλθεν ὁ 'Α. ὥσπερ ἔκ τινος ἀδύτου μεμυσταγωγημένος καὶ θεοφορούμενος.

[10] There is an interesting passage in St Basil's 198th letter; excusing himself for not having written to the Bishop of Samosata, he says: 'For even if our clergy seem to be numerous, yet it is composed of men who are not used to travel; they do not deal in merchandise, nor follow the out-of-doors life, since most of them ply sedentary crafts, deriving therefrom their daily bread.' See the recent study of E. Herman, 'Le professioni vietate al clero bizantino', *Orientalia Christiana Periodica* (Rome), x (1944), pp. 23–44.

contemporary pagan conceptions aided the great transition to
the Christian world of the Middle Ages: it made Christian
thought *salonfähig*—able to enter pagan drawing-rooms on a
footing of equality. But it was a very heavy price at which this
liberty was bought. Is God to be regarded as 'an undifferenced
ground of all existence, transcending not only Matter but
Mind, creative without will or causality, unknowable save in
the *unio mystica*, having no character save the character of
being a ground'?[11] Is God, the Absolute, simply ἄρρητον, ineffable, so that we can, it is true, say what God is not but never
what God is—all attempt at definition being reduced to a
negation, while to God even Being must be denied, for such an
attribution would be to limit the Infinite? And is there any
meeting-point between such a conception of the Godhead and
the picture given in the synoptic gospels of a Father in Heaven
Who knows what His children need before they ask Him, without Whom no sparrow falls to the ground? Is not the cleavage
between the two as great as that between man and God the
Wholly Other of the theology of Karl Barth? I know that
Origen admitted the simple Christian by the side of the Christian Gnostic, but his interest is concentrated on the latter; it
was in the language of Greek philosophy that the Christian
creeds were framed: 'The Father incomprehensible, the Son
incomprehensible and the Holy Ghost incomprehensible'—yet
'there are not three incomprehensibles but one incomprehensible'. The Creed of Chalcedon—that statement of the problem
to be solved which came to be regarded as itself a solution of
that problem—is it for the orthodox theologian of to-day an
asset or a liability? But what this 'coming to keep house together' of Christian and pagan thought meant to the
Byzantine is surely this: he accepted the definitions of the
orthodox faith as set forth by the Councils of the Church
—they were part of the tradition which went back to the
Apostles—but his religion centred not in these immensely
difficult theological statements—rather it centred in that
in which he could participate with his fellow-Christians—

---

[11] E. R. Dodds, 'Parmenides and the Neoplatonic "One" ', *Classical Quarterly*,
xxii (1928), pp. 129–42 at p. 131. For a 'queer ebullition of jargon' in the work of
Dionysius the Areopagite see W. R. Inge, *The Philosophy of Plotinus* (Longmans, 1918), ii, 112.

the liturgy.[12] And for him the liturgy was itself part of the tradition and therefore to be straitly guarded as a sacred possession. 'Even the smallest neglect of the traditions', Photius wrote, 'leads to the complete contempt for dogma.'[13] Any change in liturgical usage was thus a denial of the faith. It was no wonder that the Iconoclasts failed in their attempt to banish the icons from East Roman worship. In the drama of the Eucharist, in the pictured symbolism of the iconostasis and of the hierarchy of saints, angels, the Mother of God, and, enthroned above all, Christ the Pantocrator, the Byzantine lived a creed which he could understand. And this sacred unalterable liturgy and its significance the Byzantine faithfully handed on to his Slav disciples: if you would make vital for yourself the force of a sacred liturgical tradition you can perhaps best recapture it off Byzantine soil in Holy Russia by reading the wonderful autobiography of Avvakum the Old Believer, of which there are translations into English, French, and German.[14] Avvakum, burned to death for his loyalty to the act of benediction made with two and not with three fingers, for his loyalty to the double as against the triple Alleluia, did but illustrate by his irrefrangible heroism the devotion to the liturgy which had inspired the Byzantine opposition to the heretical innovations of the Latin West. Or, again, read the autobiography of the fifteenth-century Russian merchant Athanasius—how, when robbed on his journey to India of his books, his distress was due to the fact that he could no longer be sure of the date of the Easter

---

[12] For the significance of the Liturgy in the Orthodox Church cf. N. Arseniew, *Mysticism and the Eastern Church* (Student Christian Movement, 1926), especially pp. 17–61 on 'The Spirit of the Eastern Church'; id., *We Beheld His Glory* (S.P.C.K., 1937), pp. 112–41 on the Johannine 'Vision of Glory' in the Eastern Church; Friedrich Heiler, *Urkirche und Ostkirche* (Reinhardt, Munich, 1937), pp. 286–364; Karl Holl, *Die religiösen Grundlagen der russischen Kultur*, Gesammelte Aufsätze zur Kirchengeschichte, vol. ii (Mohr, Tübingen, 1928), pp. 418–32.

[13] 'Even the smallest neglect' . . . Photius, Ep. 13, Migne, *Patrologia Graeca*, vol. cii, 724 D. Cf. Heiler, op. cit.: see n. 12, p. 139.

[14] Jane Harrison and Hope Mirrlees, *The Life of the Archpriest Avvakum* (L. and V. Woolf, 1924); Rudolf Jagoditsch, *Das Leben des Protopopen Awwakum*, &c. [=*Quellen und Forschungen zur russischen Geschichte*, ed. Karl Stählin, No. 10, Ost-Europa Verlag, Berlin, 1930]—with introduction and commentary; Pierre Pascal, *La vie de l'archiprêtre Avvakum écrite par lui-même* (Gallimard, Paris, 2nd edn. [1938]), with full commentary; see further the biography by Pascal, *Avvakum et les débuts du Raskol* (Champion, Paris, 1938).

festival.[15] Many learned works have dealt at length with the formal theology of the Greek Church: it is especially of recent years that we have come to recognize the significance of the popular theology which has found its expression—and still finds its expression—in the liturgy. We need to bear in mind this duality if we would seek to penetrate into the thought-world of Byzantium.

And Byzantine asceticism, too, has its own duality.[16] East Roman mysticism goes back to Origen and his statement of the method of contemplation ($\theta\epsilon\omega\rho\iota\alpha$) by which man can attain to the Vision of God. As Hausherr has pointed out,[17] martyrdom is recognized by Origen as the path to Christian perfection only because martyrdom is the best means of showing that we aspire to gnosis by works worthy of gnosis. And from Origen mystical asceticism passes through Evagrius to Maximus the Confessor in the seventh century until it is renewed in the eleventh century by Symeon the New Theologian, and after a long gap issues in the Hesychasm of the Athos monasteries. But there is another line in Byzantine asceticism which seeks salvation, not in a mystical Vision of God, but in obedience and in charity shown to the other members of the monastic brotherhood. The solitary cannot practise the virtues of the true Christian ascetic precisely because he has no fellow-Christian whose presence is necessary for such practice. And this type of asceticism received its formulation from St Basil. In the days of the persecutions martyrdom was regarded, we have seen, as the highest perfection: in Basil's conception nothing is changed: henceforth martyrdom will consist in obedience absolute and unquestioning, the complete surrender of one's will to one's superior. Basil was rightly named—he was indeed a king amongst men—but he treated his monks as a monarch his subjects. It has been truly said

[15] *Die Fahrt des Athanasius Nitikin über drei Meere. Reise eines russischen Kaufmannes nach Ostindien 1466–1472.* Translated by Karl H. Meyer [=*Quellen und Aufsätze zur russischen Geschichte,* ed. Karl Stählin, No. 2] (Historia Verlag, Leipzig, n.d.) Will not someone give us an English edition with a good map?

[16] For the dualism in East Roman asceticism see I. Hausherr, 'Les grands courants de la spiritualité orientale', *Orientalia Christiana Periodica,* i (1935), pp. 114–38.

[17] Hausherr, ibid., p. 123.

that Basil could hardly have borne the weight of his own rules. These rules are often uncomfortable reading:[18] they remind one of the remark of a mother: 'Do run and find out what Tommy is doing and tell him not to do it.' And it was Basil's conception of monasticism which inspired Theodore the Studite, and his rules lay so much stress on works that they would have rejoiced the heart of St James the Apostle.

And it is not only within the Empire that it is important to trace this dual line of asceticism: it is significant that it was Theodore's conception of monasticism which was introduced into Russia after the conversion of Vladimir, and more than that: the immensely long monastic services were imposed upon the Russian laity. That burden, as you remember, proved too heavy, and since every part of the traditional liturgy was sacred and no part could be sacrificed, the difficulty was met by reciting at one and the same time four, five, and even six different parts of the service; this system of 'polyphony' as it was called must indeed have produced an ungodly hubbub. The point of interest is that when Nil Sorsky sought to reform Russian monasticism and brought the new mysticism of Hesychasm from Athos it was too late, and, disappointed, he withdrew into the forest and formed a laura on the Palestinian model. We badly need an English translation of Nil Sorsky's

---

[18] Strictly speaking there is no Basilian 'Rule'—there was 'legislation both written and unwritten' (Greg. Naz. *Or.* 43, 34), there were written 'rules and canons' (Greg. Naz. *Ep.* 6), but the 'Rules' are quite unsystematic (cf. Lowther Clarke, *St Basil the Great*, Cambridge University Press, 1913, pp. 49, 64–5, 70–1); 'They have no more order than a series of "Answers to Correspondents" in a modern newspaper' (Morison). It might be better to speak of Basil's 'Rules' as 'Rulings'. It has been suggested to me that I conveyed a false impression of harshness in my remark on the Basilian 'Rulings'; it may be that the prejudice of an incurable Victorian individualism has betrayed me, but was it necessary, because a monk wished to learn his letters or to read, to refuse him his desire (Shorter Rules, 96)? Was it necessary to restrict the learning by heart of the Scriptures to the heads of the monastery, while other monks should not be curious about anything else than their own duty (ibid. 235)? Was it necessary to limit the learning by heart even of the Gospels to those specially privileged (ibid. 236)? [Pachomius was more liberal: his monks 'learn all the Scriptures by heart', Palladius, *Lausiac History*, ch. 32 s.f., Lowther Clarke's translation (S.P.C.K., 1918), p. 116, and Byzantine monasteries later followed a more generous policy, e.g. *Life of Daniel the Stylite*, ch. 3, many books were displayed in the church, and any monk could take and read any book he chose.] Above all, was it necessary to forbid a monk to do any virtuous act unless he had been ordered to do it by his abbot (*Sermo Asceticus*, II, 324 E, Garnier, Basil's Works, 2nd edn., vol. ii, Paris, 1839, p. 453 s.f.)? I find it very difficult to believe that Basil would for himself have accepted such restrictions.

writing that we might see the impress of the Byzantine mystic tradition on a Russian of the fifteenth century.[19]

It has been contended that the poverty of East Roman intellectual life is illustrated by the fact that there is no discussion of political theory—the Greeks who had been the pioneers in political thought had lost all interest in the subject. The contention is false: it is based upon a misapprehension. Byzantine literature is interpenetrated by political thought, i.e. by the theory of East Roman monarchy. The subjects of the Empire were convinced that their polity was approved by God—it was a θεοστήρικτον κράτος—a power rooted and grounded in God and protected by Christ and by His Virgin Mother. And if you once believe that, what profits it to discuss other polities? It would be but waste of breath. It is highly significant that amongst all the Byzantine commentaries upon the works of Aristotle there is only one upon the *Politics*, and for that single commentary one has to wait until the eleventh century. And here again we find duality, the double title on which the monarch's claim to rule is based—the choice of the human electors, the Army, the Senate, and the acclamation of the people and the choice of God. The necessity for the acclamation of the people, if the claimant to the throne is to be constituted the legitimate ruler of the Roman Empire, lives on throughout East Roman history. Even under the Palaeologi that tradition is preserved.[20] How deeply this right of the electors had entered into the popular consciousness is best illustrated from the Syriac legend of Julian the Apostate which may date from the sixth century. I will quote one passage. Julian, after his revolt in Gaul, has not yet entered Rome; before his arrival the Christians have massacred the pagan priests and Julian is threatening vengeance. He turns to his counsellor Aplatos for advice and the minister replies: 'Oh King, powerful and glorified for ever, considering that as your power has not yet been seated on the throne of the kingdom of the Romans, the

---

[19] For Nil Sorsky cf. Igor Smolitsch, *Leben und Lehre der Starzen* (Hegner, Vienna, 1936), pp. 71–89.

[20] For the acclamation of people and army under the restored Empire of the Palaeologi cf. Ps. Codinus, *De Officiis* (ed. Bonn), p. 89. Cf. August Heisenberg, *Aus der Geschichte und Literatur der Palaiologenzeit*, Sitzungsberichte der Bayerischen Akademie der Wissenschaften, philos.-philol. und hist. Klasse, Jahrgang 1920, Abhandlung 10, pp. 55–7.

glorified and adored name of your power has not yet been called to take over the government of the Romans and we have not yet received the acclamations of our realm in this city which is the capital of our government and the mother of all the cities under our sovran rule. As for those who do not receive the acclamations of royalty in this city, their power is less than that of kings and it is outside of the writs of the kings among the Romans.'[21]

That is one basis of the monarch's rule. And the other is the choice of God which is clearly evidenced by the claimant's successful assumption of power. And this theory of divine election —the Emperor as Vicegerent of God—is supported alike by Eusebius' adaptation to Christian use of the Hellenistic philosophy of kingship,[22] and probably even more influentially by Old Testament precedent in God's choice of Saul and of David. Indeed, it is curious to notice to what an extent those Old Testament passages had impressed the Byzantine mind and to what uses they were put.

May I here interpolate two instances of the use made of the narrative of the choice of Saul to be king? Theodore of Sykeon had not yet become a saint: he was quite young when he shut himself up in a cave and there remained three years. When he emerged from the cave, the bishop of Anastasioupolis in Galatia Prima was present, and when the bishop saw the pus oozing from the sores on Theodore's body, when he saw the indescribable number of worms in his matted hair, when he experienced the intolerable stench which made Theodore unapproachable, the bishop was so convinced of Theodore's holiness that on the spot he ordained him lector, sub-deacon, deacon, and priest. When it was objected that Theodore was still under the canonical age the bishop had only to refer to Samuel and God's choice of Saul and all were satisfied. Then there was Euthymius who later became a famous saint. He was married and had a daughter, but he wanted to run away and become a monk. He was at a loss, however, how to escape his wife's vigilance. At length he hit upon a plan: he gave out

[21] Sir Hermann Gollancz, *Julian the Apostate* (Oxford University Press, 1928), pp. 39–42.

[22] Cf. 'Eusebius and the Christian Empire', *Annuaire de l'institut de philologie et d'histoire orientales*, ii (1933–4), pp. 13–18. See pp. 168–72 *infra*.

that he was going to look after a horse which was tethered grazing in a meadow. And his biographer writes: the son of Kish went to seek an ass and found a kingdom: Euthymius pretended to seek a horse and found the kingdom of Heaven.[23] We are not informed of his wife's reaction to that discovery. In the coronation prayer there is an express reference to the Old Testament precedent: 'Oh Lord our God, the King of kings and Lord of lords which through Samuel the prophet didst choose David Thy Servant to be king over Thy people Israel, do Thou now also hear the supplication of us unworthy', &c.

There has been much controversy concerning the constitutional significance of the coronation of the Byzantine Emperor: did the Patriarch at the coronation represent the Church or, as is generally held, did he act as the delegate of the Roman State? Since it would appear that coronation conferred no larger powers upon the Emperor than those which he already possessed as the successful candidate for the throne, was coronation from the constitutional point of view unnecessary, purely optional, or did it form an essential element in the Emperor's title to rule? May not the analogy of the coronation of English kings suggest an answer to such questions? Although, in Maitland's words,[24] 'the coronation does not seem to be a legally necessary ceremony', although it adds nothing to the legal and constitutional powers possessed by the king since the moment of his proclamation, the coronation service does set the seal of the Church upon his rule. It is difficult to believe that the Patriarch at the Byzantine coronation service did not represent the Church: here, too, surely, the Church evidences before the eyes of men the previous divine choice and sets its seal upon that election. The coronation is thus, it may be suggested, a declaratory rite—a rite not obligatory but hallowed by custom. It gives expression to the Byzantine conviction 'how fair a rule is monarchy with God for guide', as

[23] Life of Theodore the Syceote in Μνημεῖα Ἁγιολογικά, ed. Ioannu (Venice, 1884), ch. 21; 'Vie et Office de Saint Euthyme le Jeune', ed. Louis Petit in the Bibliothèque hagiographique orientale, ed. Léon Clugnet (Picard, Paris, 1904), ch. 6.

[24] F. W. Maitland, The Constitutional History of England (Cambridge University Press, 1909), p. 343. Cf. E. C. Ratcliff, The English Coronation Service (S.P.C.K., 1936), p. 28: 'Nowadays a coronation is a ratification of an accomplished fact.'

George of Pisidia, the seventh-century Poet Laureate, wrote.[25] Indeed, what is the alternative to monarchy? δημοκρατία— democracy—and in East Rome 'democracy' meant revolution, civil war. 'To Pope Gregory XVI', it has been said recently, 'the mere word freedom meant revolution':[26] to the Byzantine the mere word 'democracy' spelt chaos.[27] Can it be that this Byzantine prejudice has so deeply rooted itself in a people's consciousness that the Greek of today is incapable of estab- lishing anything which we of the West should regard as demo- cracy? Acclamation by the people, the choice of God—such is the dual title of the βασιλεύς of the Romans.

In our study of the dualism in East Roman thought we are bound to consider the relation between the inheritance from pagan civilization and the later Christian outlook. Thus I know of no treatment of the problem presented to the Byzan- tines by Greek science: was the natural science of the Greeks compatible with a belief in the providence of a God Who was also Lord of the world of Nature? And in our study we might illustrate that problem by a consideration of the Byzantine treatment of earthquakes. Thus Agathias (II, c. 15) describes

[25] George of Pisidia, *Exp. Pers.* 2, 24. For recent discussions of the signifi- cance of Byzantine coronation ceremonies cf. W. Sickel, 'Das byzantinische Krönungsrecht bis zum 10. Jahrhundert', *Byzantinische Zeitschrift*, vii (1898), pp. 511–57 (with full references to the sources); F. E. Brightman, 'Byzantine Imperial Coronations', *Journal of Theological Studies*, ii (1901), pp. 359–92; J. B. Bury, *The Constitution of the Later Roman Empire* (Cambridge University Press, 1910), at pp. 10–12, reprinted in *Select Essays of J. B. Bury*, ed. H. Temperley (Cambridge, 1930), at pp. 104–5; R. M. Woolley, *Coronation Rites* (Cambridge University Press, 1915), pp. 7–31; A. E. R. Boak, 'Imperial Corona- tion Ceremonies of the Fifth and Sixth Centuries', *Harvard Studies in Classical Philology*, xxx (Harvard University Press, 1919), pp. 37–47; Otto Treitinger, *Die oströmische Kaiser- und Reichsidee*, &c. (Biedermann, Jena, 1938), pp. 26– 31; P. Charanis, 'Coronation and its Constitutional Significance in the Later Roman Empire', *Byzantion*, xv (1940–1), pp. 49–66. Cf. *Byzantion*, xii (1937), pp. 189–95, and a criticism by F. Dölger, *Byzantinische Zeitschrift*, xxxviii (1938), p. 240. Unction, it would appear, formed no customary part of the coronation ceremony until the thirteenth century, *Byzantion*, vii (1932), p. 200.
[26] Paul Simon, *Dublin Review* (July 1946), p. 78.
[27] For the East Roman view of 'democracy' cf. Eusebius, *Triakontaeterikos*, ch. 3 (Heikel, p. 201): μοναρχία δὲ τῆς πάντων ὑπέρκειται συστάσεώς τε καὶ διοικήσεως. ἀναρχία μᾶλλον καὶ στάσις ἢ ἐξ ἰσοτιμίας . . . πολυαρχία. Note St Basil's insistence on the appointment of someone to represent the abbot in the latter's absence from his monastery so that the brotherhood does not assume δημοκρατικόν τι σχῆμα ἐπὶ διαλύσει τοῦ κανόνος καὶ τῆς παραδεδομένης εὐταξίας (Longer Rules, 45); Lowther Clarke, *The Ascetic Works of Saint Basil* (S.P.C.K., 1925), p. 218. This does not necessarily conflict with Shorter Rules, 123, where an ordered decision of the majority of the brotherhood is contemplated, in contrast with the chaos of a 'democratic' state of affairs.

the effects of a great earthquake which was experienced throughout the Near East in the year 554. Egypt, as men knew well, was not troubled by earthquakes, and thus when a mild shock was felt at Alexandria the population of the city was thrown into confusion and dismay by the complete strangeness—τῷ ἀπροσδοκήτῳ . . . καὶ παραδόξῳ—of the occurrence and by the alarming thought that, though at this time the shock was slight, it might yet recur with greater violence. Agathias is thus led to consider the causes of earthquakes and the explanations of the natural scientists—οἱ τὰ τοιαῦτα φυσιολογοῦντες—in fact the explanation given by Aristotle. Dry and smoky vapours are enclosed in the hollows of the earth; they cannot easily find a vent and circle in whirling eddies shaking everything that comes in their way until the solid earth yields before their violent motion and they force their way out. Egypt is level and has no caves or hollows within which such vapours may form and, even if they do, they can easily escape through the earth and do no harm. Agathias proceeds: 'But probably even if a part of Egypt should actually suffer from earthquake shocks those who are skilled in such questions will still find other grounds on which to defend the theory of the exhalations. And to me indeed they seem to have reached in their theories a certain degree of plausibility and likelihood so far as it is given to man by the use of such evidence as he has to arrive at a conclusion in these obscure matters, but as for attaining to the truth, they appear to me to have utterly failed. For how should anyone accurately explain things which we cannot see and which transcend our understanding? It is enough for us to know that all things are ordered by the divine mind and by a will which we cannot fathom. For to consider by human reason and to inquire into the principles of nature, their movements, and the causes of each phenomenon is perhaps not completely useless nor is it without attraction (ἄχαρι), but to think and believe that it is possible to attain to reality (τοῦ ὄντος)—that would, I fear, be presumption and more uneducated than to confess one's double ignorance.'

When later Constantinople was again shaken by an earthquake the only victim was a very wealthy sinner, Anatolius by name (v, c. 3). The news spread through the city and people

saw in Anatolius' just punishment the reason for the earthquake. Here, too, the comment of Agathias is interesting: 'I
am, however,' he writes, 'in much doubt on the point and am
unable to make any certain statement concerning the cause of
the earthquake. For there can be no question that an earthquake would be a very desirable and praiseworthy thing if it
knew how to distinguish the bad men and the good, destroying
the former and making its peace with the latter. Even if we
grant, as we have every reason to do, that Anatolius was an
unjust man, yet there were a great many others like him
throughout the city; yes, and more unjust than he. And though
Anatolius was suddenly snatched from life, the others remained unharmed. Thus in my judgement it is not clear nor
easy to determine why it was Anatolius alone who perished. . . .
In fact even if a man lives to old age and enjoys his prosperity
to the full, this is no demonstration of justice, nor assuredly is
the most atrocious form of death a proof of any special wicked-
ness.' We shall know the real answer to these questions only
after life has ended (pp. 285–7: cf., on the causes of the plague,
pp. 298–9). Elsewhere Agathias clearly expresses his own
view: those who produced oracles to explain the earthquake or
resorted to astrology were guilty of impiety in leaving nothing
over in knowledge to God—καὶ μηδὲν ὁτιοῦν πλέον γνώσεως πέρι
τῷ κρείττονι καταλιμπάνοντες (p. 288).

Aristotle's view concerning the cause of earthquakes, as we
have seen it stated by Agathias, was indeed in the opinion of
some reinforced by the ingenuity of Anthemius who was at feud
with Zeno, the owner of the flat immediately above his own.
He collected a number of large cauldrons and filled them with
water; he then put over them strong leather coverings which
tapered into tubes which were securely fixed to the ceiling.
Huge fires were lighted under the cauldrons and the steam,
unable to make its escape, so shook the floor-beams of Zeno's
flat that he and his friends were thrown into abject terror
thinking that it was another earthquake shock; they rushed in
panic into the street.[28]

[28] The whole account given by Agathias v, c. 6 is translated and discussed
by Ernst Darmstaedter, 'Anthemios und sein "künstliches Erdbeben" in
Byzanz', *Philologus*, lxxxviii (1933), pp. 477–82. For fuller references to the

Attaliates writing in the eleventh century (p. 89) admits that so far as the natural phenomenon is concerned the explanation given by Aristotle may not be out of place. It is indeed, he writes, extremely probable. But the point which I desire to make is this: the convulsion does not happen by chance, but by the will of God, since God does not govern the world of nature without instruments which perform His purpose. The rain, the thunder, the lightning, thus appear to have their share in causation, but everything in the view of religious folk is dependent upon the divine will.

In short, the Byzantine was much more interested in the meaning of the natural phenomenon than in its scientific cause. When in the fourth century a doctor urged that the plague took a heavier toll of victims from those living in basement rooms because of the staleness of the air in these unhealthy cellar-dwellings the folk of East Rome regarded him as a blasphemer—air, forsooth, what had air to do with it? In such an atmosphere Greek natural science fought a losing battle.[29]

And a similar problem arose in the field of philosophy. Here if one is studying the dualism of Byzantine thought two currents are clearly defined—the safe course of Aristotelianism and the hazardous course of the Platonist. And we humble

literature on the ancient theories explaining the causes of earthquakes see ibid., n. on p. 478.

[29] On doctors cf. Sir William Ramsay, *Pauline and other Studies* (Hodder and Stoughton), 1906, pp. 380–1: 'The medical profession had degenerated seriously from the scientific spirit of the old Greek medical schools.' Cf., however, St Basil's judgement (in a letter to the Chief Physician Eustathius) on the medical profession: 'To put your science at the head of all pursuits in life is to decide reasonably and rightly', Ep. 189 (at the beginning). C. 55 of St Basil's Longer Rules is concerned with the medical art as the gift of God and with its right use. This is the longest of all St Basil's Rulings: 'Probably', writes Lowther Clarke, 'spiritual healing was a charisma in Basil's coenobia and some concluded that it was the normal treatment of disease. Basil, whose own health was notoriously bad, treated their view sympathetically but summed up in favour of the doctor.' (Lowther Clarke, op. cit., see n. 27, p. 46.) It is of course true that for hostels and hospitals handbooks preserving in brief form the remedies prescribed by Galen and other early Greek doctors were reproduced, but it would seem that they did but transmit traditional material and did not formulate the results of new research: cf., e.g., A. Kousis, *Byzantinisch-neugriechische Jahrbücher*, vi (1928), pp. 77–94. Apparently, as a general rule, if the illness was serious you went to the church of the dead saint who might be consulted only for a specific malady (as was, for example, St Artemius for diseases of the genital organs) or else to the living holy man who might suggest the name of a doctor, as would St Theodore the Syceote.

students of history who are not philosophers are at a loss. We know of no general study of Byzantine philosophy which might render first aid to our ignorance, and, as Valdenberg has pointed out, the judgements passed upon Byzantine philosophy by modern writers are directly contradictory. East Roman study of philosophy took for its expression the form of commentaries upon Aristotle: the commentaries—volume after volume—have been published by the Prussian Academy, and of those volumes Praechter has said that in one at least of the greatest of German libraries they remain untouched, memorials of self-sacrificing philological scholarship indeed, but serving only as the resting-place of the accumulated dust of the years. Will no adventurous explorer blaze a path through the formidable forest? All that the historical student can see at present is the dominance of Aristotle the logician whom the Christian could make use of just as well as the pagan. It was the pagan Porphyry's Εἰσαγωγή, his Introduction to Philosophy, that East Roman students took as their text-book. And this recognition of Aristotelianism by Christian scholars comes earlier than we might expect. Anatolius, ordained bishop of Laodicea in A.D. 269, was an Alexandrian, learned, as Eusebius states, 'in arithmetic and geometry, in astronomy and other sciences whether of logic or of physics', and was called upon by his fellow-citizens to carry on the school of the Aristotelian tradition in the capital of Egypt.[30] It is indeed surprising that the Alexandrians, most of whom were doubtless pagans, should have elected a Christian as principal of their school of philosophy. In Constantinople, Themistius in the fourth century is widely tolerant, and, though a pagan, quotes the Old Testament. As against the Pergamene school of Neoplatonism with its theurgy and miracles, as against the embittered paganism of the school of Athens, the Aristotelian commentators in Alexandria co-operated with their Christian colleagues—it is only such names as David and Elias which suggest the religious faith of the writers. Polytheistic texts are reinterpreted in monotheistic terms, and thus after the Arab conquests these texts are already prepared for adoption by another monotheistic

[30] Eusebius, *Historia ecclesiastica*, vii, 32, 5.

religion. It is Christian versions of these texts in Syriac which
the Arabs translate and later carry to Western Europe. Thus in
the view of the Church Aristotelianism was a useful servant.
The study of the logic of the Stagirite was safe. And from the
time of Porphyry, the close of the third century, down to the
reign of Heraclius in the opening years of the seventh century
there is a continuous production of commentaries on Aristotle
—never more, as Praechter has said, than a single generation
without a new commentary. And after that there follows a
great gap: we know of no commentary on Aristotle until the
silence is broken by the immense activity of Michael of Ephesus who was apparently a contemporary of Psellos in the
eleventh century. How is that long silence to be explained?
That is the sort of problem which brings home to the student
of history the limitations of his craft: such an unanswered
question may induce a proper humility. For remember, no fear
of heresy could debar the Aristotelian from pursuing his in-
vestigations. It is otherwise with the Platonist. In the third
century the Alexandrian school of Clement and Origen had felt
at liberty to spoil the Egyptians and to make full use of the
philosophy of the Greeks, but in the fourth and fifth centuries
scruples were awakened and the latitude which Origen had
claimed became suspect, and in the sixth Origenism was condemned. Platonism was a subtle danger to orthodoxy and it
was only Neoplatonic mysticism which gained free access
through the work of Dionysius the Areopagite as interpreted
through Maximus the Confessor. In controversy with the
Iconoclasts John of Damascus might use a Platonic-sounding
argument when defining the relation of the Icon to its Prototype, but it was not until the eleventh century that Psellos,
penetrating behind the Neoplatonists, discovered his master
and proclaimed him as 'my Plato'. The Byzantine world had
found it possible to appropriate the Greek literature of the
classical period by stripping it of its pagan religious associations: the gods became literary ornaments or the subject of
ethical reinterpretation through allegory. The teeth of the
classical literature were drawn: the East Roman knew how to
combat any danger of infection. Aristotle, we have seen,
through concentration on his works on logic, had been given

rights of domicile in a Christian world, but with Plato it was a different matter; here philosophy might have the force of a religious faith: could such a faith be reconciled with orthodoxy? And for a Byzantine orthodoxy was a compelling force. And thus an orthodox Patriarch and an orthodox Emperor could crush the Platonist renaissance which Psellos had initiated. Psellos was forced to sign an orthodox confession of faith, John Italus was condemned, Eustratius had to recant his errors. In the fourteenth century in Salonica there was greater freedom of thought than was possible under Patriarchal surveillance in the capital, and there the danger of Platonism stood revealed when Gemistos Pletho openly avowed his paganism. So we see in bare outline the course of these two streams in the philosophic thought of East Rome, but the student of history needs the detail which only a student of philosophy can give. In those commentaries on the works of Aristotle which represent the lectures of Byzantine teachers— either their own lecture notes or the notes taken by those attending the lectures—is there any distinctively new thought or is it but a repetition of traditional material? Did the Byzantine merely guard the legacy from the past or did he put the talent out to interest? What on the other hand was the contribution of the East Roman Platonist and precisely how and to what extent did he violate the tradition of Greek orthodoxy? Only after some such study has been put into his hands will the historical student be able to correlate the philosophical development with other fields of Byzantine thought.[31]

[31] For commentaries on the works of Aristotle see Karl Praechter, *Byzantinische Zeitschrift*, xviii (1909), pp. 516–38 and cf. H. Usener, *Göttinger gelehrte Anzeigen* (1892), pp. 1001–22; Praechter, ibid. (1903), pp. 513–30; ibid. (1904), pp. 374–91 (oral delivery of commentaries, p. 390); ibid. (1906), pp. 861–907. For the different schools in Neoplatonism: id., 'Richtungen und Schulen im Neuplatonismus' in *Genethliakon* for Carl Robert, (Weidmann, Berlin), 1910, pp. 105–56. For later Greek philosophy: Paul Tannery, 'Sur la période finale de la philosophie grecque', *Revue philosophique*, xlii (1896), pp. 266–87; V. Valdenberg, 'Sur le caractère général de la philosophie byzantine', *Revue d'histoire de la philosophie*, iii (1929), pp. 277–95; id., 'La philosophie byzantine aux IVe– Ve siecles', *Byzantion*, iv (1929), pp. 237–68, on which cf. Praechter, *Byzantinische Zeitschrift*, xxix (1929–30), pp. 313–15; J. M. Hussey, *Church and Learning in the Byzantine Empire 867–1185* (Oxford University Press, 1937). For the work of Michael of Ephesus: Praechter, *Göttinger gelehrte Anzeigen* (1906); and for the absence of distinctively Christian interpretation in the commentaries of David and Elias: id., ibid. (1908), pp. 209–39. For the significance of Syriac translations for Arab scholars: R. Walzer, *Arabic Transmission of Greek*

And in any consideration of the influence of the pagan past upon Byzantine culture the dualism in language must find a place. The conscious archaism of East Roman writers, their arduous efforts to preserve the literary style of the classical age—these are not merely the concern of the philologist, they are part of the history of Byzantine thought. Whenever the Empire was strongest it tended to reassert its close and continuous connexion with the Hellenic past: it overleapt the Hellenistic age and allowed its literature to perish. And by this conscious literary artificiality the writers cut themselves off from the people and tended to despise the use of the popular language. That language is known to us principally from the lives of the saints written by monks for simple folk to read. This passion for the ancient Attic usage only grew the stronger under the Palaeologi when the Empire was waging its last long defensive struggle against destruction, and in the fourteenth century this passion was surprisingly united with a rebirth of *Hellenic* patriotism. The name of Hellen which for so many centuries had signified only 'pagan' recovered its former significance: the monarch becomes 'the Emperor of Hellas', 'God has shown us an Emperor of the Hellenes', and similar expressions, illustrate the change.[32] The language of ancient Hellas brings with it the desire to recover the Hellenic past. The fatal cleavage between the spoken and the written tongue has been, of course, perpetuated in the conflict of our own day between the 'pure' speech and the demotic, so that a riot could be caused in Athens by the introduction of a translation of the New Testament into modern speech. This embittered struggle for the retention of the language of the past—this attempt, in Krumbacher's phrase, to produce artificial respiration in a mummy—has had upon the literature of modern Greece a disastrous influence similar to that which a like attempt produced in the Byzantine Empire. And to the modern student of history it is exasperating when an East Roman writer feels that he cannot sully his pages with any national name which

Thought to Medieval Europe, reprint from the *Bulletin of the John Rylands Library*, vol. xxi, no. 1, July 1945. [See now B. Tatakis, *La Philosophie byzantine* in Émile Bréhier, *Histoire de la Philosophie*, deuxième fascicule supplémentaire, Paris, 1949].
    [32] Cf. O. Tafrali, *Thessalonique au quatorzième siècle*, (Geuthner, Paris, 1913), p. 157.

had not been already used by Herodotus, and 'Scythian' may therefore signify any barbarian tribe which may have settled in Southern Russia. Then indeed we feel that the past is too much with us and from the artificiality of the Court and the capital we turn for refreshment to the hagiographers writing in the language which was spoken in the provincial village.

But the aspect of this dualism which interests me most is the contrast between the intellectualism of official theology and the faith of humble folk as it worked itself out in everyday life. For the 'little men' of the East Roman world that life was often enough a heavy burden: you must have in your mind the stress and strain from the recurrent threat of barbarian invasion, must recall the oppression from the agents of the imperial administration, oppression from the *potentiores*, the wealthy and powerful, with their insatiable land-hunger driving the free peasant from his holding, evicting the soldier from his hereditary farm granted in return for service in the army; you must with sympathetic imagination recover something of the terror of the ubiquitous and deadly malice of the demons who in myriad forms were wreaking on man their remorseless and unsleeping animosity. You must *feel* how easy it was for the sheer weight of life to generate despair. Indeed, from human oppressors and demonic foes where should the little man find protection? Who would undertake his defence? And to that question the Byzantine knew the answer: his defence lay in God and His Christ and in the saints inspired by God. In a recently published book which is designed to help the general reader to understand the significance of human history Mr A. L. Rowse has written:[33] 'The idea of God has been rendered superfluous.' The East Roman knew better than that: in your study of Byzantium it is with the Christian religion and with miracle that you must begin.

Your starting-point is obvious: the Byzantine knew his Bible through hearing it read in church, even if he could not read it himself—and he believed its statements. Grant the one presupposition that man can trust the Bible, and then the East Roman argument for miracle is surely both cogent and impressive. Alike in the Old and in the New Testament God is

[33] A. L. Rowse, *The Use of History* (Hodder and Stoughton, 1946), p. 115.

stated to have performed miracles on man's behalf: is God's hand straitened now in these later days? Has a God of Love ceased to aid His worshippers when they cry to Him in their distress? Indeed, if you deny miracle in this present time you make Christ a liar, for Christ said to His disciples: Greater works than these shall ye do, because I go unto the Father. And after the Ascension even from the record of the New Testament itself we can see that Christ fulfils that promise. Folk are healed if Peter's shadow do but fall upon them: this did not happen when Jesus in His life on earth healed men. Handkerchiefs and aprons if they had but touched Peter's body could cure the sick; of Christ Himself we know of no such thing. The promise of the Risen Lord holds good: that God is Love is as true to-day as it was for the Apostle John: with God nothing is impossible. I would repeat: is not that a cogent and impressive argument?

And so for the East Roman succour and comfort are to be found in the holy man, the relic, and the liturgy. Byzantine piety had created the majestic figure of Christ the Lord of All throned in glory in the dome of the East Roman churches, and before this unapproachable majesty yourself, your needs, appeared as a very little thing: but the saint had access to the courts of Heaven: he through his mediation ($\pi\rho\epsilon\sigma\beta\epsilon\iota\alpha$) would present your needs and your requests. And with the holy man rests the God-given grace of miracle, a homely succouring power which can avail against the demons. He has only got to 'throw a procession' with prayer—$\dot{\epsilon}\kappa\beta\dot{\alpha}\lambda\lambda\epsilon\iota\nu$ $\lambda\iota\tau\dot{\eta}\nu$—it sounds quaintly modern—and disease is stayed, life is saved, flooding rivers return to their beds, savage cattle when he has blessed the yoke become docile, children are conceived when he has blessed the girdles of husband and of wife: if a neighbour through jealousy has cast a maleficent spell over you the holy man has a more powerful magic charm in the sign of the cross—the important thing to realize is that this succour of the saint enters into all the familiar details of the life of humble folk: he because of his sanctity can defend you from oppression, for he enjoys freedom of speech with governors and emperors as well as in the courts of Heaven. One can easily see that the possession of a local saint is an enormous asset, and naturally you will wish to have his body after death as a last-ing protection. But of course others will want it too, and over the body there may be free fights between rival villages. At the news of the death of Symeon the Stylite a force of Saracen horsemen rode up to seize the body: it needed a detachment of the Imperial army under a Master of the Soldiery to protect the corpse. When one saint was thought to be near death he was seized and carried off to forestall a rival: the saint later re-covered consciousness and asked to be taken back to his moun-tain. The relic—the saint's clothes, a finger or a bone—are treasured, and in relic-hunting all scruples go by the board. St Anastasius after death gave useful advice concerning the best method of stealing his own body. And the holy man, together with the gift of miracle, is granted the grace of prophecy and the power to distinguish between spirits: he can read man's heart, and thus it is to him rather than to the priest that con-fession is made and by him absolution is given. St Luke the Stylite actually granted absolution unasked. And the Ortho-dox Church might for a time be unwilling to admit new and extraordinary forms of devotion like that of the pillar-saints, but in the end it yielded: no popular form of religious emotion could be allowed to remain outside the Church. It met people on their own ground. In the lives of the saints it provided good Christian folk with light and edifying reading to take the place of immoral pagan romances, and through the liturgy it brought beauty and the companionship of the faithful into hard-pressed lives. Theodore Bent once said that any superstition mentioned in Herodotus could be found in the nineteenth cen-tury as a religious rite of the Orthodox Church. And East Roman saints, like the Byzantine church, were so delightfully practical: there had been a long drought in Galatia and the saint had arranged for a solemn procession with prayers and the people came for the procession in their best clothes: 'No, no, children,' said the saint, 'run home and change: you will get soaked when the rain comes and your clothes will be spoilt.' They did as they were told, the procession was held: the rain came down in torrents and soaked they were. Simi-larly, the saint as medical specialist was just as practical: he named the doctor you should consult, he told you when an operation was necessary, what spa you should visit, and what waters you should drink, in what hot springs you should bathe. Your Bank-holidays were the annual festivals of local patron saints when the crowds of the faithful were fed at the monastery. Students have paid too much attention to the circus parties in Constantinople or Antioch: in the provinces you had no hippodromes and no cinema or football pool to bring the chariot-races into distant homes. It is in the study of the faith of humble provincial folk that we may gain an insight into the astonishing continuity of Greek religion and religious observance.

You see, perhaps, what was in my mind when I chose as the title for this talk, 'The Thought-World of East Rome.' I do believe that an essay ought to be written on that subject. 'The Oxford Movement,' Dr Headlam once said,[34] 'made religion interesting.' Cannot someone be found to do the same for the Byzantine Empire?

[34] A. C. Headlam, *The Study of Theology* (Clarendon Press, 1918), p. 9.

III

The Byzantine State

[Delivered as one of the Grey Lectures in Cambridge on
20 February 1935. Unpublished.]

I HAVE chosen for the subject of this lecture the Byzantine
State, since it is the peculiar characteristics of this State
which above all else distinguish and differentiate East Rome
from Western Europe of the early Middle Age. If it be true
that the history of the ancient world is the history of Empires,
that the history of Western Europe in the Middle Ages is the
story of small states—Kleinstaaterei *ist* Mittelalter—then the
Byzantine Empire may be regarded as a survival into Europe's
Middle Age of the conditions and institutions of an older
world. For here set against localism and decentralization stands
a highly centralized government—a government not merely
centralized in administration, but centralized—obviously, un-
mistakably—in one single city, Constantinople. Here as
against conflicting systems of law—the law of many local circumscriptions—is a realm governed by a single law—that law
emanating from a single source, the Roman emperor, and here
is to be found that single sovranty which was lacking in
Western Europe. One can come to an understanding of East
Rome most effectually, in my judgement, if one studies its
most distinctive peculiarity—the Byzantine State.

Constantinople was a Greek city before it became the eastern
capital of the Roman Empire: it was set in the Greek sphere,
and thus in a world to which absolute rule had through the
centuries of Hellenistic civilization become second nature. The
Greek East had never understood anything of that which
underlay the conception of the Principate—the outcome of the
Romanism of the thought of Augustus. The theory of the East
Roman State was fashioned by Greek thinkers, and they
desired nothing but that form of rule with which they had long
been familiar. When one emperor of East Rome had the curious idea of converting the State into a democracy—whatever

he may have meant by the term—the suggestion appeared to
the Byzantine chronicler merely the crowning disaster of an
unfortunate reign. It has sometimes been said that political
theory died out within the Empire, stifled by the atmosphere
of absolutism. This statement does not seem to me accurately
to represent the facts. Byzantine literature is steeped in political theory, but that theory is itself concerned with the
absolutism which was for the East Roman the only practicable
mode of government. Indeed, if you believe that any particular constitutional form is willed by God and sustained by
Him, it is waste of time and breath to discuss other theories of
government which lack that essential support. It is because a
single view of the ultimate basis of the authority of the State
was held without question alike by emperor and subject that
it is worth while to attempt to formulate that belief with care
and precision.

Here as elsewhere the historical student is forced back to
the reign of Constantine the Great. It was under Constantine
the Great that Eusebius first formulated the theory of the
Christian Empire.[1] His materials lay to his hand in the conception of kingship which had been elaborated by the political
philosophers of the Hellenistic world. For the Greek of the
Hellenistic age, the king had been transformed into a god
among men; Eusebius had only to drop the godhead of the
king and to put in its place the Vicegerent of God: Constantine
rules οἷα μεγάλου βασιλέως ὕπαρχος. The State in its order and
harmony, said the Hellenistic philosopher Diotogenes, is a
mimesis—a copy—of the divine creation, the kosmos: for the
divine creation Eusebius had but to substitute the kingdom of
heaven. As the State is to the kosmos, the pagan had said, so
is the king to God: the king's duty is to imitate God. For
Eusebius the archetype of the king is in Heaven. And while
the Hellenistic king is sustained by the Logos of philosophy,
there was a Christian Logos who could support a Christian
monarch. It is only when one studies the verbal parallelisms
between the pagan writers and their Christian successor that
the closeness of the similarity between them is manifest, that
the sources upon which the Christian orator drew are demon-

[1] See *Eusebius and the Christian Empire*, pp. 168–72 *infra*.

strated beyond challenge. In Eusebius we see the new conception of a Christian Empire set forth by a political theorist, but
I cannot help feeling that far more influential in fixing the
beliefs of East Rome was the faith of Constantine himself. For
here was no theory learned from another, but rather a conviction rooted and grounded in a personal experience. As 'God's
man' the emperor is charged with a mission: to the protection
and advancement of the Christian Church and in particular to
the establishment of unity of belief within the Christian body
the whole of Constantine's religious policy is directed, for it
was his frequently repeated belief that on the unity of the
Christian Church depended the prosperity of the Roman
Empire. Within the orthodox Church the bishops had their
place but, as their colleague, the emperor was charged with
the care of heretics and pagans and the religious welfare of
heretic and pagan was his imperial concern. If students would
for a time drop inherited prepossessions, close their modern
commentaries and forget what the commentators have said
and then read the correspondence of Constantine as a whole,
I believe that they could not but be struck with the boldness
of this imperial faith, its individual stamp, its consistency and
its conviction. Here the same man speaks, not a number of
forgers scattered through the chanceries of the Empire. And
because it was a faith founded on a personal experience, the
emperor's conviction left its mark, and when towards the close
of the fourth century paganism ceased to be the official creed
of the Roman world, the Empire could appropriate the programme which its first Christian sovran had formulated.

Constantine for Eusebius was the bishop of those without
the Church: indeed it took the Christian emperor many a year
before he learned that he was not a priest. The pagan title of
Pontifex Maximus continued to be borne by Constantine and
his sons, by Valentinian and Valens: it was not till the reign of
Gratian that the Roman emperor refused the title as unfitting
for a Christian ruler. In the person of the supreme magistrate
Roman tradition had ever united the responsibility alike for
civil and religious affairs: how should that Roman tradition be
preserved now that the emperor had stripped himself of the
office on which his religious authority had been based? Must he

not possess an equivalent position in the Christian faith to that which he had held as Pontifex Maximus? It seemed only reasonable. And thus for a time in the fifth century the Roman emperor became a bishop. In that century the current Latin word for episcopus is pontifex, and accordingly the Roman sovrans adopt the title of Pontifex Inclitus—the Christian substitute for the Pontifex Maximus of a pagan past. It forms a part of the official titulary of the emperor Marcian and of the emperor Anastasius.[2] It is this fact which serves to explain both the exclamation of the assembled bishops at the synod held in Constantinople in 448, 'Many years to the pious the orthodox the high-priestly emperor'—τῷ ἀρχιερεῖ βασιλεῖ[3]—and also the greeting of the bishops gathered at the Council of Chalcedon, 'Hail to the priest, the emperor.' The Latin version renders this greeting 'Sacerdoti Imperatori multos annos', and a variant reading gives Pontifici. Agapetus, bishop of Rhodes, wrote in A.D. 457 to the emperor Leo, 'Vere namque sacerdos et natura imperator existis.' It is no longer strange that Pope Leo I in his correspondence should fifteen times—according to Kissling's[4] statistics—apply the adjective sacerdotalis—sacerdotalis animus, sacerdotalis mens, etc.—to successive emperors.

It was Justinian who finally recognized that a distinction must be made between the imperial authority and the Christian priesthood. It is true that in the emperor's view that distinction was small: 'cum nec multo differant ab alterutro sacerdotium et imperium' he wrote in his seventh novel, but the distinction had been drawn, and in the sixth novel that distinction is defined. The greatest of the gifts of God to men granted by divine generosity are the priesthood and the imperial authority (βασιλεία): the one serves divine ends, the other rules over and cares for human affairs: and each of these springs from one and the same source and each adorns the life of man. . . . For if the priest be blameless in every respect, and

[2] P. Batiffol, in *Bulletin de la Société Nationale des Antiquaires de France* (1926), pp. 222–7.

[3] [L. Bréhier, ' "Hiéreus" et "Basileus",' *Mémorial Louis Petit* (= *Archives de l'orient chrétien, I*) (Bucarest, 1948), pp. 41–5.]

[4] W. K. Kissling, *Das Verhältnis zwischen Sacerdotium und Imperium* (Paderborn, 1921), p. 91.

enjoy free access to God, and if the emperor duly and rightly adorn the State which is entrusted to him, then there will result a certain fair harmony (συμφωνία) which will furnish every good thing to the human race. 'We', continues Justinian, 'are, therefore, concerned in the highest degree for the true doctrines inspired by God and for the worthy conduct of the priests which, if they observe, we are convinced that great goods will be given to us by God and that we shall firmly hold our present possessions and shall gain in addition those which we have not yet secured.' It is the conviction of Constantine appropriated by his sixth-century successor.

Professor Diehl once wrote that the Byzantine emperor is a priest. Some support for that view can be found in the writings of late Greek canonists, but this does not, in my judgement, represent the theory of the great Byzantine sovrans. The functions of patriarch and emperor are distinct, though complementary: the patriarch has his natural place by the emperor's side. Emperor and patriarch are of necessity allies for both are *within* the Byzantine polity. The East Roman conception is most clearly expressed in the definitions of the code known as the Epanagoge[5] which was perhaps inspired by Photius. Man, says the Epanagoge, is composed of many parts, so is the organism of the State—τῆς πολιτείας ἐκ μερῶν καὶ μορίων ἀναλόγως τῷ ἀνθρώπῳ συνισταμένης (III. 8), and of that organism the two greatest and most necessary parts are the emperor and the patriarch: the emperor's task is to secure to the soul and the body of his subjects peace and happiness; the patriarch's part is to strengthen in all men agreement in a common faith—to turn them from heresies and sin, and lead them to repentance. The aim of an emperor is τὸ εὐεργετεῖν,—beneficence—and when he fails thus to benefit his subjects, he falsifies the imperial character which his predecessors have handed down to him. The aim of the patriarch is to preserve the souls entrusted to his care: to live to Christ and to be crucified to the world. Thus is formulated that co-operation which should unite emperor and patriarch in a common service.

This same distinction between Empire (βασιλεία) and

---

[5] The text of the Epanagoge in J. and P. Zepos, *Jus Graecoromanum*, vol. ii (Athens, 1931), pp. 240 sqq.

priesthood is preserved in a speech of the emperor John
Tzimisces reported in the history of Leo the Deacon (pp. 101–2).
'There is one authority (ἀρχή), the highest and the first, which
brought into being out of nothing the order of the seen and
unseen universe. And in this life of ours . . . I recognize that
there are two authorities (ἀρχάς)—the priesthood and the imperial power. To one of these the Creator has entrusted the
care of souls and to the other the government of men's bodies
that neither of these parts should fail in its duty, but be preserved in vigour and completeness.' Similar language is used
by Psellos and by John of Euchaita in the eleventh century.
Both emperor and patriarch, the latter writes, are destined
for rule by God: both are 'Christs'—the anointed of the Lord.[6]

The eleventh century saw seated on the patriarchal throne
of Constantinople a very remarkable man—Cerularius. We
possess no writings from his hand: nowhere can we consult his
own statement of his ideals and purposes. We can, however,
see that he had a passion for power. It may well be that before
his consecration he had sought to become emperor. Psellos in
a letter to the patriarch writes: 'You are democratically
minded (δημοκρατικὸς ἀνήρ),[7] and you find it difficult to
tolerate the monarchy. . . . Do not seek to rule over us, do not
play the emperor's part, for thus you will become intolerable
to the majority of men.'[8] The often-quoted line of Homer is
cited yet again: 'Let one be lord, one Basileus.' 'Formerly',
says Psellos, 'the same man was both priest and protector of
his people'—I think this must be a reference to the priest-king
Melchizidek[9]—'but now that which was single has been
divided: there have been ordained both the imperial power
and the priesthood.' In the accusation which Psellos at his
sovran's direction drew up against the patriarch he accused
Cerularius of wishing to unite that which God had divided.
'In his hand the patriarch held the cross, while his mouth
issued imperial decrees.'[10] He is μισοβασιλεύς—an enemy of the
emperor. Cerularius assumed the purple boots which it was the

[6] L. Bréhier, *Le schisme oriental du XIᵉ siecle* (Paris, 1899), pp. 75, 275.
Patrologia Graeca, 120, cols. 1163, 1183.
[7] [Cf. G. I. Brătianu, *Mémorial Petit* (see note 3 *supra*), p. 33.]
[8] K. N. Sathas, *Mesaionike Bibliotheke*, vol. v (Paris, 1876), p. 512.
[9] Cf. Kissling, op. cit. (at n. 4), p. 140.   [10] Bréhier, op. cit. (at n. 6), p. 275.

prerogative of the emperor alone to wear. According to the chronicler Scylitzes (Cedrenus II, 643), Cerularius stated that there was no difference between empire and priesthood, or at least that difference was small: the priesthood was more honourable and perhaps worthy of greater consideration. But on the patriarchal throne of Constantinople there was no place for a Gregory VII: Cerularius was deposed and the dream of a Byzantine papacy was ended. East Roman tradition was too strongly established to be shaken by the ambition of a revolutionary patriarch.

It is possible that in the heat of controversy an Iconoclast emperor may have exclaimed, 'I am priest as well as emperor,' but he spoke in haste—the consistency of Byzantine theory is not prejudiced thereby. It is only in the days of the Empire's weakness that the change came: on the fall of Latin rule after the Greeks had returned to Constantinople, the person of the emperor becomes increasingly exalted, the atmosphere of the court is ecclesiastical and hierarchic. Then canonists will indeed make of their sovran a priest, save that he cannot even so offer the sacrifice of the Eucharist. But it is important to realize that this is a late development: the really significant theory is that of the Epanagoge: patriarch and emperor, as allies not rivals, both alike essential for the prosperity of the East Roman polity—both parts of a single organism. There is in the Byzantine Empire no parallel to the Investiture Dispute of Western Europe.

Further, the Byzantine world had worked out its own conception of the imperial ideal. That ideal, like most other elements in this East Roman world, has its roots in a distant past. From the time when Augustus had founded the Principate men looked to the emperor as the efficient εὐεργετής—the power which could really get things done. Even in the government of Rome itself—in the sphere of the Senate's control— it was to Augustus that men turned for the supply of their daily needs, and new responsibilities were forced upon him: he was constrained to answer the popular demand. It is on the person of the emperor that men's hopes are set. He is the source of all initiative. A psychology of dependence is widespread. And the sovran for his part acknowledges his imperial duty—assumes

the colossal burden of responsibility. 'It is our care', wrote the
emperor Marcian, 'to provide for the welfare of the human
race; for this is our aim ceaselessly pursued by day and night
that all those who live beneath our rule should be guarded from
enemy assault by the shelter of our armed forces and that
in peace they may enjoy untroubled ease and security.' (Nov.
2, apud init.) The emperor has become an earthly Providence.
Symeon, the great Byzantine mystic of the eleventh century,
defines the essential character of βασιλεία—of empire—in a
single word πρόνοια—Providence—that unsleeping forethought
which is armed against any emergency. When the emperor Leo
the Wise abolishes the municipal senates he justifies his act by
the plea that the form of the government has changed and that
everything now depends solely on the πρόνοια of the emperor
and on his administration. In another novel he writes 'everything now depends upon the care of the emperor and with
God's help it is by this imperial πρόνοια that all things are
safe-guarded and provision made therefor.'[11] If you are prepared to study Byzantine literature with sympathy, you cannot but feel the oppression of this burden of responsibility
which was borne by a conscientious emperor, ἡ τῆς βασιλείας
ποικιλία, τὸ μέγεθος τοῦ κράτους, τὸ πολυειδὲς τῆς προνοίας—the
complexity of an emperor's task, the vast extent of his rule,
the infinite variety of that imperial forethought which was the
sovran's duty.

And in an Empire constantly beset with foes it was in the
camp of his armies that the emperor found his most significant
post. For the army, as an eleventh-century writer put it, is the
glory of the emperor and the strength of the palace.[12] The
urgent appeal of Synesius to a sovran who was no soldier
retained its validity throughout Byzantine history: 'It is for
you', writes Synesius in the *De Regno*, 'to restore the king to
his original function . . . give us back the king who is a public-
spirited servant of his kingdom. In the present state of affairs
we can no longer dally at our ease, or take a step in advance:

---

[11] Novels 46 and 47 [cf. P. Noailles and A. Dain, *Les Novelles de Léon le Sage*,
Paris, 1944 (text and translation)].
[12] B. Wasilievsky and V. Jernstedt, *Cecaumeni Strategikon et incerti scriptoris
De Officiis regis libellus* (St Petersburg, 1896) = *Zapiski istoriko-philologiché-
skago fakulteta imperatorskago Universiteta*, Chart 38, p. 101.

for all men stand on a razor's edge. For our State we need God and a King.'[13]

'We need God and a King', it is an epitome of the constant desire of the Byzantine world.

And if you proceed to ask what were the qualities which above all others the East Roman admired in his emperor, the answer is simple and can be given without hesitation: they are two, Philanthropia and Eusebeia, Beneficence and Piety. Both of these conceptions would repay careful study. The supremacy of Philanthropia and Eusebeia as royal attributes is once more a legacy from the Greek philosophers of the Hellenistic period: the pity is that modern students of Greek philosophy have never troubled to trace the history of these virtues into the Byzantine period, that is to say into the age when they gain a new interest from the fact that they practically influence the conduct of rulers and when from their association with Christianity they gain a fresh and living content. In the fourth century Themistius, philosopher and rhetorician, devotes to the subject of Philanthropia three of his most instructive speeches. Philanthropia is, he insists, the touchstone by which the character of a ruler may be tested. Just as pure gold is valuable, but is raised to a new potency when it receives the imperial stamp, so Philanthropia is the stamp which placed upon other virtues gives to each a new and imperial dignity. When subjects speak on the streets or in the public baths—wherever it may be—of that which they desire from their emperor, the one word is φιλανθρωπία. Above all φιλανθρωπία is the virtue which man can without fear or reserve attribute to God: it is also the virtue which man can share with God. Man cannot imitate the Gods in length of life, in extent of power, but only in beneficence. Through beneficence an emperor may become Godlike. The beneficent emperor is thus the perfect exemplar of imperial virtue, for his is the adornment which not even the Father of All will despise. So the pagan Themistius: with this compare a passage from Synesius which unites the praise of Eusebeia and of Philanthropia on the same level of religious exaltation: 'The Emperor himself will lead us to piety, seeking from a divine source the direction of every deed whether great

[13] Synesius, *De Regno*, § 14.

or small. More wondrous than all else is it, methinks, to hear or to behold the King'—the βασιλεύς—'when in the midst of his people he holds up his hands and bends his knee before that King Who is at once his own and that of his people. And it is reasonable to suppose that the Divinity will be rejoiced when glorified by devotion from a pious king and will make such an one His own in sacred union. Thus in addition to being a lover of God he becomes more than all else a lover of man (φιλάν-θρωπος), for he shows himself to his subjects in the image of the King by Whom he is ruled.' In such statements as these we are given a glimpse of the mysticism which sustained the Byzantine imperial ideal.

The action of Philanthropia might be exemplified in many different spheres, but it is so frequently associated with legislation and the administration of justice that it is perhaps from this field that it may best be illustrated. The Byzantine prided himself on the fact that the imperial government was no arbitrary tyranny: it was founded on the basis of the Roman law—it was an ἔννομος ἐπιστασία; so the Epanagoge (Tit. 2, cap. 1) echoing Saint Basil.[14] There was, however, some doubt whether the emperor was himself bound by the laws of the State, and there are conflicting views in our sources. Continental jurists have at times been puzzled by this contradiction, but it should present little difficulty to a student of English legal history. The English Court of Chancery was bound by the Common Law, but when that law would work injustice the Court of Chancery intervened and in effect overruled the Common Law. The position of a Byzantine emperor was not unlike that of an English Chancellor: the emperor was in fact his own Court of Equity. There is an illuminating story told of Constantine X: when he discovered that a litigant was insisting on a strict interpretation of the law in order to effect a manifest injustice: 'Oh, these laws!' the emperor exclaimed, 'they have been our ruin.'[15] The task of imperial humanity is defined in the fourth century by Themistius: punishment is a medicine: but the punishment of death takes away from him who is sick

[14] Cf. G. Vernadsky, *Recueil Kondakov*, (Prag, 1926), p. 150.
[15] É. Renauld, *Michel Psellos. Chronographie*, Tome 2 (Paris, 1928), p. 152. [*The Chronographia of Michael Psellos* (English translation by E. R. A. Sewter), London, 1953, p. 263.]

all hope of cure: the death of the criminal benefits only those who need no medicine. This is ridiculous; therefore the privilege of the emperor is to seek πρόφασιν ἐπιεικείας—an excuse for mercy. It is precisely on this ground—that punishment is remedial, an ἰατρεία—that Leo VI at the end of the ninth century abolished capital punishment for peculations by state officials (Nov. CV). The virtue of the judge, explains Themistius in another oration, lies in the strict application of the law, the virtue of the emperor as τοῦ νόμου κύριος—as lord of the law—rests in his power to correct even the law—ἐπανορθοῦν καὶ τοὺς νόμους—since he is a living law (νόμος ἔμψυχος). For it would appear that God sent from Heaven the imperial authority for this very purpose that it might be man's refuge—that from the immovable law he might flee to the breathing and the living law. God, wrote Justinian, had sent to men from Heaven the imperial authority, itself a living law. The emperor's duty is to apply the law, or in a phrase of Psellos to declare νόμου τι δικαιότερον—a decision more just than the law itself.[16] This is the privilege of imperial φιλανθρωπία in the sphere of justice. Constantine IX thought that he was no longer an emperor on a day when he had not done for his subjects φιλάνθρωπόν τι.[17]

And Eusebeia—Piety—is to the Byzantine the κρηπὶς ἀσφαλής—the firm foundation of the empire. The East Roman sovrans are πιστοὶ ἐν Χριστῷ βασιλεῖς. The army's standard is a jewelled cross: with the troops is regularly carried the icon of the Virgin of Blachernae. The ceremonial year of the Byzantine emperor with its straitly regulated succession of religious services is the imperial tribute to the same ideal of piety. It was counted to Botaniates for righteousness that he *stood* through the lengthy ritual and did not sit, that he did not leave the church after the reading of the Gospel, but bore the

[16] Psellos, *Chronographia*, Renauld (see n. 15), vol. ii, p. 146. [Sewter's translation, p. 258.]

[17] Whence did the Emperor draw his remark? It appears first attributed to Titus in Suetonius' biography of that emperor, § 8: recordatus quondam super cenam quod nihil cuiquam toto die praestitisset memorabilem illam meritoque laudatam vocem edidit: amici, diem perdidi. Similarly in a Greek Carmen Paraeneticum there is a stanza devoted to Titus where there is the equivalent ἅπαξ δ' οὐκ εὐεργέτησεν εἶπε μὴ βασιλεῦσαι. V. Lindström, *Anecdota Byzantina*, Fasc. I (Upsala, 1902), p. 13, stanza 28. I owe this reference to Professor A. D. Nock. For Constantine IX: Psellos, *Chronographia*, Renauld, ii, 54. [Sewter, p. 183.]

weight of his jewelled robes until the service ended. When in
1056 a usurper threatened the throne of Michael VI and he
was urged to defend himself, he protested that to pollute the
capital with the blood of his subjects in his own defence would
be a deed of unprincipled egoism and μισανθρωπία—a denial,
you see, of imperial φιλανθρωπία. Looking down at his purple
shoes—the symbol of Byzantine royalty—'Not for these', he
said, 'will Michael betray τὴν εὐσέβειαν.'[18] But if you would
catch an echo of what this imperial ideal of piety meant to the
folk of East Rome you must turn to the poems of George of
Pisidia when in the seventh century he celebrates the victories
of Heraclius over the fire-worshippers of Persia. Heraclius had
sailed from Africa to rescue Constantinople from a bloody
tyranny with the image of the Virgin at his mast-head, he had
advanced against the Persian invader, his army led by a
sacred icon which no human hand had fashioned: the Defender
of the Faith leads the forces of the Christ against the blas-
phemies of paganism. 'When Virgin Faith goes forth to war,
she clothes herself in Heaven's bright robe of Hope.' ὡς εὖ
κρατοῦσα σὺν Θεῷ μοναρχία: 'How fair a rule is monarchy with
God for guide!' The imperium of Heraclius is a θεοστήρικτον
κράτος—a power whose foundation is God. 'Εν εὐσεβείᾳ τὸν
στρατόν σου ῥυθμίσας. Thou who in piety hast ordered thine
army μεθ' οὗ στρατηγεῖν ἐστὶν ἀσφαλέστερον, δι' οὗ τὸ νικᾶν
ἐστιν εὐσεβέστερον, with whom it is safer to serve, and through
whom victory becomes more hallowed. The emperor's piety
hallows victory. In the moment of triumph Heraclius exclaims: 'I have lived these days unto the Lord!'

I have sought to illustrate the Byzantine imperial ideal because it would appear to me that it is through the study of this
ideal that one can most clearly gain some comprehension of
the forces which sustained the Byzantine State, which turned
its wars into crusades, which inspired those recoveries from
disaster and confusion which are the wonder of its history.
Here is the background against which the study of the material
resources of the State must be set. That study has its own
peculiar difficulties. If the student of the medieval history of
Western Europe is often paralyzed by the sheer wealth and

[18] Michael Attaliota (Bonn ed.), p. 58.

complexity of his documentary material, the student of the history of East Rome is reduced to despair by the bitter penury of documents which is most obvious for the crucial period of the seventh and eighth centuries of our era. Further, Byzantine writers seem to be possessed by an unholy passion for inventing new names for administrative posts and institutions, and it is no easy matter to determine whether the new name carries with it any real change in the administration or simply re-christens an existing institution which then continues to function as it has done in the past. Once more, our modern narratives of Byzantine history do not always give us as much help as we might expect, for they are crowded with narrative and the stage is so full that the Byzantine State is rather a presupposition of the whole drama than a character in the play. Much work scattered in many learned journals has been produced during the present century, and the time has come for a stock-taking: what general lines of development have been disclosed by recent research? We need in fact a sketch of the life-history of the Byzantine State. And in that history the army of East Rome, its recruitment and the fiscal system by which it was sustained will be of primary importance, for upon these depends the achievement of the Empire. Man-power and money-power, these for the Byzantine Basileus were the essential issues. The decline of the imperial authority in the provinces of Western Europe was, I would suggest, principally due to the bankruptcy of the central government:[19] the emperor of the West could not play the part of Universal Providence on an empty treasury. For the barbarian kingdoms formed on Roman soil did not subtract territory alone from the Roman dominion; what was even more ruinous, they withheld the revenues which the Empire drew from its Western provinces. It became impossible at one and the same time to maintain a mercenary army and a fleet in commission. If the coast of Italy were to be defended from the Vandal fleet, military action in Gaul was paralyzed. East Rome survived when Rome of the West succumbed in large measure because Constantinople retained its hold upon its Asiatic reservoirs of men and of money.

[19] Cf. *The Decline of the Roman Power in Western Europe*, pp. 83-96 *infra*.

The basis of the fiscal reform of the fourth century is to be found in the unit of taxation which was not merely a land-unit, but a unit of land and labour. For the Roman government land was of value only if it were cultivated, the human element could not be neglected. The system was one of jugatio *and* capitatio: the unit of land was so much as could be worked by a labourer, or so much as could support a labourer, the human unit was the man's labour which could keep the land unit in cultivation. The aim of the State must be to maintain a balance between land and labour. Thus fluid labour, labour free to move irresponsibly, as it would, becomes for the State a danger: freedom of movement must be checked, since at any moment it can upset administrative calculation. Thus gradually, progressively through the fourth century the government intervenes in different provinces, and the labourer, the colonus, becomes tied to the soil—a serf, adscriptus glebae. The labour capital of the Empire is immobilized, and here as elsewhere a man's condition is determined no longer by free contract but through status imposed by imperial legislation. The effort of the fourth century administrator is a continuous search for guarantees, for security. One guarantee is the denial of individual initiative through the assertion of a *hereditary* liability to serve the interests of the State, another is the assertion of *corporate* liability for the defaults of others. The duty of the collection of the taxes is thrown upon the municipal senates, and, since land must not be allowed to lapse from cultivation, the State imposes upon the deserter's colleagues the duty of cultivating the abandoned land—adjectio sterilium. Thus from above the insistence of the State presses upon all alike, and each seeks to shift the burden upon the class below him. But there is no one upon whom the free peasant can shift his burden: he seeks a shelter: he finds it in the patronage of the great landholders—the potentes: if he surrenders his land to a magnate, he secures the protection of a power which can oppose the demands of the State with success: the landholder on his side welcomes the opportunity to acquire yet wider estates. The government is not slow to realize the significance of this threat: it legislates against patrocinium, but finds itself powerless to stay the evil. It is still seeking security for its revenues—still seeking guarantees. Such guarantees the wealthy landowners can give: would it not be wiser to accept that guarantee and relinquish a fruitless struggle? The State early in the fifth century capitulates: the landowner shall collect on the State's behalf the taxes of his tenants, and assume for them responsibility: he shall furnish from his domains the recruits for the army whom the State requires in its task of imperial defence. Upon the corporate liability of the municipal senates—their members riveted to their obligations without hope of escape—upon the liability of the great landlord for the taxes of those who work his domains is based the fiscal system of the Roman State.

The emperor formulates the claims of the government: the praetorian prefect distributes the burden among the provinces: the provincial governor communicates with municipal senate and landowner, and they in their turn raise the taxation from their area. The burden is a crushing liability, and its exaction is attended with much brutality and injustice. Without money the defence of the Empire is impossible, and that necessity nullifies the good intentions of the emperor. He may issue constitution after constitution enjoining consideration for the subject, but he cannot in the last resort forgo the revenues, the collection of which is the source of the ills from which the subject suffers. And when the emperor is a dreamer of imperial dreams, as was Justinian, the contradiction—the relentless inconsistency—is only accentuated. Justinian's reign overtaxed the resources of the Roman State and bred widespread disaffection. Under Justinian's successors the fiscal system broke down, and with the opening years of the seventh century the imperial administration was threatened with total collapse. The reign of the rude soldier Phocas was marked by external disaster and domestic chaos. Persia has practically destroyed the Roman army, the Chagan of the Avars is master of the Balkans and the Slav invaders are his subjects, the feuds of Blues and Greens throughout the cities of the Empire have become so murderously embittered as to assume the proportions of a civil war. It was the exarch of Roman Africa who sent his son Heraclius to save the East Roman world from dissolution. Roman Carthage—the city which

Justinian had recovered from the Vandal—manned the fleet which carried him to Constantinople. This was perhaps the greatest service the reconquered provinces of Western Europe rendered to the Byzantine State. Yet though Phocas was overthrown, disaster followed on disaster, Palestine and Egypt were lost to the Persian, a Persian army marched through Asia Minor and encamped on the Asiatic shore opposite Constantinople, in 626 Avar and Slav confederate with Persia besieged the Eastern capital by land and sea. A new army had to be created, and every recruiting ground seemed closed to the Empire. Heraclius boldly transferred his military base to the inaccessible highlands of Armenia and the Caucasus and thence enrolled the forces which in six years of warfare defeated the Persian Kingdom. After the victory the task of internal reorganization remained. The Armenian troops were settled in their native land under an Armenian noble, who was given in this Roman province a wide civil as well as military authority. Here (as Bréhier, following Kulakovsky, has suggested) is to be found the model for the Byzantine system of the military Themes, the new administrative circumscriptions which superseded the provinces which East Rome had inherited from the early Empire. That system was gradually developed during the seventh century. While Egypt and Syria were torn from the Empire by the Arabs, the Roman power was concentrated in Asia Minor. The invasion of Anatolia by the Persians, of the Balkan lands by Avar and Slav must have in large measure broken the power of the great landed proprietors. The way was open for the creation of a free peasantry. In Asia Minor the Empire had always possessed wide imperial domains: on these and on the lands deserted by their cultivators the Roman troops were settled and granted farms on condition of military service. For the free peasant living in a free village community was issued the Farmers' Law. Both military settler and free peasant pay the land-tax, but neither is a serf: neither is tied to the land. In the seventh century it would seem, the dominance of the holders of the large estates had passed, and from the στρατιωτικὰ κτήματα—the military allotments—the Empire can maintain its standing army of cavalry troops. The infantry was, it would seem, still recruited by conscription from the population of the Empire. The new system of provincial government is based upon the territories occupied by the different army-corps: the military circumscription is also the unit of provincial administration and the civil officials are subordinated to the military chiefs. It was with the army raised from the themes of Asia Minor that Leo III, the first of the Iconoclast Emperors, met and repelled the supreme effort of the Muslim Caliphate to capture Constantinople.

The Iconoclasts doubtless brought to its full development the new administrative order; the praetorian prefecture disappears in the latter part of the seventh century and with it the civil diocese: the fiscal system of the Empire depends no longer upon the municipal senates and the great landlords: the municipal senates are a broken reed, their day was doubtless over long before they were finally abolished by Leo VI at the close of the ninth century. The central government undertakes the collection of the taxes in the provinces and for those taxes it relies in large measure on the revenue from the military allotments and from the free village community. In the free village community the State still insists on its principle of corporate liability, but the villagers are protected by their right of προτίμησις: the villager's land is his own property and he can alienate it, but, if he determine to sell his land, it must first be offered to his relatives and neighbours, who can thus prevent the admission into the community of those who might fail to maintain the cultivation of the lands and so endanger the financial stability of the village. It is only recently that this fact of the private ownership of land within the village has been clearly established, but there is no necessity to contend that the community of the village is solely fiscal, and simply created by the State to ensure that corporate liability to which it had long been wedded. The free Byzantine village is a community in a larger sense than this: it owns as a community the pastures and woodlands in which all the villagers have common rights: it may as a community own the village mill. But those common rights over the untilled land can be lost when a villager extends the area of cultivation and thereby reduces part of the common land into private ownership.

Within the Byzantine village community there is no periodic redistribution of the land: recent research has disproved any such influence of Slav custom as was formerly maintained by Russian scholars.

This is the fiscal background of the period when East Rome under the Macedonian sovrans who succeeded Basil I reached its greatest height of vigour and success, but even during that period of military triumph the foundation of the State's prosperity was being undermined.

Once more the potentes were building up great estates and were laying hands upon the soldiers' allotments, were forcing their way into the territorium of the free village community. The struggle of the State with its too-powerful subjects begins afresh and is mirrored for us in a succession of imperial constitutions by which the encroachments of the wealthy landlords were to be prohibited. Sales of soldiers' and peasants' land were invalidated, the free contract of the Roman law was abolished, and the poor and the weak could no longer enter into agreements for sale with the rich and mighty. And again the history of the earlier Empire repeats itself and the potentes —now in especial the great families of Asia Minor—carry the day. The maintenance of Byzantine civilization depended upon the preservation of a nice balance between the civil and military elements in the State. If emperor and patriarch must give to each other mutual support, so is it with the army and the civil service: they must co-operate as twin pillars bearing the strain of the great structure of the Roman polity. If the army formed, as Psellos the civilian admitted, the sinews of the Roman State, that army needed, to perform its work, the resources which the civil administration supplied. In the eleventh century the emperor's ministers in the capital grew to mistrust the great Anatolian families which provided the generals who led the Empire's armies. They were unwilling to spend the revenues of the Empire on troops which might follow their general to the capital in order to wrest power from the civilian ministers in whom the soldiers had little reason to place their confidence. And this mutual mistrust bred weakness. The State appears to be unequal to performing its essential task by means of its own servants: it falls back upon the expedient of farming out the collection of its revenues to the highest bidder. It was an expedient disastrous alike to the provincials and to the central government. The financial stability of the Empire was jeopardized and the widest of doors was opened to fiscal extortion. And the century which saw the victory of the landed proprietor over the στρατιωτικὰ κτήματα and the village community, which saw mistrust sown between the army and the civil administration, saw also the irruption of the Seljuk Turk into Asia Minor and the destruction of the Roman army on the fatal field of Manzikert. The century-long defence by the Roman State of the military allotments and of the free village community had proved powerless to avert the victory of the potentes.

The result of that victory is clear: the empire is forced to enrol mercenary soldiers in its armies on an ever-increasing scale: within its own territory there is no longer the trained force—ready at any moment to take the field—on which had once rested the East Roman defence. Conscription from the inhabitants of the Empire in the form of a tax upon land was a poor substitute, and even this tax the provincials were allowed to commute into a cash payment. Mercenaries cost money, and taxes, the collection of which was farmed out to the highest bidder, never realized an emperor's expectations. Under the Comneni in the twelfth century, when the Roman State wished to reward its generals, it so thoroughly admitted the triumph of the principle of the large estate that it adopted that principle as the basis of its own procedure. It would grant to an officer an estate containing, it might be, whole peasant villages, together with the taxes (either in whole or in part) paid by such villagers. The land thus granted—the πρόνοια—was a personal donation and no heritable estate: it reverted to the emperor on the death of the grantee: there was thus a temptation ruthlessly to exploit the unhappy peasants whom the State had surrendered to the arbitrary exactions of the holder of the πρόνοια. The system which can be traced back into the eleventh century has no necessary connexion with the beneficium of Western feudalism which it closely resembled: it grew up apparently as an independent development within the Roman Empire, but after the Latin conquest in A.D. 1204 it could be readily adopted by Frankish rulers, coinciding as it did with the conceptions which they brought with them from the West.

The extension of the landed estates of the potentes in the eleventh century must have to a large extent broken up the free village community: the application in the twelfth century of the πρόνοια system of land grants can have only hastened the decline of the class of free peasantry, and this decline reacted upon the fiscal system of the Empire. The consequence of the financial straits to which the Byzantine State was reduced was the decay of the Roman navy, and that decay in its turn led East Rome to make ruinous concessions to Venice to purchase her support at sea. Thus was awakened that envy and greed which resulted in the diversion of the Fourth Crusade and the sack by Western Christians of the Christian stronghold of the East. From that overthrow East Rome never recovered: the restored Empire of the Palaeologi never possessed an adequate financial basis on which to found the defence of its diminished territory, and the foreign policy of emperors sank into a humiliating search for subsidies from the Western powers. Attempts were indeed made to restore the system of military allotments, but they had no permanent success, and of such allotments there is no longer any trace in the second half of the fourteenth century.

This is, of course, but a hasty summary of the results of some recent work, but already the life-history of the Byzantine State is taking shape, already we are beginning to see somewhat more clearly the difficulties with which East Rome had to contend in its task of imperial defence. At least we can say that through the centuries before the decline came the Empire had so successfully kept the eastern invaders at bay that Western Europe under its shelter was given time enough to fashion its own civilization.

IV

Some Aspects of Byzantine Civilization

[A paper read at a Meeting of the Society for the Promotion of Roman Studies on 5 March 1930. *Journal of Roman Studies*, xx (1930), pp. 3–13.]

AT the outset the question may well be raised whether there is any real justification for the inclusion of a paper on such a theme in the programme of a Society for the Promotion of Roman Studies. Is Byzantine civilization—in any true sense of the word—Roman at all? To judge from not a few modern studies of the life of the East Roman Empire, the answer to that question could only be in the negative. Take what is perhaps the best-known brief presentment of Byzantine history—that of Professor Diehl of Paris—and the reader will not long be left in doubt. The preface proclaims the character of the Empire: Byzantium very quickly became, and was essentially, an oriental monarchy. In the sixth century, before Justinian's accession, one could well believe that the dream of a purely oriental empire was near its realization. Justinian delayed that consummation, but at the beginning of the eighth century a really Byzantine Empire had come into being which grew ever more and more oriental in character. Under the Iconoclast monarchs the Empire had become completely orientalized; at the end of the Iconoclast struggle East Rome was a strictly oriental empire. The words 'oriental', 'orientalisé', beat upon the mind with throbbing insistence: the monotonous repetition is almost hypnotic in its cumulative effect. The reader may without difficulty fail to note that by this subtle rhetorical device an *Histoire*, which is in fact a veiled *Tendenzschrift*, has charmed him into acquiescence. He will hardly be conscious that the 'blessed word' *oriental* is given little, if any, specific content, that general assertions are not illustrated and controlled by concrete detail, that it is left uncertain *what* Orient is intended—whether Syria, Persia, India or far Cathay. The Orient, thus undifferentiated, is a word not of historical science, but of mysticism; an unkindly critic might add—of mystification. If Professor Diehl were challenged on the point, what, we may ask ourselves, would be his reply? He would doubtless point to the προσκύνησις of a Byzantine court; he would agree with Rostovtzeff that the Byzantine theory of sovranty as a celestial trust dates from Aurelian's eastern wars and reflects an Iranian conception of the true legitimation of a monarch's authority; he might contend that the later monastic ideal of divine contemplation— of a mystic θεωρία—is cousin-german to Buddhism, while he would remind us that through the wanderings of a far-travelled tale Buddha himself has been canonized as a Christian saint. The barbarous punishments of Byzantine criminal justice, blinding, nose-slitting and other corporeal mutilations, he would perhaps suggest, were derived from ancient Persian practices which were largely responsible for the Greek view that the Persian was a barbarian. Professor Diehl does in fact point out that the Iconoclast reformers found their inspiration in those Asiatic provinces which bordered upon Armenia, and we may remind ourselves that Armenia is historically a land hostile to an art of 'Darstellung'—a representational art —and enamoured of an art of 'significant form', to borrow a phrase from Mr Clive Bell, an art which sought to express its deepest convictions in the symbolism of an ornamentation which went to nature only to borrow from it decorative motives—which never sought in the interest of mere realism to reproduce that nature. Professor Diehl might follow further in the footsteps of Strzygowski and seek to portray the whole Iconoclast controversy as a struggle between two worlds: aesthetically, a struggle between the Mediterranean man and his art of representation on the one hand and the nomad, be he of steppe or desert, with his art of symbolism on the other; architecturally, a struggle in which the congregational basilica and the flat roof of the West were matched against the confined spaces of the cupola constructions of the East; and similarly, in the religious sphere, a struggle where two worlds met in conflict—a world which had raised the iconography of the human to a point where it became a bridge of mediation leading man to the ideal and the superhuman, and a world to which such an iconography appeared as *menschlich, allzu menschlich*—a degradation of the Eternal through identification with the transience of the material. And in this Armageddon of the continents Byzantium will stand as the bridgehead, the prize for which Asia and Europe will dispute, the post where the issue is joined.

It might indeed seem as though a Society for the Promotion of Roman Studies had but little reason to concern itself with Byzantine civilization. And yet I would contend that I do not stand here to-day under any false pretence. I would claim, as a disciple of Freeman and of Bury, that there remains a reason for the use of the term Later Roman Empire, that there is a Roman element in this Byzantine civilization. That civilization represents to my mind the fusion of two traditions, the Greek and the Roman, and I would maintain that what oriental elements there are in its composition are not the essential and characteristic features of the Byzantine world. I would suggest that it is by means of a panoramic survey of East Mediterranean history that we can best picture to ourselves that fusion which *is* East Rome.

As I see the process, the turning-points in the development are marked by four outstanding figures: Alexander the Great, Augustus, Constantine and the emperor Heraclius. The first period of some three hundred years—from Alexander the Great to Augustus—created the civilization with which that of East Rome was continuous: its marked feature is that it was a culture shared widely by the men of a world where intercourse was general. Alexander had broken down the separate independence of the Greek city-state, and by so doing had destroyed much of its cherished individuality. The city-state lives on, but with a difference: its significance was necessarily dwarfed when brought into contact with empires and with scientifically organized armies before which its strength was as a very little thing. It may be doubted whether we always realize with sufficient vividness the discomfort of an age when empire-building was the fashion, when any day a Pyrrhus might arrive before the city gates, seeking a field for the satisfaction of a boundless egoism. The sheltering embrace of men's city walls availed little before the relentless individualists who march through Hellenistic history. Man felt himself alone in face of a dangerous world: the poles of Hellenistic thinking are thus the individual and the cosmos. Mr Tarn has contended that Alexander the Great never dreamed of a world-empire; but, even if this be true, Alexander did break down the traditional moulds of men's thinking and forced them to deal with problems in the light of the οἰκουμένη—as Professor Bury was fond of saying, the 'oecumenical idea' was born. In an age when the might of the gods of the city-state had dwindled before new powers, the agencies which really counted, the forces which could *do* things, were the human rulers of the Hellenistic kingdoms: they were the efficient saviours and benefactors of man. While Euhemerism was reducing to human proportions the ancient deities, men were seeing their rulers as gods. The god-king was born; the sovran did not ultimately derive his legitimation from the suffrages of his fellow-countrymen, but rather from the possession of a demonic energy which was more than the potency of any ordinary mortal. You have, you see, these two conceptions—the universe, and the divinity which raises a ruler above his kind: later these conceptions will unite, and the κοσμικὸς αὐτοκράτωρ of the East Roman world will be the result.

And together with the oecumenical idea there gradually emerged the common language, the κοινή, the necessary medium of communication in a world where the sundering barriers had fallen. And that common Greek language was the natural speech of the missionary, if he would carry his cause throughout Hellenistic society. Even the exclusiveness of the Jew yielded to the compulsion exercised by this common vehicle of thought. We are sometimes tempted to judge of all Judaism from our knowledge of Palestine of the first century of our era; but that unbending aversion from Hellenism and its ways was forged in the fires of the Maccabaean reaction, and elsewhere in the Diaspora a very different spirit reigned. The Septuagint is the permanent memorial of the conquering power of the universal language. It is in a Greek-speaking world that Constantinople was founded, and the efforts of Roman emperors to foster the spread of Latin within the Roman provinces of the East were foredoomed to failure.

Alexander's Asiatic campaigns not only carried Hellenism to the Orient, but from those campaigns was brought back the scientific material which formed the capital of the scholars of Alexandria. Aristotle had lacked that range of knowledge from which, in the Hellenistic age, new sciences were born. But the period during which this scientific renascence lasted was brief, and Greek scientific curiosity faded away. It was not killed by Christian obscurantism: the scientific age had passed before Christianity was born. This decay of the scientific interest is one of those mysterious changes in human thought which it is so difficult for the historian to explain: the mind of man reverts from the free enquiry of the unfettered reason to the acceptance of the primacy of authority—of oracle or sacred book. Among the thinkers of the fourth century of our era, Christian and pagan alike are convinced that the final authority is to be found in the scriptures: Julian, as much as any father of the Church, is assured that the plausible hypotheses of the scientists count as nothing when set against the word of God. In their lack of scientific curiosity, in the supremacy accorded to the inspired writing, the Byzantines are the spiritual heirs of the later Alexandrines.

And not in this alone: for it was the scholars of Alexandria who formed the pagan canon of the classical literature. In their work on the texts of the great authors of the past, in the collection and preservation of those texts, the scholars of Alexandria won their position as the librarians of the Greek world. The literature of the Hellenistic period is, I take it, the work of men who consciously wrote as *epigoni*, and the range of their creative originality, as in pastoral or romance, is restricted. They are already custodian-trustees. Here obviously the Byzantines are their successors: they ever sought to read their title clear to the great inheritance which had descended upon them from the past. But the very splendour of that inheritance, while it might inspire imitation, paralyzed initiative. For everything had already been achieved, and achieved with final mastery. We know the benediction passed upon the people which has no history. Byzantium had its roots in so glorious a past that its brilliance threw the present into shadow. Heisenberg is, I think, right in his assertion that there was nothing in Byzantine history which can be called a Renascence in the sense in which the West has used that word, and Bury in his Romanes Lecture showed that, even where Byzantine literature seems to appropriate Western models, it is in reality but bringing forth from its own treasure-house familiar motives. Its literary wealth was so great that there was no incentive to put the talent out to interest. But this is no new phenomenon, the fruit of a supposed sterility amongst the Byzantines: they are but continuing the task of the scholars of Alexandria; in Europe's Middle Age they are the world's librarians.

This Hellenistic culture of the centuries after Alexander's death undoubtedly contains oriental elements, but it is not always easy to isolate those debts of Greece to the East. One of the most striking features of Byzantine life is the omnipresence of demon powers; this general belief in the operation of demonic agency is another legacy from the Hellenistic period. Is this a purely Iranian conception invading a Greek world for which it was a new thing, or did the Iranian conception link itself naturally to ideas which were already widely prevalent on Greek soil though hidden by the majestic façade of the Olympian faith? It is desperately hard to determine what was the working creed of humble folk in the classical age; the literature which we still possess is so urban and so aristocratic. As the great gods lost not a little of their former authority, did the lesser powers of popular belief venture forth from their hiding-places into the light of day? The supremacy of the demons in Greek lands throughout the history of our era might suggest that in some form or another they had long been familiar to the folk of the Eastern Mediterranean.

And against this common civilization of the Hellenistic East, spread throughout the kingdoms which had taken the place of the single realm of Alexander, there stands in clear relief the power of Rome. That is the result of the wars of the third century: Carthage fallen, there remained no rival to Rome in the Western Sea; Syracuse fallen, there remained no independent centre of Hellenism west of Greece. The Greek had lost his chance of making the Mediterranean a Hellenic lake from shore to shore. Henceforth Hellenism would come to

Western Europe through Roman channels. The three centuries before Christ are thus a period of intercourse between two worlds—the Greek and the Roman. One current carries the armed power of Rome to the East, the other carries the culture of Greece to the West. Roman conservatism fights a losing battle, and for a time it might have seemed that, in spite of the victory of Roman arms, Greece would enslave her conqueror, that Rome itself would be transplanted to Alexandria. But Antony was defeated by Octavian, and the second period of our survey, inaugurated by Augustus, meant a reinforcement of the Roman tradition, it meant that Byzantine civilization could draw upon the riches of a double inheritance: the heir of Hellas was also the guardian of the legacy of Rome.

Attempts have been made to disguise this fact: men have defined Hellenism as the culture of all educated men throughout the Roman world: Otto, for instance, has said that Julius Caesar by his victories won Gaul for Hellenism. This juggling with words is a dangerous game, for it may easily obscure facts. The principate, formed of Roman materials, is a Roman building, and the culture which Rome brought to Western Europe, whether you like that culture or not, is a Roman product. That I firmly believe, and I confess that modern efforts to belittle that Roman achievement seem to me singularly ill-judged. For our present purpose the significance of the work of Augustus lies in this—that the Greek East could begin to regard Rome in a new light, not merely as an exploiting power, but as one deserving of those epithets of saviour and of benefactor which it had lavished on its own sovrans. The 'Evangel' of a Roman emperor was laying the basis for that fusion of traditions which went to the making of East Rome: it was rendering possible the day when the proudest boast of the Greek should be the assertion that he was a Roman. And further, I would repeat, Augustus saved into the new age those Roman traditions which during the last years of the Republic were threatened with dissolution; when the tide which drew Rome to the Eastern Mediterranean reasserted its force, those traditions could be transported, not to an Alexandria where there was every likelihood that they would

F   B.B.S.

simply have been submerged, but to a New Rome upon the Bosphoros which was the creation of an emperor who had already ruled the Roman West for many years.

Thus Constantine initiates the third period, the great transition in which East Rome was built, and in his own person Constantine marks a turning point in the history of the Mediterranean lands. He is not merely the result of the past, he is a new beginning. The pictures drawn by modern scholars of Constantine have been many and various, but few, if any, do justice to the boldness and originality of his achievement. Burckhardt and Costa are only representative of many who have sought to explain away Constantine's Christianity. I confess that, after a lengthy and detailed study of all those edicts and letters of his which have been preserved, I have come to the conclusion that Constantine's Christianity is indeed the key to his reign. He is the servant of God, the fellow-servant of the bishops, the man of God—a man under a sense of mission: his fortune he owes to the Christian God, and that relation to a Christian God has laid upon him a charge to defend the Church, to toil unceasingly for ecclesiastical unity. I feel that to Constantine more than to any other man the Roman world owed the formulation of its Christian theory of sovranty, for with him that theory had sprung spontaneously and vividly from his own experience. The Roman magistrate had traditionally been entrusted with the maintenance of the *Pax Deorum*; the maintenance of that peace was a matter of such vital importance to the commonwealth that the Roman State very early took religion under its efficient charge. It is to the close connexion between Roman religion and the Roman State that Warde Fowler's masterpiece is devoted. That connexion is not lost with the passage of the years, and a restoration of the Roman State habitually carries with it a restoration of the Roman religion. Augustus, Justinian, Leo III, the Iconoclast, are all in the Roman tradition; and it is in this line that Constantine has his place. The calling of the emperor to service, the mission of the emperor, the obligation of a Christian emperor, these are the themes which fill the writings of Constantine. The formal acceptance of an Iranian theory which regards sovranty as a gift of heaven is one thing, the living conviction of experienced fact is another. When George of Pisidia in the seventh century exclaims of East Roman sovranty ὡς εὖ κρατοῦσα σὺν Θεῷ μοναρχία—how fair a thing is monarchy with God for guide!— he is but echoing the thought of Constantine.

And one must ever remember that the man who led the crusade of A.D. 324 against the persecutor Licinius was the emperor who had at first left the settlement of the Donatist controversy to the bishops, and only after their failure had been forced himself to pass judgement: that is to say that Constantine came to the Council of Nicaea with the conviction that the emperor was God's chosen mediator in ecclesiastical affairs. When an emperor has issued an order in defence of the truth, a recalcitrant bishop must be taught that it is not seemly for him to disobey the imperial mandate. And because it was Constantine, the champion and protector of the Church, who formulated that principle, the Church allowed the claim. Constantine admitted the Church into full participation in the life of the Roman State: the Church—or, at least, each individual church—is recognized as a corporation before the Roman law, bishops become Roman judges, a Christian clergy enjoys the same privileges as the pagan priesthood—many other instances could be cited. And the consequence was that the Christian Church accepted the Roman State: it did not fashion a new State for a new—a Christian—empire. And with the Roman State the Church accepted the law of Rome. The law of Islam was fashioned by the religious consciousness of Islam: religion and law were inextricably intertwined. As we have seen during the last few years, for a divorce to be effectuated a completely new mould must be created for the law of a new society. But the Christian Church, professing a creed of altruism, accepted a code of law which, as Mitteis has shown, is logically so completely satisfying because consistently based on the presuppositions of an egoism untroubled by humanitarian scruples. It is once more the personality and the achievement of Constantine which rendered this reception of pagan law as the basis of a Christian State not merely a possibility, but a fact of history.

And Constantine further entertained the vision of a Roman State which should be founded upon the unity of Christian orthodoxy and find in that unity a magnet which should draw the world of barbarian peoples to know and reverence the Christian God. In the early days of the fourth century this was a prophetic vision and its realization was delayed, but that vision was realized at length in the Byzantine Empire where orthodox Christianity was the inspiration that sustained, the cement which held together, the East Roman world.

Thus, as I see the story—and I am only attempting here to outline a personal view of the historical development—Constantine was the architect of East Rome. If I am right, the strength and consistency of the emperor's convictions sprang from the immediacy of an individual experience; they were no mere logical deductions from an inherited theory. Those convictions led Constantine, as it were, by a necessity inherent in themselves to divine the fabric of the Christian State which was to be. That Christian State was being constructed within the ancient shell of the doomed pagan building. The pagan walls were already sapped and undermined: in time they would fall of their own decay.

That fall was certain, because it was preordained by the will of the Christian God. For the present man could work—and wait. But with a prescience that was almost uncanny in its accuracy the emperor forecast the lineaments of the Christian edifice which should one day be disclosed. The three centuries which stretch from Constantine to Heraclius are a period of transition, an age in which, through religious conflict and domestic disaffection, through foreign menace and barbarian *Völkerwanderung*, East Rome—the Christian State of Constantine's vision—was built. 'And the builders every one had his sword girded by his side, and so builded.'

We have but to state the problems which received their solution in this period, and that can be done in few words. First, there was the fundamental economic question: should the money economy of the old world be carried on into the new, or should the Empire lapse into a natural economy and payment in kind for service rendered? In the early years of the fourth century the Roman State strove resolutely to maintain the latter system in order that it might not be forced to expend its store of precious metal, but the unrelenting opposition of the soldier and the civil servant carried the day, and once more salaries were paid in cash. But this meant that a fluid taxation system must of necessity be retained, and it is on this system that the later Empire was based. Only so could a standing army have been kept in being and a fleet in commission: it was through its gold that Byzantine diplomacy won its triumphs. The fact is familiar, but it is not infrequently forgotten. The contrast between the western and the eastern halves of the Empire lies precisely here: the West was bankrupt; from unravaged Asia Minor the East consistently drew its taxes and thus remained solvent.

The East, like the West, was threatened with the supremacy of the barbarian: under the menace of Gaïnas and of Aspar the end of Roman and civilian authority seemed very near. The West had no counterpoise to throw into the scale against Ricimer: the East found within its own territory the barbarian who should meet and overthrow the barbarian from without. The Isaurian mountaineers saved the Empire. The result may be summarized in a sentence: in the West all real power is concentrated in the hands of the barbarian master of the soldiery—in the East the Roman civilian Anastasius reigns unquestioned. Sovranty, the undivided *imperium* of the emperor, and with it the Roman heritage of State supremacy link the East Roman State to the Rome of the Principate.

Alexandria had once challenged Rome: the answer to that challenge was the battle of Actium. And now Alexandria challenged New Rome in the rivalry of the patriarchates. Constantine's conception of the relation of the emperor to the Church could never be realized until the pride of the ecclesiastical Pharaoh, the patriarch of Alexandria, was humbled. The story of that struggle I endeavoured to outline in a paper published recently in the *Journal of Egyptian Archaeology*:[1] it need not be repeated here. At the Council of Chalcedon the patriarchate of Alexandria suffered shipwreck, and henceforth the will of the emperor and of the emperor's bishop, the

[1] 'Alexandria and Constantinople: A Study in Ecclesiastical Diplomacy', *The Journal of Egyptian Archaeology*, xii (1926), 145–56. [See pp. 97–115 *infra*.]

patriarch of New Rome, was supreme. The vision of Constantine had become an accomplished fact.

Constantinople had been built as a Christian city set in Greek-speaking lands, and the West, forgetting its Greek, drifted apart. In his African and Italian campaigns Justinian made the last great bid to restore the Roman heritage of a Mediterranean empire; he made the last great gesture of a Latin tradition in his codification of the law. Both efforts failed: the West went its own way: the Greek language triumphed, but the law, preserved in Greek texts, was Roman law: it is a typical example of that fusion of traditions which this paper is written to illustrate.

Constantine had sought, we have seen, to found the Empire upon the basis of a common Christian orthodoxy. The work of this period is the elaboration of the content of that orthodoxy. Its final formulation meant that Egypt and Syria were alienated from Constantinople, but through their loss the Empire and orthodoxy became conterminous, and a new cohesion was gained.

With the seventh century we find ourselves in a new world: Persia, the hereditary enemy of the Roman State, is overthrown, and the Empire's neighbours are the Arab and the Slav. The period of transition has been brought to a close, and the reign of Heraclius marks the beginning of Byzantine history.[2]

There follows the momentous Iconoclast struggle in which the principles formulated during the preceding centuries are directly challenged: in the field of art a challenge to an iconography which was the outcome of Greek traditions; a challenge in the ecclesiastical sphere when eastern monks were supported by the western Papacy in a demand for freedom from the intervention of the civil power; a challenge in the realm of law when Iconoclast emperors made a consistent effort to remodel the legislation of the State and refashion it upon a Christian basis. This triple challenge and its issue are indeed of fundamental significance for any student who would seek to determine the essential character of an empire which was at

[2] [I should now say that Byzantine history begins with Constantine the Great.]

this time, if we are to believe Professor Diehl, 'étroitement orientalisé'. For in this Iconoclast struggle a movement which, as we saw, took its rise from the extreme eastern provinces of the Empire—the lands bordering on Armenia—was given its opportunity to enforce its own convictions, and to that effort, which extended over a century, this Eastern Empire gave no uncertain answer. It resolutely refused to abandon its icons: despite persecution, it maintained its loyalty to a *Greek* iconography; it rejected the claims of the monks to ecclesiastical freedom: it willingly acquiesced in that interposition of the civil power in religious affairs which has behind it the unbroken tradition of *Roman* history; this Christian State, whose loyalty to the faith of the seven councils was its proudest boast, rejected with anathemas the consciously Christian legislation of the Iconoclasts and unhesitatingly reaffirmed in the code of a Macedonian sovran the *Roman* law of that intensely Roman monarch Justinian. It reconquered southern Italy, and on that Western soil it created, in Professor Diehl's words, a veritable *Magna Graecia*. What an odd thing for an oriental empire to do. Why not a Magna Syria or a Magna Chaldaea? Further, in its greatest and most self-conscious period East Rome cultivated with ardour a literature which was modelled on that of classical Greece, while an imperial scholar mobilized in the interest of the commonwealth the records of the Empire's Greco-Roman past.

And as against the insistence upon the dual tradition of Greece and Rome to what essential characteristics of Byzantine civilization can one point if one would seek to justify the dogmatic assertions of, let us say, Professor Otto of Munich? 'Here Asia won a decisive victory over Europe';[3] it is easy to make such a statement: how, we may ask, is it proposed to prove it? For myself, I can only say, in the familiar phrase of the lawyers, that I desire further and better particulars. Believe me, I am not trying to make a debating point: I am not merely pleading *pro domo*.[4] I do really want to know what these oriental elements are which are said to determine the

[3] *Kulturgeschichte des Altertums*, p. 93.
[4] The conception of East Roman civilization defended in this paper is that of my little book on *The Byzantine Empire* published in the Home University Library.

character of East Roman life. Is it contended that the Byzantine Empire is oriental because it is Christian, Christianity being in its origin an oriental religion? My difficulty is that Christianity has always meant different things in different surroundings, while the Orthodox Church, identified with a Greek theology, does not seem to me to be adequately characterized by the epithet 'oriental'. Again, monasticism may be described as an oriental movement, but once more, when the general pagan asceticism of the time of monastic origins is remembered, when one considers that the strongest influence in the formulation of the monasticism of the Eastern Church was so essentially Greek a statesman as was St Basil, it would appear to me misleading to represent Greek monasticism as distinctively oriental. Or take the etiquette of the East Roman court; here one may freely admit that there is Persian influence at work, but one is forced to ask the question: which is truly more individual, more characteristic of the Empire, that the sovran is honoured by the prostration of the subject or that with a profoundly Roman passion for efficiency the Byzantine always expected the monarch to lead the armies of the Roman State —that Byzantine absolutism was never permitted permanently to reduce the emperor to the position of a *roi fainéant*? For me the latter fact is infinitely more significant. One by one I think of the outstanding features of this East Roman civilization, and I fail to see that they are peculiarly oriental. It is not enough, for instance, simply to adduce the fact that Byzantine sovranty was absolute: *as such* absolutism is not oriental. I have even a suspicion that we are inclined to talk somewhat too glibly of the transition from the Principate to the Dominate. We naturally look at the development from an Italian standpoint. But Constantinople was set from the first not in Italy, but in a Greek land. For the folk of the Eastern Mediterranean was there ever any such thing as a Principate? Is not the interest of the letter of Claudius, recently published by Mr Bell,[5] from one side at least, just this, that it demonstrates the incomprehension of the Greek world before the unaccountable refusals of a Roman emperor? If you desire to represent the triumph of absolutism as an oriental encroachment, you must,

[5] *Jews and Christians in Egypt* (British Museum, 1924), pp. 1–37.

for the provinces of the Roman East, go back to a very early date, to the foundation of the Principate; yes, and even beyond that, for this absolutist conception of government was Hellenistic before ever it was Roman. If you would contend that the conception is fundamentally oriental, might it not be answered that it had at least become in the centuries after Alexander the Great so closely woven into the life of the Hellenistic world as itself to form a part of that Greek civilization to which Rome and Byzantium were the heirs? The Dominate, even in the West, is there δυνάμει from the first: it was the interpretation which Augustus put upon his powers which made his *imperium* something other; for, as soon as the *imperium* is deprived of its temporal limits and its collegiate character, what is the *imperium* itself but practical absolutism—if the holder of the *imperium* choose to make it so? If you desire *because of its absolutism* to represent the Eastern Empire as an oriental State, it will not be necessary to await the coming of the Iconoclast emperors.

I would repeat that until Professor Diehl and Professor Otto come into the open and put down their cards upon the table for all to see—until then—it is open to us to insist that those characteristic features which seem to us essential in Byzantine civilization are developments from, and continuous with, the civilizations of Greece and Rome. Let us briefly in closing recapitulate some of those features. First among them is a State which was maintained upon the basis of a money economy: upon that basis alone depended the Empire's standing army, its fleet in commission, its constantly adaptable art of war, continuously studied, and still represented in the surviving military manuals—the στρατηγικά: to all of which the West stands in striking contrast, for feudalism and a landed economy made all this impossible. Further, a State which resolutely maintained a single system of Roman law; and this maintenance goes right back to the founder of New Rome itself, who because he so unexpectedly offered to the Christians a full and free entry into the Roman State could do so on his own Roman terms, introducing, it is true, a few minor modifications into the law of the State, but essentially leaving the massive building unaltered. M. Maurice, in a recent book which his warmest admirers can only regret, has represented the Constantinian settlement as a Concordat between Roman State and Christian Church; but the all-important fact for the student of the later Empire to realize is surely this: that the admission of the Christians into the privileges of the State by Constantine was in essentials a unilateral act: thereby was determined the character of the later history of Roman law. When the Iconoclasts attempted to break the traditional moulds, it was already too late, for the Roman Empire had familiarized itself too intimately with the conditions of the Constantinian settlement to tolerate any change. And again in contrast with this State of the single law stands the West with its welter of local courts and systems of local law.

And the one law is maintained by a single sovranty, the direct continuation of the *imperium* of Rome—the only sovranty worthy of the name in the Europe of the early Middle Age. By the seventh century the menace of feudalism is broken in the East Roman Empire, and the centralized State is supreme. Here, in this Paradise of the Austinian jurist, all authority is concentrated in, and flows from, God's vicegerent, the Emperor.

And, as from Rome's earliest days, so now in the Christian Empire, the holder of the *imperium* is also charged with the care of religion: the *pax Deorum*, which it was the duty of the Republican magistrate to safeguard, has become a Roman emperor's maintenance of Greek theological orthodoxy, which is indeed but another instance of the fusion which I have sought to illustrate. Only to the traditional duty derived from a Western Rome there has been added a Christian missionary activity amongst the barbarians settled without the Empire's frontiers. This, too, is, as we have seen, a heritage from the founder of New Rome, for Constantine as Christian Emperor gave a new content to the title of *pontifex maximus*: he was 'the bishop of those without the Church', whether heretics or pagans, and to that mission his successors remained loyal.

In a word New Rome did not belie her name: the Empire set in Greek lands with its heart in the city of Constantine may still with reason claim the interest of the members of a Society formed for the study of the work of Rome.

V

The Decline of the Roman Power in Western Europe: Some Modern Explanations

[Read at the Joint Meeting of the Hellenic and Roman Societies on Friday, 4 September 1942. This paper originally formed part of the Sir Samuel Dill Memorial Lecture delivered in Belfast on 27 January 1933. *Journal of Roman Studies*, xxxiii (1943), pp. 29–35.]

IT is the purpose of this paper to consider a few of the more outstanding contributions towards the solution of this familiar problem propounded since the publication in 1898 of Sir Samuel Dill's book on *Roman Society in the Last Century of the Western Empire* (2nd edn., 1899). It may well appear somewhat surprising that I should venture to speak on such a topic, since my own work, such as it is, has been concerned rather with the history of the Byzantine Empire. And yet for a student of Byzantine history the problem has a special interest: he is forced to consider that problem not merely as a West European issue, but rather to compare and contrast the historical development in the western and eastern provinces of the Empire. He is compelled to raise the question: why was it that the Roman Empire failed to survive in Western Europe while it endured for a further millennium in the East? The very fact that he is primarily interested in the history of the Byzantine Empire enables him to approach the Western problem from a different angle and to treat that problem in a wider setting and not in isolation. This is my apologia for what might otherwise appear to be an inexcusable impertinence. In a word I desire to ask what general considerations can be adduced to explain the fact that in Western Europe there is a cultural break—a caesura—while in the East Roman world the cultural development is continuous, the Hellenistic and Roman traditions being gradually fused to form the civilization of the Byzantine Empire.

Of the recent explanations of the decline of the Roman power in Western Europe we may first take that of Vladimir G. Simkhovitch who in the *Political Science Quarterly* for 1916 published an article under the title 'Rome's Fall Reconsidered'[1] in which he attributed the collapse of the Roman power to the exhaustion of the soil of Italy and of the provinces. That article has been reprinted—somewhat incongruously—in the author's book *Towards the Understanding of Jesus*.[2] The evil began under the Republic: in Cato's time agriculture had already declined in the greater part of Italy. When asked what is the most profitable thing in the management of one's estate he replied 'Good pasturage'. What is the next best? 'Fairly good pasturage.' What is the third best? 'Bad pasturage.' And the fourth best? 'Arare'—agriculture. Simkhovitch admits that the Romans possessed great agricultural knowledge. 'All that is implied by the agricultural revolution,' he writes, 'the seeding of grasses and legumes, the rotation of crops, yes even green manuring, all that was perfectly known to the Romans. Why was it not practised for two thousand years or more? I do not know.' Columella was already drawing upon a literary tradition in his counsel to farmers: his mistakes prove that he had never witnessed the operations which he describes. To seed alfalfa one cyathus for 50 square feet, which amounts to several bushels per acre, is an impossible proposition. Province after province was turned by Rome into a desert: draining was neglected, and deserted fields became mosquito- and malaria-infested swamps. The 'inner decay' of the Roman Empire in all its manifold manifestations was in the last analysis entirely based upon the endless stretches of barren, sterile, and abandoned fields in Italy and the provinces. The evidence adduced by Simkhovitch is drawn for the most part from writers of the Republic or of the period of the early Principate, but from the Christian Empire he quotes Constantine's legislation in favour of the children of the poor who have not the means to provide for their offspring, and also the constitution of Valentinian, Arcadius and Theodosius giving per-

[1] *Political Science Quarterly*, xxxi (1916), 201–43.
[2] *Towards the Understanding of Jesus* (New York: The Macmillan Company, 1937), pp. 84–139.

mission to the squatter to cultivate deserted fields. Against those who would maintain that the flight from the land was caused by the oppressive taxation he contends that it was precisely the exhaustion of the soil which rendered the burden of taxation oppressive: it was because so much land was uncultivated that taxation pressed so heavily upon those who still continued the farming of their fields. The limits which confine the productivity of man's labour become for society physical conditions of existence from which it cannot escape. It was these limits set by the exhaustion of the soil which rendered the doom of Rome inevitable.

There is no doubt truth in this picture of the decline of agriculture: for the later Empire it may well be an accurate description of some parts of Italy: in A.D. 395 the abandoned fields of Campania alone amounted to something over 528,000 *jugera*; but in itself it is inadequate as an explanation of the fall of Rome. For in one country at least—Egypt—there can be no question of soil-exhaustion, and it is precisely from Egypt that we have our earliest reports of the flight from the land, of the disappearance of villages through depopulation. Modern studies of economic conditions in Egypt have demonstrated the fatal effects of the methods of administrative exploitation employed by the Roman government in that province. The burden of taxation here certainly came first, and the decay of agriculture was its result and not its cause. Further, the sweeping generalizations of Simkhovitch's paper cannot be sustained: even in the fifth century of our era where a resident proprietor supervised the cultivation of his own estate there can be no question of soil-exhaustion. Read again Ausonius' poem of his expedition in the valley of the Moselle, read the letters of Sidonius Apollinaris: still in the Gaul of the fifth century it is clear that there were smiling fields and well-cultivated farms. The real danger of the *latifundia* lay, I am convinced, in the fact that they were for the most part managed by bailiffs for owners who were absentee landlords, men who drew money from their estates in order to spend it in Rome, Ravenna, or some provincial capital. The primary cause of the agricultural decline is to be found in the abuses of the fiscal system, in the scourge of corporate responsibility for

the collection of the taxes which ruined the municipal aristocracy of the city *curiae*, and perhaps above all in the absence
of the personal supervision of the proprietor and the unprincipled use of authority by irresponsible bailiffs, controlling the
cultivation of the large estates which now absorbed so great a
part of the land of the Empire. Soil-exhaustion is, in fact, an
inadequate explanation of the collapse of the Roman power.

Another theory has been proposed by Professor Ellsworth
Huntington—that of climatic change. The great sequoias of
California—the big trees of a familiar advertisement—have
been growing for some three or even four thousand years.
Each year in the trunk of the tree there is clearly marked the
circle of the year's growth: when the tree is felled these rings
can be traced and according to their width a chronological
chart of climatic variation can be established: the years of
considerable width of ring recording the effect of favourable
climatic conditions, the narrower rings marking the result of
less favourable climate. In this way for the area of the sequoias
the variations in climate can be traced for at least 3,000 years.
On this basis Ellsworth Huntington constructed his theory.
In an article published in 1917 in the *Quarterly Journal of
Economics* on 'Climatic Change and Agricultural Exhaustion
as Elements in the Fall of Rome'[3] he suggested that the
climate of the Mediterranean world and that of California have
always undergone similar modifications: that from the chronological chart of Californian climate one is accordingly entitled
to reconstruct the changes in the climate of the Mediterranean
area during the course of the history of Rome, and from the

---

[3] On climatic change and the evidence of tree-growth, cf. Ellsworth Huntington, 'The Secret of the Big Trees,' *Harper's Monthly Magazine*, cxxv (American
edition), lxiv (European edition), pp. 292–302 (July 1912); id., 'Climatic
Change and Agricultural Exhaustion as Elements in the Fall of Rome,'
Quarterly Journal of Economics (Harvard University Press), xxxi (February
1917), pp. 173–208; Carnegie Institution of Washington, *Publication No. 192*
(1914), pp. vi, 341; Ellsworth Huntington, with contributions by Charles
Schuchert, Andrew E. Douglass, and Charles J. Kullmer, 'The Climatic Factor
as illustrated in arid America'; *Publication No. 289* in three volumes: A. E.
Douglass, 'Climatic Cycles and Tree Growth. A Study of the Annual Rings of
Trees in relation to Climate and Solar Activity' (vol. i, 1919, p. 127, Bibliography 124–7; vol. ii, 1928, pp. vii, 166, Bibliography 159–66); 'Climatic Cycles
and Tree Growth' (vol. iii, 1936, pp. vii, 171, Bibliography 166–71); *Publication
No. 352* (1925) on 'Quaternary Climates', Ernest Antevs, 'The Big Tree as a
Climatic Measure,' pp. 115–53, Bibliography 150–3.

record of such changes we may conclude that the fall of Rome
was due to a decline in the rainfall from which the Mediterranean world suffered during the fourth, fifth, and sixth centuries of our era. It is easy to object that on Professor Huntington's own showing the latter part of the second century and
the first half of the third century marked a climatic improve-
ment: it might be hard to trace any corresponding increase in
prosperity in the history of the Empire during this period. But
a more serious objection would point to the hazardous character of the fundamental assumption. Records of rainfall in the
neighbourhood of the great trees have only been kept for about
half a century; Professor Huntington prints a table of four
year-groups in order to establish the climatic parallelism between California and the Mediterranean area, [*Quarterly Journal
of Economics*, xxxi (1916–17), p. 193]:

    I   Seven years of heaviest rainfall in California.
    II   Eighteen years with heavy rainfall in California.
    III Seventeen years with light rainfall in California.
    IV Thirteen years with least rainfall in California.

The table presents the following figures:

	San Francisco	*Rome*	*Naples*
I	8·3 in.	10·7 in.	11·5 in.
II	4·5 in.	10·6 in.	11·0 in.
III	3·4 in.	9·8 in.	9·2 in.
IV	1·9 in.	9·6 in.	8·6 in.

'The columns vary', writes Professor Huntington, 'in harmony with the California rainfall.' That is true, but the dis-
parity in the amount of the decline in rainfall between
California and Rome—in California a fall from 8·3 in. to 1·9 in.,
in Rome a fall only from 10·7 in. to 9·6 in.—is very striking,
and it is not easy to see what conclusions can justifiably be
drawn from such figures.

But that is not all: the matter does not remain as it stood in
1917. In 1925 the Carnegie Institution of Washington published
further discussion of the Big Tree as a climatic measure, and it
now appears uncertain what part is played respectively by
temperature and what by rainfall in the yearly growth. Thus a

further element of ambiguity is introduced into the problem. Before this Ossa of doubt piled upon a Pelion of uncertainty the confidence of a mere student of history may well quail, and for the present I should hesitate to call in aid Nature's yard-stick as a solution of our historical perplexities. The great trees still keep their climatic secret.

From Nature we may turn to the human factor in our search for the causes of the collapse of the Roman power. Otto Seeck has, I think, found no followers in his attempt to charge the third-century Roman emperors with the responsibility for that collapse. Through their continued *Ausrottung der Besten*—the persistent extermination of capacity and individual merit— the Caesars bred a terror of distinction and encouraged the spread of that slave mentality which issued logically and natur-ally in the triumph of Christianity—the Beggars' Religion— *die Religion des Betteltums.* An inverted Darwinism stamped out originality from the Empire: no man remained with the courage to be the master of his fate—the captain of his own soul. The way was open for 'Byzantinismus', for crawling servility and fawning adulation of authority. Here the pre-judice of one who was inspired by a passionate and life-long hatred of the Christian faith has, I cannot but feel, attempted to wrest history to its own purpose. Is there indeed any single century in the annals of the Empire which can show so many men of outstanding personality as can the fourth century of our era? Surely Professor Lot is not far from the truth when he exclaims: 'If ever there were supermen in human history they are to be found in the Roman emperors of the third and fourth centuries'—men who shouldered the burden of a tottering world and resolutely refused to despair of the Republic. And beside the Roman emperors stand in the Christian camp such figures as Athanasius and St Basil in the East, as Ambrose and Augustine in the West. There is little of crawling servility in such men as these. The wonder of the fourth century to my mind is rather the heroic courage and the desperate resolution with which men strove to preserve that imperial organization which alone safeguarded the legacy of the ancient world. Further, you will not have failed to notice with what rigour Seeck presses the theory of the hereditary transmissibility of ἀρετή. So thorough-going a conviction might well rejoice the heart of a champion of an unreformed House of Lords. No, *Die Ausrottung der Besten* will not suffice to explain the decline of the Roman power.

Professor Tenney Frank, of the Johns Hopkins University, Baltimore, has approached the problem from another angle. From an elaborate statistical study of the Corpus of Latin Inscriptions[4] he concludes that Rome and the Latin West were flooded by an invasion of Greek and Oriental slaves: as these were emancipated and thus secured Roman citizenship the whole character of the citizen body was changed: on the basis of a consideration of some 13,900 sepulchral inscriptions he argues that nearly 90 per cent of the Roman-born inhabitants of the Western capital were of foreign extraction. What lay behind and constantly reacted on those economic factors which have generally been adduced to explain the decline of the Roman power was the fact that those who had built Rome had given way to a different race. 'The whole of Italy as well as the Romanized portions of Gaul and Spain were during the Empire dominated in blood by the East.' In this fact Tenney Frank would find an explanation of the development from the Principate to the Dominate—the triumph of absolutism, of the spread of Oriental religions, the decline in Latin literature and the growing failure in that gift for the government of men which had built up the Empire.

But the foundations on which this far-reaching theory rests are not above suspicion. The nationality of Roman slaves is but rarely expressly stated in the sepulchral inscriptions, and thus it is upon the appearance of a Greek name for slave or freedman that Tenney Frank has inferred an Oriental origin. The legitimacy of this inference has been questioned by Miss Mary Gordon in her able study of the 'Nationality of Slaves under the early Roman Empire', *J.R.S.*, xiv, 1924. A slave was a personal chattel, and slave-dealer or slave-owner could give to the slave any name which in his unfettered choice he might select: the slave-dealers with whom Romans first came in

---

[4] 'Race Mixture in the Roman Empire,' *American Historical Review*, xxi (1916), pp. 689 sqq.; see also by him *An Economic History of Rome* (1927), pp. 207 sqq., 211 sqq.

contact were Greeks and thus, as Miss Gordon says, 'Greek was the original language of the slave trade and this is reflected in servile nomenclature much as the use of French on modern menus and in the names affected by dressmakers suggests the history and associations of particular trades.' In fact the nomenclature of the slave in the ancient world was scarcely less arbitrary than are the modern names given to our houses, our puddings, our horses or our dogs. An attempt to determine the domicile of origin of our cats or dogs solely by the names which their owners have given them would hardly be likely to produce results of high scientific value. The outlandish names of barbarian captives reduced to slavery would naturally be changed to more familiar forms, and Latin nomenclature was singularly poor and unimaginative: the Greek names were well-known and resort to these was easy. It may be said that this reasoning is largely *a priori* and of little cogency. But Ettore Cicotti in a recent paper on 'Motivi demografici e biologici nella rovina della civiltà antica' in *Nuova rivista storica*, Anno xiv, fasc. i–ii, has adduced an interesting historical parallel. L. Livi (*La schiavitù domestica nei tempi di mezzo e nei moderni. Ricerche storiche di un antropologo*, Rome, 1928) in 1928 published documents which his father copied from the State Archives of Florence. These documents record 357 sales of slaves: the transactions date from the years 1366 to 1390—for the most part from the years 1366 to 1370. The majority of the slaves were of Tartar origin, though some were Greeks, Roumanians, etc. In these records the slave's original name is generally given and then follows the Italian name by which the slave is known. Thus the name of Lucia occurs forty-two times and represents such original names as Marchecta, Gingona, Erina, Minglacha, Saragosa, Casabai, Alterona and many others. Similarly the name of Caterina is given to slaves of Greek, Tartar, Turkish, Circassian, and Russian origin, and has taken the place of such barbarous names as Coraghessan, Chrittias, Colcatalo, Tagaton, and Melich. The parallel is very instructive.

But this is not all: the sepulchral inscriptions studied by Tenney Frank extend over a period of three centuries: suppose that Rome had during the early Empire a population of some

800,000 with an annual mortality of 2 per cent: in those three centuries the deaths would number 4,800,000. Tenney Frank has examined 13,900 inscriptions and those are derived from imperial and aristocratic *columbaria*: here the slaves would be better off and the percentage of accomplished foreign slaves would be higher: what of the nameless dead whom no record preserved, whose bodies lay in the vast common burial pits of the slave proletariat? These 13,900 dead who left permanent memorials behind them cannot be regarded as really representative of the general servile population of the city: we are not justified in using the percentage obtained from these records and applying it as though it were applicable to the whole class of slaves and of freedmen.

In the light of this criticism Tenney Frank's statistics are vitiated, and it must be admitted that the nationality of the slaves of Rome under the early Empire remains a matter of conjecture. There must have been a far greater number derived from Western Europe than are allowed for on Tenney Frank's calculations.

A somewhat different form of biological explanation is given by Professor Nilsson in his well-known book *Imperial Rome*. The most important problem for the Empire was that of race: that was decisive, for upon it depended the quality of Roman civilization. Culture rests on racial character. If the alien races and barbarian peoples were to be assimilated, they must be interpenetrated by their conquerors. Since the Roman world was of vast extent and those of alien race were very numerous, an increase in the birth-rate of the Romans was required: instead of this the Roman birth-rate declined: the blood of the Romans became more and more diluted, and in place of the Romanization of the Empire a civilization of intercommunication and intercourse resulted in a mingling of races—an unchecked 'mongrelization'. Under the Empire cross-breeding, hybridization, spread throughout the provinces, and in this widespread realm of mongrels all stable spiritual and moral standards were lost.

I confess that as soon as the word 'race' is introduced into any discussion I realize that my only safe course lies in a resolute silence, for I have never been able to understand the precise significance of that ambiguous term. But when folk begin to ascribe all kinds of moral and spiritual failings to race-mixture it will hardly be expected that an Englishman will accept the insinuation without a protest. It is beyond calculation to estimate how many races and peoples have gone to his ethnological make-up, and he will not readily admit that the results of 'mongrelization' have in his case been wholly deplorable. As an Englishman I am unlikely to discuss dispassionately the theory of Professor Nilsson. And unfortunately I am also a student of Byzantine history, and as such I am convinced that the essential condition of the prosperity of the later Roman Empire was its possession of Asia Minor—that reservoir alike of money and of men. And Asia Minor of the Byzantines was surely man's most stupendous effort in race-mixture to which history can point: it was an ethnological museum. Professor Nilsson, to be quite frank, will have his work cut out to persuade an English Byzantinist that race-mixture is of necessity so poisonous and deadly a process. I had better leave it at that: you had best form your own judgement on the theory without further comment from me.

There still remains, however, the explanation of Professor Rostovtzeff as set forth in his *Social and Economic History of the Roman Empire*, a masterpiece for which any student of imperial Rome must have a sincere admiration. Professor Rostovtzeff's explanation of the collapse of the Roman power can be briefly summarized. It was through the medium of the *municipia*—of the towns—that Rome had unified Italy, and when she extended her conquests into the West of Europe she naturally favoured the growth of towns as centres of Romanization. But the towns drew their wealth from the countryside, and the peasants bitterly resented this exploitation of their own class by the *bourgeoisie*. Under the peace of the Empire the civilian population became unfitted for the life of the military camps, and it was from the rude vigour of the peasantry that in the crisis of the third century the Roman armies were recruited. The peasant of the army made common cause with the peasant of the countryside and both waged a war of extermination against their oppressors of the city. The explanation of the downfall of the aristocracy and with them of the ancient civilization is thus to be found in a class-conscious alliance between the soldier and the worker on the land. Professor Rostovtzeff, it must be remembered, has seen in his native country an aristocratic régime overthrown by a similar alliance. And the only answer to this theory that I can give is quite simply that I can find no support for it in our extant sources. I have consulted every reference to the authorities cited by Professor Rostovtzeff, and in my judgement none of them supports his reading of the facts. So far as I can see the constant terror of the peasants is the soldier: the last menace to a defaulting debtor is (according to the papyri) the creditor's threat: 'I will send a soldier after you.' The soldier is to the peasant what Napoleon or the policeman has been to successive generations of children in English nurseries. To the Roman peasant and soldier of the third century of our era there had not been granted a revelation of the gospel according to Karl Marx.

And thus I come back as a student of Byzantine history to the difficulty to which I referred at the beginning of this lecture. I believe that there was in Western Europe a break in the cultural development, and that there was no corresponding break in the development of civilization in the eastern provinces of the Roman Empire. To a Byzantinist, therefore, the problem which we are considering necessarily assumes a dual aspect: what he must discover, if he is to gain any intellectual satisfaction from the inquiry, is precisely the *differentia* which distinguishes the history of the Western provinces from that of the *partes orientales*. And so many of the modern explanations do not provide him with any such *differentia*. 'Die Ausrottung der Besten,' civil wars, and imperial jealousy of outstanding merit did not affect the West alone: the whole Roman world suffered from these scourges: the brutality of an undisciplined soldiery was likewise an evil common to both halves of the Empire. Soil-exhaustion, climatic change, these must have affected the entire Mediterranean area. The oppression of civil servants, the decay of the municipal senates, the flight from the land—all these ills the Eastern provinces were not spared. Greeks and Orientals invaded the West and we are told caused the collapse of the Roman power there; but in the East these same Greeks and Orientals sustained the Empire against unceasing assaults for another millennium: it seems mysterious. And therefore in closing it only remains for me to state the *differentia* as I see it and to suggest an explanation of this diversity in the history of East and West—an explanation which is so humiliatingly simple that I am constrained to believe that it must be right.

You realize then that I speak as a student of Byzantine history: a Byzantinist looks at the world of Western Europe. As I conceive of it, culture is essentially a social thing: it is born of intercourse and it needs a conscious solidarity of interest in order to sustain it. Roman civilization depended upon intercommunication, upon the influences radiating from the capital and returning to the capital for reinforcement. Such free communication, however, can be preserved only within an area which is safeguarded from violence: the Roman Empire was such an area safeguarded by the civil administration and by the frontier screen of the military forces. The civil service and the army together formed the steel framework which maintained the entire structure of civilization. It is perhaps with the Emperor Hadrian that one first observes a conscious realization of this function of the Roman power. The area of civilization is delimited on permanent lines: not expansion of territory, but concentration of resources in order to protect the solidarity of culture—that is the emperor's task. The barbarian invasions broke into this area of intercourse, and the establishment of barbarian kingdoms on Roman soil destroyed the single administration which was its counterpart. And the fatal significance of the establishment of these barbarian kingdoms lay in the fact that they withdrew from the Empire not only Roman soil, but also the revenues derived therefrom. Africa lost to the Vandals, Spain occupied by Sueve and Alan and Visigoth: Southern France a Visigothic kingdom and the rest of Gaul a battleground on which Aëtius fought and fought again: Italy alone remained as a source of revenue, and Italy was an impoverished land. The Western State was bankrupt. And the defence of the Empire demanded money, for Rome had so effectually provided the area of peaceful intercourse in Western Europe that her subjects were no longer soldiers: if battles were to be won they must be fought by barbarian mercenaries, and for mercenaries to fight they must be paid. Further, Rome's effort in the West was a struggle with a double front: against the barbarian on land and against the Vandal fleet upon the sea. Rome possessed no technical superiority such as the invention of gunpowder might have given her, such as later the secret for the composition of the 'Greek fire' gave to the Byzantine navy. Thus the tragedy of the Empire in the West lay precisely in the fact that she had not the wherewithal to keep at one and the same time a mercenary army in the field and a fleet in commission. And the *differentia* which distinguishes the situation in the East of the Empire is, in my judgement, that, while the Danubian provinces were continuously ravaged, Asia Minor was for the most part untroubled by invasions: Asia Minor remained as I have said a reservoir alike of men and money. It was this reservoir which the West lacked. The West could throw no counterpoise into the scale against the supremacy of the barbarian; but the East amongst its own subjects numbered the hardy mountaineers—the Isaurians—and the fellow-countrymen of the Isaurian Tarasicodissa, whom history knows as the Emperor Zeno, could meet the menace of the barbarian mercenary and when the supremacy of the Alan Aspar had been broken, the Empire could send the Isaurian back to his mountains and Anastasius, an aged civilian who had only just escaped consecration as a bishop, could rule unchallenged. And as a consequence of the triumph of the civil power, the civil administration—the steel framework which maintained Byzantine civilization—was likewise preserved, and from the city of Constantine culture radiated and through intercourse with the capital was again reinforced. Here is preserved that conscious solidarity in the maintenance of civilization which guaranteed a real continuity. In the West there are survivals from the ancient world—true—a branch lopped from a tree may still produce shoots; but for all that the continuity of life is broken: the doom of decay is sure. Gregory of Tours is a remarkable man, but he is a lonely figure and he feels himself isolated. And against that figure I would set a scene at a Byzantine court—when the Emperor's barbarian mistress appeared in her radiant beauty at a reception, one courtier uttered the words οὐ νέμεσις: the barbarian queen did not understand the allusion, but for Byzantines the two words were enough to summon up the picture of Helen as she stood before the greybeards on the walls of Troy. So well did the aristocracy of East Rome know their Homer: such is the solidarity of Byzantine culture. In a word it was the pitiful poverty of Western Rome which crippled her in her effort to maintain that civil and military system which was the presupposition for the continued life of the ancient civilization.

VI

Alexandria and Constantinople:
A Study in Ecclesiastical Diplomacy

[This paper represents the substance of a lecture delivered at a Meeting of the Egypt Exploration Society on 26 January 1926. (*The Journal of Egyptian Archaeology*, xii (1926), pp. 145–56.) I have retained its original form and have accordingly refrained from any elaborate 'documentation'.]

SCHOLARS have often considered the diplomacy of the Pharaohs and of the Ptolemaic kings of Egypt; there is perhaps room for a brief study of the diplomacy of the un-uncrowned kings of Roman Egypt—the Christian patriarchs of Alexandria. This is the theme of the present paper.[1] I am not here concerned with theology, but with the struggle of the

[1] The following are the principal modern works on which this paper is based:
Pierre Batiffol, *La paix constantinienne*, ch. 2 (Paris, Gabalda, 1914).
Id., 'Origine du règlement des conciles', in *Études de liturgie et d'archéologie chrétienne* (Paris, Gabalda, 1919).
Felix Haase, *Altchristliche Kirchengeschichte nach orientalischen Quellen* (Leipzig, Harrassowitz, 1925).
Heinrich Gelzer, 'Die Konzilien als Reichsparlamente', in *Ausgewählte kleine Schriften* (Leipzig, Teubner, 1907), pp. 142–55.
Ed. Schwartz, 'Die Konzilien des 4 und 5 Jahrhunderts', in *Historische Zeitschrift*, civ (1910), pp. 1–37.
Id., 'Konzilstudien', in *Schriften der Wissenschaftlichen Gesellschaft in Strassburg*, 20 Heft (Strassburg, Trübner, 1914).
P. Rohrbach, 'Die Patriarchen von Alexandrien', in *Preussische Jahrbücher*, lxix (1892).
On Greek monasticism:
Karl Holl, 'Über das griechische Mönchtum', in *Preussische Jahrbücher*, xciv (1898).
Id., *Enthusiasmus und Bussgewalt beim griechischen Mönchtum* (Leipzig, Hinrichs, 1898).
J. Leipoldt, *Schenute von Atripe und die Entstehung des national-ägyptischen Christentums* (Leipzig, Hinrichs, 1903).
On Chrysostom and the Synod ad Quercum:
Ubaldi in *Memorie* of the Academy of Turin, 2nd series, lii (1903).
For Nestorius:
J. F. Bethune-Baker, *Nestorius and his Teaching: a fresh examination of the evidence* (Cambridge University Press, 1908).
G. R. Driver and Leonard Hodgson, *Nestorius. The Bazaar of Heracleides* (Oxford, Clarendon Press, 1925). (My quotations from the *Bazaar of Heracleides* are taken from this translation of the work.)
F. Nau, *Le Livre d'Héraclide de Damas* (Paris, Letouzey et Ané, 1910).
Id., *Nestorius d'après les sources orientales* (Paris, Bloud et Cie, 1911).
Ed. Schwartz, 'Zur Vorgeschichte des ephesinischen Konzils', in *Historische Zeitschrift*, cxii (1914), pp. 237–63.

Bishop of Alexandria to maintain the supremacy of his see against the upstart bishopric of Constantinople. A word is, however, necessary by way of introduction on the development within the Eastern provinces of the Roman Empire of the organization of the Christian Church as an institution.

Christianity took its rise in the *cities* of the Roman East. Paul passes from city to city founding his small Christian communities at strategic points, which were to serve as bases from which the world was to be conquered for Christ. It was thus from the provincial capital that Christianity spread to the countryside: thus that in course of time the provincial capital came to be regarded as the mother church and the natural centre of the Christian communities scattered through the province. In this way from the first the Church unconsciously adopted for its organization the same territorial divisions as those of the civil power: the communities in a civil province are regarded as collectively forming an ecclesiastical unit. While Paul writes his letters to the capital cities of Roman provinces—Ephesus (Asia), Corinth (Achaia), Thessalonica (Macedonia)—the first epistle of Peter is addressed to the congregations of Galatia, Pontus, Cappadocia, Asia and Bithynia (cf. 2 Cor. i. 1). The problem of organization in the early Church has to many become a weari-

Ed. Schwartz, 'Die sogenannten Gegenanathetismen des Nestorius', in *Sitzungsberichte d. Bay. Akad. d. Wiss.* Philosoph.-philol. u. hist. Kl., Jahrgang 1922, 1 Abhandlung (Munich, 1922).

For Cyril:
Pierre Batiffol, 'Les présents de S. Cyrille à la cour de Constantinople,' in *Études de liturgie et d'archéologie chrétienne* (Paris, Gabalda, 1919), pp. 154–79, and in *Bulletin d'ancienne littérature et d'archéologie chrétiennes*, i (1911), fasc. 4.

For Dioscoros:
Felix Haase, 'Patriarch Dioskur I nach monophysitischen Quellen', in Max Sdralek, *Kirchengeschichtliche Abhandlungen*, vi (Breslau, Aderholz, 1908.)
And cf. A. Wille, *Bischof Julian von Kios, der Nunzius Leos des Grossen in Konstantinopel* (Kempten, Kösel, 1910).
Karl Günther, *Theodoret von Cyrus und die Kämpfe in der orientalischen Kirche vom Tode Cyrills bis zur Einberufung des sogen. Räuber-Konzils.* Programm. (Aschaffenburg, Werbrun, 1913.)
For the general setting cf. L. Duchesne, *Histoire ancienne de l'Église*, vol. iii (Paris, Fontemoing, 1911).
This paper was written before I had seen
B. K. Stephanides, 'Οἱ πάπαι Κελεστῖνος ὁ Α′ καὶ Λέων ὁ Α′ ἐν ταῖς σχέσεσιν αὐτῶν πρὸς τοὺς Βυζαντ. αὐτοκράτορας καὶ τὰς ὑπ᾽ αὐτῶν συγκαλουμένας οἰκουμ. συνόδους,' in Ἐπετηρὶς Ἑταιρείας Βυζαντινῶν Σπουδῶν. ἔτος Α′ (Athens, 1924), pp. 55–85.
Ed. Schwartz, 'Aus den Akten des Concils von Chalkedon', in *Abhandlungen der Bayerischen Akad. d. Wiss.* Philosoph.-philol. u. hist. Kl., xxxii Band, 2 Abhandlung (Munich, 1925).

ness owing to the preoccupation of students with dogmatic
questions, such as the origins of the institution of episcopacy
and the Apostolic Succession: but in itself the problem of
organization is only one aspect of the intensely human question of the maintenance of intercommunication between the
several churches, and of the guardianship of the true faith
through such intercommunication. When a travelling aposto-
late, when the web of a far-flung correspondence both proved
inadequate, we hear during the latter half of the second century of the gathering of bishops in councils. And here again
these extraordinary gatherings, assembled for the discussion
of problems of pressing urgency, were gatherings of the
bishops of a civil province within the capital of the province.
About the middle of the third century from these extraordinary provincial councils there developed the regular provincial synods meeting annually in the provincial capital. Thus
the prestige and authority of the bishop of the provincial
metropolis were naturally increased: he tended to become the
standing president of the synod: he won influence over the
election of all bishops within the province. In 325 the Council
of Nicaea determines that in future such provincial councils
shall be held regularly twice in the year under the presidency
of the metropolitan, and that no episcopal election shall be
valid unless the metropolitan has given his approval. Thus in
each imperial province by the side of the civil governor there
stands the ecclesiastical head of the Christian communities
within the province.

This is definitely raised to a principle of Church organization, and, when the limits of an imperial province are altered,
there follows a corresponding alteration of the sphere of the
metropolitan: the Emperor Valens will divide the civil province of Cappadocia in order to strike a blow at the authority
of St Basil. But the provincial councils develop into gatherings
of bishops from *many* provinces, and these later councils tend
in the same way to centre round the great cities of the Empire:
Antioch, Alexandria, Ephesus; and as a result of this development the bishop of one of these great cities stands in relation
to the provincial metropolitans in the same position as do the
latter to the bishops within their several provinces—i.e. there

emerges the position of an over-metropolitan, or, as he came to be known, a patriarch. And these complexes of provinces with a patriarch at their head are identified with the larger divisions of a civil praefecture—the *dioceses* under their *vicarii*: just as the metropolitan has his parallel in the provincial governor, so the patriarch in the ecclesiastical sphere represents the *vicarius* of the praetorian praefect within the civil hierarchy. Just as the metropolitan must approve of the election of the provincial bishops, so the patriarch must give his consent to the elections of metropolitans within the civil diocese. This was the general rule, but the Patriarch of Alexandria exercised extraordinary powers, for *all* elections of bishops within the provinces of Egypt were subject to his approval. Thus had the Church in the Eastern provinces of the Empire adopted as the basis for the organization of its hierarchy the territorial divisions of the Roman administrative system. From this principle there followed naturally the corollary that the importance and precedence of a bishopric depended upon the importance and precedence within the Empire of the bishop's city. Here again the result of an historical development was raised into a general principle. Byzantium—the humble Greek city—was, as a see, subject to the bishop of Heraclea: but when Byzantium was transformed into Constantinople and in 330 became the seat of the imperial government, this subjection of the capital of the Roman East to the unimportant bishopric of Heraclea was an anomaly: the see of Constantinople was coveted by metropolitans (e.g. Eusebius of Nicomedia), even by patriarchs (e.g. Eudoxius of Antioch); at length the Council of Constantinople (381) by its third canon declared that the bishop of Constantinople should stand second in honour only to the bishop of the old Rome upon the Tiber, *because the city of which he is bishop is New Rome*. Because Constantinople *is* the capital of the Roman East, it is given the place of honour amongst the Eastern churches: the suffragan becomes the first of the patriarchs. This is indeed the crowning application of the theory of the Christian East which we have been considering: the rank of churches is determined by the prominence of cities as *civil* capitals—a principle itself deduced from the *facts* of an historical development. But the third canon of the Council of Constantinople was more than that: it was also a challenge to Alexandria. The occasion and the issue of that challenge form the subject of this lecture. But it is essential from the first to realize that this struggle between the patriarchates is no chance encounter: that indeed it is the result of an historical development which links Paul of Tarsus to the Alexandrian patriarchs. For, if the rank of a bishop depended in principle on the rank of his city, to whom in truth did the pre-eminence belong—to the bishop of the city of Alexander with its six centuries of pagan and Christian history, or to the bishop of the city of Constantine, the city of yesterday, the presumptuous intruder amongst the capitals of the Roman East?

The early history of the spread of Christianity in Egypt is notoriously obscure, but in the last great persecution Egypt had withstood the utmost fury of the imperial agents, and that fury—described for us in the pages of Eusebius—and its failure had left their mark. Egypt had defied the might of Rome, and the Empire of Rome had acknowledged defeat. That precedent, glorified in Coptic hagiography, became a treasured national possession. The Egyptian loved to be 'agin the Government': it was a reassuring conviction that what Egypt had done once, Egypt could do again. We are dealing with the *city* of Alexandria: it is, however, easy to forget and essential to remember that though the opposition to the imperial government was led by Alexandria, though that Alexandrian leadership dazzles us by the great personalities in which it was incorporated, by the spectacular splendours of the vast stage on which the drama was enacted, yet behind the façade of Alexandria lay the Egyptian people. When the last great protagonist of Alexandria had suffered shipwreck at Chalcedon, there still remained the Egyptian people for whom a Monophysite faith stood as sign and symbol of their alienation from Rome and the Roman government: it was the massive resolution of the Egyptian people to remain loyal to that Monophysite faith that yet again defeated all the king's horses and all the king's men. It is perhaps the supreme example in human history of the triumph of non-co-operation. That is the background of the valley folk; there is further the background of the desert, no longer a solitary place, but peopled by anchorites and monks. If Christian asceticism in its origins had been in large measure a protest against a Church which was making too easy terms with the world, it was a patriarch of Alexandria, Athanasius, persecuted by the Church of the Emperor, who brought back to an alliance with the Church of Egypt the protestants of the wilderness. Monasticism in general—though to the generalization there were many exceptions—was not interested in speculative theology: as Holl has reminded us, the monks were in the main concerned with practical questions of the defence of the forms adopted by Christian piety: so far as they were interested in dogmatic issues, it was in problems of soteriology, and it is, of course, a truism that soteriology from Athanasius onwards dominates the religious thought of Alexandria. The essential fact for Alexandrian piety was the Christ Who was the object of worship, rather than the Christ of logical and metaphysical definition, rather than the Christ Who, as the school of Antioch insisted, was also the man Jesus, and therefore conditioned by a human development in time and space. All conceptions which emphasized the dualism of nature in the God-Man tended to dissipate that unity of the person worshipped which was for the Egyptian a pre-requisite, if the analytic activity of the mind were to be stayed, and the heart freed for the untroubled repose of devotional contemplation. Thus, were the practical issues of cult or soteriology endangered, the monks were readily aroused to opposition, and they who were originally drawn for the most part from the people could, as propagandists, appeal with irresistible force to the people. In the fifth century the voice of the monk was what the press is to-day, and with their religious slogans the monks produced the same effect as modern newspapers with their political war cries. 'Cursèd be Nestorius!' 'Hang the Kaiser!' The slogan becomes an inebriant, and men are intoxicated with its passionate repetition: 'But when they knew that he was a Jew, all with one voice about the space of two hours cried out "Great is Diana of the Ephesians".' As it had been in the pagan city, so it was in Christian Ephesus. The patriarchs of Alexandria played upon the emotions of these monks with inherited mastery: the reputation for orthodoxy which Atha-

nasius had won attached itself to the office which Athanasius
had held: when the relentless brutality of Theophilus, the foe
of Chrysostom, had with fire and sword stamped out the
opposition of the Nitrian monks, there was no further room for
independence of thought in Egypt; no declaration of papal
infallibility was needed: the infallibility of the Papa of Alexandria was for Egypt an axiom. The patriarch was fighting his
country's battles, and his despotism was unchallenged. Henceforth the treaty of alliance which Athanasius had concluded
between the desert and the city was maintained with a loyalty
which had behind it the force of an inveterate habit. The monks
of Egypt formed the patriarch's fanatic bodyguard: theirs
not to reason why: their clubs were brandished at his nod:
their dervish bands would follow him in victory or destruction!

That is the setting: and Egypt's first champion in the duel
between Alexandria and New Rome is Athanasius. It was
Athanasius who realized the great advantage which distance
gave to an Egyptian patriarch. The Bishop of Constantinople
lived in the shadow of the imperial palace: but Alexandria lay
more than three weeks' journey from the Eastern capital.
Here it was much easier to play the essentially Egyptian game
of passive resistance—the emperor meanwhile might change
his mind! Athanasius, summoned to Caesarea by Constantine,
simply stayed where he was—and waited. But passive resistance even in a patriarch had its limits, and that limit was
reached when a strong emperor had once made up his mind
upon a course of action and refused to change it. There is
throughout the apparent vacillations of Constantine's church
policy one fixed resolution which provides the key to the
emperor's acts: the aim of that resolution was to secure the
unity of the Church, and woe to him who opposed its realization! Arius had withstood the imperial will at Nicaea and he
had been exiled: why could Athanasius defy the command to
appear at Caesarea and yet after piteous hesitation—as we
now know from the papyri of which Mr Bell has given us so
masterly an edition[2]—obey the command to present himself at Tyre? I believe the reason to be simple: as I have

[2] H. I. Bell, *Jews and Christians in Egypt* (London, 1924), pp. 53 sqq.

recently ventured to suggest in this *Journal*,[3] the reason is that
Arius had recanted, had signed an orthodox creed, and that
Athanasius who refused to rejoice over the sinner that repen-
teth and would not admit Arius to communion was the one
man who by his uncharitable bigotry barred the emperor from
attaining his heart's desire. Therefore Athanasius was sent into
exile in the West. That interview in Constantinople between
emperor and patriarch is of profound significance for the course
of the whole struggle: when a resolute emperor had once made
up his mind, a patriarch of Alexandria could resist no longer:
Alexandria won its triumphs against emperors who were
irresolute or emperors who played into the hands of the enemy.

The sufferings and triumph of Athanasius raised Alexandria
to a position of unchallenged supremacy. Constantinople under
the Arian dominance of a Valens was not a serious rival. But
when Valens fell on the stricken field of Adrianople, when
Gratian's choice had given an orthodox emperor to the Roman
East in Theodosius the Great, Alexandria immediately realized
that this change might undermine the supremacy of Egypt.
Gregory of Nazianzus had been summoned to Constantinople,
and there began to re-form a congregation of those loyal to the
faith of Nicaea. He had been recognized as bishop of the city
by Peter, Patriarch of Alexandria: the latter now repented of
this recognition and determined to impose upon the see of New
Rome a Cynic philosopher who had been banished from Egypt.
Bishops protected by sailors (from the Egyptian corn-ships?)
hurriedly performed the rites of consecration under cover of
night, and then Maximus together with his consecrators hastened to Salonica to secure the emperor's approval (380). This
Theodosius bluntly refused, and the answer to Egyptian intervention was the third canon of the Council of Constantinople
which we have previously considered. Gregory of Nazianzus
relinquished his office, and Nectarius was consecrated bishop
of Constantinople in his place. Alexandria had met an emperor who knew his own mind—and had suffered defeat.

Theodosius the Great died in 395, and his sons Arcadius and
Honorius were weaklings: Nectarius died in 397, and forthwith
Alexandria renewed the struggle. Theophilus, the Egyptian

[3] xi (1925), pp. 58–69.

patriarch, was a man of violence who knew no scruples, but he was also a consummate diplomat who knew how to bide his time. His first attempt to control the see of the capital was a failure: he proposed as candidate his personal friend Isidore, but the all-powerful minister, the eunuch Eutropius, with the support of Arcadius carried the election of Chrysostom. Theophilus protested against that election, but in vain. Eutropius threatened him with an accusation for deeds of violence committed in Alexandria: the patriarch's consent to Chrysostom's consecration was the price at which he could purchase immunity from prosecution: he considered it wiser to submit. Chrysostom thus began his ministry in the capital with the patriarch for his foe, but with the support of the emperor and of the empress Eudoxia.

I am not here concerned to describe how Chrysostom aroused the enmity alike of the court and of influential ecclesiastics in Constantinople, my purpose in this paper is simply to study the *methods* of Alexandrian diplomacy. In 399 Theophilus had quarrelled with his friend Isidore: the patriarch launched against the blameless octogenarian an odious charge: it was of course quite groundless, but the charge alone sufficed. Isidore was excommunicated, treated with brutal violence, and further accused of heresy. He fled for protection to the Nitrian monks. Massacre and arson scattered the survivors of the Nitrian community throughout the provinces of the Roman East. Some fled to Constantinople and appealed for protection and justice to Chrysostom. The bishop refused to act as judge upon the conduct of his colleague of Alexandria: his appeal to Theophilus for reconciliation remained unanswered: but Egyptian emissaries were despatched to Constantinople with counter-charges. The monks secured the support of the palace: their case was heard in the court of the praetorian praefect: their accusers were condemned to death, though stay of execution of the sentence was granted until the arrival of the Patriarch of Alexandria: Theophilus was summoned to stand his trial in Constantinople with Chrysostom for judge. The foes of Chrysostom within the capital saw their opportunity: they appealed to Theophilus 'since', as Palladius, Chrysostom's biographer, writes, 'he had experience in such matters.' The first step was to discredit the orthodoxy of Chrysostom: then a large synod should assemble in Constantinople, and Chrysostom should be condemned as a heretic. Theophilus determined to secure Chrysostom's deposition and, if possible, his rival's death. He induced Epiphanius, bishop of Salamis in Cyprus, to believe that Chrysostom had favoured Origenism, and thus exploited for his own ends the fiery orthodoxy and pious simplicity of the revered champion of the creed of Nicaea. Epiphanius, in spite of his great age, made the journey to Constantinople as the enemy of Chrysostom: in the capital he learned that he had been but the cat's paw of Alexandrian diplomacy: in his bitter disillusionment he set sail for Cyprus, only to die on the voyage. The foes of Chrysostom were checkmated.

Meanwhile Theophilus, heir to the ecclesiastical stratagems of Athanasius, did not leave Egypt unaccompanied: a regiment of Egyptian bishops preceded him by the short sea route: he himself pursued his leisurely way through the provinces of Asia, encouraging those who were prepared to support Alexandria in the struggle with Constantinople—that struggle is now a duel between the two patriarchates: the prize of victory supremacy in the Eastern Church. Theophilus no longer appeared as one who was called to meet a serious accusation: already he announced his intention of deposing a heretic bishop. At Chalcedon the foes of Chrysostom were gathered, and the emperor, who still supported the bishop of Constantinople, now called upon Chrysostom to cross to Asia and to examine the charges against Theophilus. This Chrysostom refused to do: he would give the Alexandrian patriarch no ground for his accusation that the bishop of the capital was interfering in matters beyond his jurisdiction. Here Ubaldi in his valuable study of the Synod ad Quercum—a study which has unfortunately been disregarded by English scholars—has made an illuminating suggestion. Arcadius had summoned bishops to a council, the preparations were made, the bishops assembled, and now by Chrysostom's refusal to act as judge the emperor's plans were frustrate: he was like to appear ridiculous. How could he save his face? Theophilus provided the answer: the council could still meet: there was work for it to do. If Chrysostom would not be judge, if he disobeyed the

imperial summons, he could *be judged*: the emperor would not
have made his preparations in vain. The court turns against
its bishop.

During the delay caused by Chrysostom's refusal Theophilus adduced his most cogent arguments. He had come, as
Palladius says, like the beetle, laden with the dung of the East,
laden with the gold of Egypt, with the salves and odours of
India. Two deacons deposed by Chrysostom—the one for
adultery, the other for murder—drew up at the dictation of
Theophilus the list of the charges against their bishop: a hasty
reconciliation with the Nitrian monks removed the ground for
further action against Theophilus: the council could begin its
work. To the summons of the council Chrysostom replied that
he was ready to appear before any synod in the world, if only
his personal enemies would withdraw. In his absence Theophilus, the foe of the accused, his accuser and his judge, condemned him to deposition on the ground of his contumacious
refusal to appear before the tribunal. The vacillation of emperor and empress might postpone the execution of that
sentence, but not for long: the result was the complete triumph
of the patriarch of Alexandria, and Chrysostom's successors in
the see of Constantinople took the lesson to heart and were
careful not to antagonize the uncrowned king of Egypt. Cyril
succeeded his uncle Theophilus on the throne of St Mark and
continued the policy of the dynasty.

In 428 Theodosius II chose the eloquent monk Nestorius to
be bishop of Constantinople. An honest, fearless and devout
man was head of the Church in the Eastern capital. Cyril saw
that here he could count upon no subservient submission, and
took his measures accordingly. The tragedy of Chrysostom was
to be repeated in the 'Tragedy of Nestorius'—the title which
Irenaeus gave to the great collection of 'pièces justificatives'
which he compiled in his friend's defence. This new triumph of
Alexandria was won by methods which were now traditional
with the see of St Mark. Naturally I shall not attempt here to
sketch in detail the *Vorgeschichte* of the Council of Ephesus: I
am only anxious to demonstrate that parallelism in the
methods of Alexandrian diplomacy. As with Theophilus, so
with Cyril: his unscrupulous violence had laid him open to

accusations which it would be inconvenient for him to meet: diplomacy demanded that he should be able to pose, in like manner as Theophilus had done, as the defender of threatened orthodoxy. As in the case of Theophilus, however, it was the patriarch and not the bishop of Constantinople who began the attack. The first step of Theophilus had been to secure from an Egyptian synod the condemnation of Origenism in order to charge Chrysostom with that heresy: the first step of Cyril was to attack Nestorius in his Easter pastoral of 429 and in a circular letter to the Egyptian monks: in both he carefully avoided any mention of the *name* of Nestorius. Copies of these documents reached Constantinople: here there were priests from Alexandria who were ready to provide Nestorius with material for an accusation before a council. That Cyril knew his danger is clear from his protestations contained in his first letter to Nestorius: 'let not your Piety doubt for a moment that we are ready to suffer anything even to prison and death': at the same time Cyril wrote to his own agents in Constantinople giving them their instructions: they were to paint Cyril to his Egyptian opponents as the heroic champion of the true faith, while no direct attack was to be lodged against Nestorius with the emperor, lest Nestorius should be able to complain that Cyril was accusing him to Theodosius of heresy.[4] Cyril's correspondence indeed proves that this parallelism in method was conscious. To his agents in the Eastern capital he would admit no anxiety. 'There is no need for alarm: councils sometimes, everyone knows, turn out otherwise than men expect [an obvious allusion to the Synod ad Quercum]. Let not Nestorius, poor man, think that I shall submit to be judged by him, whatever accusers he may suborn against me. The rôles will be reversed: I shall decline his competence to judge me, and I shall know how to force him to defend himself.' (Ep. 4.) The letters of Cyril to Nestorius were carefully framed so as to draw statements from the bishop which could be used as evidence against him. They produced the effect which Cyril desired. He could now appeal to Rome: Pope Coelestine should be used as Theophilus had sought to use Epiphanius. Cyril sent to the Pope a lying summary of the course of the contro-

---

[4] This letter is quoted by Nestorius, *Bazaar of Heracleides*, p. 101.

versy: the true chronology was distorted in order to disguise
the fact that Cyril had himself been the aggressor. Nestorius,
conscious of his honesty and orthodoxy, also sent a report to
Rome, but in Greek: this Coelestine was unable to read, while
Cyril with subtle diplomacy had caused all his evidence to be
translated into Latin. The Pope, who probably hardly realized
what the dispute was about—the term 'Mother of God' was
not in common use in the West at this time—now declared
against Nestorius: Nestorius must within ten days of the
receipt of the Pope's letter accept the theology of Rome *and
Alexandria* and disavow his (unspecified) heretical views. Cyril
was constituted the Pope's mouthpiece and representative. It
was more than even Cyril himself could have hoped for. He
could now with even greater success than Theophilus pose as
the champion of orthodoxy. He compiled his famous 'Anathemas', and exceeding any authority which he could rightly
claim demanded that Nestorius should subscribe to them.
'Rechtlich betrachet war dieser dogmatische Erlass des alex-
andrinischen Patriarchen eine Ungeheuerlichkeit'—a legal
monstrosity. Schwartz has pointed out[5] that in the correspondence between Cyril and the Pope the emperor is never named
—so little notice did men take of Theodosius II. Yet even
before the Egyptian bishops bearing Cyril's Anathemas had
arrived in the Eastern capital the emperor had by a constitution addressed to the bishops summoned a council to meet in
the following year at Ephesus, while in an ungracious letter to
Cyril he showed that the council would enquire into the conduct of the Patriarch of Egypt (19 November 430). The council
met: of the terrorism practised at Ephesus by Cyril's rabble I
need not speak: Nestorius had to be guarded by imperial
soldiers from assassination, and could not leave his house.[6]
The refusal of Cyril to await the arrival of John of Antioch and
the Syrian clergy is well known: his complete disregard of the
emperor's instructions, his defiance of the emperor's representative are equally familiar. Cyril *was* in fact the Council.
As Nestorius says, Cyril conferred upon himself the office of
judge (p. 117). 'I was summoned by Cyril who had assembled

[5] *Historische Zeitschrift*, cxii (1914), p. 257.
[6] Cf. *Bazaar of Heracleides*, pp. 108, 134–5.

the Council, even by Cyril who was the chief thereof. Who was judge? Cyril. And who was the accuser? Cyril. Who was bishop of Rome? Cyril. Cyril was everything.' Before such a tribunal Nestorius could obviously not appear. Its deliberations were a foregone conclusion and the deposition of Nestorius inevitable.

It was in vain that the distracted emperor confined Cyril: Egyptian gold procured the prisoner's release, and once in Alexandria Cyril was safe. Once in Alexandria his hands were free, and he fought the cause of his Anathemas with the 'benedictions'—the εὐλογίαι—of Egypt. Details of those εὐλογίαι chance has preserved to us in a document which has recently been published for the first time by the great Roman Catholic scholar Pierre Batiffol.[7] Theophilus had come to Constantinople, as we have seen, laden with the dung of Egypt: from Egypt Cyril distributed to those who had influence at the Byzantine court amongst other gifts eastern carpets, ivory chairs and tables, fine linen, ostrich eggs and a sum in hard cash which Batiffol in 1911 calculated at over a million francs. The benedictions of Alexandria proved persuasive: though Cyril was forced to approve of an Antiochene creed, he was not constrained to sacrifice his Anathemas.

The parallelism in method between the Alexandrian attack upon Chrysostom and the attack upon Nestorius is striking. Was it even more complete than has been thought? Schwartz has remarked that the summoning of the Council of Ephesus by the emperor was premature, since Theodosius had no considered policy for which negotiation might prepare the way before the assembling of the Council: Schwartz therefore concludes that it must have been the advice of Nestorius which led the emperor to his hasty decision.[8] The nature of this difficulty, first raised, I think, by Schwartz, needs perhaps a word of explanation.

Gelzer and Batiffol have shown that the Church councils of the Christian empire represent the imperial senate so far as *res divinae* are concerned. The senate of pagan Rome had discussed both civil and religious matters, and the *res divinae* as

[7] Cf. the Bibliography on p. 98 *supra*.
[8] *Historische Zeitschrift*, cxii (1914), pp. 258 sqq.

the more important came first upon the agenda. Since the
victory of Christianity there only remained for the senate the
consideration of profane matters; the Church council, formed
on the model of the Roman senate, becomes the supreme authority *in rebus divinis*. The emperor nominates and summons
the senators: it is he who determines the composition of Church
councils: he bears the expense of the bishops' journeyings, and
puts the imperial post at their service. The presidency belongs
to the emperor or his delegates: Constantine, I believe, presided in person at the Council of Nicaea: later emperors preferred to send their representatives. In the senate the presiding
magistrate does not vote: neither do the imperial delegates in
the council. The Gospels take the place of the Altar of Victory.
The *senatus consulta* need for their validity the approval of the
emperor: without imperial sanction the conclusions of Church
councils are of no effect. Gelzer entitled his famous essay 'Die
Konzilien als Reichsparlamente': but Church councils are, as
Schwartz has reminded us, Imperial Parliaments of a peculiar
kind: their members are not the representatives of their congregations or their dioceses: the old conception dating from
the days before the triumph of the Church lives on: the councils of the Church are charismatic assemblies: their decisions
are revelations of the Holy Ghost—of that Holy Spirit that
lives in the bishops through the consecration to their divinely
appointed office. There can therefore be no question of a
majority or a minority: the decisions must perforce be unani-
mous: a minority, if it persists in opposition, necessarily creates
a schism: the only course open to it is to deny to the council
with which it disagrees the operation of the Holy Ghost—to
form, as at Sardica or Ephesus, another council through which
the Holy Spirit may express the divine will. Of necessity, therefore, a far-seeing emperor, seeking, as seek he must, the unity
of the Church, is bound to prepare by previous negotiation a
solution in which this charismatic Parliament will concur: for,
if there is no concurrence, the whole is lost, and imperial policy
is foredoomed. Constantine in the *Homoousion* had his solution: what in the mind of Theodosius was to be the principal
task of the council when he summoned the bishops to Ephesus?
Here I would like to make a suggestion, based upon an obscure

phrase in the *Bazaar of Heracleides* which does not seem to have attracted the notice of students.

Addressing Cyril, Nestorius writes (p. 105): 'Thou hast stirred up [my friends against me] in order that under pretext of their souls thou mightest show thyself zealous to set them aright, because thou hadst pleasure in them, or that either I might desist from listening to thine accusers and those who were ready to accuse thee, who were already armed against thee, since, if that were to come about, it would then be easy for thee to do whatsoever thou wouldst in regard to the possessions, or otherwise in oppressing me thou wouldst make believe that for the sake of the fear of God I was thine enemy and that *for this cause I had declined mine office as judge.*' By oppressing Nestorius, Cyril would create the impression that it was because of the consciousness of his own guilt that Nestorius had declined his office as judge. I would boldly suggest that in this extremely clumsy sentence we possess the key to that premature summons of the council by Theodosius. Arcadius had summoned the Synod ad Quercum to try Theophilus: Chrysostom's refusal to act as judge had disconcerted the emperor's policy. I believe that the Council of Ephesus was called by Theodosius primarily to make inquisition into the conduct of Cyril: that suggestion is indeed borne out by the terms of the emperor's letter to the patriarch: the refusal of Nestorius to act as judge similarly frustrated the policy of Theodosius.

In each case the emperor cuts a sorry figure: and in each case, before the emperor can make up his mind to sacrifice his bishop, it is left to another to shoulder the burden of responsibility. You recall the scene in Chrysostom's case: the bishops who had led the opposition to Chrysostom were determined to force a decision: 'in our view,' they said to Arcadius, 'you, Sire, are appointed by God as absolute ruler, subject to none, superior to all: your will is law. Do not desire to be more lenient than the priests, more holy than the bishops. We have publicly declared before all: on our heads fall the deposition of John. Do not then spare one man to bring us all to ruin.' Arcadius hesitated yet a few days longer, and then the imperial order was issued: a notary was despatched to Chry-

sostom with the message: 'Acacius, Antiochus, Severianus and
Cyrinus have taken your condemnation upon their own heads.
Commend, therefore, your affairs to God, and leave the Church.'
From this scene turn to the amazingly vivid account which
Nestorius has given of the interview of the archimandrite
Dalmatius with Theodosius II (*Bazaar of Heracleides*, pp. 272
sqq.). The emperor had just said, 'Neither do I find any
cause of blame in this man [i.e. Nestorius]; I and my Empire
and my race are guiltless of this impiety' (p. 277), when
'Dalmatius and those with him cried out: "On me let this
impiety be, O Emperor; I rebuke thee and thine on account of
these things. I will make my defence for these things before
the tribunal of Christ, as having done this very deed." . . . And
after [the emperor] [had] received this promise that the responsibility for the impious deeds committed against me should
not be [his], he decreed and confirmed the things which had
been wrought against me.'

Compare these two conversations with the interview between Constantine and Athanasius with which our account
began, and you have before you the reason for the success of
the diplomacy of Alexandria.

Cyril died (444), and the East heaved a sigh of relief: a letter
attributed to Theodoret advises that a heavy stone be put on
his grave, lest he should return. The dead would soon have
enough of him and try to send him back. The 'dynasty' had
come to an end, but Dioscoros continued Cyril's policy. The
diplomacy of Dioscoros, however, has not the subtlety of a
Theophilus or a Cyril: subtlety indeed was unnecessary, for
the emperor was now under the control of the eunuch Chrysaphius, and Chrysaphius was a partisan of Dioscoros. Supported by Chrysaphius, and thus secure of imperial favour, the
Patriarch of Alexandria could snap his fingers alike at Pope
and Western emperor. Pope Coelestine had delegated his authority to Cyril, but Pope Leo the Great would delegate his
authority to none. Leo's first letter to Dioscoros on the latter's
accession gave to the patriarch his cue. Alexandria, the Pope
had said, must be one with Rome. To that demand Dioscoros
opposed the determination that Rome should find in the East
her match—that the East, too, should have her Pope. That is

the meaning of the Second Council of Ephesus: it is this which distinguishes the battle fought by Cyril from the battle fought by Dioscoros. Cyril could exploit a pope against an emperor: Dioscoros played a yet more daring game. He held the emperor a eunuch's slave, and hurled his defiance against the see of Peter. The Patriarch's Coptic biographer expresses the whole situation in a nutshell in his doubt whether Mark were not greater than Peter.

Of the 'Brigandage of Ephesus'—the *Latrocinium* of 449— it is unnecessary to speak: an analysis of Alexandrian methods would add little of value to the picture already drawn. Here Alexandrian violence overreached itself: Dioscoros—the Attila of the Eastern Church, as Amelli[9] has styled him (though this is surely an insult to Attila!)—would not even permit the reading of the Papal letters: it was amid scenes of indescribable confusion that Eutyches was reinstated and Flavian, the Bishop of Constantinople, deposed.

But with the fall of Chrysaphius and the accession of Marcian and Pulcheria the tables were turned. Pope and emperor were united, and at Chalcedon the whole structure of Alexandrian supremacy fell like a house of cards. When Marcian's first letter reinstating Ibas and Theodoret, deposed by the Latrocinium, reached Alexandria, the clergy of Egypt foresaw their doom: 'Death is in this letter, Man of God.' The words, reported by the Coptic biographer of Dioscoros, express that conviction. Pulcheria, 'the second Eve', had seduced her husband to Egypt's ruin, and the summoning of the Council of Chalcedon in spite of the dissuasion of Leo the Great was the work of the empress. But in the shipwreck of Alexandrian domination the captain never left the bridge: Dioscoros amidst the miserable recantations of the Eastern episcopate never wavered: he could have bought his throne by submission—I accept Haase's defence[10] of the historicity of the Coptic biography of the Patriarch with its account of the interview between the emperor and Dioscoros before the meeting of the council—but for the successor of Athanasius, of Theophilus and Cyril the price was too high. Dioscoros would

---

[9] *S. Leone magno e l'Oriente* (Rome, 1882). I owe the reference to Haase.
[10] In his monograph on Dioscoros: cf. the Bibliography on p. 98 *supra.*

humble himself neither before Pope nor Emperor. 'With me the faith of the fathers is destroyed.' These words of Dioscoros as he left the council—he refused to appear at the later sittings—were his challenge, addressed not to the bishops who had deserted him, but to the people of Egypt. The Council of Chalcedon came not to bring peace, but a sword, and the answer of his people to their Patriarch's challenge was the formation of the Egyptian monophysite Church. The faith of Cyril, as Egypt understood it, was not destroyed. But for the Patriarchate of Alexandria there was to be no recovery. 'God has deposed Dioscoros!' shouted the bishops gathered at Chalcedon. 'This Dioscoros,' said Bishop Leontios of Askalon, 'has become a stumbling-block to the whole assembly of the bishops, for it is his will that for his sake all should go into banishment. This "Saint" contends that he is fighting for the true faith and yet he values his own person higher than God, higher than [Rome, Constantinople and Antioch] and higher than all bishops. Even were Alexandria destroyed, should Dioscoros perish with Alexandria, yet for all that the world would not remain without a bishop.' At Chalcedon the Patriarchate of Alexandria, as the world had known it, was indeed destroyed. The melancholy history of the successors of Dioscoros has been recounted in Jean Maspero's posthumous work.[11] Yet Leontios spoke truly: the Christian East did not remain without a bishop: for the victor at Chalcedon was the patriarch of Constantinople. Henceforth Constantinople is not merely the civil capital of the Eastern Empire: the God-founded city of Constantine is also the undisputed centre of the Church of the East Roman world.

If the figure of the deserted Dioscoros departing for his distant exile in Gangra extorts our reluctant homage, our hearts go out towards a greater exile, Nestorius. In Egypt Nestorius read the Tome of Pope Leo the Great and rejoiced; in his apology he wrote: 'My dearest wish is that God should be blessed in heaven and on earth; as for Nestorius let him remain Anathema: God grant that while men curse me, they may be reconciled with Him.'

---

[11] *Histoire des patriarches d'Alexandrie depuis la mort de l'empereur Anastase jusqu'à la réconciliation des églises jacobites (518–616)* (Paris, Champion, 1923).

VII

Idolatry and the Early Church

[From the Aytoun Memorial Lecture, Birmingham, November 1930.
Unpublished.]

WE are bound to ask ourselves how came the Christian Church to overcome its opposition to a sacred art, how came it to adopt and justify the worship of the sacred picture? How shall we of the West rightly approach in worship the iconostasis—that pictured wall which divides the worshipper from the hidden sanctuary?

The origins of Christian art constitute a hotly disputed problem. I am no art critic, on such a question I am quite unqualified to speak. I can only treat the matter from its literary side and attempt to suggest one way of approach. As you know well, a school of historians of art—represented by such names as Strzygowski, Oskar Wulff, Kaufmann—would trace those origins to the Hellenistic cities of the Near East, and in particular to Alexandria and Antioch. From these eastern cities the West borrowed its types and symbols: the art of the catacombs is thus essentially derivative. As Bayet wrote in 1879: 'the East creates the types and symbols, the West accepts them.' On the other hand, such students as the veteran archaeologist Wilpert have consistently maintained the independence of the early Christian art of Rome. The pedestrian student of history owing to his training in historical method often feels himself at a great disadvantage when he reads modern discussions of artistic problems: he is constrained to ask for some evidence which might support *a priori* assertions: this need is frequently for him an acute embarrassment. Alois Knöpfler, for instance, begins an article with the assertion that there is nothing in Christianity which could possibly lead it on grounds of principle to a rejection of art: 'Christianity is not the denial of the natural capacities in man: its aim is only to purify and complete those capacities.

Gratia non destruit naturam, sed elevat et perficit. That was ever the teaching of the Catholic Church from the earliest times to the present day. The Church can therefore never have adopted on principle a hostile attitude either towards science or art.' This purely *a priori* argument leaves the historical student unconvinced: he asks, what is the evidence of the known facts? When Strzygowski derives the whole Christian iconography of Paradise and judgement from Mandaean paintings, the historical student is once more embarrassed, being unable to discover a shred of Mandaean painting by which he may test the critic's intuition. Similarly, the complete absence of any surviving Christian art of the earliest days amongst the ruins of the Near East gives him pause.[1] Is there any evidence, he asks in his perplexity, which may throw light upon the problem? He then endeavours to think himself back into this Mediterranean civilization in the midst of which early Christianity developed. And he is immediately reminded of the obvious fact that in those days the Church was lapped about by a sea of idolatry: and in that pagan world art was intimately associated with the worship of gods constantly represented in statuary and painting. He remembers, further, that the Old Testament was not the sacred scripture for the Jew alone, to that sacred literature the Christian also asserted his claim. And in that scripture there lay embedded an explicit veto upon the representation of anything that is in heaven above or that is in the earth beneath or that is in the water under the earth (Exodus xx. 4). This was surely an atmosphere which was unlikely to favour the rise of a Christian art. We turn to the Christian literature and we find on every hand a protest against idolatry: we learn from Origen (*Contra Cels.*, 3, 15) that the first task of the Church in the instruction of the neophytes is to inspire them with a καταφρόνησις τῶν εἰδώλων καὶ πάντων τῶν ἀγαλμάτων—a scorn of all idols and all images—and thus to lead them from servitude to created things which take the place of God to the thought of Him who created all things. In the epistle to Barnabas, xx. 1, we read that on the

---

[1] [But cf. now the paintings discovered at Dura and see in especial Comte du Mesnil du Buisson, *Les peintures de la synagogue de Doura-Europos 245–256 après J.C.* (Rome, 1939), and M. Rostovtzeff, *Dura-Europos and its Art* (Oxford, 1938).]

way of eternal death the first snare of the soul is idolatry. The epistle to Diognetus praises the cult of the Jews (ch. iii) because of its hostility to the idolatry of the Greeks.[2] The author of the Didache writes: 'my child, keep yourself from the science of the augurs, because it leads to idolatry. You must not look at—you must not listen to—any of these things for it is from them that the worship of idols has sprung.' (iii, 4.) The constant theme of the Christian apologists is the peril of idolatry—its absurdity and shame.

And since we are not regarding merely the community of Christians, but the whole society of which that community forms a part, we further remember that pagans as well as Christians had protested against idolatry—there was a store of ammunition ready to the hand of the Christian disputant. It is instructive to see the use he made of the arguments of his pagan predecessors. Justin Martyr in his Apology has stated in summary form the case against idolatry: let us briefly examine that statement:

(i) Justin objects to the anthropomorphism of idolatry: it is folly to give to the gods the form of men for this is not fitting to the divine.

Greek anthropomorphism had early been ridiculed by Xenophanes: 'if oxen, horses and lions had hands and could paint pictures or carve statues, they would represent the gods under the form of oxen, horses and lions, even as men who represent them after their own likeness.' God is one, and neither His form nor His thoughts are like those of man. Plutarch under the Empire did but re-echo the thought of many a devout pagan.

(ii) These images are soulless, ἄψυχα, and dead—corpses, νεκρά. Plato had long ago contrasted the statues—bodies without souls, ἄψυχα—with the living gods. Plutarch often repeats the same word—ἄψυχα—of the statues of the gods.

(iii) (a) The images of the gods are made of the same material as the most dishonourable objects. This, too, comes from the pagan armoury: cf. the story of Amasis in *Herodotus*, 2. 172, a god made out of a vessel for washing feet.

[2] Strabo similarly sees in Moses 'a true Stoic philosopher' because of his absolute condemnation of idolatry.

(*b*) It is a chance whether the workman turns out a god or a common utensil. Horace had said the same: *Sat.* 1. 8. 1.

> Olim truncus eram ficulnus, inutile lignum,
> cum faber, incertus scamnum faceretne Priapum,
> maluit esse deum.

(iv) These sacred images are the work of base and depraved handicraftsmen. Zeno, the founder of the Stoics, had written that nothing could be regarded as of much worth or holy which was the work οἰκοδόμων—those who built the temples—or βαναύσων, the common labourers who produced the statues:

Celsus (Origen, *Contra Cels.* 1. 5) speaks of the workmen as φαυλότατοι and μοχθηροὶ τὸ ἦθος, very base and depraved in their morals.

(v) The richness of the statues only served to tempt thieves, and then guardians are set to protect the gods! a thing which it is—ἀθέμιτον—unlawful to say or to think. It was an old taunt: the followers of Pythagoras had maintained that the statues were but a prey for robbers: it is the theme of Lucian's satire: the Olympian Zeus complains that robbers have made off with two of his golden curls valued at 6 minae and have escaped. Here the form of the objection is perhaps derived from the *Wisdom of Solomon* (xiii. 16): ὅτι ἀδυνατεῖ ἑαυτῷ βοηθῆσαι . . . καὶ χρείαν ἔχει βοηθείας.

(vi) The idols bear the names of demons and have their form. The pagans admitted that demons manifested themselves through the statues: Celsus allows that some demons were attracted by the blood and the fat of the sacrifices: these do not benefit man, and men must be on their guard against them. It is a recognition of the danger which attends the idolater through the pagan sacrifices in the temples.

The consideration of this single passage will suffice for the point which I desire to illustrate. Christians and pagans are alike living in the same society, and the Christian is, in his argument, exploiting a capital which has been amassed by pagan thinkers. But with this difference: the pagan philosopher in most cases felt himself bound to come to terms with the inherited forms of a traditional popular devotion: he was constrained to temper the logic of his criticism and in some measure to reconcile it with ancient usage, to justify the *mos majorum.* The Christian recognized no such obligation: for him the pagan attack upon idolatry could be allowed to retain its full force, while he could launch against those from whom his argument was borrowed the taunt of inconsistency.

Now I confess that for me this sustained attack upon idolatry running as a constant theme of the apologists through the Christian literature of the period is very impressive. Constantly these early writers refer to the divine prohibition of images contained in Exodus xx. 4. Have the historians of art taken sufficient account of the implications of this polemic? May I remind you of some further considerations? Amongst the Greek writers of the first three centuries there is no express mention of a Christian art. The studies of Hugo Koch and Walter Elliger have, to my mind, made it clear that even Clemens of Alexandria and Origen with all their readiness to learn of the Greek, to build a Christian theology with the aid of Greek philosophic teaching, were yet hostile to any art of *Darstellung*—of representation. Recall for a moment the arguments which Origen brings against the pagan use of statues:

(i) That men through paying reverence to the statues tend to fall into the belief that these statues are themselves gods.

(ii) The fear that the honour which belongs to God should be diverted, withdrawn and debased so as to be paid to matter which has been given the form of a statue.

(iii) The objection that demons take up their abode in statues and in places where statues are set. (As we have seen, this was acknowledged by the pagans themselves.)

(iv) The repetition of the Old Testament prohibition still regarded as binding upon the Christian Church: the citation of other texts, e.g. Thou shalt worship the Lord thy God and Him only shalt thou serve.

When one carefully considers these arguments one is struck once more with the force of the Christian dread of idolatry. It would appear to me that one can hardly fail to realize with a new vividness where the line is drawn between the old world and the new. Origen could appropriate so much from Greek thought and Greek life, he was the peer of the pagan philosophers of his day, was recognized as such, and moved freely in their society: but beset with an idolatrous civilization the

Christian philosopher on this point of idolatry can make no concessions: here the disagreement is absolute and no conciliation is possible.

And this argument *ex silentio*, the implications which, as it seems to me, follow from Origen's case against the pagan statues are only confirmed when we turn to the writings of Eusebius, the first Eastern Christian whose attitude towards a Christian art can be gathered from any direct treatment of this specific subject. His evidence is of such importance that it demands a more detailed treatment. From him we learn that the Christians of the town of Paneas reverenced a statue which they interpreted as representing Christ and the woman with an issue of blood. From the description of the statue given by Eusebius it is probable that it was pagan in origin and commemorated some healing miracle of Aesculapius. Eusebius did not regard the statue as erected by Christians: it was natural that pagans who had been benefited by Christ or His apostles should make images of Peter and Paul 'or even of Jesus', following in this their *pagan custom, ἐθνικῇ συνηθείᾳ*, whereby they habitually honoured their saviours. Here the contrast is clearly drawn between pagan and Christian practice. But far more significant is the letter which Eusebius wrote to Constantine's sister Constantia, who had asked him for a portrait of Christ. Did she desire, he asked, the portrait of the true unchanging Christ or of the Christ of humiliation when He appeared in the form of a servant? Of the former there could be no question: the matter was settled once and for all by Christ's own words: no one knoweth the Father but the Son, and no man knoweth the Son but the Father who begot Him. But if the latter: even 'the form of a servant' was no ordinary human form: it was *gloriâ divinitatis temperata*, even His human body was differentiated from other bodies by the glory of His divinity, and the mortal was swallowed up by life, *mortale a vita absorptum*: the rays of His glory could not be represented by lifeless colours—that glory which blinded the eyes of the Apostles on the Mount of Transfiguration. And still more was this true of the Christ who after death and ascension had cast off mortality and had changed the *forma servi* for the glory of God. In such a case all that man could do would be to follow the

I   B.B.S.

heathen practice, for the pagans when they desired to represent a god or a hero achieved neither a likeness nor anything
in the nature of a portrait but simply figures of men. Such a
practice could not be followed by Christians. If Constantia
wished for a portrait of the earthly Jesus, let her rather recall
the prohibition given by God in Exodus xx. 4. Had she herself
ever seen anything of the kind in the Church or heard of such
a thing from another? Was it not rather true that in the whole
world anything of the kind was banished and excluded from
the churches? Was it not common knowledge that it was only
for the Christians that such things were forbidden? Eusebius
himself had taken away from a woman pictures which were
supposed to represent Paul and the Saviour in order that
scandal might be avoided. It did not seem fitting that they
should be displayed to others lest it might seem that Christians carried their God about with them as did the worshippers
of idols. If, unnecessarily, a portrait of the Saviour were
desired before the day when we should see Him face to face,
then there was no better painter than the word of God itself.

Elsewhere Eusebius records the fact that Constantine had
erected on one of the fountains in Constantinople statues
representing Daniel in the Lions' Den and the Good Shepherd.
There is no criticism of the emperor's action. It is not necessary to regard this silence as inconsistent with the letter to the
emperor's sister. Here, as Williger has pointed out, we have
on the one hand a scenic composition—not a single figure—
while on the other we have a purely symbolical representation.
If we regard the fear of idolatry as the determining motive,
there is here no such danger as might arise from the statue of
a single figure of Christ or of one of the Apostles. In an idolatrous world, a world of statues, the significance of such a single
figure might easily be misunderstood by the pagans: at a time
when under Constantine's influence pagans were in great
numbers entering the Church, such a single figure might
readily prove a danger to the new converts.

But the letter to Constantia is very striking: it is a surprisingly bold warning: remember to whom it was written—to the
sister of the first Christian emperor—and it sternly refuses to
grant her request. Note that it is not against the worship of

images that the bishop makes his protest: it is directed against any representation of Christ in art. It is written further by the bishop of Caesarea—an important Christian see and yet he can ask, 'Had Constantia herself ever seen anything of the kind in the Church or heard of such a thing from another? Was it not rather true that in the whole world anything of the kind was banished and excluded from the churches?' Those are very remarkable questions and their implications are very far-reaching. Remember that Eusebius was a widely-travelled bishop: he knew Antioch, he had been present at the Council of Nicea: more than that—he had been in Egypt during the great persecution and had seen the sufferings of the martyrs there. This was in the fourth century, and yet historians of art to-day assert that centuries before this Antioch and particularly Alexandria had been vigorous centres of Christian art and had provided the models which the Christians of Rome copied in the frescoes of the catacombs. Admittedly none of this early art of the Christian East has survived: on this literary evidence can we believe that it ever existed?

Of course the problem of the Christian art of the catacombs remains, but so far as that is concerned our ignorance is almost complete. The popular view of that art has long been that it began in the first century, i.e. that the earliest surviving paintings in the catacombs were actually produced in the first century: that it was a symbolic art (though on the meaning—the *Leitmotif*—of that symbolism there is no agreement), and that it originated in the catacombs. Every one of these conclusions is now denied: Styger in a startling paper published last year contends that we possess no trace of first-century Christian art in the catacombs: that art is not symbolic, it is purely historic in character; it did not originate in the catacombs, but above-ground.[3]

All that I would suggest here is that the hypothesis of the eastern origin of Christian types and symbols which were then borrowed by the West is not without its difficulties. Once more

[3] [In 1933 Paul Styger's book *Die römischen Katakomben* was published in Berlin (Verlag für Kunstwissenschaft). It would seem, he argues, that in the early frescoes of the catacombs we must see abbreviated repetitions of wall decorations of Christian houses, though in Rome no Christian private house dated before the religious peace has been as yet discovered (pp. 356–7). The frescoes themselves are not symbolic, but historical: the fresco is a popular story-telling reproduction of the sacred scripture (p. 362).]

there is to my mind demonstrated the danger of the water-tight-compartment method in research. The historian of art works in his own sphere: the literature of early Christianity is not his concern: that is left to the patristic scholar. What would be the answer which an art-historian of this orientalizing school would give if faced by the letter of Eusebius to Constantia? I confess that I cannot easily imagine the form of that reply.

As long as we study our Church history from *within* the Christian community, it might seem to us entirely natural that Christians should, without scruple, satisfy the Mediterranean man's craving to express his beliefs through an art of *Darstellung*—a representational art. It is only when we think the Christian back into the Mediterranean civilization of which he formed a part, only when we have restored him to his place in an idolatrous world, that we can begin to understand his prejudice against any such artistic expression. The peril to true religion as he saw it daily embodied before his eyes was too instant.

Now perhaps you see the reason for my doubts concerning the validity or cogency of Knöpfler's *a priori* argument: 'Christianity can never on principle be hostile to art.' Assuredly it can when art threatens a higher loyalty—when art menaces the purity of the worship of the One God. For in the last resort the demands of a Christian God outweigh the claims of culture. There are to be found at the heart of Christianity a stark asceticism and a staggering confidence. Lactantius, Roman and rhetorician, might shudder at the thought of the passing of the Roman Empire—*horret animus dicere* he wrote of that terrifying conception: but yet he could contemplate the overthrow of the Mediterranean civilization of his day because he was more than a Roman and a rhetorician—he was also a Christian. Despite the sack of Rome—the eternal city—by the Goth, Augustine could face the future, for of him it could be truly said

si fractus illabatur orbis,
impavidum ferient ruinae:

the culture of Rome might fall shattered, but still the city of

God remaineth. 'This is the victory which overcometh the world—our faith.'

In the strength of this transvaluation of values even art might suffer banishment from the early Church: it is better to enter into life maimed than. . . .

The fear of idolatry was, I believe, a far more potent factor in the life of the early Christian community than we sometimes realize. But if it was against this idolatrous Mediterranean civilization that the Christian protested, he was still so much a part of that civilization that he fought his battle with the weapons which had been forged by the men of that Mediterranean civilization. The Christian apologetic against idolatry was simply borrowed from pagan thinkers.

It remains to show the reverse of the medal—to illustrate how a Greek Church defended its icons in precisely the same way as it had attacked the pagan statues—with the weapons that a pagan society had fashioned.

And it is with Constantine the Great that this second chapter of our story must begin, since so much of later history depended upon the personality of Constantine. The more I study the emperor's biography, the more firmly I am persuaded that here indeed is one of the few unescapable figures of European history. No impersonal *Zeitgeist*, no streams of tendency—whichever of the popular phrases you may prefer—will explain Constantine: he represents an erratic block in the course of human history which diverted the stream. You may claim that, before the Battle of the Milvian Bridge, in A.D. 312, the imperial policy of persecution was already a confessed failure; common statesmanship would have counselled toleration, but I am convinced that no common statesmanship could have led a Roman emperor of the European West to desert the massive tradition of the Roman past and to unite himself to a Christian minority. If Constantine had indeed been merely a tolerant pagan, the ultimate victory of the Christian Church might have followed none the less surely, but it would have been delayed by many years, and if the triumph had been delayed, it would have been a different triumph: it is probable that it would have proved to be in a fuller sense a *Christian* triumph. For, in face of modern statements to the contrary effect, I believe that the association of Roman emperor and Christian Church was essentially *not* a Concordat, but a unilateral act. The emperor defined the terms of that alliance and the Church accepted them. And when that transaction of offer and acceptance was complete, then the emperor used every means in his power to draw into the Church the pagan world, while imperial munificence found its opportunity in erecting churches throughout the Roman East. They should be worthy of the lavish generosity of the emperor: they rose enriched by mosaic and decorative art. And because the giver was the sovran who had, first of all the Roman Caesars, proclaimed himself a Christian, men did not scrutinize the gift too closely —their scruples were silenced. With this influx of pagans into the Church, with this outpouring of wealth upon the Christian community, a new art arose as consequence of the imperial conversion. In churches, in private houses, on the clothing of the rich and on their vessels of precious metal there were wrought scenes from the Old and New Testaments; Christ, the angels and archangels, the apostles, saints and martyrs were all represented in human form. The groynes which through the early centuries had kept art at a distance were washed away and the full tide swept into the Christian Church. Scruples were silenced, I have said, but not all: one voice at least challenged the new idolatry—the voice of Epiphanius of Cyprus.

In the later stages of the Iconoclast Controversy when the weight of the argument on either side rested upon the voice of tradition, the foes of the icons produced in support of their cause writings of Epiphanius which directly challenged any sacred pictorial art. The defenders of the images could discount the evidence of Eusebius by branding him as an Arian heretic, but no such charge could be levelled against Epiphanius, the Hammer of the Heretics, the pillar of Nicene orthodoxy. They were reduced to arguing that one swallow does not make a summer (so John of Damascus), or, more effectually, they urged that the writings themselves were recent forgeries. I believe that Holl's case for the authenticity of the fragments stands unshaken. I therefore treat them as genuine, and we may turn to consider the views expressed therein.

Epiphanius travelling in Palestine came to a village church, and on the curtain hanging before the door he found depicted the figure of Christ or one of the saints. Whichever it was, it mattered not, in his passionate resentment Epiphanius tore down the curtain, though he later gave to the church a new and harmless hanging in its place. He was so stirred by this incident that he wrote a treatise against those who εἰδωλικῷ θεσμῷ—idolatrously—attempted to make εἰκόνας representing Christ, the Mother of God, the martyrs, angels or prophets. Those who plastered the walls (κονιάσαντες, a reference to 'thou plastered wall' of Acts xxiii. 3) with representations of the saints professed to do so in their memory and honour. Rather they do them dishonour: these representations are falsely so called. John had said, 'when He shall be revealed we shall be like unto Him', Paul called the saints 'of the same form (συμμόρφους) as the Son of God'; Jesus had said of the saints, 'they shall be as angels of God'. How, then, can you desire to see those saints who are destined to shine in glory represented in inglorious, dead, dumb matter? How can you do reverence to angels, who are spirits and living for ever, ἐν νεκροῖς? And the saints themselves do not desire such reverence: Epiphanius quotes Revelation xix. 10 (John worshipping the angel): See thou do it not: I am a fellow-servant with thee ... worship God. Acts x. 26, Peter to Cornelius: Stand up: I myself also am a man. And when one attempts to represent Christ, how shall one figure the inconceivable, the ineffable, the incomprehensible? And if it is objected that because He became perfect man we represent Him as man, 'was this the object of the Incarnation', asks Epiphanius, 'that He should be represented at your hands in painting?' Is He not the likeness of the Father, does He not call the dead to life? This art is in a word a contempt of God, who has said, 'Thou shalt reverence the Lord thy God and Him only shalt thou worship.'—But the Christian bishops paid no heed to his protest: Ephiphanius turned to the Emperor Theodosius: Now, when the heresies were overcome and the idols overthrown, the devil has deceived the faithful and dragged them back to the ancient idolatry. The emperor will realize that it is not for Christians to represent God with coloured paints. Which of

the ancient fathers in church or house or on the threshold
placed a picture of Christ? who thus placarded before the eyes
of men the prophets and the apostles? These are lies: men
fashion these pictures out of their own imaginations: Epiphanius had himself seen an archangel—a spirit—represented
with sinews and bones! All these pictures should be swept
from the churches—and if mosaics cannot be moved, at least
no new mosaics should be added. But the appeal to the emperor failed, and all that Epiphanius could do was to leave in
his will a warning to his own flock: let them keep the traditions
which they had received: remember, my beloved children, not
to bring εἰκόνας into the churches or the cemeteries of the
saints: it is in your hearts that you should keep God in
memory, there that the things of God should be inscribed. If
any one should seek to represent through material colours the
divine lineaments of the Word of God incarnate, let him be
anathema!

The icons, you see, have come into the Church, but as yet
no theology has been developed which can give to matter its
place as a bridge to the spiritual: therefore for Epiphanius the
sacred pictures can only be idolatry, an invasion of paganism
into the Church. The Iconoclast will later take up and develop
alike the charge of idolatry and the Christological argument
that Epiphanius formulated: for Epiphanius, as for the Iconoclast, the incarnate Christ though fully man was never bare
man, because while man He was still God.

Before considering for a few minutes that Iconoclast controversy which in my judgement forms the decisive moment in Byzantine history, I want to sketch the character of the apologia
by which paganism defended itself from the charge of idolatry.

And one must never forget the difficulty which always faces
the apologist in religious matters: his brief is weighted with
traditional material which he must justify as best he may. The
pagan apologist was burdened with religious practices and
myths which were rooted ultimately in a primitive past: how
shall the philosopher bring within the scope of *his* statement
of religious truth this legacy of the centuries?

There is an interesting passage in Maximus Tyrius in which
the rhetorician raises the question, supposing that the

philosopher were granted a *tabula rasa*—a people possessing no religion—and were granted, too, a free hand to mould a religion for them, should he introduce images of the gods? 'For if we were to give laws', he writes, 'to other men recently sprung from the earth and dwelling beyond our boundaries and our air, or who were fashioned by a certain Prometheus, ignorant of life and law and reason, it might perhaps demand consideration whether this race should be permitted to adore these spontaneous statues alone which are not fashioned from ivory or gold and which are neither oaks nor cedars, nor rivers nor birds, but the rising sun, the splendid moon, the variegated heaven, the earth itself, and the air, all fire and all water, or shall we constrain these men also to the necessity of honouring wood or stones or images?'[4] His answer is apparently that since this worship is the common law of all men, it were better to make no innovations, but to follow here, too, the common practice. As Dion of Prusa expresses the same sentiment: One should not object that it would have been better not to raise before men any statue or any image of the gods on the pretext that we should turn our eyes only towards heavenly things. These things, that are above, every being endowed with reason adores, every man who believes in the blessed gods, even though he only sees them from afar. But thanks to that desire which draws us to the divine there is in all men a passionate longing to honour and serve the Divinity, to draw near to it, to lay hold upon it with assurance, to bring to it sacrifices and garlands. Just as little children separated from their father and their mother long for them, need them sorely and often in their dreams stretch out their arms towards them in their loneliness, so men, who rightly love the gods for their benefits towards them and because of the kinship which unites them to the divine, desire in every way to be in their presence and to company with them (xii, 60–1).

The principles of Stoic and of Neo-Platonist alike might seem to exclude images of the gods, but for each that 'common law of all men', of which Maximus speaks, was too strong and each devised ways for justifying popular devotion.

---

[4] From the translation by Thomas Taylor of the 38th Dissertation of Maximus (London, 1804).

It was easy to repel the accusation that the pagan worshipper regarded the images of stone or metal as being themselves gods. Plutarch protests against this identification, and
its falsity is, of course, assumed by philosophic writers. One
passage from an encyclical of Julian the Apostate may be
cited: 'Therefore when we look at the images of the gods, let
us not indeed think that they are stones or wood, but neither
let us think they are the gods themselves; and indeed we do
not say that the statues of the emperors are mere wood and
stone and bronze, but still less do we say that they are the
emperors themselves. He who loves the emperor delights to
see the emperor's statue, and he who loves his son delights to
see his son's statue, and he who loves his father delights to see
his father's statue. It follows that he who loves the gods
delights to gaze on the images of the gods and their likenesses
and he feels reverence and shudders with awe of the gods who
look at him from the unseen world' (294 CD).

The statues of the gods are perpetual reminders of the
deities whom man loves and seeks to serve: not being able to
comprehend God's essence, we seek assistance through fashion-
ing symbols which may recall Him to us, And in thus acting,
writes Maximus of Tyre, we are affected in the same manner
as lovers who are delighted with surveying the images of the
objects of their love, and with recollecting the lyre, the dart,
. . . and everything in short which excites the memory of the
beloved object. Or as the pagan interlocutor in the Apology of
Macarius Magnes states the same view: 'If anyone makes an
image of his friend, he does not think that the friend is actually
in the statue, nor that the members of his body are enclosed in
those of the portrait. But it is the honour paid to his friend
which appears in the image.' 'Statues of the gods were invented
in order to remind men of God, that the thoughts of those
visiting the temples might be led to God.'

And to those who contended that it was unworthy to
fashion the divine in human shape the apologist had his
answer: that answer is given by Dion Chrysostom: 'since we
know—and do not merely guess—that it is to a Being in Whom
reason dwells that we have recourse, we give to God the human
form as being the vessel of thought and reason. In the

complete absence of the original model, we seek to show forth the incomparable and the invisible by means of the visible and the comparable. We employ the power of the symbol.' Or as Julian writes: 'Our fathers established images and altars . . . as symbols of the presence of the gods, not that we may regard such things as gods, but that we may worship the gods through them' (293 A). 'The form of the statues', in the words of the pagan of the Apology of Macarius Magnes, 'is human, because man is regarded as the fairest of creatures and as the image of God.'

We do not seek to benefit God by raising statues in His honour: '*perhaps*', says Dion Chrysostom, 'God needs none of these things, whether statues or sacrifices: but it is not in vain that these objects are consecrated to them, since through this act we manifest our zeal and our disposition towards them.' Julian, who in his youth had learnt from his Christian Bible that God is not worshipped with men's hands as though He needed anything, can dispense with Dion's 'perhaps'. 'Just as those who make offerings to the statues of the emperors who are in need of nothing nevertheless induce goodwill towards themselves thereby, so too those who make offerings to the images of the gods, though the gods need nothing, do nevertheless thereby persuade them to help and to care for them. . . . For even though God stands in need of nothing, it does not follow that on that account nothing ought to be offered to him. He does not need the reverence that is paid in words. What then? Is it rational to deprive him of this also? By no means. It follows then that one ought not to deprive him either of the honour that is paid to him through *deeds*, an honour which not three years or three thousand years have ordained, but all past time among all the nations of the earth' (293–4).

The statues are, further, man's teachers: to quote from Maximus Tyrius:[5] 'a divine nature has no need of statues or altars, but human nature being very imbecile and as much distant from divinity as earth from heaven, devised these symbols. . . . Those therefore whose memory is robust and who are able by directly extending their soul to heaven to meet

[5] From Thomas Taylor's translation.

with divinity have *perhaps* no need of statues. This race is, however, rare among men, and in a whole nation you will not find one who recollects divinity and who is not in want of this kind of assistance, which resembles that devised by writing-masters for boys who give them dim marks as copies, by writing over which, their hand being guided by that of their master, they become, through memory, accustomed to the art. It appears to me, therefore, that legislators devised these statues for men, as if for a certain kind of boys, as tokens of the honour which should be paid to divinity, and a certain manuduction as it were and path to reminiscence.'

But behind the apologist lay the world of sacred legend—the weight of the past—the many stories of miracles performed by statues. Shall this past be called in doubt? Plutarch hesitates: timidly rationalistic at one moment, at the next he restores with his left hand what he has just taken away with the right. Aelian makes, it would seem, no attempt at criticism: he collects instance after instance of these miraculous tales and apparently seeks to convince by the sheer mass of his material. The miraculous element in man's worship of the statues was too firmly rooted in popular belief to give way before the exalted philosophy of the Neo-Platonist. Plotinus needed neither statue nor sacrifice. Porphyry, before he became the disciple of Plotinus, wrote his work defending the statues by the method of astrological allegory: that defence we can now study in the masterly edition of the fragments which Bidez gave us in his life of Porphyry. But Porphyry unlearned at the feet of Plotinus his early zeal, and in his old age in his letter to his wife wrote: Observance or neglect of the temple service neither helps nor harms, but if a man serves God as if God needed anything, he sets himself up, without knowing it, above God. Later Neo-Platonists admitted into their system ever greater concessions to the popular belief: Iamblichus attributed to the statues a miraculous origin: if Plotinus had allowed (*Enneads* 4, 3, 11) that the essence of the universal soul could easily be made present in everything which is disposed to receive its action and thus in some small degree to participate in its power, Iamblichus went further: for him the gods are present in the statues, or at least communicate to them supernatural virtues. Proclus taught that through secret initiatory rites the statues can be made like to the gods and fit to receive the divine illuminations. Theurgy, of which Porphyry had proclaimed the peril, triumphed and Julian left the representatives of the earlier school of Neo-Platonism for Maximus, who could illumine the torch of the statue of Hecate by his invocations. Apollo, before the god's temple in Daphne was burnt down, prophesied through a sign given by his statue to Julian that he was about to desert his temple. Credulity wins the day and the popular faith makes Neo-Platonism its captive.

This doctrine of symbolism reaches its highest point in the declaration of Dion Chrysostom that these statues of the gods in human form are intended to show in symbolic fashion the kinship (συγγένεια) which unites God and man. They symbolize *life*, as the Neo-Platonist Sallustius says—life that strange inexplicable thing which links man to the living God.

Thus the apology of the pagans for the statues is designed to show (i) that here is no idolatry: these are not gods: the great statue, as that of Zeus by Pheidias, is an expression in summary form of the mind of God, and its aim is to lead the mind of man to God; (ii) the statue is man's copybook through which he may engrave on his memory the lineaments of God; (iii) the statue through sacred rites is fitted to receive the divine: it is indwelt by a more than human power, and is thus endowed with miraculous energy; (iv) the god is fashioned in human form since man is made in the image of God: and thus in symbol is proclaimed the kinship which unites God and man.

From this statement of the pagan apologetic we turn to the Iconoclast Controversy to see how the Greek Church met the challenge by which its image-worship was attacked, by what arguments the defenders of the sacred icons won a complete and lasting victory.

In the history of the Iconoclast controversy there are, as you know, two periods: the first ends with the restoration of the icons by the Empress Irene, the second with the final triumph of the images under the Empress Theodora. But the second period, the ninth-century revival of the Iconoclast

movement, adds little to theology; it repeats the arguments
adduced by the Iconoclasts under Leo III and Constantine V
and, for the rest, falls back upon the authority of earlier church
fathers, the authority of tradition, in order to support its case.
It is, therefore, with the ideas of the initiators of the movement and the orthodox apologetic by which those ideas are
met that we are here primarily concerned.

The Iconoclast Argument

(i) *Idolatry.* At the outset the principal—though not the sole
—charge of the Iconoclasts against the worshippers of the
images was that of idolatry, and the leader of the Iconoclast
clergy, Constantine, Bishop of Nacoleia, consciously reverts to
the earlier Christian apologetic against paganism in his appeal
to the veto of the Old Testament. The Christians under the
Principate had supported their accusation of idolatry by
identifying the pagan statue with the deity that it represented:
it is thus of great interest to observe the reasoning which underlay the Iconoclast charge. The significance of this reasoning
was for the first time pointed out by Ostrogorsky in his book
Studien zur Geschichte des byzantinischen Bilderstreites. From a
fragment of the work of Constantine V quoted in the refutation of the Patriarch Nicephorus we learn what was the emperor's view of a true icon: καὶ εἰ καλῶς, ὁμοούσιον αὐτὴν εἶναι
τοῦ εἰκονιζομένου (Nicephorus, Migne, *P.G.* 100, 225 A): it must
be of the same οὐσία (substance) as that of which it is an image:
then obviously on this interpretation if statue or picture is the
same thing—of the same οὐσία—as that which it represents,
then it is indeed an idol. This even Iconodules would admit:
καὶ ταύτῃ ἀλλήλων εἰκών τε καὶ εἴδωλον ἀποδιαστέλλονται ὥστε οἱ
μὴ δεχόμενοι τούτων διαφορὰν δικαίως ἂν εἰδωλολάτραι κληθεῖεν
(Migne, *P.G.* 100, 277 B). But however closely the image might
be connected with its subject, one clear distinction for the
Iconodule there did remain—type and prototype differed in
οὐσία, and thus a convincing defence was open to the image-
worshipper against the charge of idolatry precisely on the
same lines as the pagan had used to rebut the accusation of
the Christians. That apologetic was formulated once and for

all by John of Damascus. It is not a worship of matter, but of those whom matter represents. The honour given to the image is referred to the original.

This difference between Iconoclast and Iconodule—the 'magico-oriental view', as Ostrogorsky has called it, of the image on the one hand, the Platonic view on the other—is fundamental. It seems strange to us that Theodore the Studite should be at pains laboriously to establish that there is a difference in essence between Christ and the image of Christ: it would appear to us self-evident. But to Theodore it was of supreme moment to establish that truth against the Iconoclast, or otherwise he could not defend himself from the charge of idolatry. Similarly, the Iconoclast is quite consistent in maintaining that for the Christian there is only one image which is permissible, and that is the Eucharist. For precisely in the elements *after consecration* we have a type which is of the same οὐσία as the Prototype. This *is* my body, this *is* my blood. The εἰκών is no mere likeness, ὁμοίωμα—no mere paradigm—as John of Damascus would define it, it *is* under a figure, μόρφωσις, Christ Himself.

It has not, I think, been noticed that it is precisely this view of the Eucharist which appears to Theodore the Studite so horrible a blasphemy. If the Eucharist was only an εἰκών, its virtue was challenged: the Eucharist was no image: it was itself reality. Here more clearly than anywhere else we can observe that difference in the meaning of terms which prevented Iconoclast and Iconodule from understanding each other.

(ii) *The Christological argument.* The second line of argument of the Iconoclast is the Christological: Christ is one person in two natures—and those two natures, the human and the divine, may neither be sundered nor confused. It was agreed on every hand that the Godhead could not be portrayed in art: the Divine was not circumscribed in space so that He could be delineated: He was ἀπερίγραπτος. Humanity, on the other hand, it was obviously possible to portray. But Christ both human *and divine*, how could He be represented in art?—all that art could represent was bare man (ψιλὸς ἄνθρωπος); you are making of Christ a creature, nothing more than a man, and by so doing you are adding a fourth person to the Trinity. For there cannot be an εἰκών of one who consists of two natures which represents only the form proper to one nature. The icon was bound to omit the divine element in Christ, and was therefore necessarily misleading.

And to this the reply was that if the Incarnate Christ could not be represented in art, then His full humanity and the hope of the Gospel were denied.

(iii) *Tradition.* The third line of argument of the Iconoclast was the appeal to tradition and usage.

With the pagan defence of the statues of the gods in our minds it is interesting to compare, in somewhat greater detail, the apologetic of the supporters of the images:

(i) The pagan had urged that through the image man learnt as through a copy-book the truths of religion—the nature of God.

In the same way the West of Europe, untroubled by the profound Christological problems of the East, regularly regarded the images as the Bible of the Illiterate, teaching the truths which men could not read of in books. In the East John of Damascus urges the same truth: 'What a book is to the literate, that an image is to the illiterate. The image speaks to the sight, as words to the ear: it brings us understanding.' Or again, after quoting St Basil's words, 'Let us show them forth in a sermon as if in a picture,' he writes: 'What better proof have we that images are the books of the illiterate. . . . I have not many books nor time for study and I go into a church, the common refuge of souls, my mind wearied with conflicting thoughts. I see before me a beautiful picture and the sight refreshes me and induces me to glorify God. I marvel at the martyr's endurance, at his reward, and fired with burning zeal I fall down to adore God through his martyr and receive a grace of salvation.' Elsewhere again, in a quotation from Leo, Bishop of Neapolis: 'The representations of the saints are not our gods, but books which lie open and are venerated in churches in order to remind us of God and to lead us to worship Him.'

The parallelism between the Christian and the pagan thought is complete.

(ii) The close connexion which exists between the image and that which is represented. As we have seen, while the defenders of the icons deny identity of essence, they assert, and with increasing emphasis as the controversy progresses, this close relation. As the individual thing—table, chair—is related to the Platonic idea of that thing, so are the images to their prototype. In the first book of the treatise of John of Damascus written in defence of the images we read: 'The saints in their life-time were filled with the Holy Spirit and, when they are no more, His grace abides with their spirits and with their bodies in their tombs and also with their likenesses and holy images, not by nature, but by grace and divine power.' To Theodore the Studite there is a hypostatic—a personal— identity between the image and the original—the relation of the two is like that of a man and his shadow: it is only in their substance that they are distinct. As the shadow of the apostle according to the New Testament account wrought healing, says John of Damascus, so by the virtue of the saint represented the image can work miracles: the image is so far personally identified with its original that Theodore can congratulate one who brought to the font an icon as godfather of his child. This identification is, of course, saved from the charge of idolatry because it is not the material of which the image is made which is worshipped, but Christ or the saint in the image. Matter is endued with a divine power through prayer made to those who are depicted in image. Purple by itself is simple, and so is silk and the cloak which is made of both. But if the king put it on, the cloak receives honour from the honour due to the wearer. So it is with matter.[6] Material things in themselves demand no veneration, but if the person represented be full of grace, the materials become partakers in grace, κατ' ἀναλογίαν τῆς πίστεως. I am not quite sure how those words should be translated: 'through an analogy which is the result of faith'?

Here the parallelism with the later defence of the statues by the pagans is very close: we have noticed that Iamblichus held that the gods could communicate to the statues supernatural virtues, or as Proclus put it: through consecration the statues

[6] Cf. Epiphanius, *Ancoratus*, 51.

become 'fit to receive the divine illuminations', and can thus work wonders.

The highest level reached by the pagan apologetic is to be found in the statement that the statues symbolize the kinship between gods and men. The crowning point in the whole of the Christian apologetic for the images lies in the contention that they proclaim that God became man. Throughout the argument of John of Damascus we are brought back again and again to the Incarnation and the consequent redemption of matter. The Old Testament prohibition of images is explained on this ground: is it not evident, he asks, that as it is impossible to make an image of God who is uncircumscribed and impassible or of one like to God, creation should not be worshipped as God? . . . Now, however, when God is seen clothed in flesh and conversing with men I make an image of the God whom I see. I do not worship matter, I worship the God of matter who became matter for my sake and deigned to inhabit matter, who worked out my salvation through matter. I will not cease from honouring that matter which works my salvation. Do not despise matter, for it is not despicable: nothing is despicable which God has made. This is the Manichean heresy. That alone is despicable which does not come from God, but is our own invention—the spontaneous choice of will to disregard the natural law, i.e. sin. You see that the law and everything it ordained and all our own worship consist in the consecration of what is made by hands, leading us through matter to the Invisible God.

And the Greek Church escaped from the prohibitions of an earlier dispensation through their belief in a progressive revelation. As John of Damascus writes: 'And I say to you that Moses through the children of Israel's hardness of heart and knowing their proclivity to idolatry forbade them to make images. We are not in the same case. We have taken a firm footing on the rock of faith, being enriched with the light of God's friendship.' And because of this liberation the Church could make use of those material symbols which were not permitted to Israel. 'For,' to quote John of Damascus once more, 'as we are composed of soul and body and our soul does not stand alone, but is, as it were, shrouded by a veil, it is impossible for us to arrive at intellectual conceptions without corporeal things. Just as we listen with our bodily ears to *physical* words and understand *spiritual* things, so through corporeal vision we come to the spiritual. On this account Christ took a body and a soul, as man has both one and the other. And baptism is likewise double, of water and the spirit. So is communion and prayer and psalmody; everything has a double signification, a corporeal and a spiritual.' And at the close of his last book he sums up his whole argument in the words: 'Thus, we worship images and it is not a worship of matter but of those whom matter represents. The honour given to the image is referred to the original, as Saint Basil rightly says.'

The kinship of God and man symbolized through matter— the supreme pagan justification: the reconciliation of God and man mediated through matter and therefore capable of being symbolized in and through matter—the crown of Christian apologetic. Modern writers have endeavoured to prove that the Iconoclasts were Monophysites: there is little, if anything, to be said for the view and there is no need for us to accept their contention. But there *was* a danger that the Iconoclast teaching might be interpreted in a Manichean sense—that matter was in itself evil, that a God who sought to be worshipped in spirit and in truth had no place for matter in the cultus of his church. The worshippers of the images saved the Greek world from any such oriental heresy. Matter had once for all been hallowed by the Incarnation. Professor Bury as a rationalist was attracted in his early days towards the authors of the Iconoclast movement, but in later life as a monist he acknowledged that it was the worshippers of the images who had preserved the 'higher synthesis of Christianity'. 'The material world was not left stranded, hostile, disdained and unexplained.' 'The service', he wrote in 1900, 'which was rendered by the Church in the councils of A.D. 787 and 843 and by the great champions John of Damascus, Theodore of Studion and Nicephorus the Patriarch in their writings to the development of religion was the preservation, though in an alien husk of supernatural elements, of the vital thought of the brilliant . . . synthesis of Jesus.'

Thus throughout this controversy we observe the parallelism

between the Christian and the pagan apologetic. It can indeed be traced even in quite small details. Maximus Tyrius as we have seen had urged that the statues were reminders of the gods, using the analogy of a lover's passion for anything associated with the loved one. John of Damascus, pleading for the preservation in image of the memory of the saints, uses the same analogy: 'I have often seen lovers gazing at the loved one's garment and embracing it with eyes and mouth as if it was himself', and are not the saints worthy of a similar passion? Pagan and Christian employ the same weapons.

But in the last resort for the Neo-Platonist the argument which outweighed the logical objections raised by his philosophy was the fact of a pious tradition of religious usage ordained, as Julian had written, 'through all past time among all the nations of the earth.' For Iconoclast, and to a still higher degree for the worshipper of the images, the last and most cogent argument was the tradition of the Christian Church. When the Iconoclast asked: what authority have you for images in the scriptures? Theodore the Studite will answer that though many practices of the Church are not mentioned in express words in the scriptures, they are implicitly there, and from the scriptures the living church has fashioned a progressive tradition to meet the challenge of heresy—the Homoousion, the Theotokos—examples too numerous to mention. The challenge brings to light the implicit truth, and that truth then becomes part of the heritage of the Church. John of Damascus urges the same plea; 'Where do you find in the Old Testament or in the Gospel the Trinity or consubstantiality or one Godhead or three persons or the one substance of Christ or His two natures expressed in so many words? Still, as they are contained in what Scripture *does* say and defined by the holy fathers, we receive them and anathematize those who do not.' 'For if we neglect unwritten customs as lacking in weight we bury in oblivion the most pertinent facts connected with the Gospel.' So St Basil had said. Saint John of Damascus, quoting these words, continues: 'How do we know the Holy Place of Calvary or the Holy Sepulchre? Does it not rest on a tradition handed down from father to son? And the unwritten tradition which identifies these spots does more things of the same kind. Whence come the three immersions at baptism, praying with the face turned towards the east and the tradition of the divine mysteries (=the Eucharist)? Hence St Paul says: Therefore, brethren, stand fast and hold the traditions which you have learned either by word or by our epistle. As, then, so much has been handed down in the Church and is observed down to the present day, why disparage images?' And at the close of his argument his supreme appeal is to tradition: 'We beseech, therefore, the people of God, the faithful flock, to hold fast to the ecclesiastical traditions. The gradual removal of what has been handed down to us would be undermining the foundation stones and would in no short time overthrow the whole structure.' Or again: 'We do not change the boundaries marked out by our fathers: we keep the tradition we have received.'

Greek Paganism had kept the tradition of the worship of the images until it could hand over the defence of that tradition to the Christian Church. The issue of the Iconoclast Controversy was all along the line a triumph of tradition. The image—that hymn of praise as John of Damascus called it, the lasting token of those who have fought and conquered and of demons humbled and put to flight—the image remained: the attack of an oriental art of symbolism was repulsed by Greek loyalty to a Greek iconography: the Mediterranean art of *Darstellung*— of representation—held the field and in every Greek church to-day the iconostasis proclaims alike the redemption of matter and the victory of orthodoxy. By the recognition of a progressive revelation the Greek Church had freed itself from the dead hand of a Semitic prohibition: it had maintained a place in worship for those emotions which had inspired the Greek in the defence of his pagan gods. But during the long struggle the passionate loyalty to the tradition of the fathers had so possessed the soul of the Greek Church that after the victory of the images, after the celebration of the festival of re-established orthodoxy, it ceased to believe in a progressive revelation of truth, in a tradition which should consciously adapt itself to present needs as and when fresh crises called for restatements of Christian truth. The Church became a custodian trustee of the deposit of faith: it remained the Church of the seven councils: it did not expect that leading into further truth which had been promised by its Lord. The later history of the Greek Church appears to one who is not of its allegiance as the tragedy of an arrested development.

For the student of history this controversy concerning the sacred images remains a deeply interesting chapter in the story of Mediterranean religion and in the story of that pagan civilization which gave to the Christian Church its apologetic against the idols and then in its turn provided the model for the Church's defence of the holy icons. It is through such a study that we become more clearly conscious of those common aspirations towards a worship of the spirit, that common sanctification of matter in the service of the spirit, which links men together in their common quest of the Divine.

BIBLIOGRAPHY

EARLY CHRISTIAN ART

H. Achelis, *Der Entwicklungsgang der altchristlichen Kunst* (Leipzig, Quelle & Meyer, 1919).

L. von Sybel, *Frühchristliche Kunst* (Munich, Beck, 1920).

Viktor Schultze, *Grundriss der christlichen Archäologie* (Munich, Beck, 1919).

J. Wilpert, *Die altchristliche Kunst Roms und des Orients* [= *Zeits. f. kath. Theologie*, xlv (1921), pp. 337–69] (Innsbruck, 1921).

P. Styger, 'Die altchristliche Kunst,' *Zeits. f. kath. Theologie*, liii (1929), pp. 545–63.

THE APOLOGISTS

T. W. Crafer, *The Apocriticus of Macarius Magnes* (S.P.C.K., 1919).

J. Geffcken, *Zwei griechische Apologeten* (Leipzig, Teubner, 1907).

A. Puech, *Les apologistes grecs du II siècle*, etc. (Paris, Hachette, 1912).

Bodo de Borries, *Quid veteres philosophi de idololatria senserint,* Diss. Göttingen, 1918.

Charly Clerc, *Les théories relatives au culte des images chez les auteurs grecs du IIᵉ siècle* (Paris, Fontemoing, ?1915).

ART AND THE CHURCH

Alois Knöpfler, 'Der angebliche Kunsthass der ersten Christen,' *Hertling Festschrift* (1913), pp. 41–8.

Hugo Koch, *Die altchristliche Bilderfrage nach den literarischen Quellen* (Göttingen, 1917).

Walter Elliger, *Die Stellung der alten Christen zu den Bildern in den ersten vier Jahrhunderten*, etc. (Leipzig, Dieterich, 1930).

NEO-PLATONISM

J. Bidez, *Vie de Porphyre* (Gand, 1913).
Adolf Harnack, in *Hibbert Journal*, October 1911.

EPIPHANIUS

Karl Holl, *Gesammelte Aufsätze zur Kirchengeschichte*, vol. ii, pp. 351–87 [1916] (Tübingen, Mohr, 1928).
Georg Ostrogorsky, *Studien zur Gesch. des byzantinischen Bilderstreites* (section 3) (Breslau, Marcus, 1929).
P. Maas, 'Die ikonoklastische Episode in dem Brief des Epiphanios an Johannes', *B.Z.* xxx (1929–30), pp. 279–86.
F. Dölger, in *Göttingische gelehrte Anzeigen*, cxci (1929), no. 8 (August 1929).
H. Grégoire, in *Byzantion*, iv (1929), pp. 765–71.

ICONOCLASTS

Alice Gardner, in *Hibbert Journal*, January 1904.
K. Schwarzlose, *Der Bilderstreit* (Gotha, 1890).
E. J. Martin, *A History of the Iconoclastic Controversy* (S.P.C.K., 1930).
Mary H. Allies, (transl.), *S. John Damascene on Holy Images* (London, Baker, 1898).
G. Ostrogorsky, as above.
    And see E. Bevan, 'Idolatry', *Edinburgh Review*, April 1926.

VIII

Isocrates[1]

'A great man.' Professor Werner Jaeger. 'Plato himself had to reckon with a powerful writer and thinker.' J. M. Lloyd Thomas in the *Hibbert Journal*, Jan. 1946, p. 192.

FIRST: certain claims which have been made on behalf of Isocrates may be considered:

(i) He was the pioneer who pointed the way to a union of Greek cities under the ἀρχή of Athens: the Second Athenian Confederacy was thus the natural outcome of the *Panegyricus* of Isocrates. This claim cannot be sustained, for that Confederacy was rendered possible only by the elaborate safeguards included in the instrument of foundation which were intended to secure that the evil practices which had ruined the Delian League should never recur under the new coalition. In the *Panegyricus* those evils are either denied or justified, and there is no assurance that they would not be repeated in the future. Thus in the case of the slaughter at Melos and Scione, Isocrates ignores the fact that Melos was a neutral State whose only desire was to retain its neutrality: it becomes a State at war with Athens: ἐγὼ δὲ ἡγοῦμαι . . . οὐδὲν εἶναι τοῦτο σημεῖον ὡς κακῶς ἤρχομεν εἴ τινες τῶν πολεμησάντων ἡμῖν σφόδρα φαίνονται κολασθέντες (§ 101): further, other States in similar cases had not dealt more leniently, and indeed Athens is to be congratulated that so few massacres occurred under her ἀρχή (§ 102). Such a defence was hardly likely to persuade the Greek States to gather under the hegemony of Athens, even though Isocrates added (§ 103): οἶμαι δὲ πᾶσι δοκεῖν τούτους κρατίστους προστάτας γενήσεσθαι τῶν Ἑλλήνων, ἐφ᾽ ὧν οἱ πειθαρχήσαντες ἄριστα τυγχάνουσι πράξαντες—'those will prove the best leaders and champions of the Hellenes

---

[1] A Note after reading Professor G. W. Jaeger's *Paideia*, vol. iii on Isocrates [1947. Unpublished]. I owe a special obligation to Professor A. Momigliano and to Dr P. Treves for lending me off-prints of recent foreign work on Isocrates though I am sure that neither would agree with my views.

under whom in the past those who were obedient have fared the best.' Where is there any room here for a συνέδριον of the associated cities? Obedience to the behests of Athens—that is the Isocratean programme. The enforcement upon the members of the League of democratic constitutions is upheld (§ 106); the Kleruchies were sent into the depopulated States for the protection of their territories and not for our own aggrandisement (§ 107). Nowhere in the *Panegyricus* does Isocrates seek to explain that hatred which, he knows full well, as did his contemporaries, destroyed the Delian League, and nowhere in the *Panegyricus* does he suggest any guarantees against abuses. The Second Athenian Confederacy, in a word, could never have come into being under such an Athenian ἀρχή as is defended in the speech of 380.

(ii) It has also been contended (by Wendland)[2] that it was the vision of a Greece united in ὁμόνοια which Isocrates painted in the *Philippus* that created the League of Corinth in the years after his death. On such evidence as we possess the claim cannot be sustained. The only picture of the future given us by Isocrates is to be found in the *Philippus* (69–70): 'Men of the highest renown will come as ambassadors from the greatest States to your court; you will advise with them about the general welfare . . . you will see all Hellas on tip-toe with interest in whatever you happen to propose, and no one will be indifferent to the measures which you as arbitrator will determine.' The world of Greek States remains as before, and as before these States send their ambassadors singly to the king's court: there is no suggestion of a League with cities meeting in council. The League of Corinth is a *new* thing, and in the vision of Isocrates all the elements of the picture are familiar: the King of Macedon has simply taken the place of the King of Persia (see *Panath.* § 160; *Panegyr.* § 121). Here is no bold conception of constitutional change.

(iii) Professor Jaeger has sought to establish that in the *Panegyricus* Isocrates makes a distinction between the hegemonia and the ἀρχή τῆς θαλάττης. This distinction cannot be

---

[2] The Corinthian League 'sich vielfach lehnt an das Programm des Isokrates an', P. Wendland, 'Beiträge zur athenischen Politik und Publicistik des 4ten Jahrhunderts. I. König Philippos und Isokrates', *Nachrichten der kgl. Gesellschaft der Wissenschaften* (Göttingen phil.-hist. Klasse, 1910), p. 135.

maintained: Athens in the thought of Isocrates was not intended to surrender to Sparta the hegemony provided that she could keep for herself the mastery of the sea. In 380 Sparta was still all-powerful, and therefore Isocrates was forced to use diplomatic language—to profess to contemplate sharing the leadership of the Greeks with Sparta: such arguments are to be sought οἵ τινες τὼ πόλη τούτω (Athens and Sparta) πείσουσιν ἰσομοιρῆσαι πρὸς ἀλλήλους καὶ τάς θ' ἡγεμονίας διελέσθαι (§ 17). But the whole theme of the speech is a contradiction of this standpoint: hegemony should be held by those who first won the honour or by those who rendered the most services to the Greeks: on both counts Athens has the best title (§ 22); even at the time when the sons of Heracles came as fugitives, Athens ἡγεμονικῶς εἶχε and claimed προεστάναι τῶν Ἑλλήνων (§ 57) ὥστε περὶ μὲν τῆς ἐν τοῖς Ἕλλησι δυναστείας οὐκ οἶδ' ὅπως ἄν τις σαφέστερον ἐπιδεῖξαι δυνηθείη (§ 65) (contrast § 63 for the claim of Sparta). At Salamis Athens performed distinctive deeds τῆς ἡγεμονίας ἄξια (§ 98), and after the Persian Wars the Athenians τὴν ἀρχὴν τῆς θαλάττης ἔλαβον δόντων μὲν τῶν ἄλλων Ἑλλήνων, οὐκ ἀμφισβητούντων δὲ τῶν νῦν ἡμᾶς ἀφαιρεῖσθαι ζητούντων (§ 72). In fact, the Spartans παρειλήφασι ψευδῆ λόγον ὡς ἔστιν αὐτοῖς ἡγεῖσθαι πάτριον. ἢν δὲ ἐπιδείξῃ τις αὐτοῖς ταύτην τὴν τιμὴν ἡμετέραν οὖσαν μᾶλλον ἢ ἐκείνων, τάχ' ἄν ἐάσαντες τὸ διακριβοῦσθαι περὶ τούτων ἐπὶ τὸ συμφέρον ἔλθοιεν—'perhaps they might give up splitting hairs about these questions and pursue their true interests' (§ 18). In § 99 the definite claim is raised that Athens must have the hegemony when a campaign against the barbarians is in prospect: πῶς δ' οὐκ ἄν δεινὰ πάθοιμεν, εἰ τῶν κακῶν πλεῖστον μέρος μετασχόντες ἐν ταῖς τιμαῖς ἔλαττον ἔχειν ἀξιωθεῖμεν, καὶ τότε προταχθέντες ὑπὲρ ἁπάντων νῦν ἑτέροις ἀκολουθεῖν ἀναγκασθεῖμεν. For the Athenians the ἀρχὴ τῆς θαλάττης cannot be separated from the ἡγεμονία, for the ἀρχή is only the form taken by the ἡγεμονία after the Persian Wars. Professor Jaeger does not refer to the *Antidosis* 57 where Isocrates, describing the argument of the *Panegyricus*, says that he summoned the Greeks to make war upon the barbarians while at the same time Λακεδαιμονίοις περὶ τῆς ἡγεμονίας ἀμφισβητῶν, and proceeds τὴν ἡγεμονίαν ἔτι σαφέστερον ἀποφαίνειν ὡς ἔστι τῆς πόλεως =Athens; and cf. *Antidosis*, §§ 76–7, on the *Panegyricus*: τίς ἂν πολιτικώτερος καὶ μᾶλλον πρέπων τῇ πόλει τοῦ τὴν ἡγεμονίαν ἀποφαίνοντος ἔκ τε τῶν ἄλλων εὐεργεσιῶν καὶ τῶν κινδύνων ἡμετέραν οὖσαν μᾶλλον ἢ Λακεδαιμονίων; In the *Areopagiticus*, writes Professor Jaeger, 'Isocrates does not distinguish between domination and hegemony'[3]: that is true, but it is important to realize that no such distinction is made in the *Panegyricus* between ἀρχή and ἡγεμονία. The usage of Isocrates is continuous until his argument in the *Peace*. Similarly, after Aegospotamoi the Spartans held καὶ τὴν κατὰ γῆν καὶ τὴν κατὰ θάλατταν ἀρχήν (*Areop.* 7)—ἀρχή and ἡγεμονία are indivisible.

(iv) Isocrates and Logoi—Professor Jaeger grows enthusiastic over the 'hymn' in which Isocrates celebrates the achievements which man owes to the λόγοι (*Nicocles*, §§ 5–9; *Antidosis*, §§ 253–7). It was, however, a favourite contention with Isocrates that it is the use made of things or qualities which determines their true value.[4] What was Isocrates' view of the practical function of the λόγοι? This he gives at the opening of the *Panegyricus*: the λόγοι τοιαύτην ἔχουσι τὴν φύσιν ὥσθ' οἷόν τ' εἶναι περὶ τῶν αὐτῶν πολλαχῶς ἐξηγήσασθαι καὶ τά τε μεγάλα ταπεινὰ ποιῆσαι καὶ τοῖς μικροῖς μέγεθος περιθεῖναι καὶ τά τε παλαιὰ καινῶς διελθεῖν καὶ περὶ τῶν νεωστὶ γεγενημένων ἀρχαίως εἰπεῖν (§ 8)—'to make great things mean, to invest little things with greatness, to say old things in a novel way and to give to recent events an antique air'—the function of λόγοι is purely sophistic. The comment of Longinus on this passage is surely not without its justification: "Well then, Isocrates," someone will say, "is that what you propose to do? To make the conduct of Lacedaemonians and Athenians the opposite of what it was?" For he has practically turned his eulogy of speeches into a prefatory warning to his hearers that he is himself not to be trusted.'[5] In the (doubtless fictional) dialogue at the close of the *Panathenaicus* the student of Isocrates praises his master's speech as παντοδαπῆς μεστὸν ποικιλίας καὶ ψευδολογίας (§ 246)—how should the words be

[3] *Harvard Studies in Classical Philology* (special volume 1941), p. 429, and notes 1 and 2.
[4] e.g. *Panath.* § 220, *Antidosis* §§ 251–2. Cf. *Archidamus*, § 50.
[5] Translation from T. G. Tucker, *Longinus on Elevation of Style* (Melbourne University Press, 1935), pp. 54–5 (= ch. 38).

148   ISOCRATES

translated?—'packed with all kinds of sophistic subtlety and faked history'? In reading the work of Isocrates one must always be on one's guard—the art of 'reading between the lines' was never more necessary.[6] We remember, as Isocrates tells us, that Lysimachus λέγει ὡς ἐγὼ τοὺς ἥττους λόγους κρείττους δύναμαι ποιεῖν (*Antidosis*, § 15).

(v) To the student the two 'Nicocles' speeches present special difficulties. Of the speech 'To Nicocles' Professor Jaeger remarks: 'It is not so systematic as we should expect from its beginning and from Isocrates' statement that he intends to lay down only the general principles of monarchy, . . . it consists chiefly of separate precepts which follow one another without a "close logical connexion".' He finds in it, however, 'an underlying connexion between the separate precepts. They all add up to form a portrait of the ideal ruler, a portrait whose unity lies in the ethical consistency' (p. 98). Pöhlmann, before Professor Jaeger, had sought a principle which should unify both the 'To Nicocles' and the 'Nicocles': he found it in the contrast with the democracy of Isocrates' time.[7] This search for a unifying principle, however, it may be suggested, is to do too great honour to the 'To Nicocles'; Isocrates himself thought otherwise. When in the *Antidosis* he called upon the clerk to the court to read aloud a section of the speech, he said: οὐχ ὁμοίως δὲ γέγραπται τοῖς ἀνεγνωσμένοις (=sections from the *Panegyricus* and the *Peace*). οὗτοι μὲν γὰρ τὸ λεγόμενον ὁμολογούμενον (each part agrees with the other) ἀεὶ τῷ προειρημένῳ καὶ συγκεκλειμένον ἔχουσιν (there is a close logical connexion), ἐν δὲ τούτῳ τοὐναντίον· ἀπολύσας γὰρ ἀπὸ τοῦ προτέρου καὶ χωρίς, ὥσπερ τὰ καλούμενα κεφάλαια, ποιήσας, πειρῶμαι διὰ βραχέων ἕκαστον ὧν συμβουλεύω φράζειν (*Antidosis*, 68). This was for Isocrates quite unusual; he will not break off in the middle of a subject: εἰ γὰρ τοῦτ' ἤδη ποιοίην μήτε τέλος ἐπιθεὶς τοῖς γεγραμμένοις μήτε συγκλείσας (cf. συγκεκλειμένου *supra*) τὴν ἀρχὴν τῶν ῥηθήσεσθαι μελλόντων τῇ τελευτῇ τῶν ἤδη προειρημένων, ὅμοιος ἂν εἶναι δόξαιμι τοῖς εἰκῇ καὶ φορτικῶς καὶ χύδην ὅ τι ἂν ἐπέλθῃ λέγουσιν. ἃ φυλακτέον ἡμῖν ἐστιν (*Pana-*

[6] R. v. Pöhlmann, 'Isokrates und das Problem der Demokratie', *Sitzungsberichte der K. Bayr. Akad. d. Wiss.*, Philosoph.-philologische und hist. Klasse, Jahrgang 1913 (Munich), p. 128.
[7] v. Pöhlmann, op. cit., pp. 88–90.

thenaicus, § 24). For the practice of Isocrates, cf. *Antidosis*, 11: τοσοῦτον οὖν μῆκος λόγου συνιδεῖν καὶ τοσαύτας ἰδέας καὶ τοσοῦτον ἀλλήλων ἀφεστώσας συναρμόσαι καὶ συναγαγεῖν καὶ τὰς ἐπιφερομένας οἰκειῶσαι τοῖς προειρημένοις καὶ πάσας ποιῆσαι σφίσιν αὐταῖς ὁμολογουμένας, οὐ πάνυ μικρὸν ἦν ἔργον. In thus composing the 'To Nicocles' it has been contended that Isocrates created a new literary form—the prose Paraenesis. Of this literary form Münscher writes that it 'besteht aus aneinandergereihten Gnomen (höchstens mit kurzer Begründung) ohne strenge Disposition; man sollte im Druck die einzelnen absetzen' (*P.W. Real-Encyclopädie*, ix. 2, col. 2189 s.f.). Isocrates himself tells us that in writing the 'To Nicocles' he did not seek τὰς καινότητας: in this form of composition one should ἡγεῖσθαι τοῦτον χαριέστατον ὃς ἂν τῶν διεσπαρμένων ἐν ταῖς τῶν ἄλλων διανοίαις ἀθροῖσαι τὰ πλεῖστα δυνηθῇ καὶ φράσαι κάλλιστα περὶ αὐτῶν ('To Nicocles' § 41). In ibid. (§ 43) Isocrates expressly mentions Hesiod, Theognis and Phocylides: at the close of his work (ibid.) he has the satisfactory consciousness that he has offered to Nicocles 'all the good counsels which I know'. The 'speech' is indeed a collection of gnomic remarks and maxims, many of surprising banality: one of the most curious pieces of advice is: 'Do not be contentious in all things, but only where it will profit you to have your own way' (§ 25, Norlin's translation). Polonius might well feel that he had been anticipated by Isocrates. It is surely idle to attempt to find unity in 'the ethical consistency' of such a compilation; it is presumably primarily intended to illustrate the verbal dexterity of Isocrates—φράσαι κάλλιστα in fact—τά τε παλαιὰ καινῶς διελθεῖν— we see a rhetorician at work upon his 'All Trivia'.

But the speech supposed to be addressed by Nicocles, as king of Cyprus, to his subjects is surely one of the strangest writings produced under the Athenian democracy by anyone who claimed to be a leader of political opinion. Presumably one must treat it seriously and not regard it merely as an epideictic *tour de force*, but it is not easy to guess the reason for its composition. Professor Jaeger has pointed out that Plato in his letters 'holds that the common interest of all the Sicilian Greeks justifies the concentration of all political power in the hands of the tyrant Dionysius, if he would only consent

to give his State a constitution and abandon the arbitrary rule
of despotism' (p. 73), but obviously the conditions are all-
important. And such conditions were, of course, lacking in the
tyranny of Nicocles. 'Isocrates does not attempt to limit the
tyrant's power by written laws or constitutions' (p. 87). But,
Professor Jaeger says, by Isocrates 'tyranny is made part of a
political idea and thereby legalized'. Isocrates, it is true, takes
the position of the ruler 'as a fact established by the chance of
his birth' (p. 92), but 'he does more than accept tyranny as a
given fact in power-politics. He brings it under an ideal standard so that he can then fairly explain that monarchy is the
best form of constitution' (p. 87). 'The *arete* of the monarch is
the basis on which his demand for obedience and loyalty from
his subjects can be justified' (p. 88). With well-timed discretion
Professor Jaeger adds: 'We need go no further into the social
morality of the doctrine developed in this section of the speech
about the political duties of the good subjects of a good monarch' (p. 88). Professor Jaeger may have abstained from any
such commentary since Hitler had anticipated him. The subject's duty is one of unquestioning obedience: when the tyrant
has once announced his wishes δικαίως ἂν ἤδη τοῖς μὴ πειθο-
μένοις μεμφοίμην (§ 11); his legal title to the throne being
established, τίς οὐκ αὐτὸς αὑτοῦ καταγνώσεται τὴν μεγίστην
ζημίαν, ἄν μὴ πειθαρχῇ τοῖς ὑπ' ἐμοῦ συμβουλευθεῖσι καὶ προσταχ-
θεῖσιν (§ 13); the 'counsels and commands' are not further
characterized. There follows a eulogy of *Führertum*—how the
tyrant can win people over to his side more easily than any
other form of government by persuasion, violence, or bribery
(§ 22): this, it must be presumed, is 'to bring government
under an ideal standard'. For the citizens of Cyprus there can
be no privacy: 'Never conceal from me anything that you
possess or that you are doing or that you intend to do, knowing
that privacy must of necessity bring with it great fears' (§ 52).
Everyone is to practise delation against his fellow-citizens if
he sees anyone disloyal to the tyrant's rule. 'No clubs or
associations are to be formed without my sanction.' 'Preserve
the present state of affairs and do not desire any change' (§ 55).
'Consider that my safety is your security' (§ 56). 'Teach your
children to be obedient' (§ 57). 'Expect to fare well or ill

according as you are disposed well or ill toward me' (§ 61).
'Regard my words as your law . . . this is the sum of the whole
matter' (§ 62).—'You must fuse your wills with mine' (Hitler).

It is little wonder that Isocrates was afraid of his own handi-
work. When he produced the lengthy defence of his whole life
which fills the *Antidosis*, he quoted large extracts from the
Panegyricus, the *Peace*, and from his speech *Against the Soph-
ists*, naming the speech in each case; he also quoted a lengthy
passage from the innocuous introduction (on rhetoric) to the
'Nicocles', but he studiously refrained from *naming* the speech
from which the extract was taken. The 'Nicocles' did not provide effective material for a statesman accused of oligarchic
tendencies: it was prudent not to remind Athenians of that
laudation of a 'totalitarian' State.

(vi) Professor Jaeger writes that Isocrates extends his ideal
of national culture and makes it universal (p. 79), and thus we
can 'connect the supra-national ideal of Greece—its universally
valuable paideia—with the realistic political plan of conquering Asia and settling it with Greek colonists. In fact that ideal
contains a higher justification for the new national imperialism
in that it identifies what is specifically Greek with what is universally human. . . . In Isocrates national feeling is that of a
culturally superior nation which has realized that the efforts it
has made to attain a universal standard of perfection in all its
intellectual activities are its highest claim to victory in com-
petition with other races—since these other races have accepted
the Greek forms as the absolute expression of civilization.'
And Professor Jaeger contends that 'from all [Isocrates'] words
we can feel the living breath of Hellenism [I suspect that this
is a mistranslation of the German text—'Hellenismus' here
means the Hellenistic Age]. The new era actually did fall into
the forms which Isocrates had thought out before its advent.
Without the idea which he here expresses for the first time, the
idea that Greek paideia was something universally valuable,
there would have been no Macedonian Greek world-empire
and the universal culture which we call Hellenistic would never
have existed' (pp. 80–1). This is a high claim for Isocrates—
indeed a remarkable claim when one considers that in the view
of Isocrates the proper treatment of barbarians was βιάζεσθαι

—ἔστι δὲ τὸ μὲν πείθειν πρὸς τοὺς Ἕλληνας συμφέρον, τὸ δὲ βιάζεσθαι πρὸς τοὺς βαρβάρους χρήσιμον (*Philippus*, § 16); εὐεργετεῖν was Philip's rôle with the Greeks (cf. *Philippus*, § 116), βασιλεύειν with the Macedonians, τῶν δὲ βαρβάρων ὡς πλείστων ἄρχειν (ibid., § 154), and what ἄρχειν meant in the thought of Isocrates was interpreted by the writer of *Ep*. 3 to Philip, (§ 5) ὅταν τοὺς μὲν βαρβάρους ἀναγκάσῃς εἰλωτεύειν τοῖς Ἕλλησι πλήν τῶν σοι συναγωνισαμένων κ.τ.λ. The basis of Professor Jaeger's claim is the famous §§ 49–50 of the *Panegyricus*: does it really support the claim?

It is speech, Isocrates argues in this passage, which has proved itself to be the surest sign of culture in every one of us: καὶ τοῦτο σύμβολον τῆς παιδεύσεως ἡμῶν ἑκάστον πιστότατον ἀποδεδειγμένον καὶ τοὺς λόγῳ καλῶς χρωμένους οὐ μόνον ἐν ταῖς αὐτῶν δυναμένους ἀλλὰ καὶ παρὰ τοῖς ἄλλοις ἐντίμους ὄντας (which Norlin translates 'those who are skilled in speech are not only men of power in their own cities but are also held in honour in other States'). τοσοῦτον δὲ ἀπολέλοιπεν ἡ πόλις ἡμῶν περὶ τὸ φρονεῖν καὶ λέγειν τοὺς ἄλλους ἀνθρώπους, ὥσθ' οἱ ταύτης μαθηταὶ τῶν ἄλλων διδάσκαλοι γεγόνασι καὶ τὸ τῶν Ἑλλήνων ὄνομα πεποίηκε μηκέτι τοῦ γένους ἀλλὰ τῆς διανοίας δοκεῖν εἶναι, καὶ μᾶλλον Ἕλληνας καλεῖσθαι τοὺς τῆς παιδεύσεως τῆς ἡμετέρας ἢ τοὺς τῆς κοινῆς φύσεως μετέχοντας. (Here Norlin translates 'have become the teachers of the rest of the world'.) Now it is a sound rule: if you want to understand the *Panegyricus* consult the *Panathenaicus*, since after Leuctra Isocrates could say openly what he could only hint at in 380: cf. *Panath*., § 96. Ἐπειδή περ οὖν ἐπελήλυθέ μοι τὸ παρρησιάζεσθαι καὶ λέλυκα τὸ στόμα κ.τ.λ. I would suggest that the meaning of § 50 of the *Panegyricus* can be best ascertained by a study of §§ 208–14 of the *Panathenaicus*.

In the *Panathenaicus* the argument is that discoveries in ways of living or in the arts or elsewhere are made only by men of superior endowments: ὧν Λακεδαιμόνιοι πλέον ἀπέχουσι τῶν βαρβάρων· οἱ μὲν γὰρ ἂν φανεῖεν πολλῶν εὑρημάτων καὶ μαθηταὶ καὶ διδάσκαλοι γεγονότες, οὗτοι δὲ τοσοῦτον ἀπολελειμμένοι τῆς κοινῆς παιδείας καὶ φιλοσοφίας εἰσὶν ὥστ' οὐδὲ γράμματα μανθάνουσιν κ.τ.λ. (§ 209). Isocrates then recounts how Spartan boys are taught to steal—what is there in such conduct that is good or admirable and not, on the contrary, shameful? πῶς δὲ οὐκ ἀνοήτους χρὴ νομίζειν τοὺς ἐπαινοῦντας τοὺς τοσοῦτον τῶν νόμων τῶν κοινῶν ἐξεστηκότας καὶ μηδὲν τῶν αὐτῶν μήτε τοῖς Ἕλλησι μήτε τοῖς βαρβάροις γιγνώσκοντας (§ 213). I would suggest that both this passage and that in the *Panegyricus* are directed against Sparta, and both are intended to glorify Athens. The barbarians are not mentioned in the *Panegyricus*, since that speech is a call to a crusade against the brutalities of the barbarian Persians: there it would be out of place to ascribe to the barbarians any virtues. But in the *Panathenaicus* only echoes of that crusade remain, as in the excursus on Agamemnon: here the barbarians who are capable of learning and teaching—this is quite general, there is no specific reference to *Greek* culture or a *Greek* paideia—can be opposed to the Spartans who can do neither. It can be recognized that the Spartans in their boorishness and shameful education have no part either with the Greeks or the barbarians. In the *Panegyricus*, which is likewise directed against Sparta, Isocrates is, of course, more discreet, but I fancy that to Isocrates' readers the words καὶ μᾶλλον Ἕλληνας καλεῖσθαι τοὺς τῆς παιδεύσεως τῆς ἡμετέρας ἢ τοὺς τῆς κοινῆς φύσεως μετέχοντας would not have been obscure. The point is that the passage does *not* mean 'other races have accepted the Greek forms as the absolute expression of civilization'. The Spartans have sacrificed their title based on their common Greek blood—even the barbarians can outdistance them, which for Isocrates is a striking concession—'the publicans and harlots go into the kingdom of Heaven before you'. And as for the universal paideia which is prophetically to usher in the Hellenistic Age, one more passage from the *Panathenaicus* may be quoted (§§ 219–20): οἶμαι γὰρ ἅπαντας ἂν ὁμολογῆσαι κακίστους ἄνδρας εἶναι καὶ μεγίστης ζημίας ἀξίους ὅσοι τοῖς πράγμασι τοῖς εὑρημένοις ἐπ᾽ ὠφελείᾳ, τούτοις ἐπὶ βλάβῃ χρώμενοι τυγχάνουσι, μὴ πρὸς τοὺς βαρβάρους . . . ἀλλὰ πρὸς τοὺς οἰκειοτάτους κ.τ.λ. Those arts which were the glory of Athens are not to be extended to the barbarians, but are rightly used against them.

Of his interpretation of the thought of Isocrates Professor Jaeger writes: 'This is not actually said by Isocrates; and some may object to our interpretation.' He is quite right.

The domestic and the foreign policy of Isocrates have

usually been treated in isolation; thus they are studied in
separate chapters in the admirable book by Mathieu on *Les
Idées politiques d'Isocrate* (Paris, Les Belles Lettres, 1925), but
it may be suggested that they should be brought into close
connexion for their fuller understanding. In considering Isocrates' plan for a war of *revanche* against Persia it must not
be forgotten that both he himself and his adopted son were
enrolled among the 1200 who paid the war-tax—the εἰσφορά
(*Antidosis*, § 145); he was one of the γνώριμοι—a member of
the propertied class on whom the democracy imposed such
burdensome liturgies: ὥστ' ἄλγιον ζῆν τοὺς τὰς οὐσίας κεκτη-
μένους ἢ τοὺς συνεχῶς πενομένους (*Peace*, § 128); they felt that
the demagogues were not considering by what means they
might provide a livelihood for those who were in need: ἀλλ'
ὅπως τοὺς ἔχειν τι δοκοῦντας τοῖς ἀπόροις ἐξισώσουσιν (ibid, § 131,
and cf. the theme of the *Antidosis*). Thus when Isocrates draws
the fantastically idealized picture of 'the constitution of our
forefathers', the result of the blissful state of affairs in Attica
was that αἱ κτήσεις ἀσφαλεῖς ἦσαν οἷσπερ κατὰ τὸ δίκαιον ὑπῆρχον
(*Areop.*, § 35). In his youth in the fifth century, Isocrates tells
us, property had been secure: wealth was regarded as so
respectable a thing that almost everyone affected to own more
property than he possessed, because he wanted to enjoy the
reputation which wealth gave. 'Now, however, . . . it has become much more dangerous to be thought to be wealthy than
to be detected in crime' (*Antidosis*, §§ 159–60). What Isocrates
wanted was ἀσφάλεια. But that security was threatened by the
fear of the homeless exiles and the mercenary soldiers who in
the middle years of the fourth century infested Greece, or
'were wandering with their women and children in strange
lands, many compelled through lack of the necessities of life
to enlist in foreign armies', fighting for their foes against their
friends (*Panegyr.*, *168*) or committing outrages upon whomsoever they encounter (*Philippus*, §§ 120–1), 'shaming the city
by begging from passers-by to-day, while those who are desti-
tute of means outnumber those who possess them' (*Areopag.*,
§ 83; cf. *Peace*, § 24, *Ep.* 9, §§ 9–10:—the authenticity of this
letter has been questioned.) Before one knew where one was,
these homeless and penniless outcasts might concert in a

demand for a γῆς ἀναδασμός; how could one avert this peril? A timely war was surely the best remedy; only, of course, it must not be fought on Attic soil. But though, as Demosthenes found, the Athenians were not prepared to purchase Persian aid at the price of an alliance with the Great King, the city had no desire for war: τῶν περὶ τὸν πόλεμον οὕτω κατημελή- καμεν ὥστ' οὐδ' εἰς ἐξετάσεις ἰέναι τολμῶμεν ἢν μὴ λαμβάνωμεν ἀργύριον (*Areop.*, § 82).[8] 'Those who are prosperous should set their hearts on peace, for in a state of peace they can preserve their present condition for the greatest length of time; those, however, who are unfortunate should give their minds to war' (*Archidamus*, § 50). The words which Isocrates had put into the mouth of Archidamus he might adapt to his own case. The war must, however, be made palatable to the Greek States: here the *Panegyricus* is of the greatest interest. There will be no conscription for the army which is to invade Persia. Consider § 185: καὶ μὴν οὐδὲ τὰς πόλεις λυπήσομεν στρατιώτας ἐξ αὐτῶν καταλέγοντες ὃ νῦν ἐν τῷ πολέμῳ τῷ πρὸς ἀλλήλους ὀχληρότατόν ἐστιν αὐταῖς. πολὺ γὰρ οἶμαι σπανιωτέρους ἔσεσθαι τοὺς μένειν ἐθελήσοντας τῶν συνακολουθεῖν ἐπιθυμησόντων. Pious hopes, of course, are easily manufactured, but note specially § 182: μόνος γὰρ οὗτος ὁ πόλεμος εἰρήνης κρείττων ἐστί, θεωρίᾳ μὲν μᾶλλον ἢ στρατείᾳ προσεοικώς, ἀμφοτέροις δὲ συμφέρων καὶ τοῖς ἡσυχίαν ἄγειν καὶ τοῖς πολεμεῖν ἐπιθυμοῦσιν. εἴη γὰρ ἂν τοῖς μὲν ἀδεῶς τὰ σφέτερ' αὐτῶν καρποῦσθαι, τοῖς δὲ ἐκ τῶν ἀλλοτρίων μεγάλους πλούτους κατακτήσασθαι. Precisely, ἀσφάλεια for the well-to-do who remain at home. δεῖ δὲ ... ἐκείνοις τοῖς ἔργοις ἐπιχειρεῖν ἐξ ὧν τὰς πόλεις ἀσφαλέστερον οἰκήσομεν (§ 173). But this is hardly the way to preach a war of *revanche*—or even a religious crusade. 'Business as usual' with a vengeance!

And this war will have the great advantage that it can be waged cheaply. In the earlier years of the fourth century Clearchus had to raise a military force from those living in the cities (οἱ πολιτευόμενοι), and that was very costly: ἀναγκαζό- μενοι ξενολογεῖν ἐκ τῶν πόλεων πλέον ἀνήλισκον εἰς τὰς δεδομένας τοῖς συλλέγουσι δωρεὰς ἢ τὴν εἰς τοὺς στρατιώτας μισθοφοράν for

---

[8] Demosth. iv. 21, 500 for a short period of service, the rest mercenaries: 26 (day soldiers); viii. 21, ἡμεῖς οὔτε χρήματ' εἰσφέρειν οὔτ' αὐτοὶ στρατεύεσθαι; xxiv. 99, πῶς οὐ δεινὸν εἰ ... ἄμισθος ὁ δῆμος.

ἐν ἐκείνοις χρόνοις οὐκ ἦν ξενικὸν οὐδέν (*Philippus*, § 96); but now
ῥᾷον εἶναι συστῆσαι στρατόπεδον μεῖζον καὶ κρεῖττον ἐκ τῶν πλανω-
μένων (ibid.), and, of course, by so doing relieve property-owners
from their fears. τῆς ἀπορίας τῆς περὶ τὸν βίον ἡμῶν ἀφαιρεθείσης
(*Panegyricus*, § 174).

Better still, of course, if you can get your own war fought
for you—it matters not by whom, provided he has an army,
whether it be Dionysius of Syracuse, Jason of Pherae, or Philip
of Macedon. Read again the *Philippus* carefully, and note how
it is the Macedonian army which is to wage the war; no
account appears to be taken of the Greek forces whose war of
revenge Macedonia is expected to conduct, Philip is promised
the goodwill of the Greeks—τοὺς Ἕλληνας εὔνους ἕξεις, and
goodwill is not a costly commodity (*Philip.*, § 95). Now we are
in a position to consider the fancy picture which Isocrates has
drawn of the Ionian colonization of Asia Minor. It may be
suggested that this is simply a projection into the distant past
of the war against Persia as Isocrates conceived it. The fullest
statement[9] of this Ionian colonization is to be found in the
Panegyricus, §§ 34–7; part of that statement may be quoted in
the translation of Norlin: 'Our city, seeing the barbarians in
possession of most of the country while the Hellenes were confined within a narrow space and because of the scarcity of the
land were conspiring and making raids against each other and
were perishing, some through want of daily necessities, others
through war,—our city, I say, was not content to let things be
as they were, but sent out leaders to the several states who,
enlisting the neediest of the people and placing themselves at
their head, overcame the barbarians in war, founded many
cities on either continent, settled colonies in all the islands
and saved both those who followed them and those who
remained behind; for to the latter they left the home country—
sufficient for their needs (ἱκανὴν τὴν οἴκοι χώραν κατέλιπον)—
and for the former they provided more land than they had
owned.' With this may be compared *Panath.*, 165–6: 'To the
States which were more severely rent by factions they despatched the most highly reputed of their citizens who advised

---

[9] See further *Panath.* 43 for settlement of τοὺς μάλιστα βίου τῶν Ἑλλήνων
δεομένους and cf. ibid. 190.

them regarding their present difficulties, and associating themselves with the people who were unable to gain a livelihood in
their own States or who had fallen below the requirements of
the laws—a class which is generally destructive to ordered
States—they urged these to take the field with them and to
seek to improve the conditions of their present life. And when
there proved to be many who were inclined and persuaded to
take this course, they organized them into an army, conquered
the peoples who occupied the islands of the barbarians and
who dwelt along the coast of either continent, expelled them
all and settled in their stead those of the Hellenes who stood
in greatest need of the necessities of life.' The reader of this
account will observe that the Athenians do not send a large
army to Asia, but ἡγέμονας εἰς τὰς πόλεις; or as in the *Panathenaicus*, τῶν πολιτῶν τοὺς μεγίστην παρ' αὐτοῖς δόξαν ἔχοντας
(§ 165), who organized local opposition against the barbarians.
That means, of course, that the war against Persia will in
large measure be fought with the aid of revolting satraps and
of the Greeks of Asia. Hence the catalogue of potential allies
in *Panegyricus*, 160–2, and *Philippus*, 101–4—Egypt, Cyprus,
Phoenicia, Syria, Tyre, Cilicia, Caria, while the Greeks of the
Asiatic coast-line we need not persuade to go to war: all we
have to do is not to hold them back—so the *Panegyricus*: in
the *Philippus* Isocrates dwells on the probable disloyalty of Id-
rieus, the Carian dynast (*Philippus*, § 103). And for colonization Isocrates in 356 had thought of cutting off enough land
in Thrace to furnish adequate means of subsistence to those of
the Hellenes who were in need and because of their poverty
were wandering from place to place (*Peace*, § 24). When
Philip's action had defeated this scheme Isocrates turned to
Asia: Philip should either conquer the whole of the Persian
Empire, or at least should sever from it Asia from Cilicia to
Sinope. He should then found cities in this region and settle in
them those 'who now for lack of the daily necessities of life
are wandering from place to place and committing outrages
upon whomsoever they encounter'. . . . These bands must be
employed in a war against the barbarians; the homeless wan-
derers would be collected into cities, and these cities would act
as a screen protecting the rest of the Greeks. 'For by doing this

you will not only make the homeless prosperous, ἀλλὰ καὶ πάντας ἡμᾶς <u>εἰς ἀσφάλειαν καταστήσεις</u>', *Philippus*, §§ 120–3.

The return to 'the constitution of our ancestors', which is the essential element in Isocrates' programme of domestic reform, has as its end and purpose the restoration of ἀσφάλεια for the property-holding class: for under 'the administration of our forefathers' the Athenians μετὰ τοσαύτης ἀσφαλείας διῆγον ὥστε καλλίους εἶναι καὶ πολυτελεστέρας τὰς οἰκήσεις καὶ τὰς κατασκευὰς τὰς ἐπὶ τῶν ἀγρῶν ἢ τὰς ἐντὸς τείχους, καὶ πολλοὺς τῶν πολιτῶν μηδ' εἰς τὰς ἑορτὰς εἰς ἄστυ καταβαίνειν ἀλλ' αἱρεῖσθαι μένειν ἐπὶ τοῖς ἰδίοις ἀγαθοῖς μᾶλλον ἢ τῶν κοινῶν ἀπολαύειν, *Areop.*, 52. There is a highly significant sentence in the *Peace*, § 133: ἐν ᾗ δ' ἂν ἕκαστοι τιμῶνται ταύτην βούλονται καθεστάναι τὴν πολιτείαν: precisely 'All men desire in each case to establish that form of government in which they are held in honour'. The reform of the Athenian government proposed by Isocrates would have established a purely timocratic State where wealth, and wealth alone, it seems, would determine the citizen's position in the social and administrative life of Athens. In the address *To Nicocles* he had said that it was a monstrous thing (δεινόν) that the worse should rule the better (*To Nicocles*, § 14). In the *Nicocles* (§ 14) he had said that it was perfectly monstrous (δεινότατον) that the good and the bad should be thought worthy of the same privileges: those who were unlike should not be accorded the like treatment: everyone should be honoured in accordance with his deserts. In the *Areopagiticus* itself (§ 21) he wrote that there were two forms of equality— one was to give the same rights to all whether good or bad, and the other was to give each his due. But in his own scheme of reform privilege is determined by a property qualification— it is a poor measure whereby to distinguish between the good and the bad citizen. In the *Panegyricus*, § 105, he had written of the Athenians that they thought it δεινόν for τοὺς πολλοὺς ὑπὸ τοῖς ὀλίγοις εἶναι καὶ τοὺς ταῖς οὐσίαις ἐνδεεστέρους τὰ δ' ἄλλα μηδὲν χείρους ὄντας ἀπελαύνεσθαι τῶν ἀρχῶν. That is precisely what he recommended to the Athenians in the *Areopagiticus*. The pursuits of the citizens the *Areopagiticus* determined πρὸς τὴν οὐσίαν: οἱ ὑποδεέστερον πράττοντες were 'directed' to agriculture or trade, while οἱ βίον ἱκανὸν κεκτημένοι were compelled to con-

cern themselves περὶ τὴν ἱππικὴν καὶ τὰ γυμνάσια καὶ τὰ κυνη-
γέσια—and thrown in at the end as a makeweight—καὶ τὴν
φιλοσοφίαν (*Areop.* §§ 44–5). It is a very singular order for the
employments of the well-to-do when one remembers the protests of Isocrates against giving priority to the pursuits of the
body rather than to the mind (*Antidosis*, §§ 250, 301; *Panegyricus*, §§ 1–2; *Ep.* 8, § 5). The old constitution gave to the
people, Isocrates said, τῶν τοιούτων πραγματειῶν ἀτέλειαν
(*Panath.* 147)—freedom from concerning themselves with
affairs of State: in his scheme of reform government is the
affair 'einer auserlesener Minderheit': it means 'the formation
of a new political class'. Isocrates 'nimmt es als eine natur-
gegebene Tatsache hin, dass Bildung ein Monopol des Besitzes
ist und Armut davon ausschliesst'. The new Areopagus would
become 'eine Art staatssozialistischen Arbeitsamts': there
would be no *carrière ouverte aux talents*: the test would be the
property of the parents and not the capacity of the children.
'Directed' labour for the poorer classes and an oligarchy of
wealth—such was the price which Isocrates was prepared to
pay for ἀσφάλεια.[10] When studying the policies propounded by
Isocrates one must never leave out of account the personality
of the φιλόσοφος. After expounding in the *Peace* (§ 145) his plan
for the establishment of a Pan-Hellenic ὁμόνοια, the closing
words give Isocrates' vision of the result of his policy: 'the
fortunes of philosophers would be greatly improved.' It is a
surprising climax: *parturiunt montes. . . .*

The foreign policy of Isocrates it is unnecessary to discuss:
in recent work it has been riddled through and through. For a
time German scholars interpreted it by means of Prussian
analogies of unity realized through 'blood and iron':[11] the outstanding example of this school is Drerup's *Aus einer alten
Advokatenrepublik*. But the analogies will not fit. If the Greek
States had wished for ὁμόνοια they could have had it without
the help of Philip: and if Philip's only instrument was to be
persuasion, he was as powerless as any other: to effect what
Isocrates demanded of him he would be bound to resort to

[10] The best treatment of the *Areopagiticus* known to me is that of Pöhlmann,
op. cit., pp. 109 sqq., from which I have quoted.
[11] Cf. Mathieu, *Les Idées politiques d'Isocrate*, p. 54.

force. This internal contradiction vitiates the policy of Isocrates. And the basis on which to build any stable ὁμόνοια is
singularly unpromising: all the Greek cities, Isocrates tells
Philip, 'have now been brought down to the same level (ὡ-
μαλισμένας) by their misfortunes, and so I think that they
would much rather choose the advantages to be derived from
ὁμόνοια than the profits (πλεονεξίας) from the policy which they
formerly pursued' (*Philippus*, § 40); and seeing that 'our States
care nothing about their enmities or their oaths or about anything else save what they conceive to be expedient for themselves, and since it is expediency alone that they pursue and it
is on this that they expend all their care', Philip will be able
to effect a reconciliation 'since their interest will persuade them
to this course and their present disasters force them to adopt
it' (§ 45)—and if the wind change and expediency point to war,
oaths, it seems, will count for nothing! Philip, if he read the
letter, must surely have felt that this appeal for his intervention was less than attractive. And worse than this: the naïve
belief of Isocrates that Philip had only to act as εὐεργέτης
towards Greece and would be content to play that part is
quite astonishing and curiously 'academic' in the worst sense
of that word. He might talk of Philip playing his part as king
over the Macedonians, but he never realized the duties which
for Philip that rôle carried with it. And in the end, if Rostagni
is right in his interpretation of the *Panathenaicus*, as I think he
must be, Isocrates realized his failure to win Philip to his plan,
and while still opposing any alliance with Persia sought to conciliate Thebes and thus drew nearer to the policy of Demosthenes.

But even when one has tried to read his work with some
care, Isocrates remains a puzzle—just a bundle of contradictions. If one only could be sure when he was writing a purely
sophistic epideictic speech or when he was intended to be
taken seriously! What, for instance, is one to think of the
Archidamus? Some modern students have taken the speech as
possessing actual political significance, but is this possible?

Consider § 85: 'while we [the Spartans] now have unjustly suffered disasters we shall prove to everyone that in the past δικαίως τῶν ἄλλων πλέον ἔχειν ἠξιοῦμεν'; or § 89, 'we must either πρωτεύειν ἐν τοῖς ῞Ελλησιν or perish'; or § 94, 'the Spartans ἄρξαι τῶν ῾Ελλήνων ἀξιωθέντες'. Could Isocrates have thus directly denied the whole argument of the *Panegyricus*? Could the apostle of ὁμόνοια in all seriousness have composed this bellicose exhortation to war? For myself the *Archidamus* remains a pure ἐπιδεικτικὸς λόγος. It would make matters much simpler if one could believe the same of the *Nicocles* speech, but there when the speech is written on behalf of his own student it is much more difficult to hold such a view. Has it been noted that there is one tell-tale word in the *Areopagiticus* (§ 60)—'ἐν τοῖς πλείστοις τῶν λόγων τῶν εἰρημένων ὑπ᾽ ἐμοῦ—I commend democratic governments'—this leaves room for the *Nicocles*. We should know better where we stand if we had some detailed concrete information on the paideia of the school of Isocrates. The *Antidosis* is such an exasperating work just because when it seems on the point of giving us some such information it sheers off the subject and leaves us still guessing. How did the students of Isocrates spend their time after their period of mental discipline spent on 'astronomy, geometry and studies of that sort' (*Antidosis*, §§ 261–9). It surely cannot have taken them three or four years to learn to regard a hiatus as the worst of sins. Granted that 'philosophy' meant for Isocrates the training which should enable men to meet the practical problems of life as they arose (*Antidosis*, § 184), in what did that training consist, and on what was it based? The charge which Isocrates brought against the Greek envoys who had negotiated the Treaty of Antalcidas was that they had adopted no single principle in settling the terms of the agreement: 'they ought to have adopted one view and applied it impartially to all the Greek States.' It is a very interesting criticism (*Panegyricus*, § 177). Surely to meet emergencies successfully as they arise one must have some principle on which one's decision is based. Circumstances may change the application of such a principle, but the principle itself remains stable. One misses any discussion of the principles on which a paideia which prided itself on its ethic (*Antidosis*, §§ 87, 284) was based:

οἱ δὲ φιλοσοφίᾳ καὶ λογισμῷ τὴν δύναμιν ταύτην (the capacity for speaking) λαβόντες, οὐδὲν ἀσκέπτως λέγοντες, ἧττον περὶ τὰς πράξεις πλημμελοῦσιν (*Antidosis*, § 292), but we simply do not know how this invaluable gift of judgement was acquired or fostered. Isocrates tells us that for himself he set up a more difficult standard than for others (*Antidosis*, § 51), and further it was clear that the principles in which we educate (παιδεύο-μεν) our students are those which we practise in our own lives (*Antidosis*, § 239). Now there is one principle on which Iso-crates insists: χρὴ δὲ τοὺς νοῦν ἔχοντας οὐκ ἀνωμάλως ποιεῖσθαι τὰς κρίσεις περὶ τῶν ὁμοίων πραγμάτων (*Antidosis*, § 203)—in Norlin's translation: 'Men of intelligence ought not to form contrary judgements about similar things'; οὐκοῦν χρὴ . . .μὴ περὶ τῶν ὁμοίων τἀναντία γινώσκειν (ibid. § 253); καίτοι τῶν φρονίμως διακειμένων οὐκ ἐλάχιστον τοῦτο σημεῖόν ἐστιν ἢν τὰς αὐτὰς πράξεις ἐπὶ πάντων τῶν ὁμοίων φαίνωνται γνωρίζοντες (*Peace*, § 114). Further, Mathieu writes:[12] 'Toutes ses œuvres [i.e. of Isocrates] politiques sont remplies de préoccupations morales et il veut, grâce à elles, transporter dans la vie des États les règles qui régissent la vie des individus (*Peace*, §§ 119–20). . . . Isocrate veut étendre la morale de l'individu à l'État' (*Philippus*, § 133). It is when we seek to trace the application of these principles in the works of Isocrates that difficulties arise. What is this ethic which is to be realized by the Greek State? We shall find in the 'speeches' of Isocrates the Golden Rule: καίτοι χρὴ τοὺς νοῦν ἔχοντας τοιούτους εἶναι κριτὰς τοῖς ἄλλοις, οἵων περ ἂν αὐτοὶ τυγχάνειν ἀξιώσαιεν (*Antidosis*, § 23); or of the Athenians: τὴν αὐτὴν ἀξιοῦντες γνώμην ἔχειν πρὸς τοὺς ἥττους ἥνπερ τοὺς κρείττους πρὸς σφᾶς αὐτούς (*Panegyricus*, § 81; cf. *Panathenaicus*, § 48). We shall find in the *Archidamus* (§§ 35–6, 59) such a paean in praise of justice in the relations of States as to cause the most convinced idealist to raise his eyebrows. In the *Peace*, § 30, Isocrates writes of Athens: 'as the result of keeping our city in the path of justice and of giving aid to the oppressed and of not coveting the possessions of others we were given the hegemony by the willing consent of the Hel-lenes' (Norlin's translation).[13] All this is true, but what of *Pan-*

---

[12] *Isocrate, Philippe et Lettres à Philippe*, etc. (Boccard, Paris,) p. 13.
[13] And cf. *Peace*, §§ 31–2.

athenaicus, § 117? The Athenians having the choice between
two policies considered it better 'to choose to do injury to
others rather than to suffer injury themselves, and to rule
without justice over others rather than, by seeking to escape
that reproach, to be subject unjustly to the Lacedaemonians—
a course which all sensible men would prefer and desire for
themselves, albeit a certain few who pretend (προσποιουμένων)
to be wise, were the question put to them, would not accept
this view'. What of the completely cynical defence of the conduct of Athens towards the members of the League given in
the *Panegyricus* and repeated and amplified in the *Panathenaicus* (cf. *infra*, p. 166)? In the curious closing section of
the *Panathenaicus* one defender of Sparta is answered by
Isocrates, but the advocate of an unrestrained *Machtpolitik* is
not answered, and the reader is left with the impression that
Isocrates is prepared to accept that standpoint. What is indeed the ethic which the Paideia of Isocrates was intended to
inculcate in the students of his school? 'The new rhetoric',
writes Professor Jaeger, 'had to find an ideal which could be
ethically interpreted and which at the same time could be
translated into practical political action. This ideal was a new
moral code for Greece' (p. 53). 'The paideia of rhetoric . . . as
conceived by Isocrates sets its goal in the realm of the ideal'
(p. 83). 'All his published writings . . . were ancillary to the
ethical programme of his school' (p. 54). Really one begins to
wonder whether Professor Jaeger has *read* the 'speeches' of
Isocrates; things are not quite so simple as all that!

And for the application of the principle that one should not
call the same or like things by different names—well, here one
simply is at a loss. In the work of Isocrates contradiction is
piled on contradiction and one is left in a maze. It must have
been a formidable task for Isocrates when in the *Antidosis* he
set himself to prove his own consistency. An extract from the
programme which he issued on founding his school—the Κατὰ
τῶν Σοφιστῶν—could be safely read: the speech *To Nicocles*
did not do him justice, but he could apologize for this loose
collection of aphorisms, and as an admonition to a tyrant it
would not be dangerous. The *Nicocles*, however, as we have
seen, was perilous, and though it could provide some innocu-

ous remarks on rhetoric no mention must be made of their source. The *Panegyricus* had been the statement of the claim of Athens to hold the ἀρχὴ τῆς θαλάττης as an element of her ἡγεμονία of the Greek States: the *Peace* had been a sustained attack upon the ἀρχὴ τῆς θαλάττης while maintaining in a peaceful world the ἡγεμονία of Athens. It is to be noticed that Isocrates in his account of the *Panegyricus* (*Antidosis*, §§ 57–8) from which he directs extracts to be read removes this contradiction by speaking only of his defence of the ἡγεμονία of Athens—the ἀρχή is not mentioned[14]—so that in his account of the *Peace* (*Antidosis*, §§ 63–5) he can attack the δυναστεία of Athens and her ἀρχή without appearing to run counter to the theme of the *Panegyricus*. But the real problem for Isocrates must have been to decide about the *Areopagiticus*. Was he indeed compelled to sacrifice any mention of the speech on which he had spent such anxious labour? It had been obvious to him when he wrote it that he must not employ the term πάτριος πολιτεία: that slogan of the fifth century would awake the ghost of Theramenes and memories of oligarchic reaction. It had not been easy, but he had avoided the phrase successfully: in *Areopagiticus*, § 15, he had written [ἡ δημοκρατία] ἡ ὑπὸ τῶν προγόνων καταλειφθεῖσα: in § 61 he had said οἶδα γὰρ τούς τε προγόνους τοὺς ἡμετέρους ἐν ταύτῃ τῇ καταστάσει κ.τ.λ.; in §§ 58–9 he had been bolder and had almost betrayed himself: ἀλλὰ διείλεγμαι περὶ διοικήσεως οὐκ ἀποκεκρυμμένης, ἀλλὰ πᾶσι φανερᾶς, ἣν πάντες ἴστε καὶ πατρίαν ἡμῖν οὖσαν κ.τ.λ. But it had been an astute idea to attack the Thirty Tyrants—they would act as a screen to hide the comrade whom they had murdered, to whom Isocrates owed not a little. Isocrates had then thought of the advice which he had given to Timotheus —the necessity in a democracy ἐπιχαρίτως λέγειν (*Antidosis*, § 132), or as Demosthenes phrased it πρὸς χάριν δημηγορεῖν (iii, 3; cf. viii, 70 and ix, 4, τρυφᾶν καὶ κολακεύεσθαι πάντα πρὸς ἡδονήν), Ἐγὼ δ' οἶδα μέν, Isocrates would say in the *Peace* (§ 14), ὅτι πρόσαντές ἐστιν ἐναντιοῦσθαι ταῖς ὑμετέραις διανοίαις κ.τ.λ.; so into the *Areopagiticus* he had then inserted an entirely dishonest laudation of the contemporary democracy

---

[14] It does, however, occur in § 72 of the *Panegyricus*, but only as the voluntary gift of all the Greek States.

—its 'innere Unwahrheit' is noted by Münscher (*P.W.* ix. col. 2208)—and then he had realized that he had overshot the mark and had pulled himself up: τάχ' οὖν ἄν τις θαυμάσειε, τί βουλόμενος ἀντὶ τῆς πολιτείας τῆς οὕτω πολλὰ καὶ καλὰ διαπεπραγμένης ἑτέραν ὑμᾶς πείθω μεταλαβεῖν (*Areopagiticus*, § 71).—And all had been in vain: the *Areopagiticus* had fallen on deaf ears and was suspect: there was no place for it in the *Antidosis*. Isocrates threw his cherished Jonah overboard.

The mystery of the contradictions in the works of Isocrates is increased by the fact that his 'speeches' were not delivered orally and then forgotten: they were from the first published in writing and were 'on every one's tongue' in Athens (τοὺς πάλαι παρ' ὑμῖν διατεθρυλημένους [λόγους], *Antidosis*, § 55). Take, for instance, the question of the treatment of her allies by Athens: both Isocrates and his contemporaries must have known that the representation of Athenian action given in the *Panegyricus* was fundamentally false: thus in the *Antidosis* we have a frank statement of the ill-treatment of the allies before Aegospotami (§§ 318–19), and for the ill-treatment in the fourth century see § 107, and consider the praises of Timotheus and its implications (ibid., §§ 121 sqq.). Note the admission in the *Peace*, § 42, 'we seek to enslave the cities', or ibid. § 46, where, speaking of the mercenary troops employed by Athens, Isocrates writes: καὶ τοὺς συμμάχους τοὺς ἡμετέρους αὐτῶν ἰδίους λυμαινόμεθα καὶ δασμολογοῦμεν ἵνα τοῖς ἁπάντων ἀνθρώπων κοινοῖς ἐχθροῖς τὸν μισθὸν ἐκπορίζωμεν. See, further, the *Peace*, § 29: we have reaped from the cities hatreds and wars and great expense. The point is that Isocrates knows full well how Athens should treat her allies: in the programme of ὁμόνοια set forth in the *Peace* he writes: 'And what is most important of all, we shall have all mankind as our allies—allies who will not have been forced, but rather persuaded to join with us, who will not welcome our friendship because of our power when we are secure only to abandon us when we are in peril, but who will be disposed towards us as those should be who are in very truth allies and friends' (§ 21, Norlin's translation); or again, says Isocrates, the second way in which we can improve our condition is that 'we should be willing to treat our allies just as we would our friends, not to grant them autonomy in words

while giving them up to our generals to do what they please
with them, not to stand over them in dominance, but in true
alliance' (§ 134); or in *Philippus*, §§ 146–8: 'no one would praise
our city either because she was once mistress of the sea or because she extorted such huge sums of money from her allies
and carried them up into the Acropolis, nor yet, surely, because she obtained power over many cities—power to devastate
them or aggrandize them or manage them according to her
pleasure (for all these things it was possible for her to do); no,
all these things have been the source of many complaints
against her', while because of the battles of Marathon and
Salamis she enjoys the praise of all mankind.—And then, after
all this, to return in the *Panathenaicus* to the cynicism of the
Panegyricus, to deny roundly that there were any excesses
committed by the Athenians on the allies before Aegospotami,
to affirm that the Athenians learnt late in the day the lesson
from the savagery (ὠμότης) of the Spartans, and that it is upon
the Spartans that falls the responsibility for any regrettable
incidents. It would seem that one is driven to the conclusion
that in an encomium you neither expected truth from the
writer nor an honest expression of his own views. Dionysius of
Halicarnassus[15] tells us that in case of an ἔπαινος the aim of the
writer should be only τὰς ἀρετὰς καὶ οὐ τὰ ἀτυχήματα προφέρειν
while Hermogenes[16] writes τὸ δὲ ἐγκώμιον ψιλὴν ἀρετῆς ἔχει
μαρτυρίαν. Similarly, it would appear that in an encomium the
writer is at liberty to pervert or even to 'create' history. Thus
in the *Areopagiticus* one can recognize Athenian history: Solon
is the founder of Athenian democracy and Cleisthenes its
restorer after its overthrow by Pisistratus. But in the *Panathenaicus* Isocrates invents a millennium of democratic history before Solon, Cleisthenes disappears, and the beginning of
the perversion of the primitive ideal democracy comes with
Solon—and all this startling construction is devised merely to
out-trump the Spartans: it enables Isocrates to contend that
Lycurgus took for his model the early Athenian constitution.
In the same way in the *Panathenaicus* Isocrates can freely
alter the history of the relations between Athens and Thebes

---

[15] *Ep. ad Pomp.* 751, 8 ed., Reiske. I owe the reference to Hermann Rohde.
[16] Spengel, *Rhetor. Graeci*, ii. p. 11.

in order to conciliate Theban sentiment—and can call attention to the alteration; or in the *Panegyricus* can state that Athens never occupied Euboea, which such a student of Thucydides as Isocrates must have known to be false. If this suggestion of the character of these encomia on Athens is correct, it will enable us to free Isocrates from the unpleasant thought that he was convinced in his own cynicism.

But before we commit ourselves to the judgement that Isocrates was a 'great man' or a 'powerful thinker', there is need, it may be suggested, of some further study of Isocrates the sophist.

IX

Eusebius and the Christian Empire

[From the *Annuaire de l'institut de philologie et d'histoire orientales*, ii (1933–34). *Mélanges Bidez*, Brussels, 1933, pp. 13–18.]

To the oration composed by Eusebius for the celebration of the Tricennalia of Constantine the Great scholars have hardly paid the attention which it deserves. Here for the first time is clearly stated the political philosophy of the Christian Empire, that philosophy of the State which was consistently maintained throughout the millennium of Byzantine absolutism. The basis of that political philosophy is to be found in the conception of the imperial government as a terrestrial copy of the rule of God in Heaven: there is one God and one divine law, therefore there must be on earth but one ruler and a single law. That ruler, the Roman emperor, is the Vicegerent of the Christian God. It is remarkable that the State, which had only a few years before been persecuting the Christians, on whose rulers Lactantius had poured the flood of his invective, is now transformed into a μίμησις of Heaven and that this new philosophy of the Christian Empire should have been set forth, so far as we know, for the first time by one who was primarily a scholar and not an original thinker. The question naturally arises: is this theory the outcome of the thought of Eusebius himself or is it derived from other sources? Scholars do not as yet seem to have pointed to the parallelism between the Hellenistic philosophy of kingship and the Christian theory of Eusebius. It is, however, of permanent interest to endeavour to trace the modes through which the momentous fourth-century transition was mediated, and here, it would appear, is an instance of such mediation.

In a paper published in 1928[1] Erwin R. Goodenough has

---

[1] *Yale Classical Studies*, vol. i (New Haven, 1928), pp. 55–102. See now Louis Delatte, *Les Traités de la Royauté d'Ecphante, Diotogène et Sthénidas* (Liége, 1942) = Bibliothèque de la Faculté de Philosophie et Lettres de l'Université de Liége, Fasc. 97.]

studied *The Political Philosophy of Hellenistic Kingship*, and it was this paper which suggested to me the possible source of the theory of Eusebius. In a fragment preserved by Stobaeus[2] from the περὶ βασιλείας of Diotogenes we read ἔχει δὲ καὶ ὡς θεὸς ποτὶ κόσμον βασιλεὺς ποτὶ πόλιν · καὶ ὡς πόλις ποτὶ κόσμον βασιλεὺς ποτὶ θεόν. ἁ μὲν γὰρ πόλις ἐκ πολλῶν καὶ διαφερόντων συναρμοσθεῖσα κόσμω σύνταξιν καὶ ἁρμονίαν μεμίμαται, ὁ δὲ βασιλεὺς ἀρχὰν ἔχων ἀνυπεύθυνον, καὶ αὐτὸς ὢν νόμος ἔμψυχος, θεὸς ἐν ἀνθρώποις παρεσχαμάτισται. In another fragment Stobaeus quotes from a treatise περὶ βασιλείας of Sthenidas,[3] the Pythagoraean: χρὴ τὸν βασιλέα σοφὸν ἦμεν · οὕτω γὰρ ἐσσεῖται ἀντίμιμος καὶ ζαλωτὰς τῶ πράτω θεῶ. οὗτος γὰρ καὶ φύσει ἐντὶ καὶ πρᾶτος βασιλεύς τε καὶ δυνάστας, ὁ δὲ γενέσει καὶ μιμάσει ... μιματὰς ἄρα καὶ ὑπηρέτας ἐσσεῖται νόμιμος τῶ θεῶ ὁ σοφός τε καὶ βασιλεύς. With this theory of μίμησις compare the view of Eusebius: τοῦ θεοῦ λόγος παρ' οὗ καὶ δι' οὗ τῆς ἀνωτάτω βασιλείας τὴν εἰκόνα φέρων ὁ τῷ θεῷ φίλος βασιλεὺς κατὰ μίμησιν τοῦ κρείττονος τῶν ἐπὶ γῆς ἁπάντων τοὺς οἴακας διακυβερνῶν ἰθύνει.[4] Again speaking of the divine Logos Eusebius writes τῷ τῆς κατὰ γῆν βασιλείας μιμήματι τὴν οὐράνιον ἐκτυπούμενος, ἐφ' ἣν καὶ σπεύδειν τὸ πᾶν τῶν ἀνθρώπων παρορμᾷ γένος.[5] Again ἀτὰρ δὴ καὶ βασιλεὺς ἀληθεῖ λόγῳ χρηματίσειεν [ἂν] οὗτος ὁ τῆς ἐπέκεινα βασιλείας τὸ μίμημα βασιλικαῖς ἀρεταῖς τῇ ψυχῇ μεμορφωμένος.[6] Further Constantine is described as ὁ πρὸς τὴν ἀρχέτυπον τοῦ μεγάλου βασιλέως ἀπεικονισμένος ἰδέαν καὶ ταῖς ἐξ αὐτῆς τῶν ἀρετῶν αὐγαῖς ὥσπερ ἐν κατόπτρῳ τῇ διανοίᾳ μορφωθείς.[7]

That God is the source of the imperial power—ὁ τῆς βασιλείας αἴτιος,[8] καὶ δὴ βασιλείας αὐτῆς ἀρχῆς τε πάσης καὶ ἐξουσίας καθηγεμών[9]—is of course traditional in Christian thought, while it was also the accepted belief—δόγμα—of the pagan.[10]

More interesting is the position which the Logos occupies in relation to the monarch. God, writes Plutarch,[11] has set in the

---

[2] Stobaeus, edd. Wachsmuth and Hense, vol. iv (1909), p. 265 = book iv, ch. vii, § 61.
[3] Ibid., p. 270 = iv, vii, 63.
[4] Eusebius, Τριακονταετηρικός, ed. Heikel, pp. 198, 34–199, 3.
[5] Ibid., p. 203, 17–19.   [6] Ibid., p. 203, 25–7.
[7] Ibid., p. 204, 17–19, cf. p. 202, 10–12.   [8] Ibid., p. 197, 8.
[9] Ibid., p. 202, 17–18; cf. p. 199, 6–7.
[10] Cf. F. J. Dölger, in *Antike und Christentum*, 3 (1932), at p. 124, on Celsus in Origen., *Contra Celsum*, 8, 68.
[11] Plutarch, πρὸς ἡγεμόνα ἀπαίδευτον, ch. 3.

M   B.B.S.

Heaven as a fair image of Himself the sun and the moon, and
in cities a similar μίμημα and radiance, the King, when he has
for his guiding principle the Logos of God. That image the
wise copy, modelling themselves upon it. According to Ecphantus, quoted by Stobaeus,[12] this Logos would seem to be
incarnate in the true King, and is thus the source of his power
to benefit and save men. The Logos sows the seeds of obedience, and because of human weakness dwells with men and
thus restores what has been lost through sin. With such passages as these should be compared what Eusebius says of the
Christian Logos, the Divine Word. For Eusebius the Logos is
no longer incarnate in the King, but Constantine is the friend
of the Logos and His interpreter, and thus recalls men to the
knowledge of God.[13] The Logos imparts to His disciples the
seeds of true wisdom and salvation and gives understanding
in the knowledge of His Father's Kingdom.[14] Just as the
pagan Logos working through the King saves men from sin,
so the Christian emperor τὸν αὐτοῦ σωτῆρα μιμούμενος καὶ
μόνον σώζειν εἰδὼς καὶ τοὺς ἀθέους ἔσωζεν εὐσεβεῖν διδάσκων
(Eusebius, p. 215, 23–4). For Eusebius as for Plutarch the
Logos is the necessary guide of the true king—the greater the
king the more essential is the guidance of the Logos, Plutarch
contends[15]—παρ' οὗ καὶ δι' οὗ . . . ὁ τῷ θεῷ φίλος βασιλεὺς κατὰ
μίμησιν τοῦ κρείττονος τῶν ἐπὶ γῆς ἁπάντων τοὺς οἴακας διακυβερνῶν ἰθύνει writes Eusebius.[16] It is interesting to observe that
the Spermatikos Logos of pagan philosophy underlies the
thought both of Eusebius and Ecphantus.[17]

God is the archetype of the true king. God, says Ecphantus,
ἐτεχνίτευσεν αὐτόν (i.e. the king) ἀρχετύπῳ χρώμενος ἑαυτῷ;[18]
with this cf. Eusebius ὁ πρὸς τὴν ἀρχέτυπον τοῦ μεγάλου βασιλέως ἀπεικονισμένος ἰδέαν.[19] His virtuous activity is a μίμησις of
the divine virtue. God, writes Plutarch, is angered when men
imitate His thunder and lightning, but with those who desire
(ζηλοῦντας) His virtue and model themselves πρὸς τὸ καλὸν

---

[12] Stobaeus, vol. iv (as above), p. 278 (=iv, vii, 65 s.f.); cf. Goodenough, loc.
cit., p. 90.
[13] Eusebius, p. 199.   [14] Eusebius, p. 199, 19–22.
[15] Cf. Goodenough, loc. cit., p. 97.   [16] Eusebius, p. 199, 1–3.
[17] The word σπέρματα is used by both writers in connexion with the Logos.
[18] Stobaeus, iv, p. 272 =iv, vii, 64.   [19] Eusebius, p. 204, 17–18.

καὶ φιλάνθρωπον He is well pleased and will exalt them.[20] Of Constantine Eusebius writes πράξεσί τε βασιλικαῖς τὴν τοῦ κρείττονος ζηλῶν φιλανθρωπίαν.[21] While Eusebius insists upon the εὐσεβεία of Constantine, Diotogenes had urged that an essential part of the king's duty was θεραπεύεν θεώς: the king must θεραπεύεν τὼς θεὼς εὐσεβῶς καὶ ὁσίως φύσιν θεῶ καὶ ἀρετὰν ἐκλογισάμενος: τὸ θεραπεύεν τὼς θεώς is βασιλέως ἀντάξιον · δεῖ γὰρ τὸ ἄριστον ὑπὸ τῶ ἀρίστω τιμᾶσθαι καὶ τὸ ἁγεμονέον ὑπὸ τῶ ἁγεμονέοντος.[22] The true king must attain self-mastery: ὅθεν δεῖ τὸν βασιλέα μὴ νικῆσθαι ὑφ᾽ ἀδονᾶς, ἀλλ᾽ αὐτὸν νικῆν ταύταν: so Diotogenes;[23] Constantine is χρημάτων μὲν ἀνώτερος, γυναικῶν δ᾽ ἐπιθυμίας κρείττων, νικητὴς δὲ ἡδονῶν καὶ τῶν κατὰ φύσιν.[24] The king will most truly imitate God, said Sthenidas, εἰ μεγαλόφρονά τε καὶ ἄμερον καὶ ὀλιγοδεέα παρασκευάζοι αὐτόν.[25] Philo had written ὁ μὲν θεὸς οὐδενὸς δεῖται, ὁ βασιλεὺς δὲ μόνον θεοῦ.[26] Eusebius insists at length that Constantine set no store by the pomp of royalty: ἐσθῆτά γε μὴν χρυσοῦφῆ ποικίλοις ἄνθεσιν ἐξυφασμένην ἀλουργίδα τε βασιλικὴν σὺν αὐτῷ διαδήματι γελᾷ τοὺς πολλοὺς θεώμενος ἐκπεπληγμένους καὶ τὸ φάντασμα κομιδῇ νηπίων δίκην οἷόν τι μορμολύκειον θειάζοντας · οὐδαμῶς [δ᾽] αὐτὸς τὰ ὅμοια πεπονθὼς τῇ ψυχῇ δι᾽ ἐπιστήμην τοῦ θείου περίβλημα σωφροσύνῃ καὶ δικαιοσύνῃ εὐσεβείᾳ τε καὶ ταῖς λοιπαῖς ἀρεταῖς πεποικιλμένον τὸν ἐπ᾽ ἀληθείας πρέποντα βασιλεῖ κόσμον περιτίθησιν.[27] The Hellenistic king must be the good shepherd of his subjects: δεῖ δὲ τὸν ἀλαθινὸν ἄρχοντα μὴ μόνον ἐπιστάμονά τε καὶ δυνατὸν ἦμεν περὶ τὸ καλῶς ἄρχειν, ἀλλὰ καὶ φιλάνθρωπον· ἄτοπον γὰρ ἦμεν ποιμένα μισοπρόβατον καὶ τοιοῦτον οἷον καὶ δυσμενῶς ἔχεν τοῖς αὐτῶ θρεμμάτεσσι.[28] So Constantine in his φιλανθρωπία offers himself as a great gift to his

[20] Plutarch, loc. cit., ch. 3.
[21] Eusebius, p. 200, 11–12.
[22] Stobaeus, iv, pp. 264–5 = iv, vii, 61.
[23] Stobaeus, iv, p. 265 = iv, vii, 62.
[24] Eusebius, p. 204, 13–14.
[25] Stobaeus, iv, p. 270, 20 = iv, vii, 63. Cf. Ecphantus in Stobaeus, iv, p. 276 (= iv, vii, 65) μίᾳ γὰρ ἀρετᾷ πρὸς τὸ ἄρχειν ἀνθρώπων καὶ πρὸς τὸν αὐτῷ βίον χρήσεται οὐδὲν ὡς δι᾽ ἔνδειαν ποτιλαμβάνων εἰς ὑπηρεσίαν τὰν αὐτὸς αὐτῶ κ.τ.λ.
[26] R. Harris, Fragments of Philo Judaeus, p. 104: cited by Goodenough, op. cit., p. 74.
[27] Eusebius, p. 205, 14–20.
[28] So Archytas the Pythagoraean in a fragment preserved by Stobaeus from a work περὶ νόμου καὶ δικαιοσύνης. Stobaeus, iv, p. 218 = iv, v, 61. Cf. Ecphantus: ὅλαν δὲ τὰν εὔνοιαν χρὴ παρασκευάζεσθαι πρᾶτον μὲν παρὰ τῶ βασιλέως ἐς τὼς βασιλευομένως, δεύτερον δὲ παρὰ τῶνδε ἐς τὸν βασιλέα, ὁποία γεννάτορος ποτὶ υἱέα καὶ ποτὶ ποίμναν νομέως κ.τ.λ. Stobaeus, iv, p. 276 = iv, vii, 64 s.f.

subjects, and ἅτε ποιμὴν ἀγαθός seeks to bring the souls of his flock to piety.[29]

Enough has been said to suggest that in the Hellenistic philosophy of kingship material lay ready to the hand of Eusebius when he sought to fashion a theory of State for the new Christian Empire. Diotogenes, as we have seen, had written that the king had been transformed into a god among men;[30] Eusebius had only to drop the godhead of the king and to put in its place the Vicegerent of God: Constantine rules οἷα μεγάλου βασιλέως ὕπαρχος.[31] The State in its order and harmony, said Diotogenes again, is a mimesis of the divine creation, the kosmos: for the divine creation Eusebius had but to substitute the kingdom of heaven. As the State is to the kosmos, said the Hellenistic philosopher, so is the king to God: the king's duty is to imitate God: ἐπὶ πᾶσι δὲ τούτοις μναμονεύεν δεῖ ὅτι θεόμιμόν ἐντι πρᾶγμα βασιλῆα.[32] For Eusebius, the archetype of the king is in Heaven. And while the Hellenistic king is sustained by the Logos of Philosophy, there was a Christian Logos who could support a Christian monarch. At the same time the attributes, which Greek philosophers had desired for their rulers—φιλανθρωπία, εὐσέβεια and the rest—could figure without difficulty in the panegyric of a Christian monarch and could gain a richer content from the changed setting. Was it indeed thus that the scholarship of Eusebius was employed to fashion the political philosophy of the Byzantine world?[33]

---

[29] Eusebius, p. 200, 15–19.
[30] Stobaeus, iv, p. 265, 11–12 = iv, vii, 61 s.f.
[31] Eusebius, p. 215, 31.
[32] Diotogenes in Stobaeus, iv, p. 270, 10–11 = iv, vi, 62 s.f.
[33] [L. Delatte on philological grounds would date to imperial times the documents regarded by Goodenough as Hellenistic.   Their essential doctrine about Kingship, however, seems not to be later than Philo.—*Edd.*]

X

Two Notes on the Reforms of Diocletian and Constantine

[*Journal of Roman Studies*, xv (1925), pp. 196–204.]

I. THE EFFECT OF THE EDICT OF GALLIENUS

IN 1921 Mr Léon Homo published an elaborate study in the *Revue Historique*[1] on 'Les privilèges administratifs du Sénat romain sous l'Empire et leur disparition graduelle au cours du IIIᵉ siècle'. I have not seen any critical consideration of that study: in the following note I desire to discuss the conclusions of Mr Homo so far as they are concerned with the edict of Gallienus and its application down to the military reorganization of Diocletian. Mr Homo's treatment of the problem is based upon his view of the historical value of the *Historia Augusta*: for a detailed statement of that view the student should consult his earlier paper on 'La grande crise de l'an 238 ap. J.-C. et le problème de l'Histoire Auguste'.[2] His position he has summarized thus: the *Historia* is not a vast falsification dating from the end of the fourth or the beginning of the fifth century: 'Non. Il s'agit bien d'un recueil authentique de biographies rédigé sous la dynastie dioclétiano-constantinienne, et, par conséquent, l'historien du IIIᵉ siècle n'a pas le droit de la rejeter systématiquement. Mais deux réserves capitales sont nécessaires. Tout d'abord, l'Histoire Auguste abonde en anachronismes, dus à l'information médiocre et au manque d'esprit critique de ses auteurs. Deuxièmement, les prétendues pièces d'archives qu'elle contient sont des faux composés en règle générale par les auteurs des biographies eux-mêmes. Ils ne doivent donc pas être utilisés comme des documents authentiques, mais les faits précis qu'ils avancent ne sont pas nécessairement faux, puisque le faussaire peut les avoir empruntés

---

[1] Vol. cxxxvii (July–Aug. 1921), pp. 162–203; cxxxviii (Sept.–Oct. 1921), pp. 1–52.

[2] *Revue Historique*, cxxxi (1919), pp. 209–64; cxxxii (1919), pp. 13–8.

aux sources authentiques qu'il avait à sa disposition. Quant à la nomenclature officielle qui y est donnée, elle ne vaut ni plus ni moins que celle du texte proprement dit, c'est à dire que les erreurs et les anachronismes s'y rencontrent à chaque ligne. En résumé, on n'a le droit ni d'accepter les yeux fermés, ni de rejeter a priori les données de l'Histoire Auguste, mais le premier devoir de l'histoire est de les retenir, au moins provisoirement, pour les soumettre à une critique impartiale et rigoureuse.'[3] It may be well to state at the outset that I am unable to accept this favourable view of the *Historia Augusta* as a source for the reconstruction of the history of the later years of the third century.

Mr Homo's rejection (pp. 165–80)[4] of the theory of Borghesi (*Œuvres*, v, p. 397) that Alexander Severus divided the traditional *imperium* of the Roman provincial governor by separating the military from the civil power, may be unreservedly accepted, though the arguments by which that conclusion is reached I should formulate differently. The *Vita* of Alexander Severus in my judgement is for the most part pure *Tendenz*, and it is only with extreme caution that it can be used as a historical source for the reign.[5] We can pass at once to Mr Homo's treatment of the edict of Gallienus. For this he quotes the two passages from Aurelius Victor (*Caesares* 33, 34 and 37, 6) in the following form: 'et patres quidem, praeter commune Romani malum orbis, stimulabat proprii ordinis contumelia, quia primus ipse [*sc.* Gallienus] metu socordiae suae ne imperium ad optimos nobilium transferretur, senatum militia vetuit et adire exercitum'; and 'amissa Gallieni edicto refici militia potuit, concedentibus modeste legionibus, Tacito regnante'. The latter passage he translates: 'La carrière militaire perdue (pour le sénat) à la suite de l'édit de Gallien put être rétablie sous le règne de Tacite, en raison de la modération et de la condes-

---

[3] Ibid, cxxxvii, 162–3.

[4] In this section of his paper Mr Homo's treatment of the use of the title *dux* in the third century (pp. 169–79) contains a valuable discussion of the epigraphic evidence, though the reader misses a reference to Mommsen's *Anhang* to Von Sallet's *Die Fürsten von Palmyra* (cf. *Ges. Schriften*, vi, 204 sq.), which first pointed the way to the solution of the problem.

[5] Cf. Norman H. Baynes, 'The Date of the Composition of the Historia Augusta', *Classical Review*, xxxviii, 165–9, [and the monograph, *The Historia Augusta: its Date and Purpose* (Oxford, 1926); cf. also *infra*, pp. 209–17].

cendance des légions.' The issue of the edict he would date to the last months of the year A.D. 261 by arguments which appear to me inconclusive (*Rev. Hist.*, cxxxviii, 3–5): e.g. 'une mesure aussi décisive, aussi terrible pour le sénat que l'était l'édit de Gallien ne peut avoir été prise qu'à Rome, c'est-à-dire l'empereur étant sur place et ayant les moyens de réduire immédiatement toute tentative de résistance sénatoriale qui viendrait à se produire'. This is, in my judgement, to overestimate the power of the senate. The date of the issue of the edict is, however, relatively unimportant: the essential matter is its interpretation. Mr Homo points out that the original criterion for the distribution of provinces between *princeps* and senate lay in the character of each individual province and its need of military defence: it was the *provinciae inermes* which fell to the senate. But under Gallienus the whole Roman Empire in its length and breadth was in need of military defence.[6] The emperor, himself at the mercy of the dictation of the Danube legions, with a resolute logic applied once more that original criterion to the altered circumstances of his day. All the provinces of the Empire were by his edict transformed into imperial provinces. The Empire must be preserved, no matter at what cost: it was the hour of the soldier and the capable general. 'It was not, however, in the ranks of the degenerate senatorial aristocracy that one could hope to find capable generals, but only amongst professional soldiers formed in the rough school of frontier defence' (p. 6), 'ces chefs, l'empereur ne pouvait les trouver que dans l'ordre équestre' (p. 193). The edict has thus the effect that all senatorial governors—consular or praetorian—are replaced by governors from the equestrian order, while, concludes Mr Homo, 'il semble très vraisemblable d'admettre que la transformation dans l'administration des provinces sénatoriales a été une réforme d'ensemble, et qu'elle se place précisément' in A.D. 261—the year of the issue of the edict (p. 199).

Under Claudius and Aurelian the edict of Gallienus remained in force: Aurelius Victor 'l'atteste formellement: Amissa Gallieni edicto refici militia potuit . . . *Tacito regnante.*

<hr>

[6] Cf. L. Homo, 'L'empereur Gallien et la crise de l'empire romain au IIIe siècle', *Revue Historique*, cxiii (1913), 1–22, 225–67.

Il a fallu la restauration sénatoriale marquée par le règne de Tacite pour qu'il fût abrogé' (p. 20). But Mr Homo is forced to admit that there were some exceptions to this rule: Velleius Macrinus (ὁ λαμπρότατος ὑπατικὸς πρεσβευτὴς καὶ ἀντιστράτηγος τοῦ Σεβαστοῦ *C.I.G.*, 3747–8) under Claudius must have been 'un légat impérial pris, selon l'ancienne règle, dans l'ordre sénatorial' (p. 21), while, though the name is lost, *C.I.L.*, iii, 14460, supplies us with a *legatus pro praetore* of Moesia Inferior under Aurelian. Of the reason for these exceptions we are ignorant (p. 22). With the year A.D. 275 we reach the senatorial reaction under Tacitus: for this we possess the direct state-ment (previously quoted) of Aurelius Victor and, further, the evidence of the *Vita Taciti*, 19.2, 'Nos recepimus ius procon-sulare,' 19, 3–4, 'Optinuimus quod semper optavimus, in anti-quum statum senatus revertit. Nostri ordinis sunt potestates. Gratias exercitui romano, et vere romano; reddit nobis quam semper habuimus potestatem.' From a full discussion of these and other passages of the *Vita Taciti* (pp. 35–9) Mr Homo concludes that not only was the edict of Gallienus abrogated by Tacitus, but that the senate recovered *all* its traditional rights, save only the privilege of coining bronze money.

Florian returns to the system of Gallienus; Probus comes to a compromise with the senate: *Vita Probi*, 13, 1 (pp. 40–9). In senatorial provinces Probus '*permisit* patribus ... ut procon-sules crearent', i.e. a favour granted in particular cases, but not the recognition of a right; in imperial provinces of consular rank 'permisit ... ut ... legatos ex consulibus darent'—'c'est le droit pour le sénat de fournir, non pas de nommer—la dif-férence est capitale—*des* légats anciens consuls ... et non pas *tous* les légats'; it is not a complete return to the position as it had stood before the edict of Gallienus: 'Probus déclare qu'il pourra prendre dans le sénat les gouverneurs des provinces impériales consulaires, mais il se réserve aussi le droit ... de les recruter en dehors' (p. 42—I confess that I should not, without assistance, have thus interpreted the text of the *Historia Augusta*—'Permisit patribus ut ... ius praetorium praesidibus darent', i.e. in imperial provinces of praetorian rank the governors should continue, as under the edict of Gal-lienus, to be chosen from the equestrian order (*praesides* =

'l'ensemble des gouverneurs impériaux équestres' p. 43), 'mais avec collation éventuelle du ius praetorium (= "les emblèmes de l'autorité symbolisés par les cinq faisceaux et le rang de sénateur avec les avantages qui en découlaient") par le sénat' (p. 44).

Carus and Carinus represent a military reaction and a complete reversion to the principles of Gallienus, though here, too, as under Claudius and Aurelian, exception must have been made in favour of individual senators, e.g. Marcus Aurelius Valentinianus, senatorial legate of Hither Spain (*C.I.L.*, ii, 4102, 4103).

Such in bare outline is Mr Homo's reconstruction of the third century constitutional struggle between the senate and the emperor. Of its extreme ingenuity not a moment's doubt is possible, but can it be accepted as history? I venture to think that it cannot be so accepted. The 'foundation-pillars'— to employ a term of von Soden's—of that reconstruction are the two texts of Aurelius Victor, especially the all-important words *amissa Gallieni edicto refici militia potuit.* Unfortunately Mr Homo has considered those words in isolation: the first step is therefore to restore them to their context. The passage as a whole reads: Abhinc [i.e. from the death of Probus] militaris potentia convaluit ac senatui imperium creandique ius principis ereptum ad nostram memoriam, incertum an ipso cupiente per desidiam an metu seu dissensionum odio. Quippe amisso[7] Gallieni edicto refici militia potuit concedentibus modeste legionibus Tacito regnante, neque Florianus temere invasisset, aut iudicio manipularium cuiquam, bono licet, imperium daretur amplissimo ac tanto ordine in castris degente. Verum dum oblectantur otio simulque divitiis pavent, quarum usum affluentiamque aeternitate maius putant, munivere militaribus et paene barbaris viam in se ac posteros dominandi' (c. 37, 4–7). I should translate 'Had the edict of Gallienus become a dead letter, the military service could have been reformed, . . . in that case Florian would never have rashly seized imperial power; the choice of an emperor would not have

---

[7] It is common knowledge (cf. Pichlmayr's Preface to his edition of Aurelius Victor, Leipzig, 1911) that both our MSS. of the *Caesares* are derived from a single archetype. Here the Cod. Parisinus reads amiss*a*, the Bruxellensis amisso; I prefer the reading of the Bruxellensis.

rested with the rank and file of the army had there been senators permanently stationed in the camp'. In other words: *the edict of Gallienus was in fact never repealed.* But if this essential step in the senatorial programme was never taken, what of the account of the senatorial reaction during the reign of the Emperor Tacitus as given in the *Historia Augusta*, what of the 'compromise' with the senate concluded by the emperor Probus? These are both, in my judgement, unhistorical. The *Scriptores Historiae Augustae*, composing their collection of biographies in frantic haste under Julian the Apostate, had before them the recently published *Caesares* of Aurelius Victor: of the section of that work devoted to the emperor Probus 'Vopiscus' made generous use, playing upon the theme 'brevi milites frustra fore'; running his eye down the chapter, he caught sight of the words 'refici militia potuit'; he inferred from them, as did Mr Homo, a senatorial restoration under Tacitus. This gave him his cue, and imagination supplied the rest. The senatorial reaction under Tacitus would thus be limited to the choice by the senate of a successor to Aurelian.

But, if we may conclude that the edict which banished senators from the army remained in force during the whole period from the reign of Gallienus to the accession of Diocletian, how are we to interpret it? Here I should agree with Mr Keyes[8] that it is impossible to regard all the cases of senatorial governors of provinces vouched for during this period by epigraphic evidence as exceptions from a general rule excluding senators from provincial governorships. We must, in fact, abandon Mr Homo's interpretation of the edict. The only other possible interpretation of the words of Aurelius Victor—'senatum militia vetuit et adire exercitum'—would seem to be that in the case of senatorial governors Gallienus separated the military from the civil authority, while gradually senatorial provinces, as well as imperial provinces of consular or praetorian rank, were conferred upon governors drawn from the equestrian order. The latter change was in many cases masked, as Mr Keyes has shown, by representing these equestrian governors as acting on behalf of a non-

---

[8] C. W. Keyes: *The Rise of the Equites in the third century of the Roman Empire*. Princeton dissertation (Princeton University Press, 1915), pp. 49–54.

existent governor of senatorial rank. This subterfuge was in course of time dropped, and the equestrian governor no longer adds to his title the words *agens vices legati*. Thus, if we would formulate a hypothesis in order to picture to ourselves the operation of the edict of Gallienus, we might state it somewhat as follows. In senatorial provinces the governor is—to employ the language of the fourth century—a *praeses*, i.e. he has only civil powers; he may even be superseded altogether in favour of a governor of equestrian rank. In imperial provinces the position of the senatorial *legatus* is similar; he, too, is a *praeses*, and is deprived of his traditional military imperium. In imperial provinces of equestrian rank (and indeed in all provinces where the governor is an *eques*) the position of the governor remains unchanged,[9] while the number of such provinces steadily tends to increase at the expense of imperial provinces of consular or praetorian rank. It is uncertain on whom the military authority thus withdrawn from senatorial governors was conferred; in provinces where only a single legion was stationed, Mr Keyes has suggested that the equestrian *praefectus legionis* was the successor of the senatorial commander;[10] in a province where more than one legion was stationed, the command over all the troops of that province was probably entrusted to a *praepositus* [on the inscription of Flavius Aper v(ir) e(gregius) praepositus leg(ionum) V Maced. et XIII gem. cf. Ritterling in Pauly-Wissowa, *Real-Encyc.* xii. 2, col. 1340; on Dessau, 9479 and Dessau, 8882 cf. Ritterling, ibid., 1360]. There is no undoubted reference to the later provincial military commander—the *dux*—until the year 289, when the anonymous author of the Panegyric on Maximian, *Panegyrici* ii (or in the new edition of W. Baehrens, vi), c. 3, writes, 'qui justitiam vestram iudices aemulentur, qui virtutis vestrae gloriam *duces* servent',[11] for the inscription, *C.I.L.*, v, 3329, of

---

[9] It is of course *possible* that even the equestrian governor before the reign of Diocletian was deprived of his military command; but I know of no evidence which would tend to support the view. Grosse's 'Fingerzeig' (*Römische Militärgeschichte*, Berlin, 1920, p. 11) does not impress me.

[10] Cf. his remarks upon *C.I.L.*, viii, 2572, at p. 54.

[11] Seeck's attribution of this Panegyric to Eumenius (cf. O. Seeck, 'Die Reden des Eumenius', *Jahrbücher für klassische Philologie*, cxxxvii, 713) in *Geschichte des Untergangs*, etc., ii (1901), p. 507, and *P.-W.*, v, 2, 1869, has misled Mr Homo, who quotes the passages as from the speech *pro restaurandis scholis*, Homo, p. 171.

the year 265 found at Verona which records the rebuilding of
the walls of the Colonia Augusta Verona *insistente Aur. Mar-
cellino v. p. duc. duc.* will hardly bear the weight of the
theory which F. Reiche sought to raise upon it.[12] The words
duc. duc. may have been rightly expanded by Mommsen
into *duce ducenario*, but even so it is possible that Aurelius
Marcellinus 'n'est pas un *dux limitis* mais un chef de corps,
"dux," délégué à cette tâche particulière' (Homo, p. 172),
while on this inscription Mr Keyes writes: 'The stone-cutter
may have repeated these letters by mistake [i.e. *duc.
duc.*], and the man's title may have been simply *v.p. duce-
narius*, a title which is found in another inscription of a little
later date (*C.I.L.*, iii, 1805). And the question comes to our
mind: what would a *dux limitis* have been doing at Verona?
It seems much more likely that Marcellinus was a financial
officer.'[13]

In the present state of our evidence I see no direct means of
demonstrating this general theory of the effect of the edict of
Gallienus; it could, of course, be conclusively disproved if we
could show that during this period a senatorial governor exercised distinctively military functions. I have been unable from
the inscriptions to discover any such evidence; it is clear e.g.
that a purely civil governor might restore the walls of Nicaea.[14]
There are, however, the two peculiar inscriptions *C.I.L.*, ii,
4102 and 4103, in which M. Aurelius Valentinianus (cf. *C.I.L.*,
iii, 3418) is described as 'virum clarissimum praesidem prov.
Hispaniae citerioris legatum Augusti pro praetore'. On this
title Mommsen bade the student observe 'ut munus civile cum
militari videatur coniunctum esse *extra ordinem*', and, if this
were the true interpretation of the wording, it would point to
the fact that in the year A.D. 283 it was unusual for a senatorial
governor to possess both military and civil power. I cannot
help thinking, however, that the words 'legatum Augustorum
pro praetore' are intended to *define* the preceding title *praesidem*: *praeses* was already becoming the customary qualification of *equestrian* governors; Valentinianus wished to make it

---

[12] Cf. F. Reiche, *Ueber die Teilung der Zivil- und Militärgewalt im dritten
Jahrhundert der römischen Kaiserzeit.* Programm. Breslau, 1900.
[13] p. 51, cf. Grosse, *Römische Militärgeschichte* (Berlin, 1920), p. 10 n. 2.
[14] *I.G.R.*, 39, 40.

quite clear that, though only a *civil* governor, he was yet a legate of senatorial rank.

If this should prove to be the true effect of the edict of Gallienus, Diocletian only needed to complete the process of eliminating the senatorial class from provincial governorships, while on the other hand he would have introduced into the imperial provinces of equestrian rank the same separation between the civil and the military power which since the reign of Gallienus had been practised in provinces, whether imperial or senatorial, which had been governed by men of a rank higher than that of the equestrian order.

II. The Army Reforms of Diocletian and Constantine*

The position which the *Journal of Roman Studies* has won for itself in this country carries with it no light responsibility: what the *J.R.S.* says to-day, many historical text-books will repeat tomorrow. The conclusions of Dr Nischer upon the army reforms of Diocletian and Constantine may thus be readily adopted by readers who are not themselves close students of fourth-century history, and it is well that these should be warned that the results reached by the author cannot be accepted without a careful reconsideration of the evidence upon which they are based. A scholar who possesses an intimate knowledge of the administrative history of the later Roman Empire has already stated his opinion that Dr Nischer has in the main failed to prove his contentions. 'Those contentions contradict in the most important points the results of methodical research, so that his article for the most part is of no service.'[15]

I am not capable of subjecting those conclusions to a detailed criticism; I merely desire to suggest some grounds for caution to readers of Dr Nischer's paper, and to explain the reasons for my own inability to accept his principal conclusions.

Not a few of the lists of regiments included in Dr Nischer's

* [Cp. E. von Nischer in *J.R.S.*, xiii, 1923, pp. 1-55. I have not yet seen D. van Berchem, *L'Armée de Dioclétien et la Réforme Constantinienne*, Institut Français d'Archéologie de Beyrouth. Bibliothèque Archéol. et Histor. 56 (Geuthner, Paris, 1952).]

[15] Ernst Stein in *Byzantinische Zeitschrift*, xxv, p. 387, n. 1.

paper seem to me to suggest to the reader that we possess
better information on Roman military history than is in fact
the case. I take as an example the catalogue of legions treated
by Dr Nischer as the creation of Diocletian (pp. 3–4): I Armeniaca, II Armeniaca, I Isaura sagittaria, II Isaura, III
Isaura, IV Italica, IV Parthica, V Parthica, VI Parthica, I
Pontica, II Noricorum and I Illyricorum. These are ascribed
to Diocletian on the authority of Seeck, but Seeck's only
ground for the ascription in the case of the ten first named is
that the existence of I Pontica in the reign of Diocletian—not
its creation by Diocletian—is vouched for by *C.I.L.*, iii, 236.
The name of I Pontica is formed from that of a country, the
nine other names are similarly formed, and therefore these ten
legions may be inferred to be the creation of Diocletian; in the
same fashion Seeck argues that the II Noricorum and the I Illyricorum are creations of Diocletian, since he may be presumed
to have formed the III Diocletiana Thebaeorum and the I
Maximiana Thebaeorum because of the occurrence in their
titles of his own name and that of his colleague. But the three
Isaurian legions (I–III Isaura) have been regarded by Ritterling as the creation of the Emperor Probus,[16] while the same
scholar many years ago expressed the view that Legio I Illyricorum, stationed in Palmyra, owed its formation to the
Emperor Aurelian.[17] Indeed, one would like to know what lies
behind the legend *Restitutor Exerciti* on the coinage of Aurelian.[18] 'Es ist nicht ausgeschlossen dass noch andere Neuein-
richtungen auf dem Gebiet der Grenzverteidigung, namentlich
in den von Aurelian dem Reiche wiedergewonnenen orientalischen und gallischen Provinzen, die allgemein als Schöpfungen
Diocletians angesehen werden . . . bereits auf des ersteren Initiative zurückgeführt werden müssen.'[19] In the same way I
feel that readers should have been more expressly warned of

---

[16] *P.-W.*, xii, 2, 1348.

[17] 'Diese Legion ist somit eine Schöpfung Aurelians, errichtet aus Mann-
schaften seiner illyrischen Legionen die den Sieg über das orientalische Reich
hatten erfechten helfen.' E. Ritterling, 'Zum römischen Heerwesen des ausgehenden dritten Jahrhunderts' in *Hirschfeld Festschrift* (Berlin, 1903), p. 347, and
on Legio IV Martia cf. ibid., n. 4. Similarly on IV Italica as a creation of
Alexander Severus or Gordian III, cf. Ritterling in *P.-W.*, xii, 2, 1329 sq. and
1337; IV Parthica he would attribute to Diocletian, cf. ibid., 1329 sq. with 1556.

[18] Cf. L. Homo, *Essai sur le règne de l'empereur Aurélien* (Paris, 1904), p. 200.

[19] Ritterling: *P.-W.*, xii, 2, 1346–7.

the uncertainty which attaches to any estimate of the actual
numerical strength of the legions; here Ritterling's reminder
is salutary: 'it must never be forgotten that the legions created
by Diocletian—save those formed at the beginning of his
reign—will not have maintained the full strength of the earlier
legions.'[20] Why Dr Nischer should arbitrarily have reckoned
the legions in the West and those in the E. Danube provinces
at 4,000 men apiece, those elsewhere in the East at 3,000, I fail
to understand. It is in my judgement of the first importance
that writers on the military history of the Roman Empire in
the fourth century should not play a game of bluff with the
reader, or delude him with statistics, unless these are clearly
stated to be purely hypothetical estimates.

The two cardinal contentions of Dr Nischer's paper as I
understand it are (a) that Diocletian introduced a general
system of divisional reserves, (b) that Constantine was the
great military reformer, and that the Empire owed to him the
introduction of the mobile field army or expeditionary force.
The former contention I believe to be unproven, while the
latter runs counter to such epigraphic evidence as we possess.
I desire very briefly to consider these two points.

For proof of the former contention Dr Nischer adduces the
exceptional position upon the Danube frontier of the two
legions III Herculia and IV Jovia as given in the *Notitia
Dignitatum*. This is but one instance of Dr Nischer's peculiar
use of the *Notitia* as evidence for the position of troops in the
reigns of Diocletian and Constantine. The uninstructed reader
might at times almost imagine that the *Notitia*, as we possess
it, was compiled in the first quarter of the fourth century. Has
Dr Nischer considered for a moment what must have been the
condition of the Roman frontier-defence on the Danube after
the crushing defeat of Adrianople and before the victories of
Theodosius the Great? There must have been a complete dis-
location of the Roman forces, and how Dr Nischer can simply
transfer the position of troops as given in the *Notitia* on this
frontier to the reign of Diocletian passes my comprehension.
Ritterling rightly remarks of the III Herculia that it must
have originally belonged to Diocletian's organization of the

[20] See *P.-W.*, xii, 2, 1350.

frontier defence, but that from its location in the *Notitia* we have no means of inferring in what province it was first stationed. In general the use made of the *Notitia* by Dr Nischer in this paper in order to establish the position of troops during the reign of Diocletian appears to me to be indefensible. The second instance adduced to prove the existence of a system of divisional reserves is that of the three legions I–III Julia Alpina. These legions in Dr Nischer's view were first stationed in the passes of the Julian Alps to act as a second reserve supporting the Danube defence. This is a guess, and as such can hardly claim probative force. We do not know by whom these legions were formed, whence they derived their name, or where they were originally posted. Personally I incline to prefer Ritterling's explanation,[21] but certainty is impossible. The third instance is that of the three Isaurian legions regarded as a divisional reserve for the Euphrates frontier; that an emperor, resident in Nicomedia, should have chosen the inaccessible hill country of Isauria in which to station legions intended to support the Euphrates line seems to me incredible. But it is from evidence such as this that Dr Nischer feels himself entitled to proceed to the startling generalization. 'We must suppose therefore that there were also divisional reserves for the Rhine frontier, for the eastern sector of the Danube, for Egypt and for Africa' (p. 7). Such a supposition, unsupported by any shred of evidence, surely carries with it its own condemnation. For such evidence as we possess of the way in which Diocletian recruited an expeditionary force it will suffice to refer to Ritterling in Pauly-Wissowa, xii, 2, 1359–60, and to K. F. Kinch: *L'Arc de Triomphe de Salonique*, 1890.

The second cardinal contention of Dr Nischer's paper is that the introduction of a mobile field army was the work of Constantine the Great. But the argument based on *C.I.L.*, vi, 2759 (=Dessau, 2045) and Dessau, 2782, when compared with *C.I.L.*, iii, 6194 (=Dessau, 2781), advanced by Seeck[22] to prove that at least the beginnings of a field army date from the reign of Diocletian—at latest from the year A.D. 301—appears to me to be unanswerable. As Seeck further pointed out,

[21] *P.-W.*, xii, 2, 1404–5.
[22] O. Seeck, *Geschichte des Untergangs der antiken Welt* (Berlin, 1901), ii, 483-4; cf. R. Grosse, *Römische Militärgeschichte*, etc. (Berlin, 1920), p. 59.

Dessau, 664, gives us a *praepositus equitibus Dalmatis Aque-sianis comitatensibus* in Noricum, and this inscription must be dated to a period before the time when that province passed into the hands of Constantine, 'womit der unzweideutigste Beweis gegeben ist, dass die Comitatenses vorkonstantinisch sind.' But, if this be true, it means that Constantine in developing an imperial field army was only elaborating a policy which had been already inaugurated by Diocletian, and that in consequence there is no such sharp cleavage between the two reigns as Dr Nischer would seek to establish. The inauguration by Diocletian of a mobile field army was indeed the natural result of the experience gained by the war in Egypt and the operations against Persia.

In a word Dr Nischer has in my judgement failed to establish the two principal contentions of his paper: I still remain an unrepentant disciple of Mommsen, and profess his belief that 'the army of this period must be described as the joint creation of Diocletian and Constantine'.

XI

Rome and Armenia in the
Fourth Century*

[*English Historical Review*, xxv (1910), pp. 625–43.]

T HE aim of the present paper is to inquire into the chronology and the historical value of the work of Faustus of
Byzantium, and to attempt to estimate his contribution
to our knowledge of Roman history in the fourth century. The
thesis from which the paper proceeds is that modern writers
have failed to appreciate the importance of that contribution,
because of a confusion which occupies a central position in the
narrative of Faustus; it is sought to demonstrate that when
once this confusion is recognized we may gain a new insight
into the relations between east and west, and that, further, we
are enabled to institute fresh comparisons with the account of
Ammianus Marcellinus, and to judge from the study of an
independent authority the value of his narrative. It should be
understood from the outset that we are concerned with the
internal history of Armenia only so far as may be necessary to
understand its influence upon the policy of the Roman Empire.[1]

* [In 1910 when writing this paper I accepted the account given by Faustus of
Byzantium of the capture by the Roman army towards the end of Constantine's
reign of the wife and harem of the Persian king. But in 1922 Adonts argued that
in this Faustus was mistaken: he had 'contaminated' an account of Galerius'
capture of the Persian harem in 298 with a narrative of the military operations
in Armenia under Constantine (*Khristiansky Vostok*, vol. vi, Vuipusk 3, Russian
Academy of Sciences, 1917–20, pp. 235–72. This paper on Faustus as a historian remained unfinished since, so far as I can discover, this was the last issue
of the journal). Adonts suggests that the confusion in the narrative of Faustus
was due to the fact that in 298 the Persian king whose harem was captured was
Narses, while, fighting against Constantius, a Persian prince of the name of
Narses was defeated and killed. The argument of Adonts I accept, and have
altered the text of my paper in consequence, though it is not easy to decide
which parts of Faustus' narrative at this point refer to the events of the third
century and which to those of the fourth. Cf. further P. Peeters, *Bulletin de la
Classe des Lettres*, etc., Académie Royale de Belgique, 5e Série, Tome 17 (1931),
pp. 10–47.]

[1] This paper owes its existence to H. Gelzer's study, 'Die Anfänge der
armenischen Kirche,' in *Berichte über die Verhandlungen der kön. sächsischen
Gesellschaft der Wissenschaften zu Leipzig*, Phil.-hist. Klasse, xlvii (1895), pp. 109–

The confusion in the work of Faustus to which reference has been made arises from the acceptance by the historian of the view that Nerses, the great Armenian catholicos, was consecrated by Eusebius, bishop of Caesarea (A.D. 362–70), in the presence of St Basil, and that, in consequence, this event took place in the reign of Valens. The result of this confusion has been that the name of Valens has been substituted in several cases for that of Constantius, and that, since Faustus mentions no emperor by name except Constantine the Great[2] and Valens, his chronology has been greatly obscured. In truth, as we shall see shortly, Nerses was not consecrated by Eusebius in the reign of Valens, but (presumably by Bishop Dianius) in the year 339 or 340, when Constantius was ruling over the Roman east.[3] If we ask, however, how this confusion arose, a natural explanation lies ready to our hand. Nerses had been educated at Caesarea and had adopted as his own the aims and methods of the eastern church; he carried out in Armenia the same policy as was followed by St Basil in Cappadocia; it was Basil who on the murder of Nerses refused to recognize King Pap's nominee, who was consecrated in his despite, an event which led to the independence of the church of Armenia.[4] Men who looked back upon the old *régime* with longing and who approved of the intimate connexion which had bound nascent Armenian Christianity in the closest ties of intimacy with the see of Caesarea felt that their last great catholicos[5] must at the

74. I have been unable to touch upon geographical questions and would merely refer the reader to the map of ancient Armenia given by H. Hübschmann, 'Die altarmenischen Ortsnamen, mit Beiträgen zur historischen Topographie Armeniens,' in *Indogermanische Forschungen*, xvi (1904), pp. 197–490, and to J. Marquart, 'Ērānšahr nach der Geographie des Ps. Moses Xorenac'i,' in *Abhandlungen der kön. Gesellschaft der Wissenschaften zu Göttingen*, Phil.-hist. Klasse, N.F., iii, no. 2 (1901). Being unfortunately unable to read Armenian, I have used the German translation of Faustus by M. Lauer (Köln, 1879), and it is to this book that reference is made in the following notes.

[2] Faustus, iii. 21, and cf. iii. 10.

[3] It is unnecessary to labour the point that Nerses could not have been consecrated in the reign of Valens. One argument among many may be mentioned: Gnel was assassinated by Arsak before A.D 358, and from the day of the murder the catholicos refused to appear at the king's court (see Faustus, iv. 15, v. 1). It is then impossible that Nerses should only have been consecrated at some date subsequent to the year 364. The chronology of Moses of Chorene is of course quite untrustworthy: it is, however, worth noticing that according to him Nerses was patriarch for thirty-four years: he was poisoned by Pap some time before A.D. 375 (cf. Moses Chor., iii. 38).

[4] On this subject cf. Gelzer, op. cit., p. 155 sqq.   [5] Cf. Faustus, iv. 4, s.f.

most solemn moment in his career have been brought into
touch with Basil and with the honoured bishop Eusebius,
whom the latter had served so faithfully. Thus in their view
Nerses is consecrated by Eusebius, Basil is present at the ceremony, and the holy dove only leaves the head of Basil to settle
of that of their national hero: further, an incident from the
career of Basil is related at length as an event in the life-story
of Nerses.[6] The loving reverence of Armenia has transported a
beautiful fancy into the realm of history. The remarkable fact,
however, is that this account has simply been inserted by
Faustus into the true historical framework: there has been
no consequential chronological displacement;[7] if the references to Eusebius and Basil (Barsilios) are omitted, and if
we read, where necessary, Constantius for Valens, the history
of Faustus is a consecutive chronological whole. It is this
statement which we shall now proceed to illustrate in some
detail so far as the history of the Roman Empire is concerned.

We can begin our analysis of Faustus' History with the reign
of Constantine the Great and the appeal to the Emperor of the
representatives of Armenia.

Waras, the Persian warden of the frontier in Atrpatakan,
had been offended by Tiran,[8] king of Armenia, and had
reported to the Persian king that Tiran was plotting against
him. He then treacherously seized the persons of Tiran, the
Queen and the young Prince Arsak, and having blinded Tiran
carried them all as prisoners to the Persian court. The feudal
nobility of Armenia,[9] after an unsuccessful attempt at recapture and a foray into Persian territory, called a national
assembly at which were present, it is interesting to note, not
only the great ones of the land, but also representatives of the
peasantry and the common folk.[10] Feeling their own weakness

---

[6] Compare Allard, *Saint Basile* (4th ed., Paris, 1903), p. 81 sq.; Greg. Naz. *Or.*,
xliii. 54; Socr., iv. 26; Soz., vi. 16; Theod., iv. 16, etc. (on the death of the son of
Valens in 372), with Faustus, iv. 5.

[7] Excepting only the opening words of bk. iii. 13, which are merely resumptive of the close of iii. 10.

[8] The Armenian king had failed to send him a particular horse which he
coveted (Faustus, iii. 20).

[9] Cf. Gelzer, op. cit., p. 132.

[10] Faustus, iii. 21.

before the might of Persia they determined to appeal to the allied Empire of Rome.[11] Andok and Arshavir—representatives of two old Armenian houses—were at once despatched to plead the cause of their distressed country. In their absence the Persian king marched into Armenia. The nobles fled before him and took refuge within the Empire. Now it would seem that Arsak was restored to his country by Constantius and ascended the throne of Armenia in the year 339 or early in 340;[12] but in the thirtieth year of the reign of Arsak the Armenians looked back over a period of thirty-four years of almost constant hostility with Persia.[13] We are thus led to the conclusion that this enmity began in or about the year 335. It is just at this time, as we learn from our western authorities, that Constantine raised Hanniballianus[14] to a 'kingdom' (regnum)[15] over Armenia and the allied peoples: it would appear that for the time he was to represent the captive royal house of Armenia. Andok and Arshavir were appointed generals by Constantine and after a defeat of the Persians the Emperor 'took into his own possession the land of all the Armenian satraps'. Constantine was himself on the point of driving home his success by a campaign against Persia when death overtook him. Under Constantius Tiran returned to Armenia, but refused on account of his blindness to resume his kingship and his son Arsak ascended the throne. It would seem that at this time the Emperor in order to secure the loyalty of Armenia took as hostages Gnel and Tirith, the nephews of Arsak.[16] While Julian tells us that Constantius banished those Armenian nobles who had deserted the cause of their king,[17] we learn from Faustus that Arsak broke up the power of the feudal nobility by distributing their armed followers in various parts of the country and thus weakened the force of local

[11] Ibid. (Lauer, p. 46). The treaty of Constantine with Armenia is to be accepted as historical: cf. Gelzer, op. cit., pp. 165 sqq.

[12] It is the first operation of Constantius in the East recorded by Julian in his panegyric on Constantius. Cf. Seeck, *s.v.* Constantius in *P.-W.*, iv. i, col. 1053.

[13] Faustus, iv. 50.

[14] [On Hanniballianus and a criticism of a suggestion of mine cf. W. Ensslin, *Klio*, 29, Heft 1 (1936), pp. 102–10].

[15] Hanniballiano *regi*, Amm., xiv. 1, 2.

[16] Cf. Faustus, iv. 5 sub fin.

[17] Julian, ed. Hertlein, p. 24, 20.

connexions. The one measure is manifestly a sequel of the other.[18]

The intervention of the Roman Empire brought with it the general supremacy of Greek ideas under the restored monarchy: Church and State were both alike to be reorganized, and accordingly a new catholicos was selected without delay.[19] Nerses had been educated on Roman soil, and was ready to introduce into Armenia the institutions of which he had learned from his teachers at Caesarea.[20] The account of Faustus implies that his consecration followed almost immediately upon the accession of Arsak (late in 339 or early in 340). Faustus, having described the new system inaugurated by Nerses, tells of an embassy to Constantius ('Valens') headed by the catholicos, and of the latter's detention for nine years by the Roman emperor. This account has been rejected as incredible,[21] and we must therefore consider when this embassy of Nerses took place, and whether the chronology of Faustus must be dismissed as untenable. It is essential for this purpose to have before us a scheme of the order of events according to Faustus. The following is a brief outline:

Book iv. c. 1—The restoration of Tiran to Armenia and the beginning of the rule of Arsak.

c. 2—Administrative and military reorganization of Armenia.

c. 3—Election of Nerses; sketch of his early life.

c. 4—His consecration at Caesarea and his reforms.

c. 5—His embassy to 'Valens' and his imprisonment (here the incident from the life of Basil has been introduced).[22] The persecutions of the Arian emperor 'Valens'; he restores the hostages Gnel and Tirith, and sends costly presents to the king of Armenia while detaining Nerses.

c. 6—Nerses is banished to an island, and for nine years the emperor refuses to permit his return to Armenia.

cc. 7–10—Incidents from the lives of Eusebius and Basil.[23]

---

[18] Faustus, iii. 21 sub fin., Lauer, p. 48. This was throughout his reign the policy of Arsak: cf. iv. 12, Lauer, pp. 80 sqq.; iv. 19, Lauer, p. 101; cf. Gelzer, op. cit., pp. 154 sqq.

[19] Faustus, iv. 3, Lauer, p. 51.   [20] Ibid., Lauer, p. 52.

[21] For the chronology of Faustus see Gelzer's criticisms, op. cit., p. 118.

[22] See *supra*. p. 188, n. 6.

[23] A reason for the insertion of these passages has been suggested *supra*, p. 188.

c. 11—The return of the embassy from 'Valens'; wrath of Arsak at the detention of Nerses. Wasak the Armenian leads an expedition into Roman territory as far as Ancyra, and after this for six years in succession conducts forays into Roman territory.

c. 12—Bishop Chad, the representative of Nerses during his absence, continues the policy of the catholicos and resists Arsak.

c. 13—The return of Nerses and his opposition to Arsak.

c. 14—Incident of Nerses and the master of the Harem Haïr.

c. 15—Arsak puts to death his nephews Gnel and Tirith and marries Gnel's widow against her will. Because of her continued hatred he sends to Rome for a wife and marries Olympias.

At this point we reach a date which we can check from our western authorities: we are at some year subsequent to A.D. 350.[24]

To return then to 339: Arsak was naturally anxious that his throne should be protected from Persian aggression, and that the friendship of Rome should be a real and effective defence. As soon therefore as Nerses had set on foot his reorganization of the Church, the account of Faustus gives us to understand that the king sent his greatest subject and Rome's pupil on an embassy to the emperor. We might expect that this would take place about 341. Faustus gives us no exact date, but he does tell us that at this time a great church council had been called together and that as a result many of the orthodox bishops were banished and Arian successors appointed in their place; Nerses shared the banishment of these deposed bishops. This would, however, be an accurate description of the great synod of Antioch, which after sitting for three years ultimately broke up in the year 341.[25] The detention of Nerses may thus with considerable probability be assigned to this year. What was then the reason which led Constantius to take this step? It may, of course, be suggested that Nerses was a more valuable hostage than two princes who would not be the direct succes-

[24] Probably A.D. 354, see *infra*, p. 194 (cf. Ammianus Marcellinus, xx. 11, Athan., *Hist. Ar. ad Mon.*, 69).

[25] For a convenient summary of its work cf. Seeck, *s.v.* 'Constantius', in *P.-W.*, iv. 1.

sors of Arsak, should he have a son; but the action of Constantius was probably dictated by more far-reaching considerations. His efforts at this time were directed to securing the victory of the Arian doctrine in the eastern Church: Roman influence had been re-established in Armenia: the tie which throughout its history drew Armenia towards Rome was a common faith, but no one can study the subsequent relations of the two countries without perceiving the fatal consequences of a difference in the creeds professed at Dovin and Constantinople. The emperor was not content to protect fellow-Christians; he felt himself impelled to attempt the work of their conversion.[26] It would seem that the statesmanship of Constantius had already appreciated the support which would be gained for Roman authority in the east if one and the same creed united the Church of the Empire with that of Armenia. In the latter country the cult and the forms of worship had always been imposed upon the people by authority:[27] it was, indeed, only through the activity of the monks and the work of Mesrob in the fifth century that Christianity became in any real sense a national faith: in the fourth century Christianity in Armenia was a human ordinance and was acquiesced in by the people just as they bowed to any other royal command.[28] If Constantius could convert the catholicos, he had gained Armenia. He could afford to provoke insignificant border forays if this was the price which had to be paid for a great and permanent victory in the sphere of religious diplomacy. Nerses, however, refused to bow to imperial persuasion: the school of Caesarea had done its work too well.

Nine years, says Faustus, was Nerses in exile, and nine years from 341 take us down to the year 350. Now 350 is the very year of the revolt of Magnentius, when Constantius left Asia

[26] Compare especially the history of the latter part of the sixth and the first part of the seventh centuries.

[27] Cf. H. Gelzer, 'Zur armenischen Götterlehre,' in *Berichte über die Verhandlungen der kön. sächsischen Gesellschaft der Wissenschaften zu Leipzig*, Phil.-hist. Klasse, 1896, ii. iii. (1897), p. 122: 'Der Gottesdienst wird also einfach von oben octroyirt. Im Orient ist es zu allen Zeiten so gewesen.'

[28] Cf. Faustus, iii. 13, Lauer, p. 27: 'Schon längst, von der Zeit an, da [die Armenier] den Namen des Christentums angenommen, hatten sie dieses allein als menschliches Gesetz und nicht mit glühendem Glauben, sondern als einen der Menschheit aufgenötigten Betrug hingenommen, nicht wie es sich gebührt hätte, mit Wissen, Vertrauen und Glauben.'

for his western campaign. We know from Ammianus Marcellinus[29] that when Constantius was starting in 360 to meet the usurper Julian he summoned Arsak to his court and crowded favours upon him in order to secure his loyalty: in the same way when he set forth in 350 he would seem to have bound the Armenians to the Roman alliance by restoring to them their revered catholicos. The pressing need for present tranquillity in the Roman east drove him to relinquish his wider schemes for Armenia's conversion. If this be the true explanation, it is to Faustus alone that we owe a deeper insight into the emperor's statesmanship and his loyalty to his great trust.[30]

As we have seen from the analysis previously given, after the return of Nerses, which we may provisionally place in A.D. 350, Faustus gives an account of the deaths of Gnel and Tirith and of the forced marriage of Gnel's widow Pharrantsem with Arsak. Her dislike for this union caused the king to ask a wife of the emperor. Ammianus Marcellinus informs us that Constantius complied with the request and sent Olympias to the Armenian court; she was the daughter of the former praetorian praefect Ablabius, and had been *sponsa* of the emperor's brother Constans; the latter, however, died in 350, and therefore it is only after that date that his betrothed could have become the wife of Arsak. Further, we learn[31] that Arsak did not travel in person to fetch his consort, and we therefore naturally expect to find some mention of a mission from Constantius to act as conduct for so distinguished a lady. It is thus a natural conjecture that this was the purpose of the journey into Armenia of Taurus the quaestor, which according to Ammianus took place in 354. The matter is only mentioned incidentally by the Roman historian and no reason is given, but we do know that Taurus was despatched upon his errand directly from the court of Constantius.[32] If this explanation be correct, the marriage of Arsak with Olympias took place in 354. It was not long, however, before she fell a victim to the craft of Pharrantsem, and the Armenian king might thus

---

[29] See *infra*, p. 196.
[30] As already noted (p. 188, n. 7) the insertion of the extraneous material in bk. iii. 8–10 which closes with the death of Valens has produced a confusion in the resumptive sentence at the beginning of c. 13.
[31] Lauer, p. 95.   [32] Amm., xiv. 11, 14.

naturally expect to have aroused the wrath of Rome and be
predisposed to turn to the protection of Persia. King Sapor
was absent at this time waging a long and distant frontier war,
but the forays of his generals upon Armenia were evidence of
his disapproval of Arsak's alliance with the Empire.[33] Disunion
had rent the Mamikonian house—one of the greatest families
amongst the Armenian nobility; the elder brother Wardan
favoured alliance with Persia, while the younger, the general-
in-chief Wasak, was loyal to the Empire. Sapor with the help
of Wardan induced Arsak to journey to the Persian court, and
there forced him to swear a solemn oath upon the gospel that
he would be loyal to Persia and would have no dealings with
Rome. But Wasak, envious of Wardan's success, warned the
king of Persian treachery, and Arsak fled. Supported by the
queen Pharrantsem, whose former husband had been slain by
Wardan, Wasak murdered his brother: again Armenia seemed
driven into the arms of Rome.

At this point the chronology of Faustus supports our conjec-
tural date for the marriage of Olympias. From the flight of the
king down to the time of the peace of Jovian, when hostilities
between Armenia and Persia broke out afresh (i.e. in 364),
eight years elapsed.[34] The flight of Arsak from Persia must
accordingly be placed in A.D. 356, which is precisely the period
which we might have expected. Between 354 and 356 fell the
murder of Olympias and Arsak's consequent fear of the wrath
of Rome.

But suddenly the position of affairs in the east assumed a
new complexion. Sapor's frontier wars were over and he therefore abruptly terminated the negotiations for peace which had
been opened by the praetorian praefect Musonianus.[35] A Persian embassy demanded that Mesopotamia and Armenia
should be surrendered by Rome, and an immediate invasion
of the Empire was threatened if these terms were refused.
Envoys from Constantius professed willingness to conclude an
honourable peace but would not hear of the cession of Armenia

---

[33] Amm., xv. 13, 4: 'Persici duces vicini fluminibus, rege [i.e. Sapor] in ultimis
terrarum suarum terminis occupato, per praedatorios globos nostra vexabant,
nunc Armeniam, aliquoties Mesopotamiam confidentius incursantes, Romanis
ductoribus ad colligendas obedientium exuvias occupatis.'

[4] Faustus, iv. 21.   [35] Cf. Amm. Marcellinus, xvi. 9, 1–4, xvii. 5.

or Mesopotamia.[36] Thus with every prospect of a renewal of the struggle between the two powers Arsak 'looked forth to see who first of the contending parties would sue for his support in the war. He waited, since his desire was to march to the help of the emperor of Greece, but the Greeks did not invite his assistance and showed him neither regard nor honour'.[37] The explanation is simple: Constantius was far distant in Sirmium; and affairs in Asia were in hopeless confusion, for Ursicinus had been removed and Sabinianus was utterly incapable. There was no statesman in the east to secure the support of Armenia's king. Sapor, on the other hand, sent an embassy courteously requesting alliance: 'If thou art on our side', wrote the Persian monarch, 'the victory is ours.' Arsak was won, and his general Wasak was ordered to raise an army. An attack on Nisibis was planned, which was to be supported by the troops of Persia, but, as their arrival was delayed, the Armenian soldiers forced their king to take immediate action. The foray upon the country round Nisibis was successful and the booty captured was enormous (A.D. 359). Such is the account of Faustus, and though the part played by Arsak is not mentioned by our western authorities, the latter tend to support the Armenian historian.[38]

Ursicinus had been ordered by Constantius to return to the east, but he could effect little as his position was now that of a subordinate to Sabinianus. The first act of Ursicinus was to hurry with all speed to Nisibis in order to improve its defences, and on the way he was all but captured by marauding parties of the enemy.[39] Further, we know that the Persian army was delayed by the magnitude of its preparations: it was midsummer before the Tigris was crossed. Sapor's plan of campaign had been to strike for Syria, but he was detained by the long siege of Amida. He did not intend to attack Nisibis, and the devastation about that city was only committed by *vastatoriae manus* of the enemy.[40] The narrative of Faustus at once elucidates and supplements Ammianus's account.

[36] The references are conveniently collected by Seeck, in *P.-W.*, iv. 1, cols. 1083–4.

[37] Faustus, iv. 20, Lauer, p. 101.

[38] That Wasak acted *against* as well as for Rome is also implied in the figure of the two mountains : Faustus, iv. 54, Lauer, p. 134.

[39] Cf. Amm., xviii. 6.   [40] Ibid., 7, 4; 6, 9.

Persia as a reward for this harrying of the Empire offered Armenia alliance and proposed that Arsak should wed Sapor's daughter; a new marriage should consecrate the new loyalty; the celebrations should take place in Assyria. The Armenian troops, however, refused to leave the country, for each man longed to return to his home; it has always been difficult to hold together for any long period an army composed of feudal levies. Andok, the father of the queen Pharrantsem, fearing that his own daughter might be despised if Arsak married a Persian princess, won over by wholesale bribery a noble of the Sassanid court and a large number of Armenian satraps. One and all professed that the overtures of Sapor were inspired by a treacherous desire to secure the person of Arsak. The Armenian king fled precipitately and the negotiations were fruitless.[41]

Constantius was now himself in the east: he realized the omissions of his agents; if he were to feel free to leave Asia in order to combat the rebel Julian, the loyalty of Arsak must be regained. The passage of Ammianus, xx. 11, 1–3, is highly important in this connexion:

Constantius adcitum Arsacen Armeniae regem summaque liberalitate susceptum praemonebat et hortabatur ut nobis amicus perseveraret et fidus. Audiebat enim saepius eum temptatum a rege Persarum fallaciis et minis et dolis, ut Romanorum societate posthabita suis rationibus stringeretur. Qui crebro adiurans animam prius posse amittere quam sententiam, muneratus cum comitibus quos duxerat redit ad regnum nihil ausus temerare *postea* promissorum, obligatus gratiarum multiplici nexu Constantio.

It might be suggested that in the word *postea* we have an implicit recognition by Ammianus of the truth of the account of Faustus. The western author in his turn is corroborated by the Armenian historian:

For eight years after the departure and flight of King Arsak of Armenia from the Persian king Sapor (as we have seen A.D. 356) the Persian king spoke no word of enmity. Rather he carried on negotiations adopting quite a humble tone, and besought King Arsak of Armenia to remain in close and friendly ties of alliance with him. For the king of Persia was in pressing danger of immediate and ceaseless armed attacks from the king of the Greeks. Yet King

[41] Faustus, iv. 20.

Arsak of Armenia would not yield to his entreaties or meet him, and if the king of Persia sent ambassadors to him he refused either to give presents or draw near to him at all; he would not even hear the ambassadors' names. Still the king of Persia sent very often to him presents and ambassadors, but came with all speed to terms with the king of Greece.[42]

Thus was Arsak loyal alike to Constantius and Julian, not merely rejecting the overtures of Persia, but during the war of 363–4 even ravaging Chiliocomum on Julian's instructions.[43] In 364 the peace of Jovian was signed; the terms are thus given by Faustus:

The emperor of Greece sealed and subscribed a treaty wherein was written 'I have given unto thee the town Mdsbin (Nisibis) which lies in Arovestan, Assyrian Mesopotamia, and the half of Armenia. I permit thee if thou art able to conquer and subdue the same: I will not come to their help'. Forced and in dire distress the king of Greece subscribed to this form of words as his decree and gave it to the king of Persia.

Vengeance for the ravaging of Chiliocomum and freedom to invade Armenia at his will were among the ends which Sapor sought to obtain by this treaty.[44]

[42] Ibid., 21.

[43] For the ravaging of Chiliocomum, cf. Amm., xxv. 7, 12. Why Arsak took no more effective action against Persia during Julian's campaign still remains obscure. Libanius hints at mutual jealousies amongst the Roman commanders, but it is noticeable that during the fourth century we hardly ever hear of unprovoked attacks upon Persia by Armenia. Arsak was forced to depend upon the forces of a feudal nobility who were deeply influenced by Persian thought and culture. Cf. Gutschmid, 'Über die Glaubwürdigkeit der armenischen Geschichte des Moses von Khoren' in *Kleine Schriften*, iii. p. 282 sqq. at p. 291: 'In Abstammung Sprache und Sage hing das armenische Volk mit Iran zusammen, die Cultur des Adels war eine persische und ist es in Armenien und seinen Nebenländern trotz der Verschiedenheit der Religion bis auf die neueste Zeit geblieben'; and H. Gelzer, 'Zur armenischen Götterlehre,' loc. cit. pp. 103 sqq. It is further important to notice that the natural difficulties of the march were considerable. These detained Bindoes and John when on their way to join the Roman forces under Narses in 591: they were advancing from Armenia towards the river Zab. Cf. Theophylact. Sim. v. 8, 3, De Boor, p. 202, 22: ὡς δὴ τῆς περὶ τὴν Ἀρμενίαν Ῥωμαϊκῆς στρατοπεδεύσεως διὰ τὴν δυσχωρίαν τῶν τόπων οὐχ οἵας τε οὔσης συνάπτεσθαι ταῖς ἑῴαις τῶν Ῥωμαίων δυνάμεσιν and see H. C. Rawlinson, 'Notes on a Journey from Tabriz through Persian Kurdistan,' etc., *Journal of the Royal Geographical Society*, x (1840), pp. 1 sqq., and his memoir on the site of the Atropatenian Ecbatana, ibid., at pp. 71 sqq.

[44] Cf. Amm., xxv. 7, 12: 'Quibus exitiale aliud accessit et impium ne post haec ita composita Arsaci poscenti contra Persas ferretur auxilium amico nobis semper i.e. [all through the recent war] et fido. Quod ratione genuina cogitatum est ut puniretur homo qui Chiliocomum mandatu vastaverat principis et remaneret occasio per quam subinde licenter invaderetur Armenia.' See also Zosimus, iii. 31, 2: προσαφείλοντο δὲ καὶ Ἀρμενίας τὸ πολὺ μέρος οἱ Πέρσαι, βραχύ

Ammianus himself seems not to admit[45] that by the terms of Jovian's surrender Persia was allowed a free hand in Armenia, but his history as a whole serves only to confirm the view that Faustus has given us an accurate summary of the treaty.[46] Forthwith in 364 Sapor began to enforce his conception of his rights,[47] and endeavoured to subject Armenia.[48]

Calcata fide sub Ioviano pactorum iniectabat Armeniae manum ut eam velut placitorum abolita firmitate ditioni iungeret suae. Et primo per artes fallendo diversas nationem omnem renitentem dispendiis levibus adflictabat sollicitans quosdam optimatum et satrapas, alios excursibus occupans improvisis.[49]

Faustus gives us the detailed commentary on these words of Ammianus:[50] between 364 and 369 he chronicles twenty-seven forays into Armenia. For most of these Merushan, an Armenian fugitive who had become a convert to the Magian religion, acted as guide: one expedition was led by prince

τε ταύτης ʽΡωμαίοις ἔχειν ἐνδόντες: and Libanius, Förster, ii. p. 518, l. 12, ʼΑρμενία πᾶσα was surrendered to the enemy.

[45] Cf. Amm., xxvi. 4, 6: 'Persarum rex manus Armeniis iniectabat, eos in suam dicionem ex integro vocare vi nimia properans sed iniuste causando quod post Ioviani excessum cum quo foedera firmarat et pacem nihil obstare debebit quo minus ea recuperaret quae antea ad maiores suos pertinuisse monstrabat.' In this passage Ammianus seems to base the claim of Persia on the fact of the death of Jovian: Persia by his decease was freed from her obligations. This can hardly be intended. Elsewhere Sapor's claim is that he is free to act in Armenia *because of* and not in spite of the treaty of Jovian. Cf. Amm., xxvii. 12, 1–2 (quoted *infra*, n. 49).

[46] Cf. Amm., xxv. 4, 7, 12, quoted *supra*, n. 44.

xxvii. 12, 10: 'sed pro tempore adiumentis negatis per Terentium ducem Para reducitur in Armeniam recturus interim sine ullis insignibus gentem, quod ratione iusta est observatum ne fracti foederis nos argueremur et pacis.'

xxvii. 12, 15. After the arrival of Count Arinthaeus in Armenia the Persians did not at once invade the country, 'hoc solo contenti quod ad imperatorem misere legatos petentes nationem eamdem ut sibi et Ioviano placuerat non defendi.'

xxvii. 12, 18, after Roman interference in Hiberia: 'his percitus Sapor pati se exclamans indigna quod contra foederum textum iuvarentur Armenii.'

xxix. 1, 2. Trajan and Vadomar are only to act on the defensive, 'hoc observare principis iussu adpositi ut arcerent potius quam lacesserent Persas . . . [s. 3,] operaque consulta retrocedentes ne ferro violarent adversorum quemquam primi et iudicarentur discissi foederis rei, ultima trudente necessitate congressi sunt.'

[47] Faustus, iv. 21, Lauer, p. 107; Amm., xxvi. 4, 6 (quoted *supra*, n. 45).

[48] In what follows I presume a knowledge of F. Reiche's *Chronologie der letzten 6 Bücher des Ammianus Marcellinus* (Liegnitz, 1889), and of O. Seeck's 'Zur Chronologie und Quellenkritik des Ammianus Marcellinus' in *Hermes*, xli (1906), pp. 480–539.

[49] Amm., xxvii. 12, 1–2.

[50] Faustus, iv. cc. 21–49. The numbers of the invaders are doubtless grossly exaggerated, cf. Hans Delbrück, *Geschichte der Kriegskunst*, II. ii. ch. iv. Zahlen, pp. 298 sqq.

Dekhan, of the Armenian Mamikonian house; another by Suren Pahlav, a relative of Arsak; while two others were captained respectively by Hrevshoghum, of the same race as Arsak, and Aghanaiosan, a Pahlav of the Arsacid house. The history of the Armenian writer is thus a complete corroboration of that which Ammianus says was the result of the peace of Jovian: 'Unde postea contigit ut ... Armeniae maximum latus Medis conterminans inter dissensiones et turbamenta raperent Parthi.'[51] As a result of the wholesale defections of the Armenian nobility the kingdom fell into utter disorder:[52] the king was distrusted and the counsels of Nerses were disregarded:[53] subjection to a fire-worshipping heathen seemed less terrible than the unbearable sufferings from constant rapine and slaughter. Only Andok, the king's father-in-law, and Wasak his general remained loyal,[54] and ultimately Arsak was compelled against his will to submit to Persia[55] and to journey with Wasak to the court of Sapor.[56] In the thirtieth year of his reign he gave up the long struggle.[57] This is an important point gained for the chronology of the eastern question as it affects the policy of Valens. Reiche,[58] relying only on inferences from Ammianus, had conjecturally placed the capture of Arsaces in the years 364-6: we now know that it did not occur till the end of 368 or the beginning of 369.[59]

With Arsak in his power, the Persian king began the work of the total subjection of Armenia and the establishment of fire-worship in that country. Faustus is only concerned with the history of his own people, but we learn from Ammianus[60] that Sapor took the further step of interfering in the affairs of Hiberia (in 369 it would appear). He drove out Sauromaces, who had been raised to the throne through the influence of Rome, and instated Aspacures, conferring upon him a diadem in recognition of Persia's overlordship. In Armenia the queen

---

[51] Amm., xxv. 7, 12.   [52] Faustus, iv. c. 50.   [53] Ibid., c. 51.
[54] Ibid., c. 51.   [55] Ibid., c. 52.   [56] Ibid., c. 53.
[57] Ibid., c. 54, cf. c. 51 *ad init.* Wasak was put to death in Persia.
[58] Reiche, op. cit., ch. 6, pp. 27 sqq.
[59] Arsak's death took place at a considerably later date: Faustus, v. 7. Ammianus, xxxii. 12, 3, in fact anticipates the death of Arsak. *Deinde* (in xxvii. 12, 4) means 'after Arsak's capture', which is the real subject of xxvii. 12, 3.
[60] xxvii. 12, 4.

with 11,000 men[61] took refuge in the fortress of Artagherk.[62]
At this point in his narrative Ammianus tells us that two prominent Armenian renegades, Cylaces and Artabannes, who
were besieging the fortress, played Sapor false, and failing in
their endeavours to induce Pharrantsem to surrender allowed
her son Pap (Para) to escape from Artagherk and take refuge
in Roman territory.[63] In view of the many Armenian nobles
who acted now for their country and now for the interests of
Persia,[64] it is hardly surprising that Cylaces and Artabannes
are not mentioned by Faustus.[65] He does not, however, contradict Ammianus's account: we learn from him that while the
Persians were ravaging Armenia and the long blockade of the
castle of Artagherk continued, Mushegh, son of the murdered
general Wasak, joined Pap on Roman soil and appealed to the
emperor for his support. But Valens feared to violate the terms
of the peace of Jovian; he clearly felt that his right to interfere
was doubtful, and considered that he could satisfy his scruples
by a compromise: Terentius, the Roman dux, should return
with Pap, but the troops of Rome should not oppose Persia;
the Arsacid prince should assert his own authority, if he had
the power, but the emperor would not confer upon him the
insignia of a king.[66] It was a futile step while at the moment
Sapor was harrying all Armenia, and it is remarkable that
Faustus does not date the accession of Pap from this period,
although he recognizes the goodwill displayed by Rome.[67]
Messages came from Pap[68] to Pharrantsem week after week
bidding her be of good hope and not surrender. But Rome
would give no military help, and before Sapor's ravages the

[61] So at least Faustus, iv. c. 55.   [62] Artogerassa: Amm., xxvii. 12, 5.

[63] Valens accorded him a residence at Neocaesarea, which naturally incensed
Sapor.

[64] Cf. Faustus on Merushan, especially at v. 38.

[65] Their names were well known to the Romans, as their subsequent murder
by King Pap was one of the arguments against that monarch raised by Terentius at a later date in his despatches to the emperor: Amm., xxx. 1. 3.

[66] Amm., xxvii. 12, 10.

[67] Cf. Lauer, p. 136: 'Während sie [the ambassadors] mit dem Könige der
Griechen verhandelten, vermochten sie diese, ihnen Hilfe zu bringen.' This
embassy, it may be noted, was, it seems, planned by Cylaces and Artabannes
after they had permitted the escape of Pap: 'Qua humanitate [Cylaces et Arta-
bannes] illecti [i.e. Valens' welcome to Pap] missis oratoribus ad Valentem
auxilium eundemque Param sibi regem tribui poposcerunt,' Amm., xxvii. 12, 9.

[68] 'From her son Arsak,' as Faustus says, iv. 56. This is, of course, only the
standing title of all Armenian kings; cf. Professor Bury's note to Gibbon, ii. p. 564.

Armenian prince, with Cylaces and Artabannes, was forced to take refuge in the mountainous district which divided Lazica from the territory of the Empire.[69] Faustus gives a terrible picture of pillage and rapine in Armenia (370): at length in the fourteenth month the garrison could hold out no longer; the queen was carried off to her death, and Artashat, Waghar-shapat, Sarehavan, and other towns fell into the hands of Persia.[70] Sapor appointed generals to hold the captured forts; Sik and Karen were left in command of the troops, while the Armenian renegades, Wahan and Merushan, were entrusted with the government of Armenia and the introduction of the Magian religion.[71]

At last, in 371,[72] Valens decided that he could not allow the Armenians to suffer unprotected, should the Persian ravages begin afresh; he took effective action, and despatched Count Arinthaeus[73] with an army.[74] Terentius had accompanied Pap to Armenia in the former year. It is precisely at this point that Faustus tells of the successful result of Mushegh's mission and of the accession of Pap. 'The great king of the Greeks made Pap, the son of Arsak, king over the land of Armenia, as Mushegh had prayed of him. The king of Greece became a strong support of Armenia, and sent a general, by name Terentius, and a Count Ade with six million men in the train of King Pap to Armenia.'[75] Count Ade is not mentioned by Ammian,[76]

---

[69] Amm., xxvii. 12, 11.

[70] Faustus, iv. 55. It was in the winter of 370, 'sidere flagrante brumali': Amm., xxvii. 12, 12.

[71] Faustus, iv. 58–9. Wahan was soon after slain by his own son: Lauer, p. 144. On the efforts to set up the Persian religion, compare Moses of Chorene, iii. 36, and thereon Gutschmid, op. cit., p. 290. It is interesting to notice that at this time military and civil authority are separated and the former is given to Persian officers. It might be suggested that this was due to the fact of the dis-loyalty to Persia of the Armenian Cylaces and Artabannes; cf. Amm., xxvii. 12, 5: 'Cylaci spadoni et Artabanni quos olim susceperat [sc. Sapor] perfugas com-misit Armeniam—horum alter ante gentis praefectus, alter magister fuisse dicebatur armorum—iisdem mandarat ut Artogerassam . . . exscinderent.' Apparently Armenian renegades were entrusted with the *military* command in the first instance.

[72] Cf. Reiche, op. cit., p. 29.

[73] He had recently (at the end of 369) been conducting operations on the Danube.

[74] Amm., xxvii. 12, 13.

[75] Faustus, v. 1, a good example of the Armenian's exaggeration in regard to numbers.

[76] But compare Moses of Chorene, iii. 37.

O

but it can hardly be doubted that this is the Addaeus whom we know as *comes domesticorum* under Theodosius I, and who, in 393, held the position of *magister utriusque militiae per Orientem*.[77] The army of Rome now occupied the country: the newly erected fire-temples were destroyed, while Nerses left his retirement[78] and supported the restored monarchy; the captured fortresses were recovered, and the Roman troops were quartered 'in Errand and Bachischu through the whole land of Armenia, through all the cantons'.[79] Persia did not repeat the pillage of the previous year, but resorted to diplomacy: Sapor counselled Pap that Cylaces and Artabannes were plotting against him and they were in consequence beheaded; meanwhile an embassy complained to the emperor that this support of Armenia was in breach of the terms of the peace of Jovian. But Valens had taken action and he did not repent.[80] Hiberia was partitioned, and Sauromaces, the Roman nominee, was made king over that part of the country which bordered on Armenia and Lazica, Aspacures being left to rule over the district which adjoined Persia. Once more Sapor protested and prepared for war.[81]

In this year (372) the Armenian general Mushegh invaded the territory of Persia, and attacked the camp of Sapor which was pitched at Thauresh in Atrpatakan. Many captives were taken, among them some of Sapor's wives, who were honourably restored to their master by Mushegh. It is important to notice that Faustus, in entire agreement with Ammian, states that this was a victory of the *Armenian* troops: the Roman leaders only shared the booty.[82] Terentius with his twelve legions was indeed in all probability in Hiberia at the time of this campaign.

Valens had not as yet engaged Persia directly, but in 373 came the battle of Vagabanta (Ammianus) or Bagavan (Faustus), in which the Roman troops were forced to resist the Persian army. Ammianus writes as follows:

[77] Cf. O. Seeck, *Die Briefe des Libanius*, p. 48.
[78] Cf. *supra*, p. 187, n. 3.   [79] Faustus, v. 1, Lauer, p. 147.
[80] Valens reached Antioch in April 372.
[81] For the details of these measures read Amm., xxvii. 12, 14–18. The operations were carried out by Terentius with twelve legions.
[82] Faustus, v. 2.

Exacta hieme rex Persarum gentis Sapor pugnarum fiducia pristinarum immaniter arrogans, suppleto numero suorum abundeque
firmato erupturos in nostra cataphractos et sagittarios et conductam misit plebem . . . [Count Trajan and Vadomar are bidden to
act on the defensive] qui cum venissent Vagabanta legionibus
habilem locum rapidos turmarum procursus hostilium in se ruentium acriter exceperunt inviti; operaque consulta retrocedentes ne
ferro violarent adversorum quemquam primi et iudicarentur discissi foederis rei, ultima trudente necessitate congressi sunt: confossisque multis discessere victores.[83]

The parallelism of the account of Faustus is instructive: he
emphasizes the magnitude of the enemy's forces: Urnair, king
of Aghovia, claimed gifts from Sapor and undertook to oppose
the Armenian satraps, the Persian troops were to attack the
Romans.[84] Sapor himself marched as far as Atrpatakan and
there halted; the main army he sent forward into the heart of
Armenia.[85] King Pap gave orders to concentrate his own men
in Bagavan while the Roman allies marched from Errand and
encamped near the Euphrates. Terentius[86] would not allow
the Armenian king to fight in person: his master would hold
him guilty if any harm were to come to the king. The united
forces won a great victory over the Persian host. In this battle,
in striking agreement with Ammianus, Faustus tells us for the
first time that the Roman legions took part in the actual fighting.[87] Ammianus proceeds: 'inter moras tamen utrimquesecus
tentatis aliquotiens *levibus proeliis* varioque finitis eventu
pactis indutiis ex consensu aestateque consumpta (A.D. 373)
partium discessere ductores etiamtum discordes.'[88] Faustus
gives an account of the success of the Armenians and Romans
at Gantsak in Atrpatakan,[89] and then with him, too, follows
a peace. Mushegh proceeds to subdue the disloyal Armenians
and the neighbouring peoples.[90]

[83] xxix. 1, 1–2.   [84] Cf. *conducta plebs* in Ammianus.
[85] Cf. Amm., *misit.*
[86] Terentius, though not mentioned by Ammianus in connexion with this
battle, was still in Armenia, cf. Amm., xxx. 1, 3.
[87] I have of set purpose suppressed all mention of those details in the account
of Faustus which are more directly concerned with the internal affairs of
Armenia: see the whole chapter, v. 4.
[88] Amm., xxix. 1, 4.   [89] Faustus, v. 5.
[90] Faustus, v. 8–20. Sapor retired to Ctesiphon, Valens to Antioch, Amm.,
xxix. 1, 4 (winter 373–4). The conspiracy of Theodorus engaged the latter's
attention.

Nerses had now resumed his former commanding position in affairs of state, but the catholicos was hated by his sovran. Fear of Rome alone stayed Pap's hand,[91] but at length he murdered the patriarch; and when Caesarea refused to consecrate the king's nominee, Pap broke through the long tradition and caused Iusik to be consecrated in Basil's despite. He himself began to reduce the privileges and property of the Christian Church and favoured the restoration of the national paganism.[92] Such actions and the unfavourable despatches of Terentius led Valens to extend a kingly invitation to Pap: once on Roman soil the honoured guest became a prisoner (374?), while Terentius counselled that Valens should enthrone a new king in Armenia.[93] Fleeing from Tarsus through many dangers and difficulties Pap escaped to his own country with 300 followers.[94] Of this journey into the territory of the Empire Faustus says nothing, but he tells us that soon after the death of Nerses the king began by embassies to pave the way for alliance with Persia.[95] We learn that he sent to Valens the astonishing demand: 'Caesarea and ten towns belong to us; give them up: the city of Urha was also built by our ancestors; if you do not desire to arouse confusion give them up; if you refuse then we will fight for them in violent warfare.' Mushegh and the Armenian nobles pleaded with the king that he should remain loyal to Rome; but to no purpose. The story of the order for Pap's murder sent secretly by the emperor and the method of its execution is given by both authors, the only difference of any moment being that the feast at which the king was assassinated was according to Ammianus's version planned by Trajan, while Faustus ascribes the scheme to Terentius and Addaeus. It was probably a concerted plot on the part of all three commanders.[96] The Armenian nobles determined that they could ill afford to make both Rome and Persia their enemies and decided to attempt no revenge for the death of their king.[97] Sapor, in place of Pap, whom he had had every

---

[91] Faustus, v. 23.   [92] See the highly interesting chapter, Faustus, v. 31.
[93] Amm., xxx. 1, 1–4.   [94] Amm., xxx. 5, 17.
[95] Cf. Amm., xxx. 2, 1: 'Param [=Pap] sociare sibi impendio conabatur Sapor.' Ammianus appears to regard Para as an innocent against whom Rome had sinned without provocation; not so Faustus. For this claim to Caesarea and Edessa cf. Marquart, *Ērānšáhr*, p. 160.
[96] Faustus, v. 32; Amm., xxx. 1, 18–23.   [97] Faustus, v. 33.

hope of winning to his side, saw (A.D. 375) the Roman army of occupation instal with great pomp[98] an Arsacid princeling Warasdat upon the throne as nominee of the Empire.

Persia resorted once more to diplomacy. A legate, Arsaces by name, proposed to Valens that Armenia, the apple of constant discord, should be divided between the two Empires, or, if this was not agreeable to Rome, let the emperor withdraw his garrisons from Hiberia. The embassy is important as foreshadowing the partition of 387. During the autumn of 375 and through the year 376 it would seem that the negotiations continued. Victor, the *magister equitum*, and Urbicius, the *dux Mesopotamiae*, were sent with an ultimatum: the troops of Sauromaces were to evacuate Hiberia by the beginning of 377. The ambassadors complained that a Persian king who boasted himself to be just and contented with what was rightly his own was yet wickedly coveting Armenia when its inhabitants had been granted permission to live as it pleased them best.[99] The embassy, says Ammianus, performed its duty well, save that it went beyond its scope and accepted some small districts which were offered it in Armenia. This passage of Ammianus would seem to be explained by Faustus, who relates that Warasdat advised 'the Greek princes', and through them the emperor, that a town or two fortresses should be built in every canton throughout Armenia as permanent garrison centres, and that the nobles and troops of Armenia should be armed at the cost of the Empire to be a continual protection against Persia. The emperor willingly agreed to carry the scheme into execution. The small districts mentioned by Ammianus may thus have been intended for occupation by the Roman garrisons.

In the autumn of 376 Suren headed another embassy to the emperor offering to cede to Rome the land thus occupied, but returned with little accomplished.[100] Valens was raising Scythian mercenaries for an expedition against Persia in 377, when the whole position was changed by the news of the Gothic invasion. One highly important fact is mentioned casually by

---

[98] Faustus, v. 34, 'mit grossem Glanze.' Cf. the words of Ammianus, xxx. 2, 1: 'augentique nostri exercitus alacritate formidinem.'

[99] Cf. Amm., xxx. 2, 4.   [100] Ibid., sect. 7.

Ammianus—the Roman legions were recalled from Armenia
and sent to Europe:[101] this explains the fall of Warasdat before
Manuel, which must have taken place in this year (377).
Manuel having dethroned Rome's vassal king[102] was forced to
ally himself with Persia, and received Suren with a Persian
garrison of 10,000 men, agreeing to provide for the support of
these troops and to pay tribute to Sapor.[103] The account of the
Armenian historian receives striking corroboration from Ammianus's narrative:

> Sapor ultra solitum asperatus quod ad expeditionem accingi
> rectorem conpererat nostrum iram eius conculcans Surenae dedit
> negotium ut ea quae Victor comes susceperat et Urbicius, armis
> repeteret si quisquam repugnaret et milites Sauromacis praesidio
> destinati malis adfligerentur extremis. Haecque ut statuerat
> maturata confestim nec emendari potuerunt nec vindicari quia
> rem Romanam alius circumsteterat metus totius Gothiae, Thracias
> licentius perrumpentis.[104]

In the early months of 378 Valens before leaving for Constantinople sent Victor to Persia *ut super Armeniae statu pro captu
rerum conponeret impendentium.*[105] The disaster of Adrianople
tied the hands of Rome for some years, while in Armenia
Merushan[106] sowed discord between Manuel and Persia. The
attempts of Persia to defeat Manuel were unsuccessful (378),
and for seven years he ruled as regent for Sarmanducht and
the sons of Pap (A.D. 378–385).[107] Armenia enjoyed a brief
interval of peace and prosperity.[108] Sapor in his extreme old
age was content not to interfere, for Roman intrigue in
Armenia had ceased to be a danger.

---

[101] Amm., xxxi. 7, 2: 'legiones ab Armenia ductas.'
[102] Warasdat fled to the Empire and spent the rest of his days in exile;
Faustus, v. 37.
[103] Faustus, v. 37–8.   [104] Amm., xxx. 2, 7–8.
[105] Amm., xxxi. 7, 1.
[106] Merushan was ultimately defeated and killed by Manuel: Faustus, v. 43.
Cf. Gutschmid, op. cit., pp. 293–4, for criticism of the account of Moses of
Chorene.
[107] Faustus, v. 39–41.
[108] 'Seine Regentschaft bildete einen Lichtpunkt in der armenischen Geschichte und war vielleicht, die wenig bekannte erste Zeit des Terdat abge-
rechnet, die glücklichste Periode deren sich die christlichen Armenier je erfreut
haben,' Gutschmid, op. cit., p. 293. 'Die letzte gute Zeit des Reichs war die
Regentschaft des klerikalgesinnten Adelshauptes Manuels des Mamikoniers':
H. Gelzer, in Hauck, *Realencyklopädie*, vol. ii. p. 66, *s.v.* 'Armenien'.

In 384 an embassy arrived in Constantinople announcing the accession of Sapor III to the throne of Persia. (Sapor III, 383–388.)[109] On Manuel's death the link of a common faith induced the great protector to commend the young king Arsak[110] to Theodosius the champion of orthodoxy. Many of the nobility, however, appealed to Persia, and Sapor III set an Arsacid prince, Chosroes, to reign in Armenia as his vassal, while the Persian noble Sik undertook the government. Arsak was forced to flee to the protection of Rome, and was supported by the army of Theodosius. But diplomacy and not war decided the claims of the rival sovrans. An embassy from Sapor reached Constantinople in 386, and Stilicho represented the emperor at the court of Ctesiphon.[111] The former project was revived, and Armenia was partitioned between the powers who had so long distracted the unhappy country with their rivalries. Large parts of Armenia were annexed, and while Chosroes ruled over four-fifths of the remaining territory as the nominee of Persia, Arsak as Rome's protégé was sovran over but one-fifth of the divided realm (387). 'The kingdom of Armenia', writes her greatest historian at the close of his work, 'was reduced, partitioned, brought to ruin: it had fallen from its greatness then and for all time.'[112]

Our study is at an end: it has, we believe, served to illustrate and justify Gutschmid's judgement of the high value of the

[109] See Karl Güterbock, 'Römisch-Armenien und die römische Satrapien im vierten bis sechsten Jahrhundert; eine rechtsgeschichtliche Studie' (in *Festgabe der juristischen Fakultät zu Königsberg für ihren Senior Johann Theodor Schirmer zum 1. August* 1900, pp. 1–58) at pp. 11 sqq.

[110] Arsak had married Manuel's daughter Wardanducht: Faustus, v. 44. Cf. Gutschmid, op. cit., p. 294, on Moses, iii. 41, 2.

[111] Claudian, *De consul. Stil.*, 51 sqq.

[112] Faustus, vi. 1. I have not thought it necessary to repeat the arguments of Güterbock (loc. cit.) which in my judgement have established that A.D. 387 is the correct date for the partition of Armenia. So Hübschmann, *Die altarmenischen Ortsnamen* at p. 221. Nöldeke, however (*Aufsätze*, p. 103), places it under Bahram IV (388/9–399) in 390, while Marquart, *Ērānšăhr*, p. 114, thinks that the first division of the land occurred in 384 while the kings remained: the second division occurred in 389 when 'der König Arsak III verzichtete förmlich auf seine Hoheitsrechte und trat sein Land an den Kaiser ab'. Modern historians have blamed Theodosius I for this act (cf. H. Gelzer, 'in äusserster politischer Kurzsichtigkeit', in Hauck, loc. cit.), but during the whole century Armenia had been 'perpetua aerumnarum causa' (Amm., xxx. 2, *ad init.*). Theodosius needed peace in the east for his campaign against Maximus: it was also the Empire's need. I believe that in this matter the great Roman emperor has been hardly judged.

work of Faustus; it has enabled us to appreciate the difficulties with which Rome was faced upon her eastern frontier; and lastly it has given us a new confidence in the splendid accuracy and historical insight of Ammianus Marcellinus.

XII

The *Historia Augusta:* its Date and Purpose.
A Reply to Criticism

[*The Classical Quarterly*, xx (1928), pp. 166–71.]

MY suggestion[1] that the *H.A.* was written during the reign of the Emperor Julian and in his interest has had, on the whole, 'a bad press'.[2] Reviewers who have not thought it necessary to support with argument their doubts or their rejection of the theory are in a strong position: they remain practically unassailable. 'The theory seems on *a priori* grounds improbable':[3] a historical student can only reply that so is human nature—distressingly improbable, as he knows to his cost. 'After reading this book one puts it down "met een zekere onvoldaanheid" ':[4] what can an author do save express his regret for having caused Dr Van de Weerd this discomfort? But two stalwart defenders of the conservative position—De Sanctis[5] and Lécrivain[6]—have sustained with detailed argument their unqualified rejection of my theory; in their cases it is possible to attempt a rejoinder.

One of the outstanding difficulties of which any theory of the composition of the *H.A.* must take account is the contradiction between the praise of a legitimate dynasty—the 'Claudius' *motif* —and the elaborate attack upon the *Erbkaisertum*—the 'unworthy sons' *motif.* This contradiction I endeavoured to explain by reference to Julian's Claudian descent on the one hand, and to the misrule of the sons of Constantine on the other. Commenting on this attempted explanation De Sanctis writes (p. 405):

---

[1] Cf. *Classical Review*, xxxviii, 165–9; *The Historia Augusta: Its Date and Purpose* (Clarendon Press, Oxford, 1926).
[2] But cf. *C.R.*, xli, 82–3; *Journal of Roman Studies*, xvi, 137–40.
[3] *American Historical Review*, xxxii (1927), p. 638.
[4] *Revue Belge de Philologie et d'Histoire*, vi, 373.
[5] *Rivista di Filologia*, N.S., v, 402–6.   [6] *Revue Historique*, cliv, 113–14.

'A me sembra che la contraddizione in questo modo non si risolva punto. È assurdo infatti esaltare una dinastia o anche parlare di dinastie predestinate dagli dèi alla gloria, se si ritiene che i valentuomini o morirono senza figli o ne ebbero di tali che sarebbe stato meglio non fossero nati.' There is, of course, a formal contradiction, but it arises from the facts of history as interpreted by the S.H.A. The house of the Claudii *had* a great destiny, even though Diocletian died childless, and though Constantine left behind him a legacy of unworthy sons. To those who read between the lines of the *Tendenzschrift* would this antithesis have necessarily appeared 'absurd'? De Sanctis proceeds: 'La contraddizione invece si spiega bene se realmente la *H.A.* è, come vuol essere, opera di diversi scrittori dell' età di Diocleziano e di Costantino; perchè è naturale che vi si rispecchino le due tendenze contradditorie allora egualmente sentite ed egualmente difese circa la successione, quella che la voleva determinata dal merito e quella che la voleva deter-minata dalla nascita: la prima avvalorata da ciò che era lo spirito e la base dell' ordinamento dioclezianeo; la seconda favorita dalle aspirazioni di Costanzo Cloro e degli amici di lui e del giovane Costantino.' This explanation is, however, hardly satisfactory. Diocletian, it is true, in the first instance chose his colleagues *propter virtutem*: this might explain the 'merito' *motif*; but why should writers of the time of Diocletian make so sustained an attack upon the *Erbkaisertum*? We no longer believe that the hereditary principle was excluded from Dio-cletian's ordering of the succession.[7] The colleagues chosen originally on the ground of merit were destined to be the founders of Jovian and Herculian *dynasties*: 'Diis genitis et *deorum creatoribus*' in the words of the dedication on *C.I.L.*, iii, 710. The explanation put forward by De Sanctis still leaves the 'unworthy sons' *motif* an enigma. Indeed, it might be urged that De Sanctis has taken insufficient account of the writings of the Apostate: I would suggest that neither the 'Claudius' *motif* nor the 'unworthy sons' *motif* has been invented by the S.H.A.; each has been borrowed from Julian, and only the

---

[7] Cf. especially G. Goyau, 'La tetrarchie: sommaire d'une étude d'ensemble,' in *Études d'histoire juridique offertes à Paul Frédéric Girard par ses élèves*, i, 68–85 (Paris, 1912).

elaboration of those themes is the work of the S.H.A. The
Claudius *motif* is clearly stated by Julian: τούτοις ἐπεισέρχεται
Κλαύδιος εἰς ὃν ἀπιδόντες οἱ θεοὶ πάντες ἠγάσθησάν τε αὐτὸν τῆς
μεγαλοψυχίας καὶ ἐπένευσαν αὐτοῦ τῷ γένει τὴν ἀρχήν, δίκαιον
εἶναι νομίσαντες οὕτω φιλοπάτριδος ἀνδρὸς ἐπὶ πλεῖστον εἶναι τὸ
γένος ἐν ἡγεμονίᾳ (313D). The 'unworthy sons' *motif* arose in
Julian's mind from a contemplation of the reign of his hero,
Marcus Aurelius: two blots upon the fair fame of the philosopher emperor pained his disciple. Those blots are stated in
the arraignment of Silenus: τὰ περὶ τὸν υἱὸν καὶ τὴν γυναῖκα
πολυπραγμονῶν [sc. ὁ Σειληνὸς] ἁμαρτήματα, τὴν μὲν ὅτι πλέον
ἢ προσῆκεν ἐπένθησεν, ἄλλως τε οὐδὲ κοσμίαν οὖσαν, τῷ δὲ ὅτι τὴν
ἀρχὴν συναπολλυμένην περιεῖδεν, ἔχων καὶ ταῦτα σπουδαῖον κηδε-
στήν, ὃς τῶν τε κοινῶν ἂν προύστη κρεῖττον καὶ δὴ καὶ τοῦ παιδὸς
αὐτοῦ βέλτιον ἂν ἐπεμελήθη ἢ αὐτὸς αὐτοῦ. καίπερ οὖν ταῦτα πολυπραγμονῶν ἠδεῖτο τὸ μέγεθος αὐτοῦ τῆς ἀρετῆς· τόν γε μὴν υἱέα
οὐδὲ τοῦ σκωφθῆναι νομίσας ἄξιον ἐφῆκεν (312A–C). The charge is
repeated later when Silenus τὸ τέλος ἀπορούμενος . . . ἐπιφύεται
τοῖς περὶ τὸν παῖδα καὶ τὴν γαμετὴν αὐτῷ δοκοῦσιν οὐκ ὀρθῶς οὐδὲ
κατὰ λόγον πεποιῆσθαι, τὴν μὲν ὅτι ταῖς ἡρωΐναις ἐνέγραψε, τῷ δὲ
ὅτι τὴν ἡγεμονίαν ἐπέτρεψεν (334B). Marcus pleads in defence
that he was but imitating the gods (334B–D), and that in raising his son to the purple he was instituting no new custom:
παισί τε γὰρ νόμιμον ἐπιτρέπειν τὰς διαδοχάς, καὶ τοῦτο ἅπαντες
εὔχονται (334D–335A). The weakness of the plea is manifest, and
Julian's own view is doubtless rightly represented by Libanius:
ἀλλὰ μὴν ὡς γνήσιος ἦν κηδεμὼν τῆς ἀρχῆς καὶ ὡς τἀκείνης ἦγε
πρὸ τῶν ἑαυτοῦ, πολλαχόθεν μὲν δεδήλωται, σαφέστερον δ' ἂν ὡδὶ
γένοιτο. παρακαλούμενος γὰρ ἐπὶ γάμον παρὰ τῶν ἐπιτηδείων,
ὅπως παῖδας φυτεύσειε κληρονόμους τῆς ἀρχῆς, τοῦτ' αὐτὸ δεδιὼς
ἔφη μέλλειν, μὴ κακοὶ φύντες νόμῳ παραλαβόντες διαφθείρωσι τὰ
πράγματα τὸ τοῦ Φαέθοντος παθόντες. οὕτω τὴν ἀπαιδίαν τὴν
αὐτοῦ τῆς εἰς τὰς πόλεις λύμης κουφότερον ἔκρινεν (*Or.*, xviii,
§ 181). Here we have clearly expressed the 'unworthy sons'
motif of the S.H.A. The comment of C. W. King on this passage is: 'He had a warning in his own family, the conduct of the
three sons of Constantine' (*Julian the Emperor* (London, 1888),
p. 178). Precisely so. Nor is this all: in one passage of Julian
the two *motifs* of the S.H.A. are brought into close connexion:

οἱ παλαμναῖοι δαίμονες punished the sons of Constantine for their impiety αἱμάτων συγγενῶν τιννύμενοι δίκας, ἕως ὁ Ζεὺς διὰ τὸν Κλαύδιον καὶ Κωνστάντιον (i.e. Constantius Chlorus) ἔδωκεν ἀναπνεῦσαι (336B). I would not assert that the S.H.A. had read the *Caesares* of Julian, but I am convinced that they drew from the emperor's known views the inspiration for their *Tendenzschrift*.

I had suggested that the religious attitude of the S.H.A. mirrors the conciliatory policy of Julian in the early months of his reign. De Sanctis objects that 'la posizione di Giuliano verso il cristianesimo fu sempre d'avversione e anzi di battaglia'. This is in my judgement to do less than justice to the evidence as summarized by J. Bidez in his paper, 'L'Évolution de la Politique de l'Empereur Julien en Matière religieuse', *Bulletin de l'Académie royale de Belgique*, Classe des Lettres, etc., No. 7 (1914), pp. 406–61 (Bruxelles, 1914). But the further point raised by De Sanctis is of greater weight. If the project of a Persian war was known to the S.H.A. when they compiled their work, then by that time the emperor had declared himself the open foe of the Christian religion, and that change of policy must have been mirrored in the *H.A.* But this argument suggests a further and perhaps an unanswerable question— what was the attitude of the population of the western capital towards Christianity? In the aristocracy of Rome paganism found its last stronghold in the West; but if the *H.A.* is a 'Volksbuch', directed to a popular audience, it must necessarily have taken account of the beliefs of the Roman populace. If that audience were largely Christian, the writers of the *H.A.* may have had good reason for the striking reserve and the curious caution of their pagan apologetic. It must be remembered that after the abdication of Diocletian Maxentius ὁ τὴν ἐπὶ ῾Ρώμης τυραννίδα συστησάμενος ἀρχόμενος μὲν τὴν καθ' ἡμᾶς πίστιν ἐπ' ἀρεσκείᾳ καὶ κολακείᾳ τοῦ δήμου ῾Ρωμαίων καθυπεκρίνατο ταύτῃ τε τοῖς ὑπηκόοις τὸν κατὰ Χριστιανῶν ἀνεῖναι προστάττει διωγμόν, εὐσέβειαν ἐπιμορφάζων καὶ ὡς ἂν δέξιος καὶ πολὺ πρᾶος παρὰ τοὺς προτέρους φανείη (Eusebius, *H.E.*, xiv, 1), that in pursuance of the same policy he restored to Pope Miltiades the confiscated properties belonging to the Church (Augustine, *Brev. Coll.*, iii, 34), while he issued an edict of toleration for Africa (Optatus, *De Schism. Don.*, i, 18). It was in Rome that Constantine, after the battle of the Milvian Bridge, declared his allegiance to the God of the Christians; and it might be urged that modern historians, in writing of the reign of Valentinian I, have not always apprehended the significance of the hotly contested battles fought out in the streets of the western capital between the foes and the partisans of Pope Damasus. Is it fantastic to suggest that the strength of Christian feeling in the δῆμος 'Ρωμαίων determined the tone of the S.H.A.? If the *Vita Aureliani* had really been composed in the first decade of the fourth century and before the conversion of Constantine—De Sanctis dates it between 1 May 305 and 25 July 306—the studied moderation of its plea for paganism would appear to me, I confess, inexplicable.[8]

De Sanctis then considers the passage from *Vita Cari* 9, which on my theory was inspired by Julian's projected campaign against Persia: it contains the words, 'licet plane et licebit ut per sacratissimum Caesarem Maximianum constitit Persas vincere . . . et futurum reor si a nostris non deseratur promissus numinum favor.' On this he makes 'una osservazione che mi sembra capitale per fissare la data: così ovvia del resto che stupirebbe non fosse stata già fatta da altri': no one would have given to Maximian the title of Caesar after 1 May 305, when he was created Augustus. This proves that the *Vita Cari*, or at least this particular section of the *Vita*, was written between A.D. 297 and 1 May 305. We should be grateful to De Sanctis for calling our attention yet again to this passage: really Vopiscus was a very ingenious fellow! I had never previously noticed the effect upon the reader of the insertion of the word 'sacratissimum'. 'Ut per Caesarem Maximianum constitit'—'as was proved by Maximianus when Caesar'—in that

---

[8] The 'discretezza' and 'cautela' with which Vopiscus has proceeded in his defence of paganism are emphasized by Giovanni Costa in his valuable and suggestive study of the *Vita Aureliani*: 'Un libello anticristiano del secolo iv? Il Divus Aurelianus di Vopisco', *Bilychnis*, xxii (1923), 127–33. Costa would place the composition of *Vita Aureliani*, cc. i to xxxvii, 4, between the years A.D. 343 and 360; the rest of the *Vita*, which he would regard as an appendix by another hand, he is inclined to date in the reign of Gratian, at the time of the controversy between Symmachus and Ambrose over the altar of Victory. See further his paper on 'L'opposizione sotto i Constantini' in *Raccolta di scritti in onore di Giacomo Lumbroso* (=Pubblicazioni di 'Aegyptus', Série Scientifica, vol. iii) (Milan, 1925), pp. 293–8. I had not seen either of these papers when I wrote my book.

form the statement would not have admitted of any inference regarding the date of the composition of the passage: 'Caesarem' would have been neutral; but 'per *sacratissimum* Caesarem'—the use of the honorific epithet *suggests* the writing of a contemporary. It is, indeed, a much subtler touch than the method of bald assertion employed in the *Vita Aureliani*, 44, 5, 'et est quidem iam Constantius imperator.' Vopiscus must surely have chuckled as he penned the word.

De Sanctis closes his review with the remark that 'it is singular that the author should have allowed to escape him a work which, not without value in itself, would have been for him of particular importance in view of the affinity of the thesis there sustained with his own theory'. The reference is to the monograph of M. Giri: *In quale tempo abbia scritto Vopisco le biografie degli imperatori* (Torino, 1905). As I stated on page 108 of my book, Giri's monograph was only known to me from a review by Hohl; it is in none of our public libraries, and my efforts to obtain a copy had been unsuccessful. Through the kindness of Professor Hohl I have now been enabled to read the book. Giri would place the composition of the *H.A.* under Constantius II about the middle of the fourth century; the *Vita Probi* by its reference to civil war (23, 5) is to be dated to 350–1 (outbreak of war between Constantius and Magnentius); the *Vita Aureliani*, because of the mention of the consulship of Furius Placidus as a recent event, should probably be assigned to A.D. 345 or 346. The other Vitae of Vopiscus were in Giri's opinion composed between the years 345 and 351. His general contention is that Vopiscus, writing under Constantius II, had no desire to produce the impression that he was writing at any earlier date: in *Vita Aureliani*, 44, 5, the words 'et est quidem iam Constantius imperator' refer, indeed, to Constantius Chlorus, but *est* is here a historic present. Vopiscus had no political or dynastic purpose, he is no 'forger', but a simple rhetorician living in the world of his books. Thus he reports in all good faith the Probus oracle, and apparently knew nothing of the Probi who had already been consuls (!); immersed 'nelle idee dei neopitagorici e apolliniani', wishful for peace and silence, he was a stranger to the political and administrative world of his day. He was a pagan, and viewed the senate as the natural representative and champion of the older faith; he therefore claimed a restoration of its ancient rights.

I entirely agree with De Sanctis that the main thesis of the book is indefensible, and therefore, for my own purpose, there is little in the monograph which is of significance. But it may be noted that Giri recognizes that *Vita Aureliani*, 43, 3, 4, may refer to the *camarilla* formed at the court of Constantius, while to the question 'Why is there no mention of Constantine in such a passage as Aurelian, 44, 5?' he replies that Vopiscus, as a pagan, could not have said a good word for the first Christian emperor. It may further be remarked that Giri would explain the fact that Vopiscus says so little of Constantius Chlorus by the consideration that Constantius 'apparisce infatti qui (=*Aurelian*, 44, 5) come "un trait d'union" fra Claudio II e Costanzo II' (p. 62); to this I would agree, if for Costanzo II we read 'Giuliano l'Apostata'.[9]

Having thus sought to meet the arguments adduced by De Sanctis we may turn to consider the objections raised by Lécrivain.

1. 'Pourquoi ce subterfuge de compilateurs au lieu d'un panégyrique franc et sans danger?' A pertinent question to which I can give no adequate answer. I have already suggested that in Rome it may have been politic for the pagan propagandist to proceed with caution. The difficulty is not, of course, peculiar to my theory: it is inherent in the documents themselves. Why is the apology for paganism so amazingly discreet? What would be M. Lécrivain's explanation?

2. 'Beaucoup de mesures ont pu être répétées sous différents empereurs.' As a general statement this is indisputable; I would, however, desire to accentuate the *character* of the parallels—'specific acts which, so far as I am aware, do not recur associated with a single emperor in the history of any other reign—e.g. the clearance of the palace, the corn-supply

---

[9] If Giri is right, however, in his contention (pp. 31–3) that Vopiscus has carefully constructed a chronological scheme for his authorities—written sources for the period to which oral memory would not reach (*Vita Aureliani*, 15, 2; *Vita Probi*, 3, 4); the authority of his grandfather for the period from the death of Probus until after Diocletian's accession (*Vita Saturnini*, 9, 4; *Vita Bonosi*, 15, 4; *Vita Numeriani*, 13, 3; 14; 15, 5); and that of his father for the period after Diocletian's abdication (*Vita Aureliani*, 43, 2)—then my interpretation of the last-mentioned passage (pp. 97–8 of my book) will not stand.

of Rome, favours to Jews, treatment of eunuchs, governors taken up into the imperial vehicle, etc.', as I wrote in my book (p. 149). The character of this parallelism still appears to me strictly unexampled, and, until some real analogy be adduced, I shall continue to regard it as presenting a problem which needs an explanation. That explanation I have sought to supply.

3. 'La glorification du sénat était devenue, surtout depuis Aurélius Victor, un thème banal.' I should prefer to say timely, of living interest, because under Julian the theme had become 'practical politics'. But 'surtout depuis Aurélius Victor'—the phrase is interesting when written by M. Lécrivain: does this mean that he has adopted the Theodosian dating of the S.H.A.?—otherwise, if the composition of the *H.A.* is assigned to the reigns of Diocletian and Constantine, the words are curiously irrelevant.

4. 'M. Baynes parait placer la compilation dans la première partie du règne de Julien; mais ce n'est qu' après la fin de son règne qu' ils auraient pu utiliser toute sa législation. Quel eût été alors l'intérêt de ce panégyrique posthume?' None, I agree; but the public acts of Julian to which the author of the Vita of Alexander Severus may be deemed to refer are (i) the criminal commission at Chalcedon; (ii) the purgation of the imperial court; (iii) the corn-supply of Rome; (iv) the favour shown to the senate; (v) measures in favour of the fiscus and the municipia; (vi) favour shown to the Jews.[10] Nos. i–iv all fall in the first months of the reign; (v) the reference is to the constitution of March 362 (restored by Bidez and Cumont, pp. 52 sqq. of their edition of Julian's correspondence); (vi) no certain date can be given, for the question depends on the authenticity of Julian's 25th letter (Hertlein) which is disputed. If the facts there stated can be relied upon, Julian refused at his accession to enforce a special tax which Constantius was about to impose upon the Jews. I cannot see that there is any difficulty in the supposition that news of these measures had reached Rome a considerable time before the emperor's death.

5. 'M. Baynes n'a surtout pas le droit d'utiliser pour sa théorie des textes postérieurs, notamment Socrate et Ammien

---

[10] If the conjecture 'ius confarreationis' is adopted in 26, 3, the marriage law cannot be dated, for no such constitution has been preserved.

Marcellin.' So far as I remember, I referred three times to the Church History of Socrates: on p. 66 of my book to illustrate Julian's admiration for Alexander the Great; the fact of that admiration can be demonstrated from Julian's letter to Themistius; on pp. 124 and 139 I referred to *H.E.* iii, 1, for the eunuch régime of Constantius and Julian's purgation of the court: the evidence of Libanius suffices. Let us not insist on Socrates. But when M. Lécrivain complains of my use of the history of Ammianus Marcellinus, I fail to understand the ground of his objection: the history is, of course, 'un texte postérieur', but its author was strictly a contemporary of the Emperor Julian under whom he served; as the work of a contemporary the history, I would contend, can fairly be used as evidence in the consideration of our present problem.

6. 'L'attribution à Julien du rescrit d'Alexandre sur le christianisme, dans les termes où nous l'avons, est insoutenable.' I agree; I never supposed that the words 'Christianos esse passus est' are other than a plain statement of fact, and Julian's toleration of the Christians is unquestioned.

In a word, the arguments of M. Lécrivain directed against my theory have left me impenitent.

I wish to add a postscript:[11] when writing my book I was unable to adduce any parallel passage for two statements of the Vita of Alexander Severus. In c. 18, 3, we read 'adorari se vetuit'; with this cf. Libanius, *Or.*, xviii, § 190 of Julian, οὐ γὰρ τοὺς φόβους καὶ τὰς σιγὰς καὶ τὸ εἴσω τὴν χεῖρα ἔχειν καὶ τὸ κύπτειν εἰς γῆν καὶ τὸ βλέπειν εἰς τὸ ὑπόδημα μᾶλλον ἢ τὸ πρόσωπον καὶ τὸ δούλους ἀντ' ἐλευθέρων ὁρᾶσθαι . . . οὐ ταῦτα ἡγεῖτο τὴν βασιλείαν αὔξειν. . . . In c. 4, 1, we are told 'dominum se appellari vetuit': with this cf. Julian's words in the Misopogon 343C. ἡ δὲ εἰρωνεία πόση;—the paragraph is put into the mouth of the inhabitants of Antioch—δεσπότης εἶναι οὐ φὴς οὐδὲ ἀνέχῃ τοῦτο ἀκούων, ἀλλὰ καὶ ἀγανακτεῖς ὥστε ἤδη ἔπεισας τοὺς πλείστους ἐθάδας πάλαι γενομένους ἀφελεῖν ὡς ἐπίφθονον τῆς ἀρχῆς τοῦτο τὸ ὄνομα, δουλεύειν δ' ἡμᾶς ἀναγκάζεις ἄρχουσι καὶ νόμοις κ.τ.λ. Lampridius had, I believe, good authority for his statements.

---

[11] There is one misprint in my book, for which I apologize: for *Gothic* war on p. 119 read *Gallic*.

XIII

The Goths in South Russia

[*The Antiquaries Journal*, iv (1924), pp. 216–19.]

ONE of the most revolutionary reconstructions of history propounded by Professor Rostovtseff in his recent book on *Iranians and Greeks in Southern Russia* (Oxford University Press, 1922), would appear to have passed unchallenged; and yet, if it were accepted, it would surely mean that no inconsiderable part of the history of the Roman Empire and its invaders would have to be rewritten, or at least conceived in a new light. From the results of the excavation of German graves in South Russia dating apparently from the first century B.C. and from the first and second centuries of our era, he has demonstrated that the Dnieper basin was gradually occupied by German tribes during the early period of the Roman Empire, and that it is only in the light of this fact that we are able fully to understand the invasion of South Russia by the Goths. 'The Gothic invasion was not the first, but the last act of the activity of the Germans in South Russia.'

This is undoubtedly an addition to our historical knowledge which is of the first importance. But Professor Rostovtseff goes further. He shows that the earlier Scythian and Sarmatian kingdoms in South Russia had lived on the tribute paid in kind by the indigenous subject peoples: money was not used in their social economy. In the German graves, however, of the first and second centuries there are found not only Greco-Roman pottery and Greco-Roman jewellery, but Roman silver and copper money—the universal currency of the period. While this contact with the Greco-Roman world would seem to have been liveliest in the second century from the period of Nerva to that of Septimius Severus, most of the coins belong to the age of the Antonines. This would appear to mean, Professor Rostovtseff argues, that from the first the German population of the Dnieper region entered into direct relations with the

Roman provinces, and thus came to form a kind of annex to the Roman Danube trade. Many of the Germans in their old homes in Scandinavia and on the Baltic had been daring sailors: in their new homes they sought to gain access to the sea-shore which would give them the opportunity of plundering and holding to ransom the eastern part of the Roman Empire. The capture of Olbia and Tyras, ports on the Black Sea, was the natural sequence of the Gothic settlement in South Russia because these cities with their Roman garrisons were the chief obstacle which barred the free approach to the sea-way. 'The Germans did not aim at destroying the existing commercial relations and the existing commercial centres. They tried to use these relations for their own profit.' 'The cities continued to exist for some scores of years after they were captured by the Goths. But they ceased to be important commercial centres as the Goths ... preferred to enter into direct relations with the Greek cities on the Thracian Bosphorus and the southern shore of the Black Sea. . . . The Gothic epoch was accordingly a revival of the Scythian and Sarmatian state in a new shape.'

It is obvious that if the Goths were from the time of their arrival in South Russia a trading people in close contact with Greco-Roman markets, this would imply that we must entirely reconsider our picture of Gothic civilization, for this close contact could not have proceeded for some two hundred years without profoundly modifying the social life of the Goths. But is it necessary to interpret the archaeological evidence in this way?

In the first place it would be admitted that in our sources, such as they are, for the history of the Roman Empire in the third century, there is no hint of any such long continued peaceful intercourse, and if it had in fact existed, we might surely have looked for such in the extracts from the history of Dexippos preserved by Zosimus. So far as I am aware there is no suggestion that the Gothic forays and raids of the later third century mark a change of policy toward the Empire on the part of the Goths. But it might be objected that, when the character of our sources is considered, such an *argumentum e silentio* cannot be conclusive.

Professor Rostovtseff, as we have seen, considers that the capture of Olbia and Tyras was the natural sequence of the Gothic settlement in South Russia. We do not know when that settlement took place, but if, as is generally supposed,[1] it is to be brought into connexion with the movements of peoples on the Danube under Marcus Aurelius A.D. 166–80, it was certainly long before this natural sequence became an accomplished fact. Of the precise year of the Gothic occupation of Olbia we are ignorant: though coining appears to come to an end with the first half of the reign of Alexander Severus, from the fact that two soldiers of the Roman garrison dedicated an altar to Mercury in A.D. 248, we may conclude that the occupation must have been later than that date. Zosimus (i. 42) records a Gothic raid on the valley of the Tyras under Gallienus (A.D. 253–68): it would thus appear that the town of Tyras did not fall into Gothic hands until this reign (so Minns: cf. *Scythians and Greeks*, pp. 126, 448, 470, 644). But it was only in A.D. 256 that the Goths for the first time crossed to Asia to devastate the Roman provinces on the southern shores of the Black Sea. There would thus seem to be no sufficient interval between the Gothic occupation of Olbia and Tyras and the sea attacks on the Empire, during which the Goths could have developed a peaceful trade with the Greco-Roman ports.

But this is not all. When the Goths desired to convey their warriors across the sea, they themselves possessed no ships which might act as transports for their army, and they accordingly forced the Bosporan kingdom to supply them with convoys. Even so, the Goths did not themselves navigate the ships: Bosporan sailors ferried them across to Asia and then returned to Bosporos: the Goths only managed to make their way back to South Russia ὅσων δεδύνηντο πλοίων ἐπιλαβόμενοι (Zos., i. 31). On their second incursion they did not allow the Bosporan ships to sail away after the Gothic forces had been landed on the soil of Asia. In this raid they captured a large number of ships and took as prisoners skilled seamen whom they employed in further forays (πλοίων δὲ πολλῶν εὐπορή-σαντες καὶ τῶν αἰχμαλώτων τοῖς ἐρέττειν ἐπισταμένοις εἰς ναυτι-

---

[1] So Rappaport. Dr Minns would date the settlement to the early years of the third century (*Scythians and Greeks*, p. 126).

λίαν χρησάμενοι, Zos., i. 33). On the news of this success their barbarian neighbours wished to share in the spoil: πλοῖα μὲν κατεσκευάζετο τῶν συνόντων αὐτοῖς αἰχμαλώτων ἢ ἄλλως κατ' ἐμπορίαν ἐπιμιγνυμένων ὑπουργησάντων εἰς τὴν τούτων δημιουρ-γίαν, but they did not dare to make the same bold voyage as the former plunderers, but simply hugged the shore, the in-fantry accompanying them on land. When they had arrived at Byzantium, on learning that the fisher folk had hidden themselves with their boats in the marshes, they came to terms with them: the fishermen agreed to carry the Goths across the strait from Byzantium to Chalcedon on their fish-ing-boats (Zos., i. 34). The men who dared not venture from Byzantium to Chalcedon were no sea-traders.[2]

Gothic operations at sea cover the decade A.D. 256–67 and thereafter we never hear of any naval action on the part of the Goths: even Theodoric the Great in Italy possessed no fleet, until at the close of his reign he planned to build ships for use alike against the Vandal and the Empire. The maritime forays of the Goths were rendered possible simply by the fact that others provided them with ships and men to sail them. Pro-fessor Rostovtseff's view that the Goths 'preferred to enter into direct relations with the Greek cities on the Thracian Bosphorus and the south shore of the Black Sea' is untenable: we cannot conclude, therefore, that 'the Gothic epoch was accordingly a revival of the Scythian or Sarmatian state in a new shape'.

The presence of Roman coins in German graves must be otherwise explained: they probably came from the cities on the shore of the Black Sea from which the Germans may well have demanded money payments as the price of security from German pillage. We know that as early as A.D. 238 the Roman Empire was paying subsidies to the Goths.

[2] For Gothic lack of seamanship, cf. Zos., i, 42, 43.

XIV

Justinian and Amalasuntha

[*The English Historical Review*, xl (1925), pp. 71–3.]

THE chronology of the years 533 and 534 has been discussed by Dr Kohl,[1] Dr L. M. Hartmann,[2] Dr H. Leuthold,[3] and Dr Sundwall,[4] and these scholars do not agree in their conclusions. I think that a different interpretation of a phrase of Procopius may remove some of the difficulties. The accepted view of the course of negotiations between Justinian and the Ostrogoths in these years seems to be in brief somewhat as follows: the bishops Hypatius of Ephesus and Demetrius of Philippi were sent together with the imperial envoy Alexander to Italy in 533; they all left Rome for Constantinople at the end of March 534. There followed a delay of some months before Justinian dispatched his new envoy Peter in the autumn of 534, although Procopius asserts that Peter left for the west directly after the arrival in Constantinople of the former mission. There are obvious difficulties in this view; Alexander, we know, complained of the seizure of Lilybaeum by the Goths from the Vandals and of their refusal to surrender the fortress on the demand of Belisarius; but the Roman forces only set sail for Africa against the Vandal kingdom in June 533. How could Justinian before that time have obtained any knowledge of the Gothic occupation of Lilybaeum which itself was clearly a result of the Roman successes in Africa? Dr Sundwall, it is true, endeavours to obviate this difficulty by supposing that a subsequent 'special commission' was given to Alexander by the emperor, but this supposition is excluded by

---

[1] *Zehn Jahre ostgothischer Geschichte vom Tode Theoderichs des Grossen bis zur Erhebung des Vitigis (526–36)* (1877).

[2] *Geschichte Italiens im Mittelalter*, i (1897).

[3] *Untersuchungen zur ostgothischen Geschichte der Jahre 535–7* (1908).

[4] *Abhandlungen zur Geschichte des ausgehenden Römertums. Översigt af Finska Vetenskaps-Societetens Förhandlingar*, Bd. lx, 1917–18, Afd. B. no. 2 (1919). Professor Bury, in the new edition of his *History of the Later Roman Empire*, ii, 162, has not considered the chronological problem.

the account of Procopius.[5] The truth is, I would suggest, that Alexander only left Constantinople many months after the departure of the bishops. I would reconstruct the chronology as follows.

The bishops left Constantinople in June 533—the letter of the emperor which they bore to the pope is dated 5 June 533[6] —and travelled direct to Rome. Dr Sundwall must be wrong in dating their arrival at Rome in May 533. Here they were delayed, since the pope's desire to return a favourable answer to the emperor was opposed by the senators, who did not wish for too close a dependence upon Byzantium.[7] During their stay in Rome Theodahad broached to them his proposal to surrender Tuscany to the emperor upon terms. This explains the absence of any mention of Alexander in these negotiations, which has puzzled modern historians. Alexander, in fact, was not in Rome at the time. The battle of Ad Decimum, as Dr Leuthold has shown,[8] was fought in September 533; this victory opened the gates of Carthage to the Romans. Probably as a result of this Roman success the Goths in Sicily seized Lilybaeum, and word would doubtless be sent of this seizure to Constantinople. Meanwhile though the palace at Durazzo was ready for Amalasuntha, though her treasure-ship lay in harbour there, the queen herself remained in Italy. Justinian had every reason to wish to know the cause of that delay. Lilybaeum gave him his pretext: on receipt of the news of the occupation his envoy Alexander was dispatched to Italy. We know that in March 534 the pope at length gave his reply to the bishops; it is dated 25 March 534. Dr Leuthold considers that at this time Alexander's mission was already completed; he had left the Gothic court, had travelled to Rome, and thus returned from Rome with the bishops to Constantinople. This is, I think, a misunderstanding of Procopius. A confusion has, I believe, arisen through the identification of 'the bishops of Alexander' (τοὺς ἱερεῖς αὐτοῦ, i. 3. 16) with Demetrius and Hypatius. If we do not make this identification, the course of events may be reconstructed without difficulty. The passage

---

[5] Sundwall, p. 277, n. 1; Procopius, *B.G.*, i, 3, 14–15.   [6] Cod. Just., i, 1, 8.
[7] Sundwall, p. 276; Langen, *Geschichte der römischen Kirche*, ii, 322.
[8] p. 20.

from which to start is i. 3. 13. Procopius has described the illness of Athalarich and the consequent alarm of Amalasuntha;
he proceeds ἐτύγχανε δὲ ᾿Αλέξανδρος ἀνὴρ ἐκ βουλῆς σύν τε
Δημητρίῳ καὶ ῾Υπατίῳ ἐνταῦθα ἥκων, i.e. 'it happened that
Alexander had arrived at Ravenna together with Demetrius
and Hypatius'. The latter had received their answer from the
pope on 25 March, and we may thus place their arrival at
Ravenna on their return journey at the end of March or beginning of April 534. With this point fixed the rest is simple.
Justinian was not only anxious at the delay of Amalasuntha,
his ecclesiastical policy had been brought to a standstill by the
procrastination of the pope. Alexander is therefore accompanied by some eastern bishops (i. 3. 16). The reply of the pope
is to be regarded as the result of the arrival of this new mission.
The eastern bishops who accompanied Alexander are left at
Rome to continue Justinian's ecclesiastical propaganda. Alexander himself, together with Demetrius and Hypatius (i. 3. 13),
starts north and arrives, as we have seen, at Ravenna. There
follows the public discussion of the reply of the Gothic State
to Justinian's diplomatic complaints. Meanwhile Amalasuntha's intrigue and her offer to surrender Italy to the emperor are the subject of secret conference. These negotiations
may well have taken many weeks; it may have been full
summer before Alexander and the bishops left Ravenna. There
is therefore no reason to doubt the statement of Procopius that
Peter was dispatched by Justinian to Italy on his return
mission directly after the arrival of the envoys in Constantinople. I believe that Procopius was well informed on the course
of this diplomacy, and that we have only to interpret aright
his somewhat allusive account to establish a consistent
chronology.

But if Hypatius and Demetrius were in Ravenna during the
summer of 534, we may perhaps be entitled to make some
further deductions. Episcopal tongues may well have been set
wagging and Amalasuntha may have learned the secret of
Theodahad. She could outbid the offer of Tuscany by throw-
ing the whole of Italy into the scale. Procopius says that she
did. Dr Pflugk-Harttung, Dr Hartmann, and Dr Sundwall
amongst others have doubted this statement. But Amala-

suntha, with her son's death imminent, a woman and alone, was in a desperate position and she knew it; she could not afford the luxury of scruples. There follow the condemnation of Theodahad and the order to restore his ill-gotten lands. Theodahad should have the less wherewith to bribe Justinian. The weeks passed; Athalarich was sinking; she could not await Justinian's reply. Necessity makes strange bed-fellows; one traitor had need of another. Did she use her knowledge to bend Theodahad to her will? Did she feel herself secure in the possession of the secret which she alone shared with the king of her creation? It is tempting to think that the price at which she sold her silence was Theodahad's oath that he would be king in name only.

XV

The Icons before Iconoclasm

[*The Harvard Theological Review*, xliv (1951), pp. 93–106.]

'THE feeling against ikon-worship suddenly burst out in the earlier part of the eighth century when the icono-clastic (ikon-smashing) emperors of Constantinople tried to suppress the practice by force.' So wrote Edwyn Bevan in an admirable essay on Idolatry.[1] And from modern accounts of the iconoclast movement one does generally get the impression that after the violent challenge of Epiphanius in the fourth century—when he tore down a pictured curtain which hung in a church[2]—the East Roman world had accepted without protest and without question the widespread cult of the icon, while the policy of iconoclast emperors appears as a sudden breach with a universally recognized tradition. But is such an impression justified? When we put together such frag-mentary pieces of evidence as we possess is it not rather prob-able that there was a continuous questioning of the legitimacy of the cult? May not the part played by the icon in the life and religious usage of the Byzantine world have been subjected to the constant criticism of pagans, Jews and even of Christians? And if this is so, it may help us to understand somewhat more clearly the primary motives which inspired the policy of the iconoclast rulers. It may be worth while to consider the evid-ence afresh since it has been increased by two recent publica-tions.

In 1938 Franz Diekamp published[3] a fragment from the

---

[1] The *Edinburgh Review*, vol. 243, no. 496 (April 1926), pp. 253–72.

[2] I accept the authenticity of the Epiphanian documents. For a criticism of the argument of G. Ostrogorsky, 'Studien zur Geschichte des byzantinischen Bilderstreites' (*Historische Untersuchungen*, Heft 5) (Breslau, 1929), see Franz Dölger, *Göttingische gelehrte Anzeigen* (August 1929), pp. 353–72.

[3] In his *Analecta Patristica* (Orientalia Christiana Analecta, 117) (Rome, Pont. Inst. Orientalium Studiorum, 1938), pp. 109–53, text at pp. 127–9 [and see now Paul J. Alexander, 'Hypatius of Ephesus. A note on Image Worship in the Sixth Century', *The Harvard Theological Review*, 45, no. 3 (June 1952), pp. 177–84].

σύμμικτα ζητήματα—the 'Vermischte Untersuchungen'—of
Hypatius of Ephesus contained in the Codex Parisinus 1115
ann. 1276, fol. 254ᵛ–5ᵛ. These 'Mixed Enquiries' were addressed
to Julian, bishop of Atramution (in western Asia Minor), a suffragan bishopric of Ephesus. This fragment is from chapter 5
of the first book of the work and concerns τὰ ἐν τοῖς ἁγίοις
οἴκοις—'the things in the holy churches'. This text has not,
apparently, attracted any attention from scholars, yet it is of
considerable interest since Hypatius of Ephesus was a prominent champion of Chalcedonian orthodoxy in the reign of
Justinian. Julian of Atramution was troubled by the scrip-
tural prohibition of the making of images and by the command
to destroy such images when they had been made. He will
allow representations (γραφάς) in the churches, but none on
wood or stone and no sculpture. These γραφαί may be on the
door-curtains (ἐπὶ θύραις: I suppose this is how the words must
be translated), but no more is permissible. In his reply Hypatius urges that we must consider the reason for the Old
Testament prohibition, and at the same time we must seek to
understand why the making of sacred things (τὰ ἱερά) is
allowed as it is at present. Since some, as sacred Scripture says,
thought that the Godhead (τὸ θεῖον) was like gold and silver
and stones and graven works of art, and since they made
according to their own pleasure material gods and worshipped
the creature rather than the creator, God rejected their altars
and their idols (Hypatius quotes Romans i. 25, Deut. vii. 5,
iv. 15–16, Ps. lxxi. 19), for nothing of all the things that are
is like or equal to or the same as the holy Trinity and the
Maker and Cause of all things. But we direct that the unspeak-
able and incomprehensible 'philanthropy' (φιλανθρωπία) of
God towards us and the sacred images of the saints shall be
glorified in sacred representations (γράμμασι), though we ourselves have no pleasure at all in anything formed (πλάσει) or
any representation (γραφῇ). But we allow simpler and immature folk to have these as being fitted to their natural development, that thus they may learn through the eye by means
adapted to their comprehension. For we have found that often
and in many cases both old and new divine commands have
made concessions to the weak to secure their salvation.

Hypatius instances the hierophant Moses who at God's prompting had been his people's legislator and yet had been bidden to make the images of the Cherubim. 'And in many other cases we see the divine wisdom (τὴν θεολογίαν) with "philanthropy" (φιλανθρωπίᾳ) for man's salvation releasing the strictness of the law to benefit the souls of those who still need to be led by the hand.' It is the care which guided the magi by a star and which led Israel away from idolatrous sacrifices to sacrifice to God. Therefore we, too, allow material ornament in our churches, not as though we thought that God was a god of gold and silver and silken vestments and vessels adorned with precious stones, but making a concession so that each order of the faithful may be led by the hand in a way which is proper to itself and so brought to the Godhead. Thus of these, too, some will be led by the hand to spiritual beauty (ἐπὶ τὴν νοητὴν εὐπρέπειαν) and from the many lights in our churches to the spiritual and immaterial light.

And some of those who have studied the higher life (τὴν ὑψηλοτέραν ζωὴν φιλοσοφησάντων) have learned that worship in the spirit can be offered in every place and that it is holy souls which are God's temples. . . . So then we in our churches do not remove the sacred objects, but to the immature we stretch out a helping hand; we do not allow them to remain untaught concerning the more perfect doctrines, but them, too, we hold in the knowledge that the Godhead is not the same as any created thing nor is it equal or like to any such thing.

'As for ourselves we have no delight in the icons'—did that sixth-century view persist among the bishops of Asia Minor? And if it did, it can readily be understood that any general cult of the icons in such extreme forms as later appear in the apologies of the iconodules would seem dangerous and a wrongful use of a practice which was tolerated only in the interest of the weaker members of the Church. Here is an attitude which may help to explain the action of those bishops of Asia Minor who in the eighth century inaugurated the iconoclast movement.[4]

Through the sixth-century protest of Julian of Atramution

[4] See G. Ostrogorsky, 'Les débuts de la querelle des images', *Mélanges Charles Diehl*, i, 235–55.

we can observe the Christian criticism of the place taken by
the icons in the service of the Church. We tend, however, to
forget that not all the East Romans had been converted to the
imperial faith. And in a fragment from St Symeon's work on
the Sacred Images[5] we find the pagan argument that the Christians, too, through their obeisance to the icons were praying to
lifeless idols. It could not have been easy for the Christians to
refute the charge. The pagans, it is said, traduced the Christians and gave birth to heresies;[6] what those heresies were we
are not told; did pagan criticism lead to the rejection of the
use of the icons? A passage from the work of John, Bishop of
Salonica,[7] is in its argument unexpected. The Christians, says
the bishop, do not give corporeal forms to powers which have
no body; the icons of Christ through the effect of the Incarnation represent God as seen on earth 'and not as He is conceived
in His divine nature' (καὶ οὐχ ὡς νοεῖται φύσει θεός). This the
pagans—surely surprisingly—were prepared to admit; granted,
they said, that you can represent One made Man, what of the
angels pictured on the icons as human beings though the Christians regarded them as spiritual and incorporeal (νοερούς καὶ
ἀσωμάτους)? And to this objection the Christians replied that
the angels were not completely incorporeal (ἀσώματοι) as the
pagans contended, they are of the air or of fire and their bodies
are very fine. Angels are localized, they have appeared in
bodily form to those whose eyes God opened and are therefore
rightly so painted as spiritual created beings and ministers of
God (κτίσματα νοερὰ καὶ λειτουργοὶ θεοῦ). It would seem that
the essential point for the pagans was to establish that the
Christian use of the icons was idolatrous: the Christian rever-
encing the Cross was a worshipper of a wooden god; if he worshipped the Cross he ought to worship asses. The Christian
replied that no demon trembled when he saw asses.[8] And
under Justinian pagans were given a short shrift: they were
arrested and carried in public procession, their books were
burned and so were their 'icons and images of their foul Gods'
(εἰκόνες τῶν μυσαρῶν θεῶν καὶ ἀγάλματα).[9] Did pagan criticism

---

[5] *P.G.*, 86b col. 3220 (*P.G.* = Migne, *Patrologia Graeca*).
[6] *Byzantion*, xvii (1944-5), p. 66.   [7] Mansi, xiii, cols. 164-5.
[8] Pseudo-Athanasios, *P.G.*, 28, cols. 621-4.
[9] Malalas (Bonn ed.), p. 491, 19-20.

of the icons raise doubts of their legitimacy in the minds of the Christians? Our fragmentary sources give us no answer to such a question.

It is strange that, so far as I know, no study has appeared of the appeal of Leontius, Bishop of Neapolis in Cyprus, directed to the Jews who charged the Christians with having introduced idolatry into the Church. That appeal we possess only in fragmentary form,[10] but it is of great interest as giving us the defence of the icons as it was formulated in the early years of the seventh century. Leontius knew Egypt well, he wrote the biography of the Patriarch St John the Almsgiver;[11] and from the first many Jews had settled in Alexandria. It may well have been in Alexandria that Leontius composed his apology against the Jews (ἀπολογία κατὰ 'Ιουδαίων). We have in the *Pratum Spirituale* of John Moschus an account of Cosmas, a scholasticus of Alexandria, who possessed a large library—he was πολύβιβλος ὑπὲρ πάντας τοὺς ἐν 'Αλεξανδρείᾳ ὄντας (*Pratum Spirituale*, c. 172, P.G., 87, 3, col. 3040D) and generously lent his books to all who wished to read them. John Moschus went to see him daily and always found him either reading or writing against the Jews, for he was passionately desirous to convert them to the truth, 'And he often sent me to the Jews that I might discuss with them on the evidence of the Scripture.' This is the background which must be kept in mind as one reads the appeal of Leontius. A summary of that appeal (so far as we possess it) is the simplest way of illustrating its significance.[12]

The Jews took their stand upon the God-given Law, and for the Christians also that Law formed part of their sacred scriptures, since they had laid claim to the Old Testament as their own and refused to follow Marcion in rejecting the earlier revelation. And that Law had expressly ordained 'Thou shalt not make unto thee any graven image or likeness of any thing that is in heaven above or that is in the earth beneath or that

---

[10] I do not understand the relation between the text cited from Mansi, xiii, P.G., 93, cols. 1597–1609, and the extracts quoted by John of Damascus, P.G., 94.

[11] Translated in E. Dawes and N. H. Baynes, *Three Byzantine Saints* (Blackwell, Oxford, 1948).

[12] P.G., 93, cols. 1597–1609.

is in the water under the earth, thou shalt not bow down thyself to them nor serve them' (Exodus xx. 4–5). 'You shall make you no idols nor graven image . . . neither shall ye set up any image of stone in your land to bow down unto it' (Levit. xxvi. 1; cf. Deut. v. 8). Such was the tradition; but, Leontius argued, there was another legal tradition: God had said to Moses that he should fashion two Cherubim[13] graven in gold (Exodus xxv. 18), while God showed to Ezekiel a temple with forms of palms and lions and men and with Cherubim from pavement to roof (Ezekiel xli. 18). Thus had God revoked his own ordinance. 'If you wish to condemn me', wrote Leontius, 'on account of images (εἰκόνες), then you must condemn God for ordering them to be made.'[14] And though God gave no instructions concerning the adornment of His temple, yet on the legal precedent of God's command to Moses (ἐκ νόμου λαβὼν τὸν τύπον)[15] Solomon filled the building with lions and bulls and palm-trees and men in bronze and with carved and molten images. It was important for Leontius to prove that the Christians were not innovators, they were but maintaining a tradition derived from the scriptures which were sacred alike to Jew and Christian;[16] elsewhere in a passage cited by John of Damascus (P.G., 94, col. 1273) he meets an objection that might be raised by the Jews. 'It may be objected', Leontius writes, 'that all those things which were in the tent of witness God ordered to be placed there, and I reply that Solomon made many different things in the temple, carved and molten things which God had not ordered him to make nor were they amongst the things which were in the tent of witness nor were they in the temple which God showed to Ezekiel, but Solomon was not condemned for this, for he made these shapes to the glory of God just as we do.'[17]

Others, it may be noted, carried the argument still further. Thus Hieronymus, a presbyter of Jerusalem, suggested that

---

[13] For the argument derived from God's direction concerning the Cherubim see p. 228 *supra*.

[14] Cf. *P.G.*, 94, col. 1384 A–B.

[15] Cf. John of Damascus, *De Imaginibus Oratio*, III, *P.G.*, 94, col. 1384 A–B, quoting Leontius: Solomon ἐκ νόμου λαβὼν τὸ τύπωμα.

[16] Cf. ibid., col. 1381, s.f. νομικὴ γὰρ αὕτη ἡ παράδοσις καὶ οὐχ ἡμετέρα.

[17] Cf. *Byzantion*, 17 (1944–5), p. 59, 'Et Dieu ne désapprouva pas et il l'appela le temple de son nom.'

God had allowed each nation (ἔθνος) to worship its own gods
through things made by man in order that no one might be
able to raise objection to the Christian use of the Cross and the
Christian obeisance (προσκύνησις) before the icons. So the Jews
made their obeisance (προσκύνησις) before the ark of the covenant, the Cherubim and the tables of the Law, although Moses
was nowhere bidden to do obeisance to or to reverence
(προσκυνεῖν or ἀσπάζεσθαι) these things (P.G. 40, col. 865) and
the same view is expressed in a fragment cited in a note, ibid.

The reply of the Jew was that these images, permitted to be
made by God, were not to be adored as gods, but served only
to remind us. 'Well said,' responded the Christian, 'the same is
true of our icons.'[18] Elsewhere Leontius states that the godless (πανάθεοι) call the Christians idolaters and worshippers of
wooden gods (ξυλοθέους). In P.G. 94, col. 1384B, he rejects the
charge with scorn: 'We do not make obeisance to the nature of
the wood, but we revere and do obeisance to Him who was
crucified on the Cross' (ibid., 1384D). 'We do not say to the
Cross nor to the icons of the saints, "You are my God." For
they are not our gods, but opened books to remind us of God,
and to His honour set in the churches and adored' (ibid., col.
1276A). 'If we worshipped the wood of the image, we should
not burn the icon when the representation grew faint. When
the two beams of the Cross are joined together I adore the
figure because of the Christ who on the Cross was crucified, but
if the beams are separated, I throw them away and burn
them.' This argument is adopted by other writers.[19]

One who receives an order from the Emperor and kisses the
seal does not honour the paper, but gives to the Emperor his
obeisance and respect;[20] and in the same way, when we see the

---

[18] This theme of the function of the icons to keep alive men's memory is constant, cf. e.g. the citations of Leontius in *P.G.* 94, col. 1276 A ἀνάμνησις and in
ibid., 1385 A; ὑπόμνησις in 1384 B and *P.G.* 28 col. 621 D. John bishop of Thessalonica in Mansi, xiii, col. 164, on the icons of the saints εἰς τὸ μεμνῆσθαι αὐτῶν
καὶ τιμᾶν αὐτούς . . . ὡς γνησίους δούλους καὶ φίλους θεοῦ καὶ παρρησίαν ἔχοντας πρεσ-
βεύειν ὑπὲρ ἡμῶν. Of the icons we read in *Quaestiones ad Antiochum Ducem*, *P.G.*
28, col. 621, οὕσπερ δι' ὑπόμνησιν καὶ μόνον ἐντυποῦμεν καὶ οὐ δι' ἕτερον τρόπον; cf.
Stephen of Bostra, *P.G.* 94, col. 1376 B–D.
[19] Cf. 'Les trophées de Damas', ed. G. Bardy, *Patrologia Orientalis*, tome 15,
fasc. 2 (Paris, 1920), p. 245 (75)—Isaiah xliv. 14–17 quoted; *Quaestiones ad
Antiochum Ducem*, *P.G.* 28, col. 621 B and the fragment ibid., col. 709 A.
[20] Cf. *P.G.* 94, col. 1384 D.

representation of Christ, through it we hail and do obeisance
to the Crucified. Just as children, if their father is away, cherish
his staff or his chair, so we cherish the places which Christ
visited, Nazareth or the Jordan, and remember his friends, the
saints and the martyrs. And on account of Christ and of those
things which are Christ's, we figure His sufferings in our
churches and houses, in our market-places and on our garments—everywhere—so that through seeing them constantly
we may be warned that we should not forget. Then turning to
the Jew, Leontius says:

'You do obeisance to the book of the Law, but you do not make
obeisance to parchments and ink but to the words of God contained
therein. And it is thus that I do obeisance to the icon of God, for
when I hold the lifeless representation of Christ in my hands[21]
through it I seem to hold and to do obeisance to the Christ. As Jacob
kissed the bloody coat of Joseph and felt that he held him in his
arms, so Christians think that holding the image they hold Christ
or His apostles and martyrs.

You say that there must be no obeisance paid to anything made
by human hands or created. But haven't you, when wife or children
have died, taken some garment or ornament of theirs and kissed it
and shed tears over it and were not condemned for doing so? You
did not do obeisance to the garments as to God; through your kisses
you did but show your longing for those who once had worn them.
Fathers and children, sinners and created beings as they are, we
often greet them and no one condemns us, for we do not greet them
as gods, but through our kisses we express our natural love for them.
As I have said many times, in every greeting and every obeisance it
is the purpose of the action which is in question.[22] And if you accuse
me of doing obeisance to the wood of the Cross as though it were God
why do you not say the same of the staff of Joseph?[23] Abraham
did obeisance to infamous men who sold a sepulchre, and went on
his knees before them, but not as though they were gods. Jacob
blessed the idolater Pharaoh and did obeisance to Esau, but not as
though they were gods. Do you see how many salutations and obeis-
ances I have adduced out of the Scriptures and all without blame?
    You call us idolaters when it was Christian saints and martyrs
who destroyed the temples of the idolaters.'[24]

---

[21] Cf. τῇ σαρκί, *P.G.* ibid., 1385 B, and the fragment, *P.G.* 28, col. 709.

[22] Cf. *P.G.* 94, col. 1385 B, ὁ σκοπὸς ἐξετάζεται.

[23] *P.G.* 93, col. 1601, διὰ τί οὐκ ἐγκαλεῖς τῷ Ἰακὼβ προσκυνήσαντι ἐπὶ τὸ ἄκρον τῆς
ῥάβδου τοῦ Ἰωσήφ. Jacob did not make obeisance to the wood but through the
wood to Joseph. Hebrews xi. 21. Cf. F. Nau, 'La didascalie de Jacob', *Patrologia
Orientalis*, vol. viii, fasc. 5, p. 740 (30); *Quaestiones ad Antiochum Ducem*, *P.G.*
28, col. 621.　　　　　　　　　　　　　　　　　　　　　[24] Cf. *P.G.* 94, col. 1385 D.

Leontius accuses the Jews of blindness because they fail to realize that through the relics of the martyrs, and through the icons demons are put to flight, and yet foul men pervert and mock and laugh at such things as these. Often blood will gush forth from the icons and from the relics of the martyrs, and foolish folk, though they see this, are not persuaded; they treat the miracles as myths and fables. As Leontius writes in another fragment:

'If the bones of the just are impure, how was it that the bones of Jacob and Joseph were carried back with all honour from Egypt? How was it that a dead man touching the bones of Elisha straightway stood up? And if God works miracles through bones, it is clear that he can do the same through icons and stones and many other things.'[25]

With this belief in the cogency of the argument from miracle may be compared a passage from the *Quaestiones ad Antiochum Ducem*:

'Let those who refuse to do obeisance to the Cross and the icons explain how it is that the holy icons have often poured forth streams of myrrh by the power of the Lord, and how it is that a lifeless stele when it has received a blow has miraculously given forth blood as though it were a living body. Let them say how it is that from tombs and relics and icons demons are often driven howling away.'[26]

In *Les Trophées de Damas* it is stated that the sick whether they be believers or unbelievers take their seat beside the coffins of the saints and are healed.[27]

And daily, Leontius continues, almost throughout the inhabited world unholy and lawless men, idolaters and murderers, adulterers and robbers are suddenly smitten in their consciences through Christ and His Cross, say farewell to the whole world and give themselves to the practice of virtue. Tell me, how can we be idolaters who pay our homage ($\pi\rho\sigma\kappa\upsilon\nu\epsilon\hat{\iota}\nu$) and do honour to the bones, the dust, the clothes, the blood and the tombs of those who refused to sacrifice to idols?

The Christian brings to the Creator, the Lord and Maker of all things, his adoration and worship through heaven and

[25] *P.G.* 94, col. 1272 C–D.
[26] *P.G.* 28, col. 621 C. For a story of a demon and the icon of the Virgin, ibid.
[27] 'Les trophées de Damas', ed. G. Bardy, *Patrologia Orientalis*, vol. xv, fasc. 2, p. 273 (103); and cf. ibid., p. 272 (102).

earth and sea, through stone and wood, through relics and churches, through the Cross, through angels and through mankind. For creation cannot itself directly worship its Maker, but through me the heavens declare the glory of God, through me the moon worships God, through me the stars, through me the waters, the showers and the dew, through me all creation worship and glorify God.

When a good king has made for himself a rich and elaborate crown all those who are truly loyal to the king pay their respect and honour to the crown, but it is not the gold or the pearls that they honour but the head of the king and his skilful hands which have fashioned the crown. So with the Christians: whenever they pay their respects to the representations of the Cross and to icons, it is not to wood or stone, not to gold or the perishable icon, not to the coffin or the relics that they bring their worship, but through these they bring their respect and their worship. For the honour paid to His saints courses back (ἀνατρέχει) to Himself. Thus it is that men destroying or insulting icons of the Emperor are punished with extreme severity as having insulted the Emperor himself and not merely the painted board. Man made after God's image is God's icon indwelt by the Holy Spirit. It is right therefore that I should honour and make obeisance (προσκυνεῖν) to the icon of the servants of God and glorify the dwelling of the Holy Spirit.

If the Jews accuse the Christians of idolatry they should be covered with shame, for they did obeisance to their own kings and the kings of other nations. Everywhere the Christians have armed themselves against the idols: against the idols we sing our hymns, against the idols we write, against the idols and the demons we pray. Supposing that an idolater had come into your temple and seen the two sculptured Cherubim and had blamed the Jews as being themselves idolaters what, asks Leontius, could you reply? For the Christian the Cross and the icons are not gods: they remind us of Christ and His saints that we should do them honour: they are there to beautify our churches; and he who pays his worship to Christ's Mother carries the honour to Him and he who honours the apostle honours Him who sent him forth.[28]

[28] Cf. *P.G.* 94, col. 1276 A.

If then prophets and righteous men bowed to the earth before idolaters because of services rendered why do you blame me when I bow before the Cross and before representations of the saints through whom from God I receive ten thousand good things?

On this appeal of Leontius Dr E. J. Martin writes (*A History of the Iconoclastic Controversy*, p. 141): 'The views . . . are so complete an anticipation of the Iconoclastic struggle and its very arguments that the authenticity of all the passages attributed to Leontius must be gravely suspect.' He conjectures that Leontius is really the champion of orthodoxy, George of Cyprus. This judgement seems to me perverse. I am struck by the great skill with which Leontius presents his case: the whole argument is based throughout on the Old Testament, the common ground of Jew and Christian. Leontius may have known the theological justification, deduced from the Incarnation, of the icons of Christ, but he makes no use of it: it would have had no cogency for the Jews. 'The principle stands that we must either not argue with a man at all or we must argue on his grounds and not ours.'[29] Leontius knows St Basil's doctrine that the honour paid to the icon passes to the prototype (ἡ τῆς εἰκόνος τιμὴ ἐπὶ τὸ πρωτότυπον διαβαίνει); he may well have known that key-text, but nowhere in the fragments which we possess does he cite a Christian Father of the Church. The only distinctively Christian argument which he employs is the evidence of those miracles performed through the icons for which the Jew was in duty bound to furnish an explanation, since Leontius was persuaded that the fact of miracle was incontrovertibly established. The plea of Leontius is thus widely different from the later Iconodule propaganda and deserves close study.[30] Indeed it may be suggested that the repetition, in a series of works against the Jews, of the arguments of Leontius in defence of the icons was indirectly intended to meet the scruples of Christians impressed by the Jewish contention. It is to be observed that it is a Christian who asks Antiochus for a justification of the disregard of the Old Testament prohibition of images.[31]

[29] G. K. Chesterton, *St Thomas Aquinas* (1933), p. 110.
[30] It would, for example, be of interest to know whether there are parallels to the view of Leontius that the world of nature needs the help of man before it can worship its Creator.   [31] *P.G.* 28, col. 621.

It is not necessary to consider in detail that series of works against the Jews, since the argument concerning the icons for the most part does but reproduce the plea of Leontius. Thus in *Les trophées de Damas* the Jewish charge of idolatry is repeated—the Christians are falling back into old pagan practices (τῇ παλαιᾷ ὑμῶν τῶν ἐθνῶν συνηθείᾳ),[32] they do obeisance to things made by human hands (χειροποίητα καὶ κτιστὰ πράγματα). The Christian in reply points to the ark of the covenant, to Moses and the (second) tables of the Law and to the Cherubim. The book of the Law is brought from the synagogue and the Jews do obeisance to it and so prove the Christian's argument.

A. C. McGiffert's edition of the *Dialogue of Papiscus and Philo*[33] (Marburg, 1889) is not accessible to me, but the text of the curious brief section on the Cross and the icons is cited by F. Nau in his edition of the *Didascalia of Jacob*.[34] This, again, only repeats the arguments which we have met with previously: the Jew asking why the order which was given by God forbidding to do obeisance to things made of wood (μὴ προσκυνεῖν ξύλοις) was disregarded by the Christians in their use of the Cross and of icons, and the Christian replying, Why do you do obeisance to the book of the Law and why did Jacob do obeisance on the top of Joseph's staff (ἐπὶ τοῦ ἄκρου τῆς ῥάβδου τοῦ Ἰωσήφ)? In respect of the book of the Law the Jew answers that he does not do obeisance to the nature of the skins but to the meaning of the words of the Law, while Jacob did not do obeisance to the wood of the staff, but he honoured Joseph who held it.

In the summary of Leontius' argument references have been given to parallels in the Pseudo-Athanasian *Quaestiones ad Antiochum Ducem*, P.G. 28, Quaestio 39, col. 621; there is no fresh development. A fragment added to the *Quaestiones* (ibid., col. 709) does but give a variant to the text of Leontius: 'For if Christ is not present to my lips in His body, nevertheless with heart and mind I am present with Christ in the spirit.' It

---

[32] 'Les trophées de Damas', ed. G. Bardy, *Patrologia Orientalis*, vol. xv, p. 245.

[33] On this dialogue see A. Lukyn Williams, *Adversus Judaeos* (Cambridge, 1935), pp. 169–74.

[34] 'La didascalie de Jacob', *Patrologia Orientalis*, vol. viii, 5, p. 740.

is interesting in such passages as this to catch an echo of the emotion which inspired the cult of the icon: in the *Quaestiones ad Antiochum Ducem*: 'We make our obeisance to express the attitude and the love of our souls (τὴν σχέσιν καὶ τὴν ἀγάπην τῆς ψυχῆς ἡμῶν) for those represented in the icon,'[35] or 'to show our longing (πόθος) for them just as we greet fathers and friends;[36] through the Cross we express the true attitude of our souls (τὴν τῆς ψυχῆς ἡμῶν γνησίαν διάθεσιν) towards the Crucified.'[37] The very simplicity of the wording seems to carry with it an assurance of genuine feeling.

There remain to be considered two documents recently translated from the Armenian, a seventh-century apology for the icons and a letter of the vardapet John Mayragometsi taken from the history of Moses Kaghankavatsi.[38] The apology begins on lines which must have become traditional: the Old Testament prohibition of images is met with references to the Cherubim, and to Solomon's Temple—God did not disapprove Solomon's initiative, He called the Temple the Temple of His name. The Christian paintings are not the true God, but we paint them in the name of God 'tel qu'il apparut'—a precise parallel to the passage quoted from John, Bishop of Salonica (*supra*, p. 229). The writer of the apology is addressing Christians and therefore he can proceed to quote from John Chrysostom, Severian of Gabala and Gregory the Illuminator, and can translate from Eusebius his account of the statue of the woman with an issue of blood at Paneas. Heretics consider the icons to be idle, for they can neither speak nor understand: 'What of the ark', is the reply, 'when it overturned Dagon?' And the Cross raised the dead in the Holy City and still performs numberless miracles down to our own day—the Cross which is the pride of angels, the salvation of men and the terror of the demons. But the special interest of this apology

---

[35] *P.G.* 28, col. 621 B.   [36] Ibid.

[37] *P.G.* 40, col. 865. It may be noted that the cult of the Cross was not extended to embrace other objects connected with the Passion—the ass, the holy lance, the sponge, the reed—and when Christians asked the reason for this ἄγια γάρ εἰσι καὶ ταῦτα καθὰ καὶ ὁ σταυρός it was not easy to find a satisfactory answer, see *P.G.* 28, col. 624; *Trophées de Damas*, p. 249.

[38] Sirarpie der Nersessian, 'Une apologie des images du septième siècle', *Byzantion*, xvii (1944–5), pp. 58–87. By her translation of these texts and her fully documented commentary Miss der Nersessian has rendered a great service to those of us who cannot read Armenian works.

lies in the statement that in Armenia two monks are preaching the destruction of the icons—'l'impie et l'égaré Thaddée et Isaïe et leurs compagnons qui entraînèrent à leur suite un grand nombre de personnes,' and from the letter we learn that when the leaders of the movement were arrested and were asked why they refused to accept the image of the incarnate God they replied that that was alien to the commandments 'et c'est l'œuvre des idolâtres qui adorent toutes les créatures; quant à nous nous ne nous prosternons pas devant les images car nous n'en avons pas reçu l'ordre des saintes écritures. Alors, leur ayant parlé des images de l'autel de Moïse, des diverses sculptures du temple de Salomon, et expliqué que nous représentons les mêmes choses dans nos églises; leur ayant donc dit ceci, et d'autres paroles semblables, nous corrigeâmes leur erreur.'

Thus the story which begins with the scruples of Julian ends with an active Iconoclast movement in Armenia and Albania. I would suggest that too little attention has been paid to this evidence as forming the background of imperial policy. Need we doubt that Iconoclasm was primarily religious in its inspiration? Is there ány reason to believe that 'Iconoclasm was but an outgrowth and indeed the climax of the caesaropapistic theory and practice of the State as represented by some of the most successful Byzantine Emperors'?[39]

---

[39] So Gerhart B. Ladner, 'Origin and Significance of the Byzantine Iconoclastic Controversy', *Mediaeval Studies*, ii (1940), Pontifical Institute of Mediaeval Studies, pp. 127–49. I prefer Louis Bréhier's summing up of 'Les caractères généraux et la portée de la réforme iconoclaste', *Revue des Cours et Conférences* for 11 April 1901, pp. 226–35.

XVI

The Finding of the Virgin's Robe

[*Annuaire de l'institut de philologie et d'histoire orientales et slaves*, ix (1949, Mélanges Grégoire), pp. 87–95.]

THE invitation to contribute a short paper to this congratulatory volume could not be allowed to pass without a response. Professor Grégoire has included within the astonishing range of his interests the hagiographical literature of the Orthodox Church and he would, it may be hoped, support the plea of a student of East Roman history for more detailed comparative studies of Byzantine hagiographical documents. How did later writers treat earlier accounts when they sought to tell a story afresh? What were their methods? Where we have such comparative material it might help us to gain some insight into the way in which the writers handled their sources. It so happens that the story of the finding of the Virgin's robe and of its transference to Constantinople to become the Palladium of the city has been preserved in different forms; it may be worth while to consider the differences in these accounts.

The simplest version was published by Basilius Latyšev in his edition of an eleventh-century Menologium containing the calendar for the months of February and March, June, July, and August (Petropoli, 1912, fasc. 2, pp. 127–32). The story tells how when Leo the Great and his wife Verina were ruling the Empire, at a time when undisturbed peace was being enjoyed by the Romans, there lived in Constantinople two brothers, Galbius and Candidus, patricians, who were related to Ardaburius and Aspar, and who were in consequence Arians. Afterwards ($\mu\epsilon\tau\grave{\alpha}$ $\tau\alpha\hat{\upsilon}\tau\alpha$) the grace of the Spirit brought them to the truth. (But what is the precise date of this conversion? Is it after the finding of the robe?) They desired to travel to Jerusalem to visit the Holy Places. The Emperor gave his approval, and a large company of friends and attendants

started on their journey. When Galbius and Candidus reached
Palestine they preferred to take the road into Galilee rather
than to follow the sea-route as they wished to see Nazareth
and Capernaum. On their way through Galilee they were over-
taken by the darkness of a night when no moon was shining
and in a small village they obtained shelter from a woman
remarkable for her purity and dignified behaviour. Her age
and white hair made her reverend, and she was rendered much
more radiant by the beauty of her virtues. It was she who had
been constituted guardian of the Virgin's robe and how
should this have been if she had not been adorned by virtues
and purity of soul? And yet the woman was a Jewess—for the
truth is precious (φίλη γὰρ ἡ ἀλήθεια)—and one would have
said that, though her soul was unillumined, it was ready and
completely fitted to receive the light. This is a remarkable
passage: for an East Roman the Jews are 'sons of the Devil', a
χριστόκτονος συμμορία and δαιμόνων κατοικητήρια.[1]

It was indeed the ordering of Providence which had brought
Galbius and Candidus to the village, while the woman would
naturally have wished to keep her secret undisclosed; that she
should have declared that secret would make it the more
readily believed.

When Galbius and Candidus were called to supper they saw
an inner room bright with many lights and odorous with much
incense. They wished to know the meaning of the sight and
asked the woman to share with them their supper. But she
declined their pressing invitation: a Jewess cannot share a
Christian's food. 'But bring your own food,' they said, 'and
eat with us,' and then she consented. 'What things happen in
the inner room?' they asked, and she told them of the miracles,
but did not tell them by whom the miracles were wrought.
'You see, sirs,' she said, 'the multitude of sick folk, and here
demons are driven out, the blind see, the lame walk and the
deaf hear.' 'When did this power begin to show itself?' they
questioned her. She replied: 'With us Jews there is a story
handed down from our forefathers which still holds good that
God was seen in this spot by one of our fathers and since then

---

[1] Von Dobschütz, 'Christusbilder', *Texte und Untersuchungen*, edd. von
Gebhardt and Harnack, N.F., vol. iii (Leipzig, 1899), pp. 244**–245**.

this grace has been preserved here.' They were confident that she was not speaking the truth, and so implored her only the more earnestly to tell them truly what she knew. Her answer still was that she knew only that the place was filled with divine grace, and they for their part were still convinced that she was lying. So they determined 'to leave no stone unturned'. They forced her to swear that she would speak the truth. With a groan and with tears, 'Sirs,' she said, 'never until this day have I disclosed to any man this sacred mystery, for under an oath my ancestors gave this secret to one woman who was a virgin, and she was to hand on the mystery from generation to generation.' But since she saw that they were devout men, and since (this, too, she would tell them) she was the last virgin in her family, she was ready to tell them the truth, 'and you, I think, will keep the account a secret.'

'The Virgin', she said, 'at her death gave to two virgins two robes (ἐσθῆτας) of hers as a benediction; one of these virgins was a member of my family and she took the gift and placed it in a little coffer and this was inherited by a virgin successively within the family. This little coffer is now hidden in the room as you see, and it is the robe within it which is the cause of all these miracles. Sirs, this is the truth which you sought: only let none of those in Jerusalem know.' They fell at her feet and said 'Mistress (we call you Mistress—despoina—since you have been deemed worthy of such mysteries) do not fear that we might betray to anyone in Jerusalem that of which we have spoken. We call the Theotokos herself to witness.' Then they asked for one more favour—that they might be allowed to sleep where the divine power dwelt—and their request was granted. And so they spread their mattresses and spent the night in prayer and weeping, thanking the Virgin for what they had heard and seen. When they were sure that all the sick had fallen into deep slumber they took accurate measurements of the little coffer and they noted of what wood it was made. In the morning they asked the woman whether there was anything which they could do for her in Jerusalem and then continued their journey.

In Jerusalem they distributed alms to the poor, and later gave instructions for the making of a replica of the coffer and had fashioned a covering for the coffer worked in gold thread. On their return they were allowed to sleep in the inner room as before, and here they prayed: 'Virgin, Mistress, thy servants are not ignorant that they are guilty of many sins and unless thou biddest us we are unworthy to touch this precious reliquary (σορός) within which so great a treasure is stored. Be thou favourable and grant us the wish of our hearts. For the removal is to thine own city which is the queen of all others and has ever honoured fervently anything of thine. We hasten to carry this precious gift to the city for her security and for her glory which shall never be extinguished.' And with the Virgin's approval they exchanged the coffer, leaving the covering which they had brought with them, and said farewell and went on their way.

When they reached Constantinople they told neither the Patriarch nor the Emperor and Empress for fear their treasure should be taken from them, but, again with the approval of the Virgin, they built a church (οἶκον) and in order to maintain secrecy they dedicated the church to St Peter and St Mark, and there they placed the robe and they made provision for continuous hymnody, for unfailing lights and the sweet odour of spices (ἀρώματα).

But once more the Virgin intervened: so great a good she was unwilling to be known only to Galbius and Candidus, and she moved them to declare their secret. Great joy filled the hearts of all who heard their story and the finders of the robe were publicly honoured. Leo and Verina built in the quarter of Blachernae an imperial church dedicated to the Virgin, and the robe was placed in a reliquary of silver and gold.

In the course of a long *Oratio de S. Deipara* (B) published by Latyšev, op. cit., pp. 347–83, the author included a revision of this account (A) of the finding of the Virgin's robe. The longest addition to the text of (A) concerns the precise date of the conversion of Galbius and Candidus; surely the Virgin would not have employed as her agents two Arian heretics. It must be placed beyond a doubt that their conversion preceded their departure on their pilgrimage. In (B) both Galbius and Candidus are generals, both are brothers in virtue and greatly distinguished, with few to equal them. And the one blot—

their Arianism—is excused as a hereditary taint arising from their close connexion with Ardabur and Aspar. God's grace had converted them, and they were not only orthodox but filled with missionary zeal, striving to bring any heretic to the true faith and making generous gifts to the poor as a return to Christ for their recognition of the truth. The Virgin's choice of Galbius and Candidus is thus satisfactorily explained.

The story of their journey is unaltered, but it is of interest to observe that the route through Galilee is preferred to the 'delights' of the coastal road (p. 377, 27). One sentence is added: 'there was nothing remarkable about the house [of the Jewess] save that which was hidden there; there was nothing great, indeed the house was extremely simple' (p. 378, 12). When the travellers asked what was happening in the inner room we read ἐνόμιζον νομικόν τι εἶναι καὶ τῶν σκιωδῶν ἐκείνων καὶ παλαιῶν (p. 378, 31). Even to an East Roman this sentence appeared to need some explanation (see *infra*, p. 246). The reviser of the text cannot resist the temptation to insert the traditional comment on the inability of doctors to heal the diseases of the sufferers (p. 379, 4). When the Jewess would not disclose the truth the editor puts into the mouth of her visitor 'And if you will have no regard for anything else, at least consider that all the labour of this journey of ours has no other object than to see the Holy Places and to have sacred talk filled with the love of God' (p. 379, 14). The Virgin inspired in Galbius and Candidus a passion to discover the truth so that their hearts began to burn within them as it had been with those who were with Cleopas (Luke xxiv. 32, p. 379, 23). In (A) the suggestion that the Jewess might want something from Jerusalem is very briefly expressed; in (B) the suggestion is developed. In the morning they greeted the reverend woman; if she wanted anything from Jerusalem they encouraged her to ask them to procure it; she must not hesitate. They would be coming back the same way. But she said she wanted nothing except their prayers and to see them again in good cheer. It is interesting to observe how the revision keeps true to the original tone and maintains throughout the deep respect for the Jewess.

When Jerusalem has been reached and the order given for

the making of the duplicate coffer a little touch is added to the account in (A): the wood must be old wood so that it may exactly resemble the original. Returned to the village they are warmly welcomed ὡς ἤδη συνήθεις (p. 381, 23): the Jewess suspects nothing οὐδὲν τὸ παράπαν ὑπιδομένη (p. 381, 25). In their prayer to the Virgin a reference to the fate of Uzza (Zan) after touching the ark[2] is introduced (cf. the reference to Cleopas *supra*). But the only really striking alteration in the text of (A) occurs at the point in the story when the genuine coffer is carried off from the shelter of the inner room: (A) has 'O blessed hands! O sight that none can blame!' ὦ μακαρίων χειρῶν, ὦ βλέμματος ἀψόγου (p. 130, 32). The editor writes: 'O blessed hands! O theft which is above all blame!' (ὦ μακαρίων χειρῶν, ὦ κλέμματος ψόγου κρείττονος (p. 382, 9). This is a bold and interesting change. Finally it may be noted that the holy reliquary—the ἁγία σορός—is housed in the imperial church, not containing the tables of the Mosaic law, but the very precious robe on which there were still the marks where the Virgin's milk had dropped as she nursed the infant Christ.

There is no other notable addition to the earlier text and the conservative treatment of (A) by the editor is remarkable; surely he must have realized the charm of the simplicity with which the story had been told.

And then in the seventh century[3] our second document is revised, and the writer of this third text[4] prefaces his version by a long and highly rhetorical confession of his inability to do justice to so magnificent a theme. This introduction, so far as concerns the account of the finding of the Virgin's robe, can only be formal and traditional, since the writer has throughout closely followed the earlier document.

At the outset of the story as told by the seventh-century editor (C) it is interesting to observe in what high esteem the

---

[2] I Chron. xiii. 9.

[3] V. Vasilievsky, *Viz. Vremennik*, iii (1896), pp. 83–95; not ninth century as Loparev, ibid., ii (1895), pp. 581–628.

[4] F. Combefis, *Graecolat. Patrum Bibliothecae novum auctarium*. Tomus II (Tomus Historicus et Dogmaticus), *Historia Haeresis Monothelitarum* (Paris, 1648), Εἰς κατάθεσιν τῆς τιμίας ἐσθῆτος τῆς Θεομήτορος ἐν Βλαχέρναις, coll. 751–74 (wrongly numbered 764). The latter part of the document relates the repulse of the Avars, through the intervention of the Virgin, in their attack on Constantinople (pp. 6774–86).

Emperor Leo I, the Great, ὁ μέγας, is held amongst East
Roman hagiographers. In (B) he is ὁ εὐσεβὴς Λέων; for the
writer of (C) that is not enough: he expands the single word
into τὰ 'Ρωμαίων εὐσεβῶς ἐκόσμει βασίλεια, ἀνὴρ τῆς ἀμωμήτου
πίστεως φύλαξ ἐπίσημος, βίῳ καὶ ἔργῳ σεμνύνων τὴν ἁλουργίδα
καὶ τὸ διάδημα (col. 758A). The heresy of Galbius and Candidus
and their conversion are related with only verbal changes, but
there is added an explicit credal statement of their faith in a
Trinity which is ὁμοούσιος καὶ συνάναρχος, in a Theos Logos born
in the flesh and ὁμοούσιος with the Father, while the Virgin
Mother of the great God is τὸ τῆς ἀφθαρσίας ὄντως ἀρχέτυπον
ἀπεικόνισμα 'as we have all believed' (col. 758). The Virgin
wished to give to her own city an inviolable treasure which
none should take away and it was she who inspired the desire
of Galbius and Candidus to visit the Holy Places. In (B) it had
been said that the arrival at the village was οὐκ ἀθεεί: the view
is elaborated in (C): καὶ τοῦτο δὲ πάντως ἐκ θείας οἰκονομίας
συμβέβηκεν· ἄλλο γὰρ ἦν ἐφ' ὅπερ ὅ τε Θεὸς καὶ ἡ Θεοτόκος
ἐκάλεσαν. A comparison of the text of (B) and (C) shows with
what scrupulous care the writer of (C) read his source. In (B)
we are told that the village was small and the inhabitants were
οὐκ ὀλίγοι. The writer of (C) noticing the contradiction writes:
'There were of course others inhabiting the village, but they
were few—they could easily be counted' εὐαρίθμητοι (col.759C).
The curious sentence ἐνόμιζον νομικόν τι εἶναι καὶ τῶν σκιωδῶν
ἐκείνων καὶ παλαιῶν in (B). p. 378, 31, he felt to be ambiguous;
he recasts it and writes 'Εβραικὸν γάρ τι σκιῶδες[5] τῶν κατὰ
νόμον ἀκούσειν ἐνόμιζον (col. 762C), and for him any reference to
the 'blameless theft' is too bold and the sentence is suppressed
(col. 770A). He retains the biblical parallels—Cleopas and Uzza
—which were inserted by the writer of (B) and he further adds
one of his own: the Jewess was 'another Anna, the daughter of
Phanuel,[6] looking for the consolation of Israel and giving
thanks to God night and day—not in the temple which
Solomon built but in the holy workshop of her own heart' (col.
759C–D). Verbal changes from the text of (B) introduced into

---

[5] I do not know what σκιῶδες means here: is it 'ancient Hebrew rites which
were foreshadowings of Christian truth'?
[6] Luke ii. 36.

(C) are of small significance, but two insertions are of considerable interest. In (B) we read that after supper both Galbius and Candidus together asked the Jewess to tell them the truth and keep nothing back (p. 378, 29). The editor in (C) writes 'and when they had taken their fill of food it was not that "Ajax nodded to Phoenix but another marked it", both of them made one and the same request to the woman'. This citation of *Iliad*, ix, 223, is a characteristically Byzantine addition (col. 762c). The second insertion is the appeal to the Jewess: 'We adjure you by the divine power which you have believed is in this house—which you have ventured to believe has worked all the miracles which you have seen—tell us the whole truth and hide nothing from us. For you yourself will suffer no harm through telling us, God forbid! and we should glorify God the more. For our God and your God is one and the same God.' For an East Roman writer that is surely a remarkable petition.

And at the close of the account as it is given in (C) we have the statement of what it meant to the folk of Constantinople that the Virgin had her church in Blachernae where the holy reliquary— the ἀγία σορός—was preserved. 'That church, it might be said, contains the whole μυσταγωγία—the secret and the power of Christians. Here in very truth all sickness, all grief and all despondency finds healing, all joy and rejoicing and the hope of better things gains confirmation' (col. 774, printed 764).

The aim of the present paper has been to illustrate the fidelity with which the Byzantine writer of a hagiographic document may reproduce his source and can do this even when anti-Jewish prejudice might naturally have led him to change the tone of the text upon which he is working.[7] A student of history would wish to know whether in other Byzantine hagiographic writings there can be found such a liberality of view as that of the present narrative.[8]

[7] For the Jew in Byzantine literature see James Parkes, *The Conflict of the Church and the Synagogue* (Soncino Press, London, 1934), pp. 271–306.

[8] It may be noted that the lection for the commemoration of the deposition of the Virgin's robe in the church at Blachernae is apparently derived from a different source, *Acta Sanctorum, Propylaeum* (November, Brussels, 1902), col. 793. Thus in this account the Virgin neither inspires nor approves of the action of Galbius and Candidus; the lights and incense are ἐν ἑτέρῳ ταμείῳ from that where the sick are congregated; the genuine coffer is dispatched in advance to Constantinople in charge of the servants of Galbius and Candidus.

XVII

The Supernatural Defenders
of Constantinople

[*Analecta Bollandiana*, 67 (1949, Mélanges Paul Peeters), pp. 165–77.]

THOSE who study the history and civilization of the Byzantine Empire have good reason to be grateful to Père Peeters: through the years he has shown them how much material for their studies can be won from hagiographical sources if the interpreter comes to them with sympathy and a readiness to understand. It is a pity that the size and weight of the volumes of the *Acta Sanctorum* make the reading of them so formidable an undertaking and thus repel intimacy. Modern writers on East Rome, convinced that 'miracles do not happen', have quietly banished miracle from their histories and have thereby falsified the picture, for there can be no doubt that the Byzantine lived in a world where miracle could happen and did happen, and that belief in miracle is itself a fact of history which the student ignores at his peril. The Christian faith in a God who can and does work miracles is expressed with lapidary brevity by the monk Theognostos: 'Whatever God wills that He can perform and where God wills there the order of nature is overcome.'[1] If the shadow of Peter falling on the sufferer could bring healing (Acts v. 15), if God had wrought special miracles by the hand of Paul so that after contact with his body handkerchiefs or aprons brought to the sick release from disease and banishment of evil spirits (Acts xix. 11–12), how much more should the robe of the Mother of God work miracles![2] It is true that Photius is reported to have said in a sermon that earthquakes are not caused through the

---

[1] Ὅσα θέλει ὁ Θεὸς δύναται, καὶ ὅπου Θεὸς βούλεται νικᾶται φύσεως τάξις. M. Jugie, *Homélies mariales byzantines* (=*Patrologia Orientalis*, xvi (1922), fasc. 3), p. 460: Encomium in Dormitionem Beatissimae Mariae Virginis by the monk Theognostos.

[2] *BHG*., 1058: Narratio historica in Depositionem Vestis S. Mariae, in F. Combefis, *Historia Haeresis Monothelitarum* (Paris, 1648), col. 779.

multitude of men's sins but through the flooding of water;[3] but it was precisely the unusual character of this view which led Symeon Magister to report it: when a violent disturbance in the sea had wrecked the fleet besieging Constantinople this disturbance was not to be explained impiously as a natural occurrence: it was the work of the Mother of God.[4] The conviction that the city of Constantine was God-guarded, that the Empire was based on God's will—that it was a $\theta\epsilon o\sigma\tau\acute{\eta}\rho\iota\kappa\tau o\nu$ $\kappa\rho\acute{a}\tau os$—the consciousness that the capital was under the special charge and protection of the Virgin, this sense of supernatural support must surely have had a profound psychological significance. It might be worth while to study in detail the effects of that conviction, perhaps to translate the principal documents in which that conviction is mirrored. This paper does but attempt to suggest the interest and the historical importance of this belief of the East Romans in supernatural succour.

The Byzantines were fully conscious of the absolutely essential part played by the great fortress of Constantine's foundation; the territory of the Empire might for a while be restricted, as it was in 626, to the space enclosed within the city walls, but if the imperial power-house remained inviolate, recovery remained a possibility. Constantinople, 'the eye of the faith of the Christians,'[5] could continue to preserve the treasure of which it was the guardian. And to gain assurance of this inviolability the rulers of East Rome—patriarchs and emperors—sought to secure the aid of as many supernatural defenders and defences as they could, and in this amassing of spiritual guarantors they were aided by God, by Christ, by the Virgin and by the holy dead who as saints had freedom of speech ($\pi\alpha\rho\rho\eta\sigma\acute{\iota}\alpha$) in the court of Heaven. We are familiar with the accounts of the relics which the crusaders carried back to

---

[3] Symeon Magister, ed. Bonn, p. 673.

[4] *BHG.*, 1140: Sermon attributed to Andrew archbishop of Crete in the Bodleian MS. text published in *Néa Σιών*, vi (1907), pp. 826–33; attributed to Theodore Ducas Lascaris in the MS. of the *'Εθνικὴ Βιβλιοθήκη* in Athens published in *Σωτήρ* (Athens), xvi (1894), pp. 186–92—a better MS.: σήμερον βρασμὸς ἐν θαλάσσῃ οὐ κατὰ τοὺς πάλαι βρασμούς· ἐκείνους γὰρ φυσιολογοῦσιν Ἕλληνες ἀσεβῶς, τὸ δ' ἐν ἡμῖν γεγονὸς ἡ μήτηρ εἰργάσατο τοῦ Θεοῦ.

[5] Leo Sternbach, 'Analecta Avarica', in the *Rozprawy* of the Academy of Cracow (1900), p. 304, 15: τῆς Χριστιανῶν ὀφθαλμὸν ὑπάρχουσαν πίστεως.

the West after the great brigandage of the Fourth Crusade; we do not always bear in mind what these relics must have signified in previous centuries for the folk of Constantinople. This effort κατασπλουτίσαι τὴν βασιλεύουσαν[6]—to enrich the imperial city—was indeed most natural, and East Rome believed that God must share the desire to increase the wealth of this astonishing treasure-house. In the Synaxarium for the commemoration of the bringing to Constantinople of the image of Christ from Edessa on August 16 this belief is expressed: Ἐπεὶ δὴ πρὸς τὴν βασιλεύουσαν τῶν πόλεων τὰ πανταχόθεν συνερρύη κάλλιστα, ἦν δὲ ἄρα θεῖον βούλημα καὶ τὴν ἱερὰν ταύτην καὶ ἄχραντον εἰκόνα μετὰ τῶν ἄλλων ἀποθησαυρισθῆναι καλῶν. . . .[7]

And, further, it must have seemed only natural to the Byzantines that the holy dead should be conscious of their powers; if their relics were duly honoured they would be prepared to use their freedom of speech to move God to exercise His pardoning mercy or to stay the evils from which the Empire might be suffering. An illustration of this belief is to be found in the different versions of the discovery of the body of St Stephen the Protomartyr. After Stephen had been stoned by the Jews, his body was left outside the city-walls of Jerusalem. Later it was secretly buried by Gamaliel, and Gamaliel himself together with his young son and Nicodemus had their graves near that of the martyr at Kapargamala.[8]

Years passed and the graves were neglected until to Lucianus, priest at Kapargamala, Gamaliel appeared and in a vision bade the priest inform the Patriarch: the graves must be found: let the dead be honoured as was their due in order that 'through us God may open the door of His philanthropia for the world'. 'The martyrdom (ἄθλησις) must be proclaimed that

---

[6] Synaxarium Ecclesiae Constantinopolitanae (=Propylaeum ad Acta Sanctorum, Novembris, Brussels, 1902), col. 899, 27.

[7] Synax. Eccl. CP., col. 899, 21; cf. the parallel text in the eleventh-century Menologium published by B. Latyšev, fasc. 2 (St Petersburg, 1912), p. 284: Ἐπεὶ δὲ τῇ βασιλίδι τῶν πόλεων εἰς ἣν τὰ πανταχόθεν ἄκρα συντρέχει καὶ ᾗ πάντα τὰ καλὰ τεθησαύρισται, μετὰ τῶν ἄλλων ἔδει καὶ ταῦτα τὰ θεῖα προσεῖναι, τὸ δὲ καὶ Θεὸς πάντως εὐδόκησεν ὁ τῶν ἀγαθῶν παροχεύς . . . and texts in Ernst von Dobschütz, Christusbilder (=Texte und Untersuchungen, N.F. 3, 1899), pp. 72** and 73**.

[8] For place names in these documents relating to St Stephen, see F. Nau, 'Sur les mots πολιτικὸς et πολιτευόμενος et sur plusieurs textes grecs relatifs à Saint Étienne', in Revue de l'Orient chrétien, xi (Paris, 1906), at pp. 203, 207, and cf. p. 205.

God may be once again glorified in us and, being moved to pity, may become merciful towards the sins of the people.' In another version of the priest's vision it is St Stephen himself who demands that his body should be discovered, and this account is more explicit: 'Why have you delayed,' St Stephen insists, 'and not told the Patriarch John what I said to you last Thursday? Don't you know how great a drought and how much distress oppress the world? And yet you never went and told the Patriarch that he should open up our graves in order that through us the Lord may have pity on His world.'[9] And for the result of the Patriarch's action we have to go to the Latin translation of Lucian's letter *ad omnem ecclesiam:* 'Et tunc in tempore iugis et infinita siccitas erat. Sed eadem hora pluvia magna descendit et abundanter inebriata est terra.'[10]

The remarkable self-consciousness of the saint illustrates the practical value set by the inhabitants of Constantinople upon the possession of the relics of the sainted dead. Similarly Constantinople guarding the head of John the Baptist would be more revered ($\sigma\epsilon\mu\nu\acute{\nu}\nu o\iota\tau o$) and from the transference to Constantinople the relic itself would be more revered, since it would be more highly honoured and be celebrated with greater acclamations of praise.[11]

It might seem at times that a precious relic was brought to Constantinople through a simple human mistake, but to view the event in that way would be to ignore God's overruling care for the imperial city. When the body of St Stephen had been rediscovered, in Jerusalem, to shelter it a church was built by a senator, Alexander by name, and the saint's body was placed in a sarcophagus of persea wood. Five years later Alexander died, and in his will he directed that his coffin, fashioned like that of St Stephen from the same wood, should rest close to the holy relic. After some time his widow wished to return to Constantinople where her family lived and asked the Patriarch to allow her to carry to the capital her husband's coffin. The

---

[9] See *BHG.*, 1649 and 1651: '$M\alpha\rho\tau\acute{\nu}\rho\iota o\nu$ $\tau o\hat{\nu}$ $\dot{\alpha}\gamma\acute{\iota}o\nu$ $\pi\rho\omega\tau o\mu\acute{\alpha}\rho\tau\nu\rho o\varsigma$ $\Sigma\tau\epsilon\phi\acute{\alpha}\nu o\nu$ $\kappa\alpha\grave{\iota}$ $\dot{\eta}$ $\epsilon\ddot{\nu}\rho\epsilon\sigma\iota\varsigma$ $\tau\hat{\omega}\nu$ $\lambda\epsilon\iota\psi\acute{\alpha}\nu\omega\nu$ $\alpha\dot{\nu}\tau o\hat{\nu}$,' in A. Papadopoulos-Kerameus, '$A\nu\acute{\alpha}\lambda\epsilon\kappa\tau\alpha$ $\dot{I}\epsilon\rho o\sigma o\lambda\nu\mu\iota\tau\iota\kappa\hat{\eta}\varsigma$ $\Sigma\tau\alpha\chi\nu o\lambda o\gamma\acute{\iota}\alpha\varsigma$, vol. v (St Petersburg, 1898), pp. 28–53; $\Lambda\acute{o}\gamma o\varsigma$ $\dot{\epsilon}\gamma\kappa\omega\mu\iota\alpha\sigma\tau\iota\kappa\grave{o}\varsigma$ $\ddot{\alpha}\mu\alpha$ $\kappa\alpha\grave{\iota}$ $\dot{\iota}\sigma\tau o\rho\iota\kappa\grave{o}\varsigma$ $\pi\epsilon\rho\grave{\iota}$ $\tau\hat{\eta}\varsigma$ $\dot{\epsilon}\nu$ $K\omega\nu\sigma\tau\alpha\nu\tau\iota\nu o\nu\pi\acute{o}\lambda\epsilon\iota$ $\dot{\epsilon}\lambda\epsilon\acute{\nu}\sigma\epsilon\omega\varsigma$ $\tau o\hat{\nu}$ $\tau\iota\mu\acute{\iota}o\nu$ $\lambda\epsilon\iota\psi\acute{\alpha}\nu o\nu$ $\tau o\hat{\nu}$ $\dot{\epsilon}\nu$ $\dot{\alpha}\gamma\acute{\iota}o\iota\varsigma$ $\pi\rho\omega\tau o\mu\acute{\alpha}\rho\tau\nu\rho o\varsigma$ $\tau o\hat{\nu}$ $X\rho\iota\sigma\tau o\hat{\nu}$ $\kappa\alpha\grave{\iota}$ $\dot{\alpha}\rho\chi\iota\delta\iota\alpha\kappa\acute{o}\nu o\nu$, ibid., pp. 54–69.

[10] Migne, *P.L.*, 41, col. 815.

[11] *BHG.*, 841: Migne, *P.L.*, 67, col. 434–46 at col. 444.

Patriarch, fearing a disturbance in Jerusalem, refused her request. But through her father she secured from the Emperor a letter ordering the Patriarch to grant her wish. This σάκρα the Patriarch was unable to withstand—τοῦ ἀρχιερέως μὴ δυναμένου ἀντειπεῖν—and the widow took with her what she thought was her husband's coffin. In fact it was that of St Stephen, and the saint throughout the journey performed many miracles. The account of that journey is full of interest, but the essential element in the story is the fact that God had induced the mistake: it was divine providence which added to the treasures of the capital the relics of the first Christian martyr.[12]

And just as it was the divine will that precious relics should come to Constantinople, so the human possessors of relics would seem at times to have admitted the claim of the capital. There is a curious vision given in the account of the finding of the body of St Stephen when the priest Lucian hears the Patriarch say that of the oxen which work for Jerusalem two and a calf would suffice (this appears to refer to Nicodemus, Gamaliel and Gamaliel's son), but the great ox must be surrendered to the imperial city—St Stephen's body cannot be withheld by Jerusalem.

Similarly when St Symeon the Stylite died, it was to Constantinople (if we are to believe the account given in the Life of Daniel the Stylite) that a disciple, a monk named Sergius, carried the precious leather tunic of the pillar saint to be given to the Emperor Leo 'by way of benediction'.[13] And just as St Stephen showed no objection to be carried off from his church in Jerusalem, so St John the Baptist's head, exiled in a little town like Comana, disclosed its presence so that it might be borne to

[12] The widow had been θεία τινὶ προνοία περιπλανηθεῖσα. Synax. Eccl. CP., col. 863, 34. Stephen's relics were placed in a church in the district of Constantinae (Constantinianae), cf. A. Banduri, Imperium Orientale, II (Paris, 1711), pp. 641–2; Synax. Eccl. CP., col. 784, 19. The Festival of St Stephen was celebrated on 27 December, Synax. Eccl. CP., col. 349–50, while the memory of the discovery of his body was observed in Constantinople on 16 September, ibid., col. 52, 4. There is a fragment of an account of the journey from Jerusalem to Constantinople (from the arrival at Sosae) in BHG., 1650: A. Banduri, op. cit., ii, pp. 646–7.

[13] Life of Daniel the Stylite in H. Delehaye, 'Les Saints stylites' (Subsidia Hagiographica, vol. xiv (Brussels, 1923), ch. 22). Cf. P. Peeters, Anal. Boll., lxi (1943), p. 59; E. Dawes and N. H. Baynes, Three Byzantine Saints (Oxford, 1948), p. 19, and note on p. 75.

Constantinople. This wondrous gift—δῶρον ἀξιοθαύμαστον—St John explained he would never have decided to give to any ordinary city—οὐ τῇδε ἢ τῇδε τῇ πόλει—only to the city greater than all others, only to the imperial city of Constantine, would he disclose where the relic could be found.[14]

It is important to realize that the customary canons of ethical behaviour do not apply where relics are concerned: the recognition of any title to property in a relic is suspended. There is a good example of this attitude in the Life of the ascetic Isaac who was born in Mesopotamia but had lived in Constantinople from A.D. 383 to A.D. 438. Here no attempt is made to disguise the use of open violence. After Isaac's death the Emperor sent a litter to bear the body to the Great Church (St Sophia) where watch was kept all night. At dawn Nectarius with his clergy and the citizens went forth chanting hymns carrying the saint to his tomb. But an *illustris* named Aurelian had constructed in front and to the south of the monastery of Isaac a martyrion dedicated to the protomartyr Stephen in order to place in it the holy corpse of Stephen when it reached Constantinople from Jerusalem. Failing in this—Stephen was laid to rest in Constantianae—Aurelian planned that the corpse of the blessed Isaac should be placed in the martyrion instead of Stephen εὐλογίας χάριν—to sanctify it. And this came to pass. At the time when Isaac was being buried, Aurelian placed a troop (βοήθειαν)—a large number of men— near the road which led to the monastery in order to carry off the corpse as it passed and to convey it into the oratory. 'And this they did with the permission of Christ our God Who directs everything, and so his holy body had to be placed in the church of the holy protomartyr Stephen on the right of the holy table within the choir.' One hardly expected that Aurelian would obtain the divine permission so easily, but the corpse still remained in the capital and Constantinople was not deprived of the protection of the precious relic.[15]

[14] Migne, *P.L.*, 67, col. 444.

[15] F. Nau, op. cit.—Thus the Virgin approved the theft of her robe, *infra*, p. 257. St Anastasius in the seventh century supported and advised those who stole his body: H. Usener, *Acta Martyris Anastasii Persae* (Bonn, 1894). The Ἐπάνοδος τοῦ λειψάνου τοῦ ἁγίου μάρτυρος Ἀναστασίου ἐκ Περσίδος εἰς τὸ μοναστήριον αὐτοῦ [in Jerusalem] (*BHG.*, 88) is a strictly contemporary document (pp. 12–14) and the story is vividly told.

There is, however, one account which insists on a much more rigorous ethical standard. In the reign of Heraclius, the nuns of a convent in Melitene fled to Constantinople before the Persian invasion and as refugees brought with them their holy picture not made by human hands. The nuns were given shelter in the capital by the Patriarch, who took the picture into his own possession. But he suffered many ills and in a vision it was explained to him that he would be cured only if he returned to the nuns their picture. 'Don't you know', he was asked in the vision, 'that they are strangers here, and they have none to console them seeing that they come from a foreign land?' The Patriarch gave back to the nuns their picture. It is a pleasant story.[16]

And thus through the centuries the number of the supernatural defences of the Queen of cities grew and it was a proud triumph when as a result of his victories John Curcuas in 944 carried to Constantinople the famous portrait of Christ which had been granted to Abgar King of Edessa.[17] What did that bringing of the portrait mean to the folk of East Rome? They 'believed that the image would be for the glory of the faithful, for the safety of the Emperors, for the preservation of the entire city and of the κατάστασις of the Christians'. What is the true translation of κατάστασις?[18] Is it the 'constitution' of the Christian Empire or is it not rather the Christian 'way of life'? 'Constantinople would thereby acquire greater strength and would be kept for all time unharmed and unravaged.'[19]

Such is the background, such the complementary supernatural protection which gave confidence to the population of the capital. But these relics were only a supplement; for the protection of Constantinople the constant pledge, the unfailing guarantee, was the succour and mediation of the Blessed Virgin: God had given her to be the acropolis, the fortress, the wall of defence for the capital: the city was *her* city: the appeal

[16] Dobschütz, op. cit., pp. 126*–7*.
[17] On the portrait cf. Dobschütz, op. cit., pp. 102–96, 158*–249*, 29**–156**; Steven Runciman, 'Some Remarks on the Image of Edessa', in *Cambridge Historical Journal*, iii (1931), pp. 238–52.
[18] Dobschütz, op. cit., p. 85**, and cf. the whole of ch. 65, ibid.
[19] Dobschütz, op. cit., p. 83**.

through the centuries is always the same: as in the past, so now, defend *thy* city. It is through a study of the East Roman hymns to the glory of the Virgin that the modern student can gain some realization of the intensity of the passionate devotion with which the citizens of 'her city' honoured the Theotokos.[20] The churches dedicated to her in Constantinople outnumbered any other dedication: they were 'countless'. 'You would not find any public place or imperial dwelling, no reputable inn or private house of those in authority where there is not a church or an oratory of the Mother of God.'[21] And as 'head and metropolis' of all these churches and oratories there stood the church at Blachernae[22] at the N.W. extremity of the landward walls. It was known that the Virgin delighted in this church, so that Christians building churches in other places called them Blachernae after the church in the capital.[23] 'And to Blachernae, if there had been any private or public good fortune, all classes—patriarchs, emperors, those in high rank or public office and ordinary citizens—would hasten to give their thanks to God and to the Virgin; and if they were burdened with disasters, they came in confidence to Blachernae to be relieved of the weight of their burdens.'[24] 'For in the church at Blachernae and from that church we have received and shall receive whatever good thing there is or shall be.'[25] And in the church of the Virgin the worshippers feel themselves to be in Heaven: 'there, while glorifying the Theotokos, we feel that we join the angelic choirs', as the Patriarch Germanus said in a sermon.[26]

And of course the Byzantines conceived of the Virgin as dwelling with them in Constantinople; where else should she dwell? In the story of a miracle (which was deemed to be of sufficient significance to be related in a separate document) to

---

[20] Cf. e.g. the Akathist Hymn: Greek Text and English verse translation by W. J. Birkbeck and G. R. Woodward (Longmans, Green and Co., 1917); Migne, *P.G.*, 92, cols. 1335–48; the vast *Mariale* of Joseph the Hymnographer: Migne, *P.G.*, 105; the homily on the Akathist Hymn published in Σωτήρ (*supra*, p. 249, n. 4). For the Syriac hymns on which Byzantine hymns were modelled, see the Italian translation by G. Ricciotti, *Inni alla Vergine* (Turin, 1939), and E. Wellesz, *A History of Byzantine Music and Hymnography* (Oxford, 1949), pp. 7–8, and Index *s.v.* Ephraem.

[21] Combefis, op. cit., col. 754.   [22] Ibid.

[23] Ibid., cols. 754–5.   [24] Ibid., col. 755; cf. col. 771, § 2: 774, § 1.

[25] Ibid., col. 755.   [26] *BHG.*, 1086: Migne, *P.G.*, 98, col. 381.

a girl who had been plagued by a demon for seven years the
Virgin in a vision says quite naturally and simply: 'I am in
Constantinople and I wanted to bring you there and heal you,
but since your mother, if she were to find your bed empty,
might be driven mad by excess of grief, I have left you in your
bed and not carried you to my church, as I should otherwise
have done.'[27] It was sympathy and consideration such as this
which endeared the Virgin to the Romans of the eastern
capital.

Thus it was only natural that the Virgin should feel herself
to be exiled if she is not amongst her own people in the capital.
It is this passionate desire of the Virgin to be reunited with the
folk of Constantinople which gives interest and significance to
the narratives of the 'Roman Virgin'. Under Leo III, when the
Emperor had begun to enforce his iconoclastic policy, the
Patriarch took the sacred image of the Virgin down to the sea
and to save it from destruction launched it on its voyage to the
western capital. Standing upright on the water the icon reached
Rome in twenty-four hours. It was welcomed by the Pope and
was hung in the church dedicated to St Peter. Years passed; at
length imperial policy was reversed and the icons were restored.
Of this change Rome had no knowledge, but the icon knew that
it was time for it to return; it struggled to free itself from its
fastenings and made a violent rattling noise which spread dismay among the congregation. The hymn-singing ceased and
gave place to the appeal of the Kyrie eleison. And then the
icon liberated itself, went down to the Tiber and thence to the
open sea. Standing upright on the water, in a night and a
day it reached Constantinople and there it found a home in
the Virgin's Church in the district of Chalkoprateia near St
Sophia. Periodically the icon was to be carried 'throughout the city which the Virgin had chosen for her dwelling-
place'.[28]

Of course the theologians knew that the mediation of the

---

[27] *BHG.*, 1076: Papadopoulos-Kerameus, *Varia Graeca Sacra* (St Petersburg,
1909), pp. 151, 7–11, 152, 29–33.

[28] On the 'Roman' Virgin see Dobschütz, op. cit., pp. 233**–266**, and his
further study 'Maria Romaia', in *Byz. Zeits.*, xii (1903), pp. 173–214. Cf. *BHG.*,
1066–8. A brotherhood was formed to take charge of the icon: *Byz. Zeits.*, loc.
cit., p. 202, 4, p. 203, 13. For the weekly procession: p. 202, 6, and Dobschütz,
Christusbilder, p. 258**.

Virgin embraced in its scope the whole world,[29] but it can hardly be doubted that the popular belief in the local presence of the Theotokos within *her* city must have meant much to the population of the capital. The Virgin, it is true, might go out to her church of the Sacred Source (Pege), but that was only a short distance from the city walls near the Golden Gate, and here by the sacred spring, where there was a monastery, the Virgin through the city's history worked her miracles of healing. Members of the imperial family often sought relief from sickness at Pege, and the Byzantines recorded with gratitude the benefits which the Theotokos had conferred upon them, bidding them either to drink the water of the spring or, mixing the water with earth, to use it as an ointment.[30]

The inhabitants of Constantinople believed that Constantine had 'transferred the arcana of the might of Rome, the Palladium of Troy, to his new capital and hid it under the porphyry column on the top of which stood his own image'.[31] But in the fifth century the capital of the Christian Empire acquired its own Palladium, the robe ($\dot{\epsilon}\sigma\theta\dot{\eta}s$) of the Virgin. The robe was discovered by two patricians, relatives of Ardaburius and Aspar, in a small village of Galilee. It was stolen by them and carried to Constantinople after they had prayed to the Virgin beseeching her to approve the deed, for, they said, 'it is to *thy* city that the robe is being transferred, the city which is the Queen of all other cities, whose first charge it has always been to honour anything of thine.' And the Virgin answered their prayer and gave her consent.[32] It was in the Virgin's

---

[29] Παντὸς τοῦ κόσμου προστασία καὶ σκέπη, *Byz. Zeits.*, xii, p. 201, 35, and cf. e.g. *Patrologia Orientalis*, xvi (1922), fasc. 3, 'Homélies mariales byzantines', p. 462; *Varia Graeca Sacra*, ed. Papadopoulos-Kerameus, p. 151, 6: ἐγώ εἰμι ἡ τὸν κόσμον κρατοῦσα καὶ περιέπουσα ; L. Sternbach, *Analecta Avarica* (see p. 249, n. 5), p. 337, 8: κοσμοσώτειρα δέσποινα.

[30] For a description of Pege see the Ecclesiastical History of Nicephorus Callistus Xanthopulus, xv, cs. 25 and 26, Migne, *P.G.* 147, cols. 72–7. For the miracles at Pege see *BHG.* 1072 and 1074: Διήγησις περὶ τῆς συστάσεως τῶν ἐν τῇ Πηγῇ τῆς Θεοτόκου ναῶν καὶ περὶ τῶν ἐν αὐτοῖς γενομένων θαυμάτων, in *Acta Sanctorum*, Novembris t. 3 (November 8), pp. 878–89, and cf. *Commentarius praevius*, ibid., p. 860; Petrus Lambecius, *Commentariorum de augustissima Bibliotheca Caesarea Vindobonensi*, vol. viii, 2nd edition, opera A. F. Kollarii, cols. 119–31, with a summary account of the miracles by Nicephorus, ibid., cols. 120–3.

[31] A. Alföldi, in *Journal of Roman Studies*, 37 (1947), p. 11.

[32] There are several versions of the story. Cf. (i) 'Depositio Vestis S. Deiparae in Blachernis', in B. Latyšev, *Menologium* (11th century), fasc. 2 (St. Petersburg,

church at Blachernae that the robe as the Palladium of the capital remained through the centuries.[33] The city also possessed the Virgin's shroud, her girdle ($\zeta\acute{\omega}\nu\eta$) and the swaddling-clothes ($\sigma\pi\acute{\alpha}\rho\gamma\alpha\nu\alpha$) in which Jesus had rested against his Mother's breast. Still upon them they bore the marks of the drops of the Virgin's milk. So human, so intimate were these treasured relics that one could not be blamed, said a Patriarch of Constantinople, if one felt that one could converse with them.[34]

And in the succession of perils which threatened Constantinople through the centuries the Byzantines were persuaded that they owed their rescue to the succour of the Virgin; and as the cycle of commemorative rites came round in the calendar of the Church the congregation heard the reading which recalled the past and the intervention of the Virgin: the aid of the city's Defender was not allowed to pass into oblivion. We do not always bear in mind what these lections must have meant for the faithful, especially when they were learned by heart.[35] We still possess the text of some of these readings perpetuating the repulse of the Persians, Avars and Slavs in 626, the defeat of the Arab attacks—year by year for seven years—in the seventh century and the culminating victory over the Arabs by Leo III. In the ninth century the armada of the Russians was wrecked and the invaders retired discomfited. And in every case salvation came from the robe, the girdle, the icon, the mediation of the Virgin. This succession of defeats suffered by the assailants of the Empire is very impressive: for the Byzantines it must surely have created a guarantee that

1912), pp. 127–32; (ii) 'Oratio de S. Deipara', in Latyšev, op. cit., fasc. 2, pp. 377–83; (iii) 'Narratio historica in Depositionem Vestis S. Mariae, *BHG.* 1058, in Combefis, op. cit., cols. 751–86; (iv) 'Oratio de S. Maria', in Migne, *P.G.* 115, cols. 560–6, a Latin version based on (ii). [See above, pp. 240–7.]

[33] For the church at Blachernae: Jean Ebersolt, *Sanctuaires de Byzance* (Paris, 1921), pp. 44–53.

[34] For the sermon of Germanus, *BHG.* 1086: Migne, *P.G.* 98, cols. 372–84 at col. 376. It is not necessary in this place to add references to the sources which concern the girdle. There is a suggestion that there was a rivalry between the church at Blachernae with its ἁγία σορός containing the robe and the church at Chalkoprateia with its ἁγία σορός containing the Virgin's girdle. We might see in the Encomium on the Virgin's girdle—so the title—which asserts that equal devotion should be paid to both girdle and robe—an effort to reconcile such rivalries. F. Combefis, op. cit., cols. 790–802 (*BHG.* 1147).

[35] Migne, *P.G.* 100, col. 1081c.

past mercies would be repeated: whatever else happened, the city must survive inviolate. At the outset the invaders might cause great sufferings for the provincials—the suburbs sacked and churches burnt—and these reverses were explained, in homilies addressed to the population of the capital, as God's punishment for sin; Photius, for instance, enlarges on the theme at the time of the Russian invasion of A.D. 860. If this were so, it did but make it the more essential to secure the mediation of the Virgin that so the pity of God should be aroused. To that traditional explanation there is one exception, and that exception in its simplicity is surely very impressive. Cananus has described the brutalities of the Muslims and the devastation of the countryside, and then he writes: 'But how and whence and for what reason this disaster and destruction and these most terrible hardships fell upon the luckless and wretched Romans—on all this it has seemed better to us to keep silence.'[36] The time-honoured explanation was indeed all too facile an escape from an agonizing problem. Cananus deserves our respect.

And it must always be remembered that the belief in supernatural aid did not relieve man from the duty of playing his part in self-defence. Just as Joshua and Gideon[37] had participated in the victory granted by Jehovah, so in the siege of the capital in 626 the citizens of Constantinople were reminded of their duty: δεῖ γὰρ μετὰ τῆς ἄνωθεν βοηθείας καὶ ἡμᾶς τὰ προσήκοντα ἐνεργεῖν.[38] And in that defence children and old men alike could take their share, even if it were only in prayers, the spiritual armour of sword and breastplate. 'God wished not that those who flee to Him for help should be idle and inactive.'[39] And perhaps no better example of the effect of a fresh realization of the Virgin's aid could be found than the account given by Cananus of the Muslim attack on Constantinople in 1422. The capital was in complete despondency when the citizens became newly conscious that they had the support, the πρεσβεία, of the Theotokos. They were filled with ardour, armour was improvized from tables or from covers of butts,

---

[36] Cananus, Bonn ed., p. 459.
[37] Sternbach, *Analecta Avarica*, p. 303, 38–9; cf. p. 305, 18.
[38] Akathist Synaxarium: Migne, *P.G.* 92, col. 1349; cf. col. 1357.
[39] Sternbach, op. cit., p. 303, 36; cf. p. 319, 25.

while unarmed stone-throwers exposed themselves as though they had been protected *cap à pie*. Here we have one of the most vigorous pieces of writing that the Eastern Empire has left us.

To the last the same appeal to the Virgin sums up the city's need. At some time between 1451 and 1453 Dorotheus, Metropolitan of Mitylene, preaches that defeat has been the punishment of sin; 'our only hope, our only refuge, is the Virgin: our prayer to her must be: Save thy city as thou knowest how'.[40] But this time this appeal to the Theotokos was in vain: in 1453 the Turk carried the day.

As the background of Byzantine history the alliance of God and the Virgin is the factor in East Roman thought which the student forgets at his peril. It runs, for instance, as a constant element through the long contemporary account of the repulse of the Avars in 626,[41] and the confidence in the succour of the Virgin is mirrored in the extreme devotion which is rendered to the Theotokos. I know of only one passage where she is called 'God' (Θεός),[42] and one wonders what precise significance that word—written without the article—may have had for a Byzantine. But an East Roman could say to the Virgin: 'In the multitude of our sins we were pursued by God; through thee we sought for God and found Him.' 'Give unto us eternal life.' The Virgin can ransom the sinner from eternal punishment. 'Thy help, Theotokos, avails for salvation: no other mediation with God is needed.' 'For no one is being saved except through thee.' 'No one is being redeemed from terror save through thee.'[43] Such is the reliance of the Christians of Constantinople upon their wall of defence, their all-victorious general, their supernatural champion on earth and their mediator in Heaven.

---

[40] Loparev, in *Viz. Vrem.*, 12 (1906), pp. 166–71.

[41] Sternbach, op. cit., cf. e.g. 300, 26; 302, 11; 302, 32; 303, 8; 303, 18; 303, 28; 310, 17; 311, 12; 313, 24 (cf. 317, 37); 318, 4; 319, 38; 320, 25. God would never have allowed the city to be captured, ibid., p. 313.

[42] Καὶ μετὰ τὸν Θεὸν Θεὸς φιλάνθρωπος, Dobschütz, op. cit., p. 263**.

[43] See the Oratio by Archbishop Germanus, Migne *P.G.* 98, col. 372–84, at p. 380, and cf. *Byz. Zeits.*, xii, p. 206 at end.

XVIII

The *Pratum Spirituale*

[*Orientalia Christiana Periodica*, xiii (1947), pp. 404–14.]

IT is surprising that those who have written on the history of the Byzantine Empire have not made fuller use of the *Pratum Spirituale* of John Moschus. Unlike much hagiographical writing it can be dated with precision: it reflects the conditions within the Empire in the sixth and the early years of the seventh century. Again, unlike much hagiographical writing, it is free from tortured rhetoric: it can be read not merely as a painful duty laid upon the historical student, but as a positive pleasure. When one sees what Sophronius, the friend and companion of John Moschus, could make of four lines of a simple statement in the life of St Anastasius,[1] one can only be grateful that he refrained from re-writing the *Pratum Spirituale*.

It may be worth while to suggest the kind of contribution which these monastic stories can make to our understanding of the thought-world of the East Romans. We do not need to ask how far these stories are historically accurate; it is enough for us to feel confident that they are reported as they were related to John, remembering that he had a wide experience of the ascetic life of his day. He had taken his monastic vows in the famous monastery of St Theodosius near Jerusalem; from the coenobium he had made his way to the sacred river of Jordan and lived as an anchorite there and later in the New Laura of St Sabas. When the Persians attacked the eastern provinces of the Empire he withdrew to Antioch, and on the Persian invasion of Syria he retired to Alexandria, and from Alexandria he visited the monasteries and the solitaries of Egypt until on the occupation of Jerusalem by the Persians he sailed to the West and died in Rome. John knew well the life of which he wrote.[2]

---

[1] Hermann Usener, *Der heilige Tychon* (Teubner, Leipzig, 1907), pp. 102–3.

[2] Usener, ibid., pp. 80–100; S. Vailhé, *Échos d'orient*, v (1901), pp. 107–16.

The Christian worship of the early Church and its ritual practices often enough appear to us as formal usages when they are stated in the text-books; in these stories of the *Pratum Spirituale* the ritual comes alive: it is restored to its setting of daily actuality. Conon, a priest from Cilicia, John tells us, was a powerful man, a member of the monastery of Penthoukla, and so he was appointed to baptize the converted. But when he had to anoint women in baptism he was embarrassed (ἐσκανδαλίζετο) and was contemplating leaving the monastery. A beautiful Persian woman came for baptism, and Conon could not face the ordeal. There was a delay of two days, and when the Archbishop heard of it he wanted to appoint a deaconess to administer the rite, but he refrained from doing so because traditional usage did not permit a woman to baptize. St John the Baptist at length intervened and secured that Conon in future did not recognize the sex of the postulant (c. 3). We begin to realize the practical problems which might arise. A young man was brought to a monastery desiring to be received as a monk. One of the Fathers through his gift of discrimination said at once that the youth had not been baptized. The candidate was asked who he was and whence he came. He said that he came from the West, his parents were pagans (Ἕλληνες), and therefore he did not know whether he had been baptized. So he was taken to the Jordan and baptized in that sacred river (c. 138). Another practical problem relating to baptism led to an interesting discussion. On the outbreak of war a party of young men fled to Palestine and among them was a Jewish youth. In the desert the Jew fell ill and at last collapsed. Feeling that he was dying he desired to become a Christian, but his companions were at a loss: they could not baptize him—'We are lay folk,' they said, 'only bishops or priests can baptize.' But with oaths and tears the Jew implored them not to deprive him of so great a gift, and so in the end they yielded. With great labour they stripped him of his clothes, stood him upright and baptized him with the desert sand, giving him the name of Theodore, and each of them said Amen after the invocation of each name of the Holy Trinity. And then the sufferer recovered strength and they all reached Ascalon and reported what they had done to the bishop. He was in grave doubt and summoned all the clergy of the city to consider whether this was a valid baptism. And some said 'Yes' because of the miracle of the youth's recovery and some said 'No': they quoted the discussion of Gregory of Nazianzus of the different kinds of baptism and none of these met this case. They cited Christ's words to Nicodemus, but others urged that the Apostles were not baptized and it surely would not be held that they did not enter into the Kingdom of Heaven. Finally the bishop decided to send Theodore to the Jordan for baptism in the river (c. 176).

We may easily fail to take account of the realism of popular thought on the sacraments. Thus a brother in the monastery of Choziba had learnt the prayer of consecration at the Eucharist and one day, when he had been sent to procure bread for the communion-rite, on his way instead of repeating a psalm he recited the consecration prayer. At the celebration of the Eucharist the priest did not see, as he was accustomed to do, the descent of the Holy Spirit. In deep dismay and fearing that he had committed some sin, he threw himself down, weeping, on the floor of the diakonikon; there an angel explained to him that the bread was already consecrated by the words of the brother. Henceforth, it was laid down, no one not ordained to the priesthood should learn the prayer of consecration, while the prayer should never be repeated save at the altar (c. 25). It would seem that children did not as a rule communicate before they were two years of age; indeed, Gregory of Nazianzus advised that baptism should be postponed, unless there was fear of death, until the child was three years old. The children in Syria at the celebration of the Eucharist stood nearest to the altar after the priests and communicated first. And here in some places the priests were accustomed to repeat the prayer of consecration in a loud voice (μεγάλως ἐκφωνεῖν) so that the children learnt it by heart. As they were shepherding the flocks the children decided to act the celebration of the sacrament; they selected a flat stone to serve as an altar and chose from their number a priest and deacons, and over their food repeated the prayer of consecration. But they were prevented from breaking the consecrated bread by a fire which fell from heaven and burned up the Eucharist and the altar-stone (c. 196).[3]

In Seleucia near Antioch there was a rich merchant, a pious Monophysite; the trusted manager of his business was a Chalcedonian. According to the custom of the country the latter communicated on Thursday in Easter week, and took home with him some pieces of the consecrated bread for domestic celebration of the sacrament. The bread he put in a casket and locked it up in his safe. After Easter he was sent to Constantinople; he gave the key of the safe to his employer but forgot the Eucharistic bread. When the merchant opened the safe he found there the bread and waited for the manager's return. The latter, however, was kept in the capital for a year. When Maundy Thursday came round the merchant, knowing that the Eucharistic bread must not be kept for more than a year, was at a loss: he as a Monophysite could not eat the bread which a Chalcedonian had consecrated, so he determined to burn it. When he opened the safe he found that all the pieces of bread had put forth ears of wheat. At the sight of this miracle he and all his family were converted to the orthodox faith (c. 79).

The same realism is shown in the East Roman belief in the descent of the Holy Ghost in the form of a cloud over the altar, and thus a celebrant will repeat the prayer of consecration until the cloud appears (cs. 27, 150). When once an altar has been consecrated, even though the monks are driven from the monastery or a solitary leaves his cell, an angel is charged by God with keeping perpetual watch and ward over it (cs. 4, 10).

In the *Pratum Spirituale* the sacred icon plays its part in popular devotion. The demon of harlotry well knew the icon's power: he had long been tormenting a monk and the latter grew desperate. 'Swear that you will not adore ($\pi\rho o\sigma\kappa\upsilon\nu\epsilon\hat{\iota}\nu$) the icon of our Lady bearing the Christ Child', said the demon, 'and I will trouble you no longer' (c. 45). A woman had spent large sums of money on digging a deep well and still could find no water. One day she saw someone saying to her, 'Send and

---

[3] Cf. a similar story dating from the Arab period but included amongst the narratives of the *Pratum Spirituale, Byz. Zeits.*, xxxviii (1938), pp. 361-5.

fetch the icon of St Theodosius of the monastery of the Rock
and God will supply you with water'. She immediately sent
two messengers, the icon was brought and lowered into the
well and straightway water began to flow (c. 81). In a monastery some twenty miles from Jerusalem a solitary had his
cave, and in it was an icon of the Virgin with the infant
Christ; when going on a journey he would light a candle and
pray to God that he might travel safely. Then turning to the
Virgin he would tell her that he would be away for many days
and would ask her to be sure to keep her candle burning until
his return, 'for I leave having your help as my companion on
my way'. He might be absent from the cave for five or six
months, but however long his absence he never found the
candle extinguished (c. 180). Such is the devotion which the
Iconoclasts challenged.

From the *Pratum Spirituale* we learn that some of the
extravagances of Syrian devotion have penetrated into the
monastic life of Palestine. Thus in his youthful fervour Christopher, who had come to Palestine from Rome, used at night
to visit the cave of St Theodosius for prayer. Leading down to
the cave were eighteen steps, and at each step Christopher
prostrated himself one hundred times. But this discipline
proved insufficient and he departed to the desert of Sinai (c.
105). In another chapter we are told that the πλάξ (was it of
stone or wood?) on which the monk stood for prayer was hol-
lowed four fingers deep where his knees and hands were placed
when he prostrated himself (c. 184). It must not, however, be
forgotten that alongside of the ascetism of bodily exercises
there is also a generous recognition of the asceticism of the
spirit (cs. 65, 153, 194).

When the social history of the Empire comes to be written
the *Pratum Spirituale* must not be neglected, for in it we see
reflected the insecurity of life in the Eastern provinces. There
is a report of war in Africa in the account of a Roman stan-
dard-bearer (δρακονάρις) of an engagement with the Maurit-
iani and the flight of the imperial troops (c. 20). Egypt and the
Thebaid suffer from the bloodthirsty (αἱμοβόροι) barbarians
always ready to carry off folk and hold them to ransom (c. 34).
The Mazikes lay waste the whole district of the Oasis, they kill

many monks and carry off others as prisoners. When the local church could not produce the twenty-four numismata demanded by the barbarians as ransom for their captives the monk Leo offered himself in their stead and was beheaded (c. 112). For the ransom of a notary of the church of Antioch his captors demanded eighty-five numismata (c. 34). The monks of Skiti were scattered by barbarian attack (c. 55). We are given an account of the siege of Salonica with barbarians laying waste the whole countryside (cs. 69–70). Saracens in Palestine are ready to assault a traveller: thus they meet and kill a solitary on the shore of the Dead Sea (c. 21 and cf. c. 133). Under Maurice the Saracen tribal chief Names raids Roman territory; Saracens solemnly promise their priest that if they capture any specially valuable booty they will bring it for sacrifice and in consequence of that promise they refuse to accept a ransom for a youth who was their prisoner (c. 155).

And there are not only barbarians: there are robbers organized, it may be, in a band of thirty under a robber chief. They have no hesitation in killing their victims (c. 143). Near Emmaus Cyriacus was a robber who was so pitiless that men knew him as 'the Wolf'. His gang was composed of Jews and Samaritans as well as Christians. In the absence of Cyriacus the newly-baptized who were returning from Jerusalem to their homes were attacked by his followers and, while the men fled, the children were dashed to the ground. When Cyriacus arrived and discovered the atrocity he beheaded the perpetrators and provided a guard for the women (c. 165). The hostility of the Jews and their readiness to kill a Christian may serve to account for this brutality (cf. c. 15).

And yet despite this insecurity one of the most striking features of the world of asceticism is its extreme mobility: monks seem to be constantly on the move. You might wish to go to the Holy City to worship at the hallowed places or to the sacred river of Jordan or to the wilderness. You might have a passionate admiration for the martyrs as had a certain John the anchorite, who went to visit St John in Ephesus, St Theodore in Euchaita, St Thecla in the Isaurian Seleucia and St Sergius in Saphas (c. 180). George an archimandrite goes to Constantinople to discuss with the Emperor Tiberius the af-

fairs of his monastery (c. 93), while an anchorite performs a
miracle at sea when returning from Constantinople (c. 174).

And John Moschus gives us some hints of the way in which
the provincials regarded the central government of the Empire. It must always be remembered that Palestine and Egypt
did not see the Emperor in person: these provinces knew the
sovran only as an authority demanding ever higher taxation
or brutally intervening through his agents to ruin men. A
story such as that told in c. 186 is thus instructive: a merchant
of Tyre was accused to the Emperor of having dissipated τὰ
κομερκίου—was he trading on behalf of the State? His property was seized, and he himself, clad only in his shirt, was
carried off to Constantinople and thrown into prison. Every
day he heard that the Emperor intended to put him to death
and he had already despaired of life. It was only by a miracle
that the merchant was saved (c. 186). This is the fashion in
which Syria becomes acquainted with the Emperor. And with
this narrative may be compared the story of the scandalous
bishop of Salonica who relapsed into the worship of idols and
was excommunicated by the Church. But he was not at the
end of his resources, for he could appeal to the authorities in
Constantinople where gold could remove every obstacle. To
these authorities in the capital the words of Isaiah (v. 23)
could aptly be applied, for 'they justify the wicked for bribes
and rob the righteous of his righteousness'. That is an illuminating judgement (c. 43). Indeed it is only to his face that the
Emperor is praised: the monk is praised whether present or
absent (c. 210).

We need a study of the virtues which were most highly
valued in the Eastern provinces of the Empire. Thus the
model bishop is generous in almsgiving, he does not cherish
the memory of injuries, he possesses the gift of tears and has
great sympathy with sinners (c. 140). Of Alexander the Patriarch of Antioch it was said that his almsgiving and his sympathy were so unbounded that it embraced those who had
robbed him. The remark was repeated that nothing was more
profitable than to have wronged Alexander (c. 34). And in this
Byzantine world almsgiving is the supreme virtue. The East
Roman took his New Testament seriously: his Lord had said

'Give to him that asketh thee' (Matthew v. 42) and he sought to obey that commandment. The West is inquisitive in its almsgiving: it seeks, as did St Basil, to estimate the moral worth of the object of its charity and the use to which its alms will be put. Not so the East Roman: enough for him that Christ had said 'Inasmuch as ye have done it unto one of the least of these my brethren, ye have done it unto me' (Matthew xxv. 40). This Byzantine faith is beautifully illustrated in one of John's stories. In Syrian Antioch there were many charitable institutions, and at the head of one of them was a Christ-loving man who distributed linen clothing which had been bought from Egypt. To him there came a brother and asked for clothes—not once or twice only, but three times. When he came for the fourth time the distributor objected that others needed help and he was not to come again. At night the distributor saw Christ come down from the sacred icon, saw Him raise His cloak, and underneath the cloak Christ showed him His garments; 'Look,' He said, 'one; look, two; look, three; look, four! Do not be grieved, for, believe Me, from the moment that you gave these to the poor they became My clothing' [*Byzantinische Zeitschrift*, xxxviii (1938), pp. 367–8]. There one gets to the heart of East Roman faith. On festivals of the Church the monasteries distributed food to the poor; in the *Pratum Spirituale* we are given particulars of the distribution made in one monastery on Maundy Thursday and Good Friday—half a bushel of grain, five eulogiai (what were these, one wonders), five small coins (ἀπὸ φαλερῶν έ), a pint of wine and half a pint of honey (c. 85). But perhaps no story more vividly reflects the value set by the Byzantine on the virtue of almsgiving than that told by John Moschus in c. 175. A woman prayed to the Virgin for her aid: the Emperor Zeno had wronged her daughter and she sought to be avenged. She prayed, with tears, for many days, and at length the All-Holy Mother of God appeared to her. 'Believe me, lady,' she said, 'many a time have I wished to avenge you, but his right hand prevents me.' John's comment is 'for he was very liberal in almsgiving'.

It is indeed their sheer friendliness which makes some of these holy men so attractive: a village ascete when he knew that a neighbour was too poor to buy seed-corn would take his own oxen and his seed-corn under cover of night and plough and sow his neighbour's field. On the high-road between Jericho and Jerusalem if he saw a weary child he would take him up on his shoulder and seeing another would perch the second child on the other shoulder. If he met a man or a woman with their shoes needing repair he would sit down and mend them: he used to carry with him the necessary tools. And if on his way he came across a dead man, he would say over him the prayers for the dead and then bury him (c. 24). There is a delightful account of the monk whose charity embraced all living creatures. He would get up very early in the morning and feed all the dogs in the monastery; he gave flour to the small ants and grain to the bigger ants. He soaked biscuits and put them out on the monastery roofs for the birds (c. 184). It is from such homely pictures as these that we shall best realize why the common folk of the East Roman provinces held the holy men in deep affection.

It is not easy to divine the interpretation of some of the stories in the *Pratum Spirituale* (e.g. cs. 50, 129). Take, for instance, the narrative in c. 76. A sea captain on his voyage saw ships bound for Alexandria, Constantinople, and other places sailing without any difficulty while his ship alone was held fast for a fortnight and could not be moved. All were in great distress and none could account for the happening. The captain, recognizing his responsibility for the crew and the passengers, began to pray for help to God, and one day he heard a voice saying 'Throw Mary down (βάλε κάτω Μαρίαν) and you will have a fair voyage'. But who Mary might be he had no idea. The voice repeated: 'Throw Mary down and you are saved.' So the captain called for Mary loudly. Mary was lying on a mattress and answered 'What do you want, sir?' The captain replied 'Do me the kindness to come here', and she rose and came to him. 'You see, sister Mary,' he said, 'my sins, and on my account you are all going to perish utterly.' But she, groaning deeply, said 'My master, I am the sinner.' He replied: 'What kind of sins have you, woman?' Her answer was that there was, alas! no kind of sin which she had not committed: 'I had a husband and two children, one was nine years old and the other five years when my husband died. For some time I remained a widow. There was a soldier living near me and I wanted him to marry me, but he said he would not marry a woman with children born of another husband, and since I loved him I killed the two children and sent to him saying "Now I have no children". When he heard what I had done he said "As the Lord liveth dwelling in Heaven, I will not have her". And so, fearing that what I had done might become known and I be put to death, I fled.' On hearing her story the captain was still unwilling to throw Mary overboard; so he devized a scheme (ἐσοφισάμην): he said 'I will get into the ship's boat, and if then the ship sails on, you will know that it is my sins which are holding back the ship'. So he ordered the boat to be lowered and stepped aboard, but neither ship nor boat moved at all. The captain came back to the ship and said to Mary 'Now you go into the boat'. And when she went down into the boat it turned round in a circle five times and sank without leaving a trace. Then the ship sailed on and in three and a half days completed a voyage which usually took fifteen days.—That is a very strange and uncomfortable story: what would a Byzantine have made of it?—what lesson did it inculcate? God's conception of moral action does to a modern reader seem very singular.

But at these pious stories an East Roman might surely on occasion be allowed to smile. Thus John Moschus heard in the Thebaid of a monk whose cell was near Antinoe; he had ten disciples, but one of these took no care for his soul and disregarded all the monk's warnings. The disciple died and the monk was greatly troubled. So he prayed to God that it might be revealed to him how it had fared with the disciple's soul. And falling into an ecstasy he saw a river of fire and in the fire a multitude and among them his disciple wrapped in fire up to his neck. 'My child,' he said, 'was it not on account of this punishment that I begged you to have a care concerning your soul?' And his disciple replied: 'I give thanks to God, father, that at least my head is free of the fire. For through your prayers I am standing on the head of a bishop' (c. 44). A Byzantine must surely have enjoyed that edifying tale.

The *Pratum Spirituale* in a word is full of diversified interest: it has been unduly neglected.

XIX

The Death of Julian the Apostate in a Christian Legend[1]

[*Journal of Roman Studies*, xxvii (1937), pp. 22–9.]

T HE Emperor Julian stood to the Roman world of the fourth century as the personification of the older faith, and with him died the hopes of a pagan restoration. His death came at a critical moment, and both pagan and Christian felt that it could have been no human hand which dealt the fatal blow. To Kallistos Julian was the victim of a demon: Κάλλιστος δέ, writes Socrates, ὁ ἐν τοῖς οἰκείοις τοῦ βασιλέως στρατευόμενος (i.e. as one of the imperial *domestici*), ἱστορήσας τὰ κατ' αὐτὸν ἐν ἡρωικῷ μέτρῳ, τὸν τότε πόλεμον διηγούμενος ὑπὸ δαίμονος βληθέντα τελευτῆσαι φησίν.[2] The comment of the Christian historian is interesting: ὅπερ τυχὸν μὲν ὡς ποιητὴς ἔπλασε, τυχὸν δὲ καί οὕτως ἔχει· πολλοὺς γὰρ ἐριννύες μετῆλθον. Libanius pictures the blessings which men anticipated under Julian's rule and adds ταῦτα καὶ ἔτι πλείω προσδοκώμενα χορὸς φθονερῶν ἀφείλετο δαιμόνων.[3] To the Christian similarly it was the saints who had fulfilled the will of Heaven in removing the Apostate persecutor of the Church, though a human assassin could hardly have been condemned—σχολῇ γε ἄν τις καὶ αὐτῷ μέμψαιτο διὰ Θεὸν καὶ θρησκείαν ἣν ἐπήνεσεν ἀνδρείῳ γενομένῳ.[4] Thus Sozomen wrote somewhat as follows:

[1] Cf. De Buck in *AASS*, October, x, pp. 572–3; G. Reinhardt, *Der Tod des Kaisers Julian nach den Quellen dargestellt* (Cöthen, 1891); Th. Büttner-Wobst, 'Der Tod des Kaisers Julian. Eine Quellenstudie', *Philologus*, li (1892), 561–80; Robert Graf Nostitz-Rieneck, 'Vom Tode des Kaisers Julian', *XVI Jahresbericht des öffentlichen Privatgymnasiums an der Stella Matutina zu Feldkirch* 1906–7, 1–35 (see H. D. in *Anal. Boll.*, xxvii (1928), p. 98 sq.); W. R. Halliday, 'St Basil and Julian the Apostate: a fragment of legendary history', *Annals of Archaeology and Anthropology*, vii (1914–16), pp. 89–106; P. Peeters, 'Un miracle des SS. Serge et Théodore et la vie de S. Basile dans Fauste de Byzance', *Anal. Boll.*, xxxix (1921), pp. 65–88.

[2] Socrates, *HE*, iii, 21; cf. *Anal. Boll.*, xxxix, 82, for quotation from Michael the Syrian.

[3] Libanius, ed. Förster, ii, 360 (=R. 618).

[4] Sozomen, *HE*, vi, 2. The reference to Greek views on the justification of tyrannicide is interesting.

'I have learned (ἐπυθόμην) that one of Julian's friends had a divine vision (θεία ὄψις) which I shall now proceed to describe. He had, it is related, started on a journey to Persia with the intention of joining the emperor. While on the road he found himself so far from any habitation that he was obliged one night to sleep in a church.[5] He saw that night either in a dream or in a vision many of the apostles and prophets assembled together; they were complaining of the injuries which the emperor had inflicted on the Church and were taking counsel concerning what should be done. After long deliberation and while they were still, as it were, in doubt, two of them arose in the midst of the assembly, desired the others to be of good cheer and, as though intending to deprive Julian of the imperial power, hastily departed from the conclave. He who saw this surprising vision did not attempt to pursue his travel, but awaited in horrible suspense the conclusion of the revelation. He laid himself down to sleep again in the same place, and again he saw the same assembly. Then suddenly, as though coming from a journey, the two who had seemed to depart the preceding night to effect their purpose against Julian returned, and announced to the others that the emperor had been put to death.'[6]

From this legend turn to the history of Faustus of Byzantium: unfortunately I cannot read Armenian, so that I can only give an English rendering of Lauer's German version.[7]

King Valens commanded that search should be made in order that a learned man might be seen and found who should be capable of writing a refutation of the Christian faith. He was told that a learned sophist lived in a certain city; so the emperor sent *magistriani* with orders to travel with all speed and to bring the man to him without delay. They took him and straightway brought him with them.

As they went on their journey towards the shelter for the second night they came across another small town. Outside the town was the martyr-chapel of a holy lady, by name Thecla. When the

---

[5] 'A fate that may well befall the modern traveller in the Levant': Halliday, op. cit., p. 101.

[6] Sozomen, *HE*, vi, 2.

[7] M. Lauer, *Des Faustus von Byzanz Geschichte Armeniens* (Köln, 1879). For a Latin version, cf. P. Peeters, *Anal. Boll.*, xxxix (1921), pp. 70–3.

sophist reached the spot, he dismounted and took up his abode in the chapel. The *magistriani* lodged in the town. When the sophist had eaten his meal, he threw down a mattress and shut the doors of the chapel. He cast himself upon the mattress and determined to lie upon his side. While he was still awake, he saw with eyes unclosed the doors of the chapel unexpectedly open, and there was a great gathering of many martyrs who appeared in glorious splendour. Before them walked the holy lady Thecla, adorned with great brilliance; for rays streamed from her as though from a light. They greeted one another and the lady Thecla spake to them: 'It is well that ye are come, dear friends and labourers of Christ.' After that they had greeted each other and seats had been set for them all, they sat down in order. Then the saints began to speak and said: 'The saints of the Lord who are not yet departed from the earth live here in persecution, some in bonds, some in prison, some in exile, others in other forms of violence, shame, need, and misery. We have with haste gathered ourselves together that we should not through negligence delay to become the avengers for the faithful of the Lord. Many labourers of the Lord are hindered, many fields lie untilled and many vineyards are laid waste. We must do away with Valens, the hinderer of the labourers, that every labourer can go to his work. The diligent labourer Barsilios is hindered at his work. Come then, let us send two of our number to go and remove the evildoer Valens from life.' One of these two was called Sargis, the other Theodoros. They sent them away, arranged a time and said: 'At the same time you and we will come.' Then they arose, went and parted.

When the sophist who was in the chapel had heard all this and had seen the vision with open eyes he was filled with wonder and remained sleepless until break of day. Early in the morning the *magistriani* came and said to the sophist: 'Up! let us go on our way.' He, however, pretended that he was ill and could not leave the spot. As they began to force him, he fell into a swoon, breathed with difficulty each single breath and could give no answer to their words until the evening. When it was evening, the *magistriani* left him in the chapel and went to their quarters in the town. The sophist shut the doors of the chapel and laid him upon his side in his place, when suddenly he saw once more the doors of the chapel opening, and the martyrs came and assembled, and the chapel was full of them. They met each other with great joy and greeted each other; then they set their seats, formed a circle and took their places in a predetermined order. Then there came also the two, Sargis and Theodoros, from the work to which they had been sent, and stepped into the midst of the assembly of the saints. The whole assembly of the saints looked up: 'How have ye accomplished your work to which ye went?' They answered and said, 'Since we departed from among you we have slain Valens, the enemy of the truth, and, see! at the appointed time we have come back to you.' The whole assembly arose, praised our Lord Jesus Christ and departed each to his place. And the sophist was in great distress until the break of day.

The stories are obviously variants of the same legend; 'Valens' in the history of Faustus is the title of the Roman emperor and not a personal name (cf. the use of the title 'Caesar'), and at this point in the work of Faustus 'Valens' stands for Julian.[8] It has been argued[9] that both stories do in fact refer to the Emperor Valens, but this contention cannot be sustained.

When we compare these two versions as given by Sozomen and Faustus we can, I think, suggest the domicile of origin of the legend and the route by which it reached its new home in Armenia. In Sozomen's account Julian is in Persia and his friend is on his way to join the emperor. In Faustus, Valens sends from a distance for one who should write a confutation of the Christian faith. Julian, we remember, started on his Persian campaign from Antioch; it was at Antioch or, if we may believe Jerome,[10] during the Persian expedition that the Emperor wrote his work against the 'Galilaeans'.[11] We should thus naturally identify the 'learned sophist' of the history of Faustus with Libanius of Antioch, and our surmise is confirmed when we find that in the Pseudo-Amphilochian *Life of Basil*, alongside of the Caesarean version of the legend (see *infra*), a similar vision was seen by Libanius the sophist.[12] But this is not all: in Faustus we read that St Thecla presided over

[8] Cf. 'Rome and Armenia in the Fourth Century', *supra*, pp. 186–208.

[9] By Peeters (see *supra*, p. 271, n. 1).

[10] 'Julianum Augustum vii libros in expeditione Parthica adversum Christum evomuisse.' *Ep.* 70 to Magnus (i, 425 E, Vall.).

[11] For a full discussion of the evidence for the date of composition of the work cf. C. J. Neumann, *Juliani Imperatoris librorum contra Christianos quae supersunt* (Leipzig, 1880), pp. 5–8.

[12] In this form of the story Libanius is in Persia with Julian, acting as quaestor: ἰσοδύναμον δὲ ὄναρ ἐθεώρει τῇ αὐτῇ νυκτὶ καὶ Λιβάνιος ὁ σοφιστὴς συνὼν τῷ Ἰουλιανῷ ἐν Περσίδι καὶ τὴν τοῦ κοιαίστωρος ἀξίαν διακοσμῶν. F. Combefis, *SS. Patrum Amphilochii Iconiensis Methodii Patarensis et Andreae Cretensis opera omnia quae reperiri potuerunt* (Paris, 1644), 182. There is no reason, now that the legendary character of the Pseudo-Amphilochian life is recognized, to assume the existence of a Libanius other than the famous sophist of Antioch (so Combefis, op. cit., p. 269 sq., n. 83), though it is surprising to find this consistent champion of the ancient faith converted to Christianity as is related in the *Vita*, 169 sqq.

the heavenly council. The virgin Thecla, ἀπόστολος as she is called in the *Menologium*, τῆς ἁγίας πρωτομάρτυρος καὶ ἰσαποστόλου Θέκλης (*Horolog. Graecorum* at date 24 September), τὴν ἁγίαν καὶ πολύαθλον πρωτομάρτυρα Θέκλαν as we read in Evagrius 3, 8[13]—was the glory of Antioch: here was her *martyrium*—her martyr-chapel;[14] on her festival was doubtless preached the homily, *De sancta Thecla*, a fragment of which is preserved and attributed to Chrysostom.[15] The legend in fact bears clear traces of its Antiochene origin.

Further, since Gelzer's masterly study of 'Die Anfänge der armenischen Kirche',[16] we might expect that the story would have reached Armenia by way of Caesarea; and in fact this chapter of Faustus is imbedded in a section devoted to St Basil of Caesarea.[17] Not only so, but in the legend as recounted by Faustus there is a direct reference to Basil: 'the diligent labourer Barsilios is hindered at his work.' It is thus evident that Caesarea was a stage on the legend's journey.

In Armenia the two saints who carry out the death sentence are Sargis and Theodoros. Who are these saints? Sargis is St Sergius who is commemorated in the Armenian calendar together with his son and fourteen companions.[18] He is usually associated with St Bacchus. He was 'primicerius scholae gentilium' (see *AASS*, October, iii, p. 835)—a military saint—and as a soldier well qualified to carry out the task of slaying the emperor. St Theodore is a martyr who suffered under Maximian or, according to another *Vita*, under Maximian and Maximin, and therefore in his lifetime had nothing to do with the Apostate. The fact of his name occurring in the legend as the slayer of Julian suggests that the saint was already associated with the familiar legend of the κόλλυβα—the cooked corn—which under the guidance of Heaven St Theodore had

---

[13] I owe these citations to the 'Monitum ad Homiliam de Sancta Thecla', Chrysostom's works (ed. De Montfaucon, Paris, 1837), ii, 896.

[14] V. Schultze, *Altchristliche Städte und Landschaften*, iii (Gütersloh, 1930), p. 320.

[15] Chrysostom (ed. De Montfaucon), ii, 896–9.

[16] *Berichte über die Verhandlungen der kön. sächsischen Gesellschaft der Wissenschaften zu Leipzig* (Phil.-hist. Klasse), xlvii (1895), pp. 109–74.

[17] On this connexion with St Basil cf. P. Peeters, op. cit. (p. 271 *supra*, n. 1), pp. 65–70.

[18] Cf. N. Nilles, *Kalendarium manuale utriusueq ecclesiae orientalis et occidentalis* (Innsbrück, 1897), ii, 572.

supplied to his fellow-citizens of Euchaita at a time when Julian had contaminated the food-stuffs on sale in the market-place by mixing with them the blood of pagan sacrifices.[19] Since both SS. Sargis and Theodoros are *stratelatai*, it was prob-ably their character as military saints which primarily deter-mined the choice of the Armenians when they adapted the legend which they had received through Caesarea, while in the case of St Theodore the story of the κόλλυβα may also have played a part in that selection.

We have still to consider the form which Caesarea gave to the story. In this connexion it is important to remember that in the fourth century the cult of the saints was solely local in character. Each town or diocese honoured only those saints which specially belonged to it, and their cult long remained limited to the place and the land where they had lived, worked or suffered—the solitary exceptions to this rule would seem to have been St Stephen, the protomartyr, and St John the Baptist.[20] Thus, if a church desired to appropriate a legend it would naturally seek to accommodate it to its own calendar. This happened at Caesarea. In the Pseudo-Amphilochian *Life of Basil* the whole story centres in Basil himself, though, as we have seen, it is parenthetically acknowledged that a similar vision was granted to Libanius; it is no longer in an Antiochene chapel of Thecla, but in the *martyrium* of the Caesarean saint, Mercurius, that the revelation is given; the president of the heavenly conclave is now not Thecla but a nameless glorious female form which suggests the Mother of God herself, while it is now Mercurius who slays the tyrant. The Caesarean guise of the legend appears in many forms. The first mention in our existing literature of St Mercurius as Heaven's executioner would appear to be in the Syriac romance on Julian which Nöldeke assigned to the first half of the sixth century: here Marcur reveals to Jovian, Julian's successor, the future doom of the Apostate. This comparatively late appearance of Mer-curius is, it would seem, due only to the fact that we do not

[19] For St Theodore cf. H. Delehaye, *Les légendes grecques des saints militaires* (Paris, 1909), pp. 11–43, 127–201.

[20] I summarize the conclusions of K. A. H. Kellner, *Heortologie*, 3rd edn., 1911. For the 'partikuläre Verehrung' of the martyrs cf. pp. 161 sqq.: for St John the Baptist and Stephen, pp. 165 sqq.

chance to possess any earlier treatment of the Caesarean version. This version became the generally accepted form of the legend, though in Malalas, the *Paschal Chronicle* and John of Nikiu, Christ Himself takes the place of honour formerly occupied by S. Thecla. Did it seem to the Byzantine world unfitting that a woman, however exalted, should preside over the senate of Heaven? In Western Europe through a ninth-century Latin translation of the Pseudo-Amphilochian *Vita* the legend, now definitely associated with the Virgin, becomes a constant element in the Mary-cycle of the Middle Ages.[21]

With that western development we are not concerned, but there remains one eastern variant of the legend which has not been noticed in previous studies of the Mercurius story. It is to be found in the *History of the Patriarchs of the Coptic Church of Alexandria,* and here Julian himself realizes that his death is the work of the saint. The story is as follows:[22] 'But as for Julian, the unbelieving prince, he marched on into Persia and God delivered him into the hand of his enemies on account of the saints whom he had imprisoned and threatened before his march. His death was thus. He saw in the night an army which came down upon him from the air, and one of the soldiers struck him with a lance on the head so that it pierced him through the body. Then, knowing that it was one of the martyrs, he filled his hand with his blood and threw it upwards saying, "Take that, Jesus, for thou hast conquered the whole world."[23] And after blaspheming thus, he fell dead. Thus

[21] For the Syriac text of the romance cf. G. Hoffmann, *Julianos der Abtrünnige. Syrische Erzählungen* (Kiel, 1887); for dating, Th. Nöldeke, 'Über den syrischen Roman von Kaiser Julian', *Zeitschr. d. deutschen morgenländischen Gesellschaft,* xxviii (1874), pp. 263–92. Translation: H. Gollancz, *Julian the Apostate now translated for the first time from the Syriac original, etc.* (London, 1928); for the visions of Marcur cf. pp. 153–5, 190–2. Latin translation of the visions, P. Peeters in *Anal. Boll.,* xxxix (1921), pp. 79 sqq. See also R. Förster, 'Kaiser Julian in der Dichtung alter und neuer Zeit', *Studien zur vergleichenden Literaturgeschichte,* v (1905), pp. 1–120 at pp. 9 sqq. For the Mercurius legend see in particular H. Delehaye, *Légendes grecques des saints militaires,* pp. 92–101 (with references to the sources which are not repeated here), Nostitz-Rieneck (*supra* p. 271, n. 1) and for modern versions of the legend Halliday (ibid.). For a representation of the death of Julian in a Byzantine miniature of the ninth century, cf. Büttner-Wobst (*supra* p. 271, n. 1), pp. 577–8. For an acute Byzantine criticism of the legend cf. Glycas (Bonn ed.,), p. 471.

[22] *Patrologia Orientalis,* i (1907), pp. 419–20. For Julian's vision in another form cf. Malalas, 332; *Chron. Pasch.,* 550–1.

[23] For different versions of Julian's last words cf. Büttner-Wobst (*supra,* p. 271, n. 1), pp. 572–9.

God delivered His people and the Romans returned to their
own country. And Basil, the holy man, three days before the
death of Julian, being in prison, had awaked from his sleep
and said to the two who were with him, "I have seen to-night
the martyr St Mercurius entering into his church and taking
his lance saying, 'In truth I will not suffer this unbeliever to
blaspheme my God'. But when he had said this he disappeared
from me and I did not see him again." Then both his companions said to him, "Verily I also saw the same thing". So
they said one to another, "We believe this firmly that it is so".
And they sent to the church of the martyr St Mercurius that
they might look for his lance which was kept there to see
whether it was still there or not. And as they could not find the
lance they were assured of the truth of the dream. And after
three days the letters with the news of Julian's death arrived
at Antioch.'

One would almost have expected 'at Caesarea'; is this an
echo of the original Antiochene legend?

There remains to be considered one further text; Nicephorus
Callistus Xanthopulos repeating in his *Church History* the legend and using Sozomen's account as his source—here it will be
remembered the saints are anonymous—adds Ἀρτέμιον δὲ
καὶ Μερκούριον λόγος ἔχει τούτους (i.e. the two saints) εἶναι.[24] I
know that this addition has been treated with scant respect[25]
—'ce n'est là qu'une licence de plagiaire. Tout ce que Nicé-
phore connaît de l'anecdote il l'a copié dans Sozomène et il ne
paraît pas qu'il se soit mis en frais de recherches érudites pour
retrouver ou deviner les noms de ces deux personnages sans
individualité définie'.[26] But St Artemius at least does possess a
marked individuality: he was originally an Arian saint, he
appears as a hero in the history of Philostorgius and that
Eunomian historian ἐκθειάζει τὸν μάρτυρα, πολλήν τινα τὴν
ἔνστασιν καὶ ἀκρίβειαν τῶν αὐτοῦ πράξεων ποιησάμενος, ἐκ τῶν
ἄνωθεν χρόνων τὴν τοῦ μάρτυρος προσοῦσαν εὐγένειαν ὑποσημη-
νάμενος καὶ πρὶν ἢ τῶν τοῦ μαρτυρίου ἀγώνων ἐφάψασθαι (*Artemii
Passio* in Philostorgius (ed. Bidez), 154). He suffered martyr-

[24] *HE*, x, 35: Migne, *PG*, cxlvi, 552.
[25] Cf. H. Delehaye, *Les légendes grecques des saints militaires*, p. 97.
[26] P. Peeters, *Anal. Boll.*, xxxix, 74–5.

dom at Antioch under Julian the Apostate[27] as a result of his protest against the tortures inflicted by the Emperor upon the Christian priests Eugenius and Macarius (cf. Μαρτύριον τοῦ ἁγίου καὶ ἐνδόξου μάρτυρος Ἀρτεμίου in Philostorgius [ed. Bidez], pp. 167–8). Artemius was later regarded as an orthodox martyr and saint, but at what date he was so recognized I do not think that we can say. It is true that in the 'Altes Martyrium des Artemius' it is stated that a pious (εὐσεβής) διάκονος Ariste secured from Julian permission to preserve the body of St Artemius: having embalmed it, she sent it to Constantinople with the idea of building there a worthy shrine for the precious relic.[28] In the *Martyrium of St Artemius*[29] we are further told that she was unable to do this: the relics διέμεινεν εἰς δεῦρο τῷ τοῦ Προδρόμου ναῷ. But the deaconess Ariste is as suspect a person as is the Εὐσεβία . . . φερωνύμως εὐσεβῶς ζῶσα who performed a similar service for the remains of St Theodore.[30] It has indeed been stated that the translation of the relics took place under the Emperor Anastasius, A.D. 491–518,[31] but I do not think this can be deduced from the *Patria Cp.* which reads[32] Ἡ Ὀξεῖα ὁ ἅγιος Ἀρτέμιος· τὸν δὲ ναὸν τοῦ Προδρόμου ἀνήγειρεν Ἀναστάσιος ὁ Δίκορος ὁ ἀποσιλεντιάριος ὁ Δυρραχιώτης. Ὄντος γὰρ αὐτοῦ πρωτοασηκρήτης ἐκεῖσε ᾤκει. μετὰ δὲ τὸ κομισθῆναι τὸ λείψανον τοῦ ἁγίου Ἀρτεμίου ὠνομάσθη ὁ ναὸς οὕτως. The church was still known by its original dedication in the seventh century and the date of the translation remains uncertain—any time between 491 and the middle of the seventh century is possible. The *Passio S. Artemii* attributed to John of Rhodes,[33] and therefore not the work of John

---

[27] Cf. the 'Altes Martyrium' in Philostorgius (ed. Bidez), p. 175.

[28] Ibid., pp. 174–5.   [29] Migne, *PG*, cxv, col. 1212.

[30] On Eusebia cf. H. Delehaye, *Les légendes grecques*, pp. 135, 146, 188 sqq., and the comment at p. 41. Note that Ariste becomes the deacon Aristos in the texts of the Armenian *synaxaria* translated by P. Peeters in Philostorgius (ed. Bidez), p. xlviii.

[31] By H. Delehaye in *Anal. Boll.*, xxxi (1912), p. 239.

[32] *Patria Cp.* ed. Preger, fasc. 2, p. 235, 21. For the Oxeia cf. the documents published by A. Papadopoulos-Kerameus on the miracles of St Artemius, *Sbornik grecheskikh neizdannuikh bogoslovskikh Tekstov*, iv–xv vyekov (St Petersburg, 1909), pp. 5, 3; 6, 5; 8, 19; 13, 3; 26, 19; 42, 28; 46, 15; 61, 30; 66, 10; 76, 11–13.

[33] Printed in A. Mai, *Spicilegium Romanum*, iv, 340 sqq.; *AASS*, October, viii, pp. 856 sqq.; Migne, *PG*, xcvi, coll. 1252 sqq., and see the better text of the beginning of the *Passio* in Philostorgius (ed. Bidez), pp. 151 sqq. On the *Passio* and its sources ibid., pp. xliv–lxviii.

of Damascus,[34] is also undated save that it must have been composed after the reign of Justinian I and probably before that of Basil I:[35] it cannot be by the same hand that wrote the διήγησις τῶν θαυμάτων τοῦ ἁγίου . . . ᾽Αρτεμίου, composed between the years 660–668.[36] In sum, it would seem that we can say no more than that by the middle of the seventh century Artemius was recognized as a ἅγιος μεγαλομάρτυς by the orthodox of Constantinople. Certain it is that the martyr who was extolled so highly by Philostorgius is never mentioned by Sozomen.

Now it has always appeared a singular fact that the saints in Sozomen's version of the legend remain anonymous. 'On ne supposera pas', writes Père Peeters, 'que Sozomène a biffé ces deux mots par souci de brièveté; mais il est encore moins croyable que le rédacteur primitif les ait laissés en blanc. Les héros de ces histoires ne sont jamais anonymes, et s'ils le sont devenus ici, ce ne peut être que par un accident de la transmission.'[37] It would seem unlikely that so remarkable an omission was due to accident. I would suggest that the legend in its original Antiochene form was imagined in honour of two Arian saints—Artemius (for this there is the support of Nicephorus) and Macarius, the confessor championed by Artemius. In Caesarea the name Macarius naturally brought to mind the name of the local saint Mercurius; Sozomen, who knew the legend in its original form and for whom Artemius remained a heretic, adopted the story, but discreetly suppressed the suspected names. Thus we could explain the curious anonymity of the heavenly messengers. Later when the lapse of time had wiped out the stigma of heresy, when the martyr's revered remains had been translated to the capital and had found a resting-place in the church of St John the Baptist, when, too, he had become the great specialist for the healing of diseases of the genital organs, then Artemius could be restored to his old position in the legend (the evidence of Nicephorus), but meanwhile Mercurius had for ever, both in East and West, usurped the place of Macarius. But I would repeat that

---

[34] As in Migne, *PG*, xcvi.
[35] Cf. Th. Büttner-Wobst (supra, p.271, n. 1), p. 576, n. 40.
[36] Cf. Papadopoulos-Kerameus, op. cit., pp. i–ii.
[37] *Anal. Boll.*, xxxix, 74.

this is only a suggestion, and of it I can offer no shadow of proof.

If the considerations of this paper have any validity, the interest of this chapter of Faustus lies in the fact that it helps us to trace the rise of a legend at Antioch, its transference to Caesarea and thence into Armenia—all within the space of a few years, for Julian died in A.D. 363, and though the precise date of the composition of the history of Faustus is still a disputed point, it may well be that his work was written before the close of the fourth century. Thus rapidly did Christian hatred and Christian triumph find in legend their justification and explanation.

XX

An Athanasian Forgery ?

[From 'Athanasiana', *Journal of Egyptian Archaeology*, xi (1925), pp. 58–69 at pp. 61–65.]

O TTO SEECK had studied the literature of the fourth century, both ecclesiastical and civil, so long and so thoroughly that his *Geschichte des Untergangs der antiken Welt* will for many a year remain the standard introduction to the history of that century. It is, however, fatally easy to read the text of that work without consulting the *Anhänge*, and there is at times the danger that Seeck's peculiar views of certain sources upon which that text is based may be insufficiently taken into account—in particular his views as to documentary forgeries of the period.[1] Athanasius was for Seeck the arch-forger: the habit of forging documents only grew upon him with the flight of the years; Athanasius 'im Verlauf der Jahre immer dreister in seinen Lügen wird'.[2] The principle laid down by Seeck as the basis of his enquiries into the fabrications of Athanasius can hardly be questioned: 'Wenn aber in *einem* Falle sicher nachgewiesen ist dass Athanasius ein Fälscher war, so werden damit alle anderen Urkunden zweifelhaft die auf seine Autorität zurückgehen,' though it is going very far when he adds '*oder zurückgehen können*'. That crucial instance of a forged document Seeck thought that he had discovered in the letter by which Constantine is alleged to have summoned the bishops from the Council of Tyre to Constantinople; with the detection of that forgery the whole Athanasian account of his first banishment is proved to be a tissue of lies. It is perhaps worth while to consider briefly this instance of Seeck's theory.

The '*Vorbericht*' to the Festal Letters (Larsow, 28) states that Athanasius fled from Tyre to Constantinople; he arrived

---

[1] For a criticism of Seeck's view of forgeries in Optatus, cf. Norman H. Baynes, 'Optatus', *Journal of Theological Studies*, xxvi (1924), pp. 37–44.
[2] *Zeitschrift für Kirchengeschichte*, xxx (1909), p. 419.

in the capital on 2 Athyr, and after eight days was seen by the emperor: 'und als er Muth gefasst, setzten seine Gegner den Kaiser durch allerlei Beschuldigungen in Schrecken, und so ward er auf der Stelle exilirt, und ging am 10 Athyr nach Gallien zum Caesar Constans.' Athanasius is eight days in all in Constantinople—from 29 October to 6 November 335. It is thus impossible that during these eight days the eastern bishops should have been summoned from Tyre, that their leaders should have travelled to the capital, should in the emperor's presence have accused Athanasius of a threat to detain in Alexandria the Egyptian corn-ships and that Constantine should only then have banished Athanasius to Gaul. This account of Athanasius is therefore simply a *Märchen*—a fabrication to prove that his banishment did not depend upon the judgement of an ecclesiastical tribunal—the Council of Tyre: he was banished on a purely civil charge (*Geschichte des Untergangs*, etc., iv, 57).

Seeck has tested all the *day* dates as well as the *year* dates of the *Vorbericht*: the inaccuracy in year dates can be explained, and only one error in the day dates can be proved—25 Mechir 364 for 19 Mechir (=the date of the return of Athanasius to Alexandria).[3] This one error Seeck would attribute to a scribal 'Verwechslung von Zahlzeichen'.[4] We are therefore bound to accept the accuracy of the *Vorbericht* in its statement that Athanasius left Constantinople for Gaul on 10 Athyr.

Of the letter of Constantine there are *three* versions: all are forgeries of Athanasius, each more unscrupulous than the former; (i) the first version can be reconstructed from the letter of the Egyptian bishops to Pope Julius: this is a document dictated by Athanasius; (ii) the second form of the letter is given in *Apologia c. Arianos*, c. 86; (iii) the third version is known to us from Gelasius of Cyzicus: it is derived from the *Synodicus* of Athanasius—a work of his old age. The conclusion is obvious: 'Dass eine Urkunde die mit dem Älterwerden desjenigen der sie uns überliefert hat, immer wieder eine andere Gestalt annimmt, von mehr als zweifelhafter Art ist, bedarf wohl keines weiteren Beweises' (*Geschichte*, etc., iv, Anhang, 407–8).

[3] *Zeitschrift für Kirchengeschichte*, xxx, pp. 401–18.   [4] Ibid., p. 409.

Further, Socrates and Sozomen cannot be cited in support of the account of Athanasius, for they themselves used the writings of Athanasius; they *may* have used such a source (e.g. the *Synodicus*) in their account of the first banishment of Athanasius, and though this cannot be strictly proven, so long as the supposition remains a *possibility*, their account can have no independent value.

Such is Seeck's argument: is it conclusive? In the first place it is to be noted that of the dated events recorded in the *Vorbericht* all refer to happenings in Alexandria save the two already cited and the death of Julian, and the death of the Apostate was an event which deeply stirred the imagination of the whole Christian Church. In the case of the dating in the *Vorbericht* of events which occurred in distant Constantinople it is obvious that confusion would be far easier.

To turn to the alleged three different versions of the letter of Constantine. Considering that both the character and the date of the *Synodicus* of Athanasius are hotly contested:[5] considering further that it is quite uncertain from what source Gelasius drew his version of Constantine's letter (for the unknown Johannes suggested by Loeschcke is admittedly but an x[6]) and that therefore Seeck's version (iii) cannot be with any certainty traced to Athanasius, we might in strictness forgo any consideration of this form of the letter, for we are for the present only concerned with forgeries for which Athanasius can be deemed responsible. But I cannot escape the conviction that the version of Gelasius does indeed represent the original form of the letter which Athanasius has abbreviated. Apart from what we may regard as redactional variations, and apart from the closing sentence which is not quoted by Athanasius, the main difference between versions (ii) and (iii) is the lengthy passage in Gelasius, 180, 20–34. The version of the letter given by Athanasius breaks off just before the words οὕτως τετα-

---

[5] Cf. Fr. Geppert, *Die Quellen des Kirchenhistorikers Socrates Scholasticus* (Leipzig, 1898), pp. 82–111; P. Batiffol, 'Le Synodikon de S. Athanase', *Byzantinische Zeitschrift*, x (1901), pp. 123–43; Ed. Schwartz, 'Zur Geschichte des Athanasius' in *G.G.N.*, *Philol.-hist. Klasse* (1904), pp. 394 sqq.; Heinz Fromen, *Athanasii Historia acephala* (Diss. Münster, 1914), pp. 11 sqq.

[6] Cf. Gerhard Loeschcke, *Das Syntagma des Gelasius Cyzicenus* (Bonn, 1906), and preface to the edition of Gelasius by Loeschcke and M. Heinemann (1918), pp. xxviii–xxxviii. I quote from this edition.

πεινωμένον καὶ κατηφῆ τεθεάμεθα τὸν ἄνδρα ὥστε ἡμᾶς εἰς ἄφατον οἶκτον ἐπ' αὐτῷ περιπεσεῖν: and in the previous sentence Athanasius has omitted the words πενθῶν δὲ καὶ ὀλοφυρόμενος (Gelasius, 180, 15). I would suggest that the abbreviation of the imperial text at these two points is intentional: Athanasius was not anxious to perpetuate the picture of his own abject plight in the year 335; Constantine's portrayal of the primate of Egypt was *menschlich—allzu menschlich*! But this picture is confirmed by the Melitian papyrus recently published by Mr Bell:[7] the luggage packed and put on board ship—only to be taken off again because of the indecision of Athanasius; πάνυ ἀθυμεῖ 'Αθανάσιος (*P. Lond.* 1914, 38): οὕτως τεταπεινωμένος καὶ κατηφής: πενθῶν δὲ καὶ ὀλοφυρόμενος: the two descriptions are wonderfully congruous. Here, I believe, is no Athanasian forgery, but Athanasian suppression of embarrassing veracity. The version of the letter of Constantine given in the *Apologia c. Arianos*, c. 86, has been 'edited' by Athanasius.

But the strength of Seeck's case rests upon the alleged differences between version (i) and version (ii) of the letter of Constantine. And here Seeck is simply in error, for the letter to which the bishops refer is indeed extant, but it is not the letter addressed to the bishops assembled at the Council of Tyre; it is the letter written, as the bishops themselves state (πρὸ τούτου, c. 9), at an earlier date to Athanasius himself when the emperor had learned that Arsenius had been found alive. It is further of interest to note that so far from concocting a forgery are the bishops that they are studiously careful to preserve in their summary the precise wording of Constantine's letter. A brief comparison will make this clear. The bishops write: (c. 9) ὁ μὲν γὰρ βασιλεύς, πρὸ τούτου γράφων, τὴν συσκευὴν ἐμέμψατο, τὴν ἐπιβουλὴν ᾐτιάσατο, τῶν Μελιτιανῶν κατεψηφίσατο, ἀθεμίτους, ἀρᾶς ἀξίους, τὰ δεινότατα ἐγγράφως εἰπών. Constantine had in fact written περὶ δὲ ἐκείνων τῶν πάσης ἀρᾶς ἀξίων, τῶν Μελιτιανῶν δηλαδὴ τῶν σκαιοτάτων καὶ ἀθεμίτων οἵτινες . . . μόνον φθόνῳ καὶ ζάλῃ καὶ θορύβοις τὰ ἄτοπα κινοῦσι, τὴν ἀθέμιτον αὐτῶν διάνοιαν ἐπιδεικνύντες ταῦτα φθέγξομαι κ.τ.λ.: and later ὅπερ δηλονότι, πρᾶγμα αὐτοῦ τοῦ φωτός, ὡς εἰπεῖν, ἐστὶ τηλαυγέστερον, ὅτι τῇ σῇ συνέσει ἐπιβουλεῦσαι

---

[7] H. I. Bell, *Jews and Christians in Egypt* (London, 1924).

ἐσπούδαζον (c. 68). The bishops write (c. 17) ἀπεστείλαμεν δὲ καὶ τὴν τοῦ πατρὸς τῶν βασιλέων ἐπιστολήν· ἔνθα οὐ μόνον ἐπ' Ἀρσενίῳ δυσχεραίνει ὅτι ζῶντος ἀνθρώπου φόνος ἐνεκαλεῖτο, ἀλλὰ καὶ ἐπὶ τῷ ποτηρίῳ ἐθαύμαζε τὸ ποικίλον τῆς κατηγορίας καὶ πεπλανημένον ὅτι πὴ μὲν Μακαρίου τοῦ πρεσβυτέρου, πὴ δὲ Ἀθανασίου τοῦ ἐπισκόπου κατηγόρουν, ὡς κλάσαντος ταῖς χερσὶ τὸ ποτήριον. The emperor writes (c. 68) τίς δὲ ἡ μετάβασις καὶ ποικιλία καὶ διαφορὰ τοῦ πράγματος, ὡς νῦν εἰς ἕτερον πρόσωπον τήν κατηγορίαν τοῦ ἐγκλήματος τούτου μετάγειν; and later καὶ συνορῶσιν ὅτι πεπλασμένων καὶ ψευδῶν πραγμάτων εἰσὶ κατήγοροι.

There still remains, however, the question of the historicity of Constantine's summons of the eastern bishops to Constantinople. If it is only a fabrication of Athanasius, the consistency of the accounts is skilfully arranged. Constantine, riding through Constantinople (the reminiscence of the eye-witness), meets Athanasius μετὰ ἑτέρων τινῶν οὓς [ὧν Gelasius, 180, 14] περὶ αὐτὸν εἶχεν (c. 86). When the bishops arrive in Constantinople and make their charges (οὐκέτι μὲν τὰ ἐν Τύρῳ θρυλούμενα παρ' αὐτῶν, περὶ σίτου δὲ καὶ πλοίων ἐποχῆς ὡς Ἀθανασίου ἐπαγγειλαμένου δύνασθαι κωλύειν τὴν ἀπὸ Ἀλεξανδρείας εἰς τὴν Κωνσταντινούπολιν τοῦ σίτου μετακομιδήν) ταῦτά τινες τῶν ἐξ ἡμῶν ἔνδον ὄντες μετὰ Ἀθανασίου ἀκηκόασι τοῦ βασιλέως ἀπειλοῦντος: so the bishops. In c. 87 in which Athanasius gives his own account of the scene we read καὶ τοῦτο (the charge of the Eusebians) πάροντες μὲν Ἀδαμάντιος, καὶ Ἀνουβίων, Ἀγαθάμμων, Ἀρβεθίων, Πέτρος, οἱ ἐπίσκοποι, ἤκουσαν. ἔδειξε δὲ καὶ ὁ θυμὸς τοῦ βασιλέως κ.τ.λ. The τινες of the bishops' letter are here named. It is at least an adept fabrication.

But Athanasius further tells us who of the Eusebians were present at the interview. They were Eusebius, Theognius, Patrophilus, ἕτερος Εὐσέβιος, Ursacius and Valens. But the *Apologia contra Arianos* was no secret libel like the *Historia Arianorum*: it was clearly intended from the first as public propaganda to be widely circulated. The date of its first publication is doubtful (348–350?);[8] but whatever the precise year, though the Eusebii were dead, Patrophilus was still one

[8] Cf. Otto Bardenhewer, *Geschichte der altkirchlichen Literatur*, iii (Freiburg, 1912), p. 61.

of the most active of the enemies of Athanasius, while Ursacius and Valens had recanted and were in high favour with Constantius. Is it conceivable that Athanasius could have thought that he could for a moment have made his lie credible when he states that his most prominent living foes were present at the all-important interview? His account must stamp him the clumsiest of liars: and Athanasius, even were he knave, was certainly not a fool. The supposition is incredible.

Lastly we may turn to the evidence of Socrates, i, 35, and Sozomen, ii, 33. It is clear that these historians did not derive their account of the proceedings *solely* from any extant work of Athanasius: even to the list of the Arians present at Constantinople given by Athanasius Socrates adds Maris. But Seeck suggests that Socrates may have used a lost work of Athanasius—the *Synodicus*. This is an unhappy suggestion, for Socrates adds, after quoting Athanasius by name, φασὶ δέ τινες τοῦτο (sc. the exile of Athanasius) πεποιηκέναι τὸν βασιλέα σκοπῷ τοῦ ἑνωθῆναι τὴν ἐκκλησίαν ἐπειδὴ ᾿Αθανάσιος πάντη κοινωνῆσαι τοῖς περὶ ῎Αρειον ἐξετρέπετο. Socrates clearly possessed for the proceedings at Constantinople non-Athanasian sources: this suggested explanation of Constantine's action is nowhere, so far as I can remember, adduced by Athanasius. We can hardly doubt that here we have the *vera causa* of the banishment of Athanasius.

As regards the dating of the '*Vorbericht*', I would suggest that it rightly records the day of the first interview with Constantine and the fact that the exile of Athanasius immediately followed *an* interview with the emperor, but by a confusion the two interviews have been reduced to one. Between those two interviews Constantine did summon the eastern bishops to Constantinople. The imperial letter of summons Athanasius 'edited', but did not forge. On examination Seeck's crucial instance of an Athanasian forgery falls to the ground.

XXI

The Political Ideas of St Augustine's
De Civitate Dei

[Historical Association Pamphlet No. 104, London (1936).]

[This essay was written to form one of a series of lectures on Social and Political Ideals which was arranged by the South-West London Branch of the Association. The Branch suggested the subject, and the lecture was designed to form an introduction to the study of the modern literature on the subject. It raises no claim to originality.[1]]

IT might perhaps be questioned whether the *De Civitate Dei*, Augustine's vast work—he himself called it an *ingens opus* —can rightly claim a place in a series of lectures devoted to the study of political and social ideals: it is primarily concerned neither with politics nor social ideals. It is designed as a defence of the Christian religion; it is the last and the greatest of the Apologies for Christianity produced by the early Church. But from the *De Civitate Dei* the Middle Ages did undoubtedly derive political doctrine: sentences from Augustine became the slogans of contending parties or were used as brickbats with which to lay low political opponents. Here we are rather concerned with Augustine's own thought, and not with the interpretations put upon it by later generations. And it must always be remembered that the composition of the *De Civitate Dei* occupied Augustine during some thirteen years, that it was published in parts and could not, in consequence, be revised as a whole when the work was completed. Augustine was never a systematic thinker: he did not sit down in cold blood to compose a philosophic treatise. He reacted to an external stimulus, and his writings are answers to provocations which came to him from without. Upon him as a bishop devolved the care of the churches, the problems of education, of protection of his

---

[1] I desire to thank Dr E. Langstadt for help given in talks with him.

Christian flock from tyranny or oppression, of the defence of
the faith alike against heresy and schism. He was no recluse
working in the calm of his study: he wrote the *De Civitate Dei*
in moments snatched from countless distractions; the work
was undertaken in answer to a definite challenge—the capture
of Rome by Alaric the Goth in A.D. 410—but through the years
it grew under his hands, often the scheme with which he
started it is lost to sight, and with difficulty he returns to that
scheme, escaping from a digression which has for the time
being absorbed his interest. The audience to which the work
was addressed was very varied; pagans to be attacked, Christians to be strengthened in their faith: uneducated folk, and
philosophers prepared to follow highly abstract arguments;
different parts of the work are on very different levels of
thought. All this must be remembered by the modern reader.
The study of the *De Civitate Dei* can never be an easy undertaking.[2]

There is no need to speak here of Augustine's life or of the
Roman Empire in the fourth century. To the last great persecution of the Christians by the Roman State Constantine
had put an end. He had adopted for himself the Christian faith,
and, though he could not make it the religion of the Roman
State, he could throw his influence into the Christian scale.
And he could educate his sons as Christians. The reaction of
Julian was short-lived, and the imperial power passed once
more into Christian hands, until towards the close of the fourth
century Theodosius the Great was free to proclaim Christianity
as the religion of an orthodox Roman State. Augustine was
born half-way through the fourth century, in the year 354, in
Thagaste, a small town in the Roman province of Africa: his
mother Monica was a Christian, his father a pagan. From
Thagaste he moved to Madaurus for his schooling, and thence,
after an interval, to the University of Carthage. Here he taught
rhetoric until he left Africa for Rome: it was at Milan, the city
of Ambrose, that he was converted. He returned to Africa
where, as priest and bishop, he spent his life. The North
African church was rent by schism; the Donatists—so called

---

[2] For an analysis of the *De Civitate Dei*, see Joseph Rickaby, *St Augustine's
City of God* (Burns, Oates & Washbourne, London, 1925).

from the founder of the schism, Donatus—contended that they alone formed the true Church of Christ. Caecilian, the Catholic bishop of Carthage, had, they said, been consecrated by a *traditor*—by one who had given up the sacred scriptures to the State authorities in the great persecution. From a church thus dishonoured the Donatists withdrew, and despite persuasion and persecution persisted in their schism. Augustine was unwearied in his championship of the Church Catholic, in his efforts to constrain the Donatists to re-enter the Catholic communion.[3] From the Christian teaching of his childhood Augustine had passed through the period of the sowing of his wild oats; his first conversion had come through the reading of Cicero's lost work, the *Hortensius*—a conversion to philosophy; then he was attracted for a time by the dualistic religion of the Manichaeans,[4] and, disappointed there, lapsed into scepticism, until, through Neoplatonism, he returned to his mother's faith and to the defence of the Church Catholic. Augustine knew both worlds—the pagan as well as the Christian.

When Rome, the eternal city, the centre of the civilized universe—of the οἰκουμένη—fell before the Goth, it seemed at first the death-blow to civilization itself. Why, men asked, had this devastating catastrophe occurred in their day? Through the centuries, from the Republican period onwards, the Romans had attributed the growth of Rome and the victorious expansion of Roman power to their fidelity to their national gods, their scrupulous observance of the pagan cult. This disaster, men concluded, must be due to the wrath of the gods angered by the neglect of their worship under a Christian State. The Christians were responsible for the fall of the city which had unified the Mediterranean world. This was the challenge to which the *De Civitate Dei* was designed as an answer: the gods of polytheism had not caused the greatness of Rome, they were powerless to bring happiness to men either in this world or the next. Thus the first part of the work is negative in its general argument. From controverting the pagans Augustine turns in the second part to his positive contention: he contrasts the

[3] On Donatism, cf. Paul Monceaux, *Histoire littéraire de l'Afrique chrétienne*, vol. iv (Leroux, Paris, 1912).

[4] Cf. F. C. Burkitt, *The Religion of the Manichees* (Cambridge University Press, 1925).

two *civitates*—the *civitas* of God and the *civitas* of the Devil. Through a study of the history of these two *civitates* Christianity is justified as the sole source of blessedness.

Now in the meaning which Augustine gives to the word *civitas* he is not consistent—it can mean 'city', in a few instances it is employed in the signification of our word 'State', but students are now, it would seem, agreed that neither word adequately represents Augustine's fundamental conception; that is best rendered by some such word as 'society': it is the history of two communities which is the theme of his work. And neither of these communities is fully incorporated in any earthly society, for the angels and the saints form part of the *civitas Dei*, while the demons are members of the *civitas Diaboli*. Primarily the use of the term *civitas* is allegorical—it is used, as Augustine himself would say, '*mystice*'. When Augustine is expounding the *theory* of his conception of history the *civitas terrena*—the society of earth—is not the State: the *civitas caelestis*, the heavenly society, is not the Church, but when he comes to consider the *representatives* of these two societies on earth—when he is treating the matter, not purely theoretically, but empirically—then the Roman State comes to be regarded as the earthly *civitas*, and the Church as the divine society. Thus the Middle Ages could see in the two societies the State and the Church.

The conception of the two 'cities' comes ultimately from the Bible: Jerusalem, the holy city, is contrasted with Babylon: but, more directly, modern research has tended to show, Augustine derived his theme from Ticonius, the Donatist, who in his work on the Apocalypse had interpreted the Book of Revelation on similar lines. Here the two *civitates*—the *civitas* of God and the *civitas* of the Devil—are contrasted. The latter seeks to serve the world, the former to serve Christ: one desires to rule in this world, the other to flee from this world; one slays, the other is slain; one labours for damnation, the other for salvation. It is thus from the schismatic that Augustine would seem to have borrowed the great contrast on which his work is founded. The *civitas* of Faith is opposed to the *civitas* of Un-faith—Belief ranged against Unbelief. The city of Heaven is characterized by humility and obedience—the city of earth by pride and lust of rule. In his preface, Augustine quotes the text 'God resisteth the proud, but giveth grace unto the humble'.[5] It is the contrast between *superbia* and *humilitas*, between the flesh and the spirit.

Between the flesh and the spirit—this is the great opposition which dominates the thought of Augustine, because the struggle between the flesh and the spirit had dominated his own life. Readers of the *Confessions* will remember the agonies of that search for truth and the despair from which he was only freed by his submission to the authority of the Church. Not through reason, but through revelation: it was God's grace that had brought the solution: it was no human achievement. And thus throughout Augustine's thought there runs this dualism—the powerlessness and the sin of man: the irresistible grace and mercy of God. Here is the root of Augustine's profound pessimism concerning man and human life and human character. Misery and mortality are the lot of man on earth. 'All men, so long as they are mortal, must of necessity be miserable.' 'What river of eloquence could ever suffice to set forth the wretchedness of this life?' The only thing that counts for man in this life is his relation to God: what matters it under what form of government a man lives—man with his brief life, man under the doom of death—provided only that he may serve his God? 'It is a man's character', says Fichte, 'which determines his philosophy': it was Augustine's own experience which determined the thought of the *De Civitate Dei*. Two loves formed two cities: the earthly city was formed by love of self leading to contempt of God, the heavenly city was formed by love of God leading to contempt of self. Therefore the one glories in itself, the other in God.

It is not that social life is inherently an evil: God designed man to be a social being. In Paradise he fashioned man and gave to him as helpmate a woman; in that human pair was the faculty of generation of other humans—here lay the germ of family life, itself the cell of every wider association. And generation, as God intended it, was a pure act of untroubled will: it was man's misuse of his free will which brought about the Fall, which gave birth to sin, which gave rise to passion in the

[5] 1 Peter v. 5, cf. James iv. 6.

act of human generation, which laid upon man the curse of Adam, the burden of inherited sin. The Fall vitiated that social life of free intercourse for which man was created; the State, or the City, was founded by Cain, the murderer of his brother, and the subjection of man by man is the bitter fruit of Adam's sin, just as the institution of slavery is itself another fruit of sin. And Augustine's theory of the State is essentially individualistic: the State is not for him an entity in itself: the State *is* the human beings of which it is composed, its character is determined by the character of its citizens: if there is no justice in the individuals who make up the State, without doubt there can be no justice in the State itself. This is the background which one must have in mind as one approaches the discussion in the *De Civitate Dei* of the true definition of the State. Augustine takes Cicero's definition of the republic— the State: 'an assemblage associated by a common acknowledgment of right and by a community of interests,' and proceeds, 'and what Cicero means by a common acknowledgment of right he explains at large, showing that a republic cannot be administered without justice. When therefore there is no true justice there can be no right,' and therefore there is no republic where there is no justice. Justice is that virtue which gives to every man his due. But, as we have seen, for Augustine, man's end is the worship of the true God: where then is the justice of man when he deserts the true God and yields himself to impure demons? Is this to give every one his due? Or is he who keeps back a piece of ground from the purchaser and gives it to a man who has no right to it unjust, while he who keeps back himself from the God who made him and serves wicked spirits is just? Augustine thus finds himself placed before the alternative of denying that the State of Rome was a republic at all or of omitting justice from the definition of the State. He chooses the latter alternative, and puts forward a definition of his own: 'a State is an assemblage of reasonable beings bound together by a common agreement concerning the objects of their love.' Pause for a moment and consider the effect of this discussion upon Augustine's view of the character of a State. There was in the early Church a strong tradition that the maintenance of justice was an essential part of the purpose of the State: St Paul had urged obedience to the State upon the ground that the State rewards the good and punishes the evil. Clement of Alexandria had defined a king as one who rules according to law, while Ambrose, Augustine's own master, had contended that justice and beneficence are the essential virtues for any community: justice—*aequitas*—is the strength of the State and injustice spells its dissolution. There have been attempts made to show that Augustine does not really mean to exclude justice from the definition of the State—he is speaking here, it is urged, of divine justice: human—natural—justice remains in the State. Mr Carlyle quotes the famous saying of Augustine, 'Set justice aside, and what are kingdoms but great robberies?'[6] and considers the meaning of the saying to be that the only point of distinction between a band of robbers and a kingdom is that the latter has the quality of justice. But as Mr Christopher Dawson has written, 'the actual tendency of the passage appears to be quite the contrary. St Augustine is arguing that there is no difference between the conqueror and the robber except the scale of their operations, for he continues, "What is banditry but a little kingdom?" and he approves the reply of the pirate to Alexander the Great, "Because I do it with a little ship, I am called a robber, and you, because you do it with a great fleet, are called an emperor." '[7] There cannot be much doubt that Augustine meant what he said. 'If he did, I cannot but feel', says Mr Carlyle, 'that it was a deplorable error for a great Christian teacher.' But, after all, Augustine's conclusions follow naturally from the premises which we have already considered. And Augustine's view was echoed with great vigour by Cardinal Newman:[8] 'Earthly kingdoms are founded, not in justice, but in injustice. They are created by the sword, by robbery, cruelty, perjury, craft and fraud. There never was a kingdom, except Christ's, which was not conceived and born, nurtured and educated, in sin. There never was a State, but was committed to acts and maxims, which

[6] 'Remota iustitia quid regna nisi magna latrocinia.' *De Civitate Dei*, iv, c. 4.

[7] *A Monument to St Augustine*, p. 63. In support of the view that Augustine did intend to deny the possession of justice to the pagan State, cf. his repeated expressions of scorn for the 'justice' of the pagan emperor Julian the Apostate: see e.g. *Contra Litt. Petiliani*, ii, §§ 203, 205; *Ep.*, 105, § 9.

[8] From 'Sanctity the Token of the Christian Empire', in *Sermons on Subjects of the Day*, p. 273 (first edition). Cited by Mr Dawson.

it is its crime to maintain and its ruin to abandon. What monarchy is there but began in invasion or usurpation? What revolution has been effected without self-will, violence or hypocrisy? What popular Government but is blown about by every wind as if it had no conscience and no responsibilities? What dominion of the few but is selfish and unscrupulous? Where is military strength without the passion for war? Where is trade without the love of filthy lucre, which is the root of all evil?' It is a pessimism as profound as Augustine's own.

But even if the earthly State cannot claim justice as its prerogative, even though it was founded by a murderer and is vitiated from the first by the inheritance of the sin of Adam, still the State is part of the divine Providence and rulers are chosen by God and ordained by Him. Here the early Church had adopted the Jewish view of earthly authority which it found in the Old Testament. It was not only the kings who worshipped Jehovah who owed to Him their thrones: pagan monarchs who persecuted the followers of Jehovah were appointed by Him: Daniel, speaking to Nebuchadnezzar, can say, 'Thou, O King, art king of kings, unto whom the God of Heaven hath given the kingdom, the power and the strength and the glory' (Daniel ii. 37). In the Book of the Wisdom of Solomon we read, 'Hear therefore, O ye kings, and understand, for power is given you of the Lord and sovranty from the Highest' (Wisdom of Solomon vi. 3). Christians remembered that their Master had bidden Peter to take a shekel as tribute and 'give unto them for me and thee' (Matt. xvii. 27): they recalled His words to Pilate, a Roman governor, 'Thou wouldst have no power against me, except it were given thee from above' (John xix. 11). Such texts as these inspired the thought of Paul the Apostle; they lie behind his declaration: 'For there is no power, but of God; the powers that be are ordained of God. Therefore he that resisteth the power, withstandeth the ordinance of God: and they that withstand shall receive to themselves judgement' (Romans xiii. 1–2).[9] In the original intention of God man was not created to exercise domination over man:

[9] Cf. Franz Joseph Dölger, 'Zur antiken und frühchristlichen Auffassung der Herrschergewalt von Gottes Gnaden', *Antike und Christentum*, iii (1932), pp. 117–27.

this is the starting point for Augustine: but that original intention had been thwarted by man's sin: it is this changed condition with which God is faced, and to meet sin coercive government has a place as at once punitive and remedial. As a reaction against sin even the earthly State has a relative justification; it beareth not the sword in vain. Ultimately God's ways
are beyond our understanding: He chooses such rulers for man
as man deserves. Thus a tyrant, such as Nero, the traditional
example of the worst type of ruler, is appointed by divine Providence. Because rulers are chosen by divine Providence, the
servants of Christ are bidden to tolerate even the worst and
most vicious of States, and that they can do by realizing that
on earth they are but pilgrims, and that their home is not here
but in Heaven. It is not in a pagan State that Christians can
expect to find the realization of their hopes.

The *civitas terrena* is represented by the succession of the
empires which dominated the ancient world. Of these Augustine takes two as standing for the series: Assyria, the empire of
the East, and its Western successor, Rome. But since the
treatment of Rome is much fuller, it will suffice for our present
purpose to illustrate the history of the *civitas terrena* by reference to Rome. Sallust, in the introduction to his monograph
on the Catilinarian conspiracy, had traced the growth of
luxury and the consequent decline of the Roman Republic
through the period which followed the Second Punic War.
Augustine quotes Sallust at length, but he goes further back
in the history for his pessimistic picture of the Roman State.
That State was founded, as was Cain's city, on a brother's
murder, and no sooner were the early kings of Rome expelled
than the patricians began to rule oppressively. The aim of the
Roman of the Republican period was glory: glory the Romans
most ardently loved, for it they wished to live, for it they did
not hesitate to die. Freedom secured by the expulsion of the
kings, they sought domination. It was eagerness for praise and
desire of fame which led them to perform many wonderful
things—things laudable doubtless, and glorious according to
human judgement. But these achievements were essentially
the work of a few virtuous men. These men were granted to
Rome by God to achieve His purpose that the empire of Rome

should be greater than the empire of Assyria, which it was to supersede. Through this desire for glory the Romans suppressed many other vices: yet since desire for glory is itself a vice, this discipline did not make the Romans holy (*sancti*), but only less base (*minus turpes*). The true aim of virtue is not that we may be seen of men, but that we may glorify our Father who is in Heaven. Yet for their virtues—even though directed to the service of an earthly kingdom—these men who despised their own private affairs for the sake of the Republic, and who for the profit of its treasury resisted avarice, who took counsel for the good of their country in a spirit of freedom— they have received their reward: they imposed the laws of their Empire upon many peoples, and at this day, says Augustine, both in literature and history they are glorious among almost all nations. The condemnation of the Roman State lies in the fact that there is no true virtue except that which is directed towards the highest and ultimate good of man. And yet God helped the Romans: *secundum quandam formam terrenae civitatis*—according to the relative standard of the earthly state—they were good men. And in rewarding them God had in view a further purpose—that the Romans might on their own level be an example and an inspiration to the Christians. What did the Romans not despise, what did they not endure, what passions did they not subdue, to win human glory! And shall those who know the meaning of true virtue and serve the true God do less for their higher purpose than did the Romans of the pagan State? Augustine is even prepared to admit that the Roman wars were just, for they were fought in self-defence, since their neighbours were less virtuous than they.

There is, I know, another picture of the vices of Rome given in books I to III of the *De Civitate Dei*, where in particular Augustine holds up to reprobation the immoral games celebrated in honour of the Roman gods: but it must be remembered that the unrelieved blackness of that chronicle of successive wars forms part of the apologetic of Augustine—part of his counter-attack against the charges of the pagans, while what perhaps appears to us as a somewhat unbalanced onslaught upon the immorality of the games is inspired by contemporary

u   B.B.S.

events—by the fact that many fugitives who had escaped to
Africa from the Gothic capture of Rome rushed to the games,
forgetting everything else in their passion for these obscene
spectacles. That sight had filled Augustine with shame and
disgust. It is the vices of the men of his own day which have
excited some of the bitterness of the first three books: when he
looks back subsequently upon the history of Rome during the
early Republican period, when Roman discipline was not yet
undermined, he writes, it is true, as a Christian bishop, but also
as a Roman who realizes what sacrifices went to the building
up of the Roman Empire. Rome is still the representative of
the *civitas terrena*: its aims were earthbound, but within those
limitations the Romans had proved themselves worthy of an
empire.

Civitas terrena = *civitas Diaboli*—such is the equation: it has
been said by some critics that Augustine in the *De Civitate Dei*
not only condemns the pagan State, but condemns every State
—the State as such. Now it may be admitted that from a first
reading of Augustine's treatise this is a natural conclusion, but
it can hardly be doubted that it would be an error. We must
always remember that the pagan State is only the representative of—it is not the *same thing* as—the *civitas terrena*, the
civitas Diaboli: that is a far greater and an invisible society of
angels, the dead, the living and those yet to be. In the *De
Civitate Dei* Augustine is attacking the pagans, he is criticizing
the pagan State and the essentially pagan elements in the State
of his own day. The Christian State as such does not enter
directly into the sphere of discussion. But Augustine's treatment of the State in the *De Civitate Dei* does not exclude a more
favourable judgement if the character of the State were different from that of pagan Rome. Indeed it may be urged that
Augustine refuses to include the concept of justice in his definition of the State, because when considering the pagan State he
is implicitly contrasting it with his ideal of a Christian State
wherein dwelleth justice. He will not extend to *every* State
that which is the peculiar prerogative of a Christian kingdom.
In Augustine's view, as we have seen, man was fashioned by
God as a social creature: the family, united by bonds of love
and mutual service, is a natural association: here that passion

for domination which has characterized earthly empires is absent. We have further seen that in his own definition of a State which he substitutes for that given by Cicero the test of a State is that its citizens should be united in a common love: if the citizens of a State were to be united, not in a passion for domination, but in a passion for the service of the true God, there is no reason why his judgement upon such a State should not be completely favourable. From his individualistic standpoint, which declines to regard the State as an entity independent of the citizens who compose it, it is the character of those citizens which determines the character of the State.[10] Change the character of the citizens, you change the character of the State, and at the same time you change the character of the judgement to be passed upon it. In Chapter 17 of Book xix of the *De Civitate Dei*, Augustine says that, while the *civitas terrena* worshipped many gods, the celestial city knew that one God only was to be worshipped, and thus it has come to pass that the two cities could not have common laws of religion, and that the heavenly city has been compelled in this matter to dissent and to become obnoxious to those who think differently and to stand the brunt of their anger and hatred and persecutions. That opposition is directed against the religious policy of the pagan State. The *civitas terrena* seeks an earthly peace: the celestial city avails itself of this earthly peace in its pilgrimage towards heavenly peace. Augustine admits that between the two cities there is a harmony so far as earthly peace is the goal. This harmony on the lower plane does not exclude the possibility that a State could adopt the higher goal. For the statement of Augustine's views upon the justification of a Christian State one must look beyond the *De Civitate Dei* to the writings inspired by his controversy with the Donatists.[11] The Christian empire is the fulfilment of prophecy: it is *secundum propheticam veritatem* that sovrans are

[10] 'Perhaps Rome will not perish: perhaps Rome has been scourged but not destroyed. Perchance Rome will not perish if the Romans do not perish. They will not perish if they will praise God: they will only perish if they blaspheme Him: for what is Rome but the Romans?' *Sermo*, 81, § 9.

[11] I have not cited the 'Ad Catholicos epistola contra Donatistas vulgo De unitate ecclesiae', Migne, *P.L.*, 43, coll. 391–446, since its authenticity is doubtful: cf. K. Adam, 'Notizen zur Echtheitsfrage der Augustin zugesprochenen Schrift De unitate ecclesiae', *Theol. Quartalschrift*, 91 (1909), pp. 86–115.

now obedient to the yoke of God, their Lord.[12] It was in the
book of Daniel that Augustine found prefigured the great conversion from the pagan to the Christian State: at the first
Nebuchadnezzar ordered the just to worship the idol and on
their refusal cast them into the fiery furnace: later the same king
commanded that any of his subjects who did not worship the
God of Shadrach, Meshach and Abednego should suffer death
(Daniel iii. 29–30). The first order typifies the period during
which apostles and martyrs suffered, the second *significavit
tempora posteriorum regum iam fidelium,* under whom it is the
impious who suffer.[13] Now kings serve God in fear, when formerly they had taken counsel together against the Lord and
against His Christ.[14] Their commands are the commands of
Christ,[15] their heart is in the hand of God,[16] they are the children born of the Catholic Church through the Gospel.[17] The
kingdoms which put their trust in demons have been overthrown.[18] 'They bear not the sword in vain'—this was not said
of any ecclesiastical authority, the sword is not the spiritual
punishment of excommunication: this is clear from the context.[19] The sword is the sword of Caesar and Christ had bidden
His followers render unto Caesar that which is Caesar's. And
an emperor, now that he is 'most pious and most faithful',[20] 'most
merciful and most religious',[21] has his own peculiar function to
perform: the service of the ordinary citizen consists in a life
lived faithfully, the service of an emperor, which he alone can
perform, is to be found in his activity as law-giver, strength-
ening the good, suppressing idolatry and heresy.[22] And the

---

[12] *Contra Cresconium,* iii, § 51. *Ep.,* 105, § 5: The duly appointed powers, 'quas
Deus secundum suam prophetiam subdidit Christo'. *Ep.,* 93, § 3: giving thanks
to God, 'quod sua pollicitatione completa qua reges terrae Christo servituros
esse promisit, sic curavit morbidos' (cf. *Ps.,* lxxi. 11); *Ep.,* 87, § 7; *Ep.,* 105, § 6;
Ep., 185, § 20. *Enarratio in Ps.,* ci: *Sermo,* ii, § 9. See *Contra Litt. Petiliani,* ii,
§ 211.
[13] *Ep.,* 93, § 9; *Ep.,* 185, § 19; *Ep.,* 105, § 7; *Contra Cresconium,* iii, § 56.
[14] *Ps.,* ii, 11, contrasted with ii, 2. *Ep.,* 93, § 18 *apud inet*; *Ep.,* 185, § 19.
[15] *Ep.,* 105, § 11. 'Hoc iubent imperatores quod iubet et Christus; quia cum
bonum iubent, per illos non iubet nisi Christus.' Cf. *Contra Litt. Petiliani,* ii, § 132.
[16] *Ep.,* 105, § 12.   [17] *Ep.,* 51, § 3.
[18] 'Regna quae de culturis daemonum praesumebant.' *Ep.,* 105, § 15.
[19] *Contra Epist. Parmeniani,* i, § 16 (cf. *Ep.,* 87, § 7). Here, as elsewhere (cf.
e.g. *Ep.,* 100, § 1; *Ep.,* 134, § 3), Augustine quotes Romans xiii.
[20] *Ep.,* 97, § 2.   [21] *Ep.,* 97, § 3.
[22] Cf. *Ep.,* 185, §§ 19–20; *Contra Litt. Petiliani,* ii, § 210; *Contra Cresconium,*
iii, § 56.

Church through the scriptures guides the king and counsels him: 'Be ye wise therefore, O ye kings, be instructed, ye judges of the earth. Serve the Lord with fear and rejoice with trembling.'[23]

For such a study of the basis of the Christian monarchy the reader will search the *De Civitate Dei* in vain; but in the closing chapters of the fifth book Augustine has set forth wherein consists the happiness of Christian princes. That happiness is to be found in the justice of their rule and in freedom from pride. Their aim must be 'to make their power their trumpeter to divulge the true adoration of God's majesty';[24] their inspirations no desire for empty glory, but a love of eternal felicity.

On the duties of subjects, in his letter to Marcellinus,[25] Augustine wrote, 'Let those who say that the doctrine of Christ is incompatible with the State's well-being give us an army such as the doctrine of Christ requires soldiers to be, let them give us such subjects, such husbands and wives, such parents and children, such masters and servants, such kings, such judges, in fine even such tax-payers and tax-gatherers, as the Christian religion has taught that men should be, and then let them dare to say that it is adverse to the State's well-being! Nay, rather let them no longer hesitate to confess that this doctrine, if it were obeyed, would be the salvation of the State.' And with this compare a passage from the second book of the *De Civitate Dei*:[26] 'If the kings of the earth and all their subjects, if all princes and judges of the earth, if young men and maidens, old and young, every age and both sexes, if they whom the Baptist addressed, the publicans and the soldiers, were all together to hearken to and observe the precepts of the Christian religion regarding just and virtuous conduct, then should the republic adorn the world in this present life with its felicity, and should ascend aloft to reign in bliss through life eternal.'

Thus it was that Augustine constantly sought to influence the magistrates of the Empire. Writing to a member of a municipal senate he quotes[27] with approval Cicero's assertion that for good men there can be no limit, no end, to their efforts in the service of their country. In this letter Augustine recurs

---

[23] *Contra Litt. Petiliani*, ii, §§ 210–11 (the lesson from Nebuchadnezzar).
[24] Translation of John Healey. [25] *Ep.*, 138, § 15.
[26] Ch. 19 [27] *Ep.*, 91, § 3.

to the theme of the early books of the *De Civitate Dei*: it is paganism and the immoralities of the pagan gods which are the foes of society.[28] Let these follies be done away with, let men be converted to the true worship of God, then you will see your *patria*—your country—flourishing, when this *patria* of the flesh in which you were born has become a portion of that country into which we are born by faith.

At all costs pride and the *cupiditas dominandi* must be banished—that desire for domination which had been the outstanding sin of the pagan empire of Rome. It is thus that Augustine is led to profess his own preference for a number of small states living in peace with each other rather than for a single great empire. Law for Augustine has its basis in the consent of the governed: his small states would be like large human families. 'It is always', Figgis remarks, 'on the analogy of the family that Augustine thinks.'

In the *De Civitate Dei* Augustine has not propounded a theory of the Christian State, but neither did he condemn the State as such, nor exclude the possibility of a State raised upon a Christian basis.

From the *civitas terrena* we turn to the *civitas Dei*: from the State to the Church. Now it is undoubted that at times Augustine does identify the Church with the *civitas Dei*, but fundamentally the latter is more than that and at the same time less than that. It is the communion of saints, while there are in the visible Church many who are not of the number. The Church is the body of those who are on the way to the celestial city, it is 'the organ and representative in the world of the eternal City of God' (Dawson). It is universal—the Catholic Church—not restricted to one province of the Empire, as was, almost exclusively, the Donatist church. It was through the Church that grace was mediated. As Figgis says, for Augustine 'the Church, the visible Church, recruited by baptism, nourished by sacraments, governed by bishops, was the one true family of God, and Christianity meant belonging to that family,[29]

---

[28] Ibid., § 3. 'Nihil enim homines tam insociabiles reddit vitae perversitate quam . . . deorum imitatio.'

[29] The Church 'is the point at which the transcendent spiritual order inserts itself into the sensible world, the one bridge by which the creature can pass from Time to Eternity' (Dawson).

while here and now it is the Millennial Kingdom of God of the Book of Revelation. The Second Coming of Christ is the Church. Between the visible Church and the earthly State what should be the relations? Now it is important to remember that the *De Civitate Dei* is not directly concerned with this problem, and that here again Augustine never formulated a complete theory of that relation. The theory which the Middle Ages developed *may* be deduced from Augustine's writings: our task is rather to enquire what Augustine himself thought. The spheres of Church and State are distinct and different, but that distinction could not be maintained completely, for the State had since the reign of Constantine called in the Church to aid it in its civil administration: in particular it had entrusted the Church with the protection and the education of orphans. It had imposed upon the Church the ungrateful duty of settling civil disputes in ecclesiastical courts: it had even appointed bishops as 'defenders' of cities to control the administration of its own officials—a difficult and burdensome responsibility. 'We do not want to have dealings with the powers that be' (*Sermo* 302, § 19), said Augustine once, when wearied with tasks which took him away from his true work. The Church, on its side, claims that the State should do all in its power to favour the worship of the true God: Augustine approves and justifies the suppression by the State of pagan rites; it is the duty of the Church to decide what that true faith is which the State must defend. At the same time, so long as their faith is not violated, Christians must obey the laws and pay the taxes of the State: they must render unto Caesar the things which are Caesar's. Here the freedom of the State is unrestricted, and we have already seen that Augustine is prepared to carry the duty of a subject's obedience to great lengths. But the crucial issue in any consideration of the relation of Church and State lay in the question whether it was the duty of the State to persecute heretics and schismatics. In his early controversy with the Manichaeans Augustine answered unequivocally in the negative: the State could not force the free will of man in matters of belief. And this was at first his attitude in the Donatist controversy:[30]

---

[30] Cf. *Ep.*, 23, § 7. 'Intellegant non hoc esse propositi mei ut inviti homines ad cuiusquam communionem cogantur. . . . Re agamus, ratione agamus.'

it is extremely interesting to watch through a detailed study
of his writings his gradual change of view. At the last he
came to think that it was not so much the State which had
a right to persecute the Donatists as that the Church had a
right to demand this service of the State. Yet the very
length and elaboration of Augustine's pleas in defence of
the use of force would suggest that he was seeking to persuade *himself* that such persecution was justified. 'Compel
them to come in': it has proved a fatal text in the history of the
Church. It is not pleasant to think of Augustine as the spiritual
father of the Inquisition.

Church and State for Augustine have their independent
spheres of action: true: but through his other-worldly conception of human history it is to the Church that the primacy
belongs, and he is mainly concerned with the State as the hand-
maid of the Church in religious matters.

Augustine is in his political theory, I would repeat, no
systematic philosopher: he is never rigorously consistent: you
cannot construct from his writings a single water-tight conception either of State or Church. As the particular need of the
moment called for his intervention, so he wrote. Alaric captured Rome and that fall of Rome was charged against the
Christians: Augustine replied by an attack upon the pagan
State. The Donatists urged against the Catholics the latter's
alliance with the Roman emperors: Augustine defends that
alliance, and contends that emperors, because they have the
resources of the Empire behind them, can serve God in a way
in which private citizens cannot serve Him. Thus the reader
who seeks for Augustine's view *as a whole* on any particular
subject is embarrassed and finds himself at a loss. Augustine
throws off in the course of an argument striking phrases, and,
tearing them from their context, men have read *out of* them or,
if you prefer it read *into them*, complete theories which *in that
form* are something other than the thought of Augustine. The
Church, said Augustine, is here and now the Millennial Kingdom: he was contending against those who sought to date in
the near future the Second Coming of Christ. If this be true,
argued later thinkers, the earthly head of that kingdom must
have royal powers: and thence may be derived the claims of

the medieval Papacy. But the medieval Papacy is not in Augustine. The State, if it is to be based on justice, must acknowledge the worship of the true God. You can argue that since the Church is the guardian of the true faith, the State is therefore subject to the Church. But Augustine proclaimed the independence within its own sphere of the earthly State. It is all too easy to make Augustine responsible for views which others have deduced from his work.

But if, in closing, we look on Augustine's thought of the State, we shall notice in particular that for him man is essentially a social creature, so formed by God: and since all men come ultimately from a single pair, Adam and Eve, *all* men are by that fact united in common ties. For Augustine there can be no Aryan clause: there are no pariahs, for all men have a common source and a single Father in Heaven.

And again, just because Augustine himself had experienced what it was to know the right and to be unable to *will* the right, *will* is the paramount factor in human life. The last word is not with the *mind*, but with the emotions—with what one *loves*. To Augustine forms of government are really irrelevant: the character of the State is determined by the character of the citizens who compose the State. The two great *civitates* of Augustine's vision are distinguished by two *loves*: 'Two *loves* formed two cities'—love of self leading to contempt of God— love of God leading to contempt of self. 'A State is an assemblage of reasonable beings bound together by a common agreement *concerning the objects of their love*.' If you would achieve, it is not enough to *know*: knowledge must be reinforced by passion. And human history has a meaning because it forms part of a great plan which was conceived when time was not— for time and creation began together—and shall be consummated when time is no more. Human history is not, as Stoics thought, a cyclic recurrence: human history has a goal. That is the thought which lies at the heart of the *De Civitate Dei*.

And for this very reason the only State which is truly eternal is the kingdom in which Christ reigns supreme. For Augustine Rome is not the eternal city. 'The things which God Himself has made will pass away, how much sooner that which Romulus founded.' Augustine could look beyond the fall of Rome—

the centre and source of the civilization of his day—because there was a *civitas* which was greater than any earthly State: the *civitas Dei* remained. That is the victory of faith, and it was this supreme confidence which enabled the Church to fulfil its mission to the barbarian conquerors of Rome when at length the empire of Rome in the west of Europe was but a memory—the memory of a lost unity which haunted the dreams of men in Europe's middle age.

XXII

1. The Peasantry and the Army in the Third Century

2. M. Pirenne and the Unity of the Mediterranean World

From a review of F. Lot, *La Fin du Monde antique et le Début du Moyen Âge*, Paris, 1927; Henri Pirenne, *Les Villes du Moyen Âge*, Brussels, 1927; and M. Rostovtzeff, *The Social and Economic History of the Roman Empire*, Oxford, 1926.

[*Journal of Roman Studies*, xix (1929), pp. 224–35 at pp. 229–33.]

1. *The suggested alliance between the peasantry and the army*. In M. Lot's book Professor Rostovtzeff's theory of an alliance between the peasantry and the soldiers and of their united attack upon the *bourgeoisie* of the cities finds no place. One has now had time to consider that theory at leisure, and as one re-reads the eleventh chapter of *The Social and Economic History of the Roman Empire* one finds it increasingly difficult to accept the view. 'Ce n'est pas un tableau imaginaire que je trace ici. Je pourrais l'appuyer sur beaucoup de documents.' So Rostovtzeff wrote in 1923; but the trouble is that the documents now adduced seem to tell a different story, and it is not easy to reconcile even the text of the *History* with the theory. From the papyri quoted by Rostovtzeff it is clear that the soldier was the bogey-man of Egypt. 'When one of the magnates . . . is at the end of his wits to know how to enforce his orders on a recalcitrant φροντιστής (manager) or some other subordinates, he always resorts to the threat of sending soldiers: "Do it at once," says Alypius, "lest you should be forced to do it by a soldier"; "do not be negligent about it lest a soldier should be sent against them [those who did not pay the arrears]"; and

he adds "a soldier was about to be sent against them. It was I that stopped him." One sees what the sending of a soldier meant to the population of a village' (pp. 436–7). 'Very instructive is the private letter *P.S.I.* 842, l. 7 sqq. διὸ γνώτωσαν ὅτι ἐὰν ἀμελήσωσιν ἐλθεῖν . . . Σαραπίων αὐτοῖς πράγματα κινήσει. ἤμελλε γαρ στρατιώτην πέμψαι κ.τ.λ.' (p. 626). It is the signature of the age. 'The instruments of oppression and exaction were soldiers in accordance with the regular administrative practice of the third century. They were a real terror to the population' (p. 436). 'The situation was aggravated by the policy of terror and compulsion which the government adopted towards the population using the army as its instrument' (p. 440). These papyri do not illustrate the sufferings of the citizens of Alexandria: they come from the humble folk of the villages of Egypt. And the inscriptions cited by Rostovtzeff surely only serve to support the evidence of the papyri. In the famous inscription first published by J. G. C. Anderson in *J.H.S.* xvii—the complaint of imperial tenants on an estate in Asia Minor—we read of στρατιῶται ἐπεισε[ρ]χόμενοι καὶ καταλιμπάνοντες τὰς λε[ω-φόρους ὁδοὺς[1] καὶ ἀπὸ τῶν] ἔργων ἡμᾶς ἀφιστάντες καὶ τοὺς ἀροτῆρας βόας ἀνγ[αρέυοντες τὰ μηδὲν ὀφειλ]όμενα αὐτοῖς παρα-πράσσουσι καὶ συμβαίνει οὐ [τὰ τυχόντα ἡμᾶς ἐκ τ]ούτου ἀδικεῖσθαι διασειομένους. If we pass to Europe, the story is the same: take the petition presented to the emperor Gordian παρὰ κωμητῶν Σκαπτοπαρηνῶν: here we read πρὸς δὲ τούτοις καὶ στρατιῶται ἀλλαχοῦ πεμπόμενοι καταλιμπάνοντες τὰς ἰδίας ὁδοὺς πρὸς ἡμᾶς παραγείνονται καὶ ὁμοίως κατεπείγουσιν παρέχειν αὐτοῖς τὰς ξενίας καὶ τὰ ἐπιτήδια μηδεμίαν τιμὴν καταβαλόντες (Dittenberger, *S.I.G.* ii. 3, 888, p. 606) . . . συμβέβηκεν τοίνυν τὰ δοκοῦντα τῆς κώμης ταύτης πλεονεκτήματα τῷ χρόνῳ περιεληλυθέναι αὐτῆς εἰς ἐλ[αττ]-ώματα διὰ γὰρ τὰς προειρημένας ταύτας προφάσεις πολλοὶ πολλάκις στρατιῶται ἐνεπιδημοῦντες ταῖς τε ἐπιξενώσεσι καὶ ταῖς βαρήσεσιν ἐνοχλοῦσι τὴν κώμην διὰ ταύτας τὰς αἰτίας πρότερον αὐτὴν καὶ πλουσιοτέραν καὶ πολυάνθρωπον [μᾶλλον] οὖσαν νῦν εἰς ἐσχάτην ἀπορίαν ἐληλυθέναι (ibid., p. 609). It might, however, appear that there is evidence in support of the theory to be found in the early sections of the 47th oration of Libanius. But one cannot

---

[1] Cf. infra in the same inscription μεσόγειοι γὰρ [τυγχάνοντε]ς καὶ οὐ παρὰ τ[ὴν ὁ]δὸν κατοικοῦντες.

help wondering what would have been the statement of the case given by the peasant owners of land in the village if they had been afforded an opportunity of explaining their refusal to pay the φόρος. Soldiers have been settled upon the village (τοὺς ἱδρυμένους στρατιώτας, Förster, vol. iii, p. 405, 17); they are permanently stationed there (διὰ τῶν ἐγκαθημένων στρατιώτων, p. 407, 1–2). In the light of the papyri and the inscriptions the question may be raised how far were 'the fruits of the earth —the πυροὶ and κριθαὶ—καὶ τὰ ἀπὸ τῶν δένδρων, the χρυσὸς ἢ χρυσίου τιμή' (p. 405, 19–20) supplied by the villagers to the soldiers voluntary gifts? And if the soldiers were enjoying these 'presents', what was left to the villagers wherewith to pay the φόρος? When faced with fresh demands, desperation may well have made them bold—τὸ τολμᾶν ἐπίδοσιν λαμβάνει (p. 407, 2). The soldiers do not intervene in behalf of their hosts: the weapons mentioned are the missiles of the villagers —λίθοι (p. 407, 24). It may be doubted whether the exactions of the soldiery were not even more burdensome to the peasants than would have been the φόρος which they refused to pay. The Skaptoparenoi in their petition threaten in despair to desert their ancestral holdings: the farmers who, as Libanius complains, failed to cultivate their lands, or turned brigands, may simply have lost heart in their struggle against the rapacity of the troops. We must never forget that the oration of Libanius is an *ex parte* statement: an advocate's brief is a doubtful source from which to draw impartial history. An emperor might listen to an account of the offences of peasants more readily than to the story of the misdoings of his own soldiers. And apart from this oration of Libanius is there any evidence for the supposed alliance against the *bourgeoisie*? It is matter for regret that Rostovtzeff's account of the third-century crisis is frequently distorted by this unfortunate theory. The Romans of the third century were not indoctrinated into the teachings of Marx, and M. Lot was well advised in his refusal to adopt Rostovtzeff's view.

2. *M. Pirenne and the unity of the Mediterranean world.*—But one recent theory—that of M. Pirenne—has been accepted by M. Lot (p. 423); on further consideration some modification of

that theory might have appeared advisable. For M. Pirenne the unity of the Mediterranean world was maintained unbroken into the eighth century of our era: that unity was only shattered as a result of the Arab conquest of Africa.[2] Upon the continent that theory has been vigorously canvassed and directly challenged; it gave rise, I understand, to the debate which most successfully enlivened the proceedings of the International Congress of Historical Studies at Oslo.[3] To it British scholarship has paid little attention—a disquieting sign of that general lack of interest in the early European Middle Age which is now prevalent in this country. Yet the problem raised by M. Pirenne is of the greatest significance alike for the history of the later Roman Empire and for the understanding of the whole period of transition which separates the reign of Theodosius the Great from the age of Charlemagne. The central issue at stake is the position of Merovingian Gaul, and in particular the question of the part played by the Syrian merchants of the West in the economic life of the Merovingian kingdom.[4] Here Gregory of Tours is, of course, our principal authority. The *History of the Franks* is an extensive work and it will probably be admitted that it has its *longueurs*: the most blood-thirsty reader can become sated by the story of incessant assassinations. Thus it may be suspected that the *History* is more often consulted than it is read through from beginning to end. Yet it is only by such a reading that one can gain an impression of the range of Gregory's interests and contacts. After such a reading I should like to take this opportunity to record my own personal impressions. M. Pirenne writes 'La Méditerranée ne perd pas son importance après la période des

[2] Cf. M. Pirenne's articles 'Mahomet et Charlemagne' in *Revue belge de philologie et d'histoire*, i (1922), pp. 76–86; 'Un contraste économique: Mérovingiens et Carolingiens', ibid., ii, 223–35; his book *Les villes du moyen âge* (Bruxelles, 1927) and his paper 'Le commerce du papyrus dans la Gaule mérovingienne' in *Comptes rendus de l'Académie des Inscriptions et Belles Lettres* (1928), pp. 178–91.

[3] Cf. *Bulletin of the International Committee of Historical Sciences*, no. 6 (May 1929) (=vol. ii, part I), pp. 61–4, and cf. further F. Vercauteren (of Gand), 'La vie économique dans les villes de la Gaule mérovingienne' in *Actes du premier congrès national des historiens français* (April 1927) (Paris, 1928), p. 30 sq.

[4] This question has not been discussed either by Mr Dalton in his introduction to his translation of Gregory of Tours (Oxford, 1927), i, pp. 175–6, or by Sir Samuel Dill in his *Roman Society in Gaul in the Merovingian Age* (Macmillan, 1926), p. 244.

invasions. Elle reste pour les Germains ce qu'elleétaitavantleur arrivée: le centre même de l'Europe, le *mare nostrum*.'[5] In what sense and to what extent is this true? How far can we prove direct contact between, let us say, Antioch or Alexandria and the ports of Merovingian Gaul?

In the first place two remarks must be made: (i) Students of economics have been tempted to give to terms used in our early medieval sources a modern significance which is foreign to their context. If a 'merchant' is mentioned, they tend to presume that he is engaged in far-reaching, even transmarine, transactions. The remark of von Below concerning the German 'merchants' of the Middle Ages must never be forgotten: 'Man hat die Erwähnung von Kaufleuten in den mittelalterlichen Quellen arglos im Sinne neuer und neuester Verhältnisse gedeutet. Es ist hier ein Punkt an dem sich die Übertragung moderner Zustände in die Vergangenheit besonders verhängnisvoll geltend gemacht hat.'[6] The merchant may be solely concerned with local trade.[7] (ii) From the mention of 'Syrians' in the Western sources during the early Middle Ages there is not infrequently drawn the inference that these eastern immigrants remained in close commercial relations with their country of origin, or that the population of these colonies was being constantly reinforced by new arrivals from the East.[8] This presupposition underlies all M. Bréhier's work upon the subject.[9] That there was such commercial intercourse under

[5] *Les villes du moyen âge*, p. 12.

[6] von Below, *Probleme der Wirtschaftsgeschichte*, ii, 323.

[7] Cf. the arguments drawn by economists from the mention of a *tonlieu* in our sources, e.g. Pirenne, *Les villes du moyen âge*, pp. 16–17. Thus M. Coville writes of Lyons under the Merovingians: 'Il y avait toujours à Lyon un tonlieu, c'est à dire la perception d'un droit de circulation sur les marchandises importées à Lyon ou qui y passaient en transit' (*Recherches sur l'histoire de Lyon du Ve siècle au IXe siècle* (Paris, 1928), p. 534, quoting *Formulae*, ed. Zeumer, p. 107), and proceeds, on p. 536, 'ce qui prouve que la ville était bien encore sur une grande voie commerciale'. But does the simple mention of a *tonlieu* justify us in inferring anything beyond the intercourse of the countryside with its neighbouring town?

[8] Cf. the argument of Bréhier drawn from the existence of Jewish colonies in Merovingian Gaul: 'Ces Juifs du VIe siècle étaient trop nombreux pour être seulement les descendants de ceux établis dans le pays aux premiers siècles de l'ère chrétienne. Bon nombre d'entre eux étaient certainement des nouveaux venus.' *Congrès français de la Syrie* (3, 4 and 5 January 1919). *Séances et Travaux*, Fasc. 2 (Marseille, 1919), p. 79.

[9] L. Bréhier, 'Les colonies d'orientaux en Occident au commencement du moyen-âge, Ve–VIIIe siècle' in *Byzantinische Zeitschrift*, xii (1903), pp. 1–39;

the early Empire cannot be doubted: this it was which brought the Orientals to Western Europe. The evidence was collected by P. Scheffer-Boichorst.[10] Such intercourse continued through the fourth and into the early fifth century,[11] but its persistence into the Middle Age of Merovingian Gaul cannot simply be assumed; the prior question must be asked: is there any justification for such an assumption?

Perhaps the best method of approach is to study Gregory's knowledge of foreign countries: what is the range of his information? Of affairs in Visigothic Spain he was fully informed: embassies were frequent, and he himself questioned Chilperic's envoys to Leuvigild on the condition of the Spanish Catholics (vi, 18). Agilan, Leuvigild's envoy, passed through Tours (v, 43) and disputed with Gregory, and the bishop was present at a banquet given by Oppila (vi, 40; cf. viii, 35, 38; ix, 20). Of N. Italy Gregory naturally knew something owing to the Frankish invasions of the country, but of S. Italy he seems to have known little: he can make the remarkable statement that Buccelin captured Sicily and exacted tribute from it (iii, 32). Of Rome or of the Popes of the time we hear nothing, save of

'Les relations de la Provence et du Levant du Vᵉ siècle aux Croisades', *Congrès français de la Syrie* (see note 8), pp. 75–98.

[10] P. Scheffer-Boichorst, 'Kleinere Forschungen zur Geschichte des Mittelalters, iv. Zur Geschichte der Syrer im Abendlande', in *Mitteilungen des Instituts für österreichische Geschichtsforschung*, iv (Innsbruck, 1885), pp. 520–50. Cf. J. Baillet, 'Les Marseillais dans le Levant aux temps romains', *Congrès français de la Syrie* (see n. 8), pp. 148–50; and see further, F. Cumont, *Les religions orientales dans le paganisme romain*, 4ᵐᵉ édition, revue, illustrée et annotée (Paris, 1920), pp. 210–11.

[11] Cf. the letter of Honorius to Agricola, *Praef. Galliarum* of the summer of 418, *MG. EPP.*, iii, p. 13. Jerome. *Com. in Ezechielem*, viii, c. 27, *P.L.* xxii, col. 255; on Salvian, *De Gubernatione Dei*, iv, § 69. 'Nam ut de alio hominum genere non dicam, consideremus solas negotiatorum et Syricorum [so Halm, MSS. siricorum] omnium turbas, quae maiorem ferme civitatum universarum partem occupaverunt, etc.,' and see Raymond Thouvenot, 'Salvien et la ruine de l'empire romain', in *Mélanges d'archéologie et d'histoire*, xxxviii (1920), pp. 145–63 at pp. 151–2. 'Si les colonies de Grecs et d'Orientaux étaient importantes, elles étaient cantonnées dans certains ports comme Marseille, ou les grands centres d'échange comme Lyon. Mais au Vᵉ siècle Salvien ne connait plus les commerçants gaulois; s'ils avaient conservé quelque importance, il n'aurait pas manqué l'occasion, je pense, de flétrir en eux les hommes d'argent. Mais il ne s'en prend qu'aux Syriens. J'en conclus que le commerce occidental, au moins dans le sud de la Gaule, avait à peu près sombré durant les invasions, que les Orientaux désormais sans concurrents avaient accaparé les affaires, à Marseille surtout où ils étaient déjà nombreux sans doute et organisés. Originaires de provinces épargnées par les Barbares, ils avaient conservé intacts leurs capitaux et leur outillage, et, mercants sans scrupules, ils en profitaient pour exploiter les pays d'Occident où nulle concurrence n'était plus à craindre.'

the appeal to John III in the case of the bishops Salonius and Sagittarius (v, 20). In book x, however, we are given a long account of affairs in Rome, showing Gregory's readiness to be interested in the subject when information could be obtained. The reason for this sudden extension of the range of Gregory's vision (x, 1) lies in the fact that a deacon of Tours, who had been sent on a mission to Rome to acquire relics of the saints, had just returned from Italy. If the reader will consider the character of the information there recorded, and Gregory's general silence on Roman matters he will, I think, infer that Gaul was at this time not in regular contact with Italy. I myself cannot believe that ships and traders were customarily passing between Italy and Merovingian Gaul.

If we pass to the history of the Roman Empire in the Eastern Mediterranean the result is curiously similar. Of Justinian we hear nothing save the appointment of Narses in place of Belisarius in Italy (iii, 32, told in connection with Theudebert's invasion of N. Italy) and the campaign in Spain (iv, 8, mentioned in connection with Visigothic history. Note, however, *In glor. mart.* 30). But of Justin's reign we learn more: of his character, of the capture by the Persians of Syrian Antioch—Antioch is placed in Egypt!—of the Persian war and of the association by Justin of Tiberius as colleague. This sudden expansion of the narrative is due to the fact that envoys of Sigebert returned at this time to Gaul from an embassy to the imperial court at Constantinople (iv, 40). From the reign of Tiberius we are given legends of the emperor's liberality (v, 19), an account of the plot to dethrone him in favour of Justinian, Justin's nephew,[12] and of his Persian war (v, 30); but of the stubborn defence of Sirmium against the Avars Gregory knows nothing. The source of his information and the reason for his silence may be conjectured from the fact that Chilperic's embassy to Tiberius returned to Gaul, it would appear, in the year 580 (vi, 2). The operations against the Avars belong to the years 580–582. We take up the eastern story once more with the death of Tiberius and the accession of Maurice (vi, 30). Here again the information doubtless came through the imperial envoys who brought a subsidy of 50,000 pieces of gold to in-

[12] On this account cf. E. Stein in P.W. *sub voc.* Justinianus II.

duce Childebert to attack the Lombards in Italy (vi, 42; viii, 18).[13] Gregory's interest in the affairs of the East when he could obtain first-hand knowledge of happenings there is shown from his account of the capture of Antioch by the Persians derived from the refugee bishop Simon, the Armenian (x, 24). The conclusion which would seem to result from this analysis is that Gregory had no regular source of information for eastern affairs such as would have been furnished by traders had they been in continued relation with the ports of the eastern empire.

Further, it is remarkable that Childebert's envoy to Constantinople, Grippo, did not sail directly to the East, but went to Carthage and there awaited the praefect's pleasure before he was allowed to proceed to the imperial court (x, 2). M. Bréhier points out that Gundovald left Constantinople and ultimately arrived at Marseilles (vi, 24; vii, 36).[14] True, but Gregory gives no hint of his route; did he, too, travel by way of Carthage?

How far does Gregory's own narrative support this negative inference? There is a Syrian merchant at Bordeaux (vii, 31) who possessed a relic of St Sergius, but at a time when pilgrimages[15] and relic-hunting[16] were familiar who shall say how this finger of the saint reached Bordeaux? There were Syrians and Jews in Paris (viii, 1), and one of them, a merchant, by name Eusebius, secured by bribes the bishopric; a Syrian of Tours helped Gregory to translate into Latin the legend of the Seven Sleepers of Ephesus (*In glor. mart.*, c. 94), but there is nothing to connect them with their Syrian homeland. In Merovingian Gaul the Bretons had ships (iv, 20; x, 9); we hear of a ship owned by a Jew coasting from Nice to Marseilles (*Glor. Conf.*, c. 95); the Visigoths of Spain possessed ships (iii, 10), a ship sailing from Spain 'with the usual merchandise' arrives at Marseilles (ix, 22), while ships sailing from Gaul to Galicia are plundered by Leuvigild (viii, 35). Nowhere, so far as I can see, in the work of Gregory of Tours is there any suggestion of a

[13] No further information attributable to the mission of Grippo in 588 (x, 2) can be traced in Gregory's history.

[14] Cf. L. Bréhier, *Congrès français de la Syrie* (cf. n. 8, on p. 311), pp. 78, 91.

[15] Cf. e.g. *Sermo de vita sancti Honorati, P. L.*, L., col. 1255.

[16] Cf. O. M. Dalton, *The History of the Franks*, etc., ii, p. 653 *s. v.* 'Relics'.

direct contact of Merovingian Gaul with the eastern Mediterranean. If Justinian was constrained to resort to measures of fiscal oppression to compel shipowners to trade with the new imperial conquests in Italy and Africa,[17] it is hardly likely that East Roman merchants would readily sail to the ports of Gaul. That products from the East reached Merovingian Gaul is clear (cf. e.g. iv, 43; v, 5 and the legend of Hospicius of Nice, vi, 6),[18] but the problem is whence did they come *directly*? Was it from imperial territory in Spain or from Carthage?

My own belief is that the unity of the Mediterranean world was broken by the pirate fleet of Vandal Carthage and that the shattered unity was never restored. A Merovingian might have pepper to his meat, the wine of Gaza might be a bait to lure a man to his assassination (vii, 29)[19] but Gaul of the Merovingians, so far as vital contacts with the empire were concerned, was from the first marooned. Gregory with all his advantages only gained occasional fragments of information upon the doings of Romania.

It may be objected that in this statement no account has been taken of the famous passage in the *Vita Genovevae*, c. 27, concerning Symeon the Stylite: 'fuit quidam sanctus in partibus orientis valde contemptor seculi nomine Simeon in Siria Ciliciae eminus ab Anthiocia constitutus in columna annis fere quadraginta. Quem aiunt sedole *negotiatores euntes ac redeuntes* de Genovefa interrogasse, quam etiam veneratione profusa salutasse et ut eum in orationibus suis memorem haberet poposcisse ferunt.' If this *Vita* is a late fiction,[20] there is no need for comment. But if the work is authentic,[21] and if the account is

---

[17] Bréhier's interpretation of Procopius, *Hist. Arc.*, c. 25, in *Byzantinische Zeitschrift*, xii, 20.

[18] Ambassadors brought works of art from the imperial court as gifts to Frankish kings. On this subject cf. L. Bréhier in *Byzantinische Zeitschrift*, xii, 22 sqq.

[19] One cannot but wonder whether this wine in Merovingian Gaul was really imported from Palestine or whether it should more strictly be described as 'of Gaza type'. What is today drunk as port wine has not necessarily come from Oporto.

[20] So Krusch: *Neues Archiv*, xviii (1893), pp. 11–50; xix (1893), pp. 444–59; xl (1916), pp. 133–81, 267–327. This chapter might be only a sixth-century legend: there were Syrians, as we have seen, in Paris, and Symeon the Stylite was known and even imitated in sixth-century Gaul (cf. viii, 15; x, 24).

[21] Cf. G. Karth, 'Étude critique sur la vie de Sainte Geneviève', in *Études franques*, ii (Bruxelles, 1919), pp. 1–96.

historical,[22] it refers to a date prior to 24 July 459 (the probable day of St Symeon's death)[23] and the 'negotiatores euntes et redeuntes' would thus belong to a period before the Vandals had put an end to free communication between the East and the West of the Mediterranean.

If, then, the view which I have endeavoured to set forth has any foundation, it is misleading to state that for the Franks of the sixth century the Mediterranean still remained '*mare nostrum*';[24] we can only accept with qualifications the statement that 'le grand commerce mediterranéen qui fleurit en Gaule durant le Bas-Empire subsiste au vi[e] et même au viie siècle';[25] it is only true at a remove that 'de Byzance, d'Asie Mineure et d'Égypte des marchands juifs, mais surtout des marchands syriens continuent de l' (=Gaul) approvisionner d'objets de luxe, d'étoffes précieuses, de vins fins'.[26]

[22] Ibid., pp. 64–5; H. Delehaye, *Les saints stylites* (Bruxelles, 1923), pp. xix–xxi. On p. xxxi he writes: 'L'Occident lui-même, l'Espagne, la Bretagne, la Gaule envoyèrent des visiteurs à Tellnešin (Theodoret, 11) et il ne paraît dès lors plus si difficile d'accepter qu'il ait pu y avoir des communications entre Symeon et Ste. Geneviève.'

[23] Delehaye, op. cit., p. 15; S. Geneviève was born in 420.

[24] Pirenne in *Revue belge de philologie et d'histoire*, i, 82.

[25] Vercauteren in *Actes du premier congrès national des historiens français*, p. 30.

[26] Pirenne, in *Revue belge*, etc., i, 83.

XXIII

The Chronology of the Campaigns of Valentinian

From a review of ERNST STEIN, *Geschichte des spätrömischen Reiches*, vol. i.

[*Journal of Roman Studies*, xviii (1928), pp. 217–25 at pp. 222–4.]

Ammianus Marcellinus and the chronology of the campaigns of Valentinian. Walter Heering in a recent dissertation[1] has reconsidered the chronology of Valentinian's campaigns against the Alamanni and has sought to establish a scheme of dating which conflicts with that maintained by Seeck and accepted by Schmidt. The dissertation has been highly praised by De Sanctis;[2] Dr Stein has rejected Dr Heering's results, and I believe that he is right in so doing. It may readily be admitted that the establishment of a precise chronology for these campaigns is in itself of small historical moment, but the study of the problem may prove of some significance if it leads us to a better comprehension of Ammian's literary methods. It is often forgotten that Ammian set out to write a history, and not merely a chronicle, that his aim is the production of a work of literature, and that in consequence he is concerned—and necessarily concerned—with the arrangement and grouping of his material. Seeck, operating with his theory of a year which ran from spring to spring—a winter-and-summer year—is far too mechanical in his treatment, and a failure to consider the problem from the point of view of literary composition has, I think, misled Dr Heering. A brief analysis of the small section of Ammian's history which deals with the years 364–6 may illustrate the true method of approach.

Ammian has brought Valentinian to Milan and despatched Valens back to Constantinople. In 26, 5, 6, he writes *agentes igitur in memoratis urbibus principes sumpsere primitus trabeas*

---

[1] Walter Heering, *Kaiser Valentinian I (364–375 n. Chr.)*, Jena Dissertation, 1927 (Faber'sche Buchdruckerei, Magdeburg).

[2] *Rivista di Filologia*, vi (1928), pp. 578–9.

consulares omnisque hic annus dispendiis gravibus rem Romanam adflixit—it is the year 365, the year of the Alamannic invasion in the West, the year of the revolt of Procopius in the East. Ammian is thus faced with two series of events which are independent of each other and must from the point of view of the literary artist be recounted as wholes: to carry on the history of the western and eastern provinces concurrently would only be to produce confusion. Ammian decides to describe first the revolt of Procopius and then later the operations in Gaul. This decision he explains to the reader in 26, 5, 15. But how comes it that Valentinian takes no part in the suppression of the revolt of Procopius, that he is apparently regardless of his brother's difficulties? The situation of Valentinian in the West must be briefly sketched in order to give to the reader the true setting for the single-handed struggle of Valens. The dangers which detained Valentinian in the West, the motives for his abstention from supporting his colleague in the East, these must be anticipated in order that the story of the revolt of Procopius may be read with full comprehension: those dangers will be recounted at length when Ammian turns to describe the *bella barbarica.*

It is this summary anticipation of the western history which has misled modern students; they have failed to realize that it is the same story as is later told in detail. Let us look at Ammian's summary. The course of his thought runs as follows: the consulship of the two emperors was a fatal year for the Roman state in West and East, since the Alamanni, the claims of their envoys having been harshly rejected, invaded Gaul, and about the same time—or rather a little later—*et circa id tempus aut non multo posterius,* 26, 5, 8—Procopius in the East raised the standard of revolt. [The Alamanni, as he tells us in 27, 1, 1, invaded Gaul *statim post Kalendas Januarias* (365); Procopius revolted in September of the same year.] When Valentinian was on the point of reaching Paris, the news of these *gravia dispendia*—of the revolt of Procopius and of the failure of the Roman defence in Gaul—was brought to him on one and the same day.[3] Dagalaifus was forthwith ordered to

[3] The mistake of Ammian is that he has not *expressly* said that it was the news of the Roman defeat which was brought to the Emperor; his text might

march against the Alamanni, who retreated before his advance. Valentinian after considerable hesitation decided that, since Procopius was the foe only of his brother and himself, while the Alamanni were the enemies of the whole Empire, his place was in Gaul. He marched to Rheims, so as to be near the threatened frontier, and took his measures to secure the protection of the western provinces. Ammian has set the stage: he can proceed with his account of the suppression of the eastern revolt.

Seeck, commenting upon this summary, remarks: the visit of the envoys of the Alamanni to Milan and the rejection of their demands both belong to the year 364, but they are recounted under the year 365; this means that Ammian is basing his history on a year which ran from spring to spring— a *Frühlings-jahr*.[4] No such inference is justified; Ammian is writing as an historian, and not as an annalist. He is giving, and giving in its natural place, the *reason* for the invasion of Gaul by the Alamanni.

When Ammian has brought to a close his account of the rebellion of Procopius, he begins a new book of his history; now he is going to tell in full the story of those events in the West which he has for his own literary purpose anticipated. He links his account to what has gone before by a reference to that summary: *Alamanni . . . ob causam expositam supra Gallicanos limites formidati iam persultabant* (27, 1, 1). There follows a narrative of the invasion and of that disaster to the Roman arms—the defeat and death of Charietto—news of which, we remember, had been brought to Valentinian on his approach to Paris. We now get in its new setting the despatch by the emperor of Dagalaifus *from Paris* (27, 2, 1) of which we have previously heard. In the former passage this was only mentioned in order that we might understand Valentinian's position: now we are informed of its sequel—the dilatoriness of Dagalaifus and his recall by Valentinian on the honourable pretext of assuming the consulship with Gratian for the ensuing year 366.

suggest that the message only informed him of the Alamannic *invasion*. Of that he must have heard in Italy, and it was doubtless that invasion which had caused him to leave Milan. It is the failure of Ammian to mention in so many words at this point in his summary the defeat of Charietto which has misled modern students of his history.

4 *Hermes*, xli (1906), p. 490.

Through a failure to realize Ammian's literary disposition of his material, Dr Heering assumes *two* distinct invasions of Gaul by the Alamanni and *two* separate campaigns of Dagalaifus. Dr Stein is fully justified in rejecting such a theory. Ammian's history is a work composed with conscious literary art, and the first duty of the student is to acquaint himself with the style and method of the last great historian of Rome.

XXIV

Lactantius, *De Mortibus Persecutorum*

Review of KARL ROLLER, *Die Kaisergeschichte in Laktanz 'De Mortibus Persecutorum'*, Giessen Dissertation, 1927.

[*Journal of Roman Studies*, xviii (1928), pp. 226-8.]

The enthusiasm with which the hunt for an author's written sources is now pursued threatens to become a positive danger; every historical writer of the ancient world is fair game, and discrimination is thrown to the winds. It is easy to forget that to trace the sources of such a compilation as the *Historia Augusta* is one thing, to seek to establish the use of a written source for such a work as the *De Mortibus Persecutorum* of Lactantius is another. Lactantius lived through the persecution which he described, he was a highly-cultured man: when he wrote the pamphlet recording the history of the decade of persecution, it is not obvious why he should need to incorporate in his work a pagan history of the same period published in the same year as his own account. Such, however, is the contention maintained in Dr Roller's dissertation. Already the theory is being treated as though it were proven, and an attempt has been made to trace the influence of the same pagan history upon the *Historia Ecclesiastica* of Eusebius.[1] It is high time that the justification for Dr Roller's suggestion should be considered.

His view may be briefly summarized: the theme of Lactantius is the *deaths* of the persecutors; an account of the evil which they did during their lives in other than the religious sphere is simply irrelevant. In this account as given by Lactantius the outlook is that of a pagan and of a Roman who is impressed by the traditions of a Roman, and not a Christian, past. We must therefore conclude that a foreign source has been incorporated by Lactantius and only very slightly modified by him. As this foreign source apparently carried the

[1] Richard Laqueur, *Eusebius als Historiker seiner Zeit* (De Gruyter, Berlin, 1929), pp. 154–5.

story down to the death of Maximin, it must have been published in the same year as was (in its original form) the *De
Mortibus*.

If we would seek to test the justification for this theory, we
must remind ourselves that Lactantius is a Christian apologist:
we cannot regard his work in abstraction from the tradition
formulated by Christian apologetic. In that apologetic the
attempt had early been made to maintain the position that
only bad emperors—emperors condemned by the judgement
of the pagan world—had persecuted the Christians.[2] Thus to
prove that a persecutor was in other respects a bad ruler of the
Roman world—be he a Nero or a Domitian—is strictly
relevant to the Christian case. 'Quis enim', as Lactantius asks,
'iustitiam nisi malus persequitur' (ch. 4 § 1)? But such an emperor might be a bad ruler in his relation to his subjects, and
yet be a fortunate sovran: disaster only overtook him when
from oppression of his subjects he turned to persecution of the
Christians. This is the view clearly expressed by Lactantius of
Domitian: 'qui cum exerceret invisam dominationem, subiect-
orum tamen cervicibus incubavit quam diutissime tutusque
regnavit, donec impias manus adversus dominum tenderet.
Postquam vero ad persequendum iustum populum instinctu
daemonum incitatus est, tunc traditus in manus inimicorum
luit poenas' (ch. 3 § 1–2). And not only did the Christian God
inflict upon him a righteous vengeance, but the senate condemned his memory so that it overthrew his statues, destroyed
his inscriptions and 'gravissime decretis etiam mortuo notam
inureret ad ignominiam sempiternam' (ch. 3 § 3). Such is the
background of the thought of Lactantius.

Further, it must not be forgotten that Lactantius had been
in his earlier years a pagan, that he came from the West to
Nicomedia at the summons of Diocletian. He was a Roman of
North Africa, for whom the western capital was the head of
the world. As a student of Christian apocalyptic he might be
compelled by the authoritative pronouncements of the scriptures to predict the dissolution of the Roman Empire. But that

[2] Cf. C. Guignebert, *Tertullien* (Paris, 1901), ch. 3; Saverio Anfuso, 'Lat-
tanzio, autore del "De Mortibus Persecutorum",' *Didaskaleion*, N.S. iii (1925),
at pp. 63–4.

idea he could not contemplate with the exalted assurance of an Augustine: that the Empire of Rome should be overthrown filled the Roman Lactantius with dread and dismay (*horret animus dicere*).[3] This was the man who wrote the *De Mortibus* with passion, undoubtedly, but the more closely the pamphlet is studied the stronger grows the conviction that it was history —and no mere farrago of lies—that Lactantius wrote.

To turn to the grounds adduced by Dr Roller for his theory of a pagan contemporary written source. (i) The evils, he argues, which accrued to the Empire from the reforms and civil administration of Diocletian, his colleagues and successors are irrelevant to the theme of the work.—No, because the persecutor is a bad emperor, even for his pagan subjects, while the Westerner and the Roman in Lactantius both alike disapproved of the imperial innovations.[4] (ii) The rule of Diocletian as painted in the *De Mortibus* is disastrous for the Empire—'cum rem publicam talibus consiliis et talibus sociis everteret, cum pro sceleribus suis nihil non mereretur'—but Lactantius can proceed—'tamdiu tamen summa felicitate regnavit quamdiu manus suas iustorum sanguine non inquinaret'. Here is a contradiction: the former view is pagan and comes from the incorporated source: the latter is Christian and represents the opinion of Lactantius.—Not at all: the treatment of Domitian's reign, already cited, forms a complete parallel. Both parts of the picture are relevant, and each is a consistent part of the thought of Lactantius. (iii) The man who had portrayed Diocletian's reign as ruinous for the Roman State could not have written of the emperor when urged to persecution by Galerius 'diu senex furori eius repugnavit ostendens quam perniciosum esset inquietari orbem terrae, fundi sanguinem multorum': it is an obvious contradiction to make the tyrant care for the interests of the State.—But one may condemn a man and loathe his acts, and yet recognize that in all his misdoings he is distressingly conscientious. And in this chapter, it must

---

[3] See the remarkable passage in ch. 15 of the 7th book of the *Divine Institutions.*

[4] With Galerius as *hostis Romani nominis*, ch. 27, § 8; cf. *Div. Inst.*, 7, 15, 11, for the cause of the confusion which will herald the destruction of the world: 'cuius vastitatis et confusionis haec erit causa *quod Romanum nomen quo nunc regitur orbis* ... tolletur de terra'.

be insisted, Lactantius is boldly facing a difficulty which no student of Diocletian's reign can escape. What is the explanation of the remarkable change of policy by which at the very end of his reign the emperor—with hesitation and by successive steps—abandoned toleration and adopted persecution of the Christians? At least Lactantius realizes—as Stade in our own day failed to realize—that here lies the problem of the reign, and to that problem he gives his answer. The tribute paid by Lactantius to Diocletian's care for the peace of the Roman world is worthy of the 'Christian Cicero'. (iv) In his account of the Battle of the Milvian Bridge, Lactantius has given two inconsistent explanations of Constantine's victory: Constantine conquers because it is the will of the Christian God (=Lactantius); he wins the day because Maxentius is deserted by his subjects and betrayed by the response obtained from the Sibylline books (=the supposed pagan source).—There is no such contradiction: the fate of the pagan persecutor is the reprobation of his pagan subjects (cf. the Domitian parallel again), he is lured to destruction by the demons in whom he trusts—'instinctu daemonum incitatus est, tunc traditus in manus inimicorum luit poenas'. It is a purely Lactantian philosophy of history. (v) The account of the victory of Licinius over Maximin is again composed of two inconsistent strands: the heavenly vision, the prayer, the assurance of success (=Lactantius): the attempt of Licinius to come to an agreement with Maximin before the battle, the failure of the attempt, the enforced engagement (=the supposed pagan source).—Once again I see no such contradiction. Licinius with far inferior forces had not hoped for victory: his aim was to delay Maximin's advance. There come the vision and the consequent assurance: the army is taught the supernatural litany, and it, too, is inspired with a new courage. Only because both the general and his men are persuaded that, if the battle comes, they will surely triumph can Licinius venture to open negotiations in the face of his troops in order to stay even at the eleventh hour the suicidal butchery of the Roman armies. Here again the persecutor is his own worst foe, and his determination to force the issue on the field of battle results in his flight to Asia. The implication of the narrative of Lactantius is surely that Licinius entered into an attempt at conciliation at that moment because his troops were assured of victory: otherwise his action would have dismayed his outnumbered army. The dream remains the presupposition alike of the conduct and of the success of Licinius. (vi) When writing of the famous meeting of Licinius and Constantine at Milan in A.D. 313 Lactantius only records the marriage alliance which united the two emperors: he does not mention the settlement of their religious policy. Here, therefore, he is merely copying the pagan source.—I hardly think that this is a necessary inference. We now know that there was no 'Edict of Milan'. Lactantius is writing for the Eastern provinces. For them the all-important date was not the interview at Milan, but the overthrow of Maximin and the declaration granting freedom of worship to the Christians issued by Licinius after the victory of Adrianople; the inhabitants of the Eastern provinces could place no confidence in Maximin's ambiguous compliance with the instructions of Constantine as senior Augustus. The declaration of Licinius was the charter of liberties for the East. There is thus a reason for the silence of Lactantius: the supposition of a pagan source is unnecessary.

Finally Dr Roller cites from the *De Mortibus* instances of linguistic usage which Brandt once thought incompatible with Lactantian authorship: these he would attribute to the pagan source. He has not noticed that Brandt, the profoundest student of the style of Lactantius, publicly disavowed his error, and admitted that the language of the *De Mortibus* furnished no ground for refusing to include the pamphlet amongst the genuine works of the author of the *Divine Institutions*.[5]

Dr Roller has, in my judgement, failed to prove his case: the *De Mortibus* is a unity. The 'pagan-source' of Lactantius cannot be called in aid to explain the Ecclesiastical History of Eusebius.

[5] *Berliner philologische Wochenschrift* (1903), col. 1257.

XXV

Stilicho and the Barbarian Invasions

From a note on PROFESSOR BURY's *History of the Later Roman Empire*.

[*Journal of Roman Studies*, xii (1922), pp. 207–29 at pp. 207–20.]

The Date of the Battle of Verona: A.D. 402 *or* A.D. 403?

Professor Bury holds that after the defeat at Pollentia in A.D. 402 Alaric withdrew from Italy, and then in the early summer of A.D. 403 again crossed the Italian frontier and attacked Verona (i, p. 162). He adds in a note 'Birt determined the true date as 403'. The question of the date of the Battle of Verona is in itself unimportant, but with regard to our historical tradition it does become of significance. For the question raised is this: Was there in the year 403 a second invasion of Italy by Alaric of which no hint has been preserved in any source save only in Claudian's poem on the Sixth Consulship of Honorius? If this is a necessary inference from Claudian's poem, we must of course accept an affirmative answer to that question, but it would in itself be an unwelcome and surprising conclusion. Is it, however, a necessary inference?

The *De Bello Gothico* of Claudian, recited in the presence of Stilicho, precedes the poem on the Sixth Consulate: in the *Gothic War* the central point is the battle of Pollentia which is described at length; the only other engagement expressly mentioned is that on the Timavus (v. 562). When Claudian is called upon to produce a poem on the Emperor's consulship he must seek new material for his subject matter. If a fresh invasion of Italy by Alaric had really been repelled by Stilicho *since* the publication of the *De Bello Gothico*, the new theme was ready to the poet's hand: he had only to take up the story from the point where he had broken off in his former poem— the Battle of Pollentia. But there is no such new warlike theme:

arma Getarum
nuper apud socerum [= Stilicho] plectro celebrata recenti.

adventus nunc sacra tui libet edere Musis
grataque patratis exordia sumere bellis.

(De VI Consulatu Honorii, 123–6.)

This seems to me to exclude any successful intervening campaign: the old story must be told with new incidents. We are
accordingly given fresh epic material with the appeal of the
river gods to Eridanus, and naturally all the rivers crossed by
Alaric in his invasion which must be recrossed by him in his
retreat are summoned. To argue, with Birt, that because the
Timavus is introduced into this scene (v. 197) which is then
followed by the mention of Verona (v. 201) Alaric must have
recrossed the Timavus *before* the battle of Verona is surely
entirely to misconceive Claudian's use of his divinities as epic
material.

It has been further argued that, if the battle at Verona had
preceded the composition of the *De Bello Gothico*, it **must** have
been mentioned in that poem: but the argument is not conclusive, for the *moenia vindicis Hastae* (v. 203) are only referred to in the later work, and, so far as I know, it is universally admitted that this incident must be placed *before* the
battle of Pollentia. Further, since the defence of Hasta and the
engagement at Verona are apparently regarded as of almost
equal importance in determining the result of the war, no valid
conclusion can be drawn from the silence of the earlier poem.
Indeed, a reason for that silence can easily be suggested: the
terms of the agreement with Alaric must have been (*inter alia*)
that he should not march on Rome, nor attempt to occupy
Gaul or Raetia; he was needed by Stilicho in Illyricum. On
his retreat Alaric apparently repented of these terms, and contemplated crossing one of the Alpine passes into Raetia or
Gaul (*VI Cons.* 229 sqq.): such a march must be prevented:
hence the engagement at Verona. But though Alaric had
clearly intended to violate the terms of the treaty, he was once
more allowed to escape, and it is manifest alike from the
charges of Zosimus v. 29, from Orosius vii, 37. 2, and from
Claudian's own laboured defence in the *De Bello Gothico* 91–
165 that Stilicho was in consequence accused of treachery. In
a panegyric recited in Stilicho's presence it was, therefore, far

wiser to ignore the ambiguous incident of Verona, and to concentrate all attention upon the earlier stages of the campaign.
Later, when new material for a fresh poem was needed, the
poet grew bolder, Verona was introduced with a proud flourish
to mask previous hesitancy: Alaric's escape must still be
excused, it is true, but the blame is discreetly thrown upon the
leader of the Alan auxiliaries. What Claudian does *not* say is
frequently of the highest significance.

But the positive grounds for viewing the poems as a treatment of one and the same campaign are more instructive.
Alaric's speech *after* the Battle of Verona should be carefully
compared with the narrative sections of the two poems: such a
comparison, I think, excludes Birt's hypothesis. Alaric is viewing in retrospect the whole course of the Italian invasion:
which of his disasters shall he lament first? (*VI Cons.* 280
sqq.)—not Pollentia (=*B.G.* 580–603), not the loss of treasure
(=*B.G.* 604–15), then he had still his forces at his back: he
reaches the Apennines, and plans a march on Rome. Stilicho
ensnares him from his goal by *foedera saevo deteriora iugo*. This
rescue of Rome by Stilicho is, we remember, the theme of *B.G.*
95 sqq. *consulitur Roma tibi*: it is this which excuses Stilicho's
clementia. In his speech Alaric thus describes the result of that
intervention of Stilicho after Pollentia:

> dum parcere fingit
> rettudit [*rettulit* alii] hostiles animos *bellumque remenso
> evaluit transferre Pado.*
>
> (*VI Cons.* 301.)

But this passage has its parallel in Claudian's own narrative at
the time when he is describing the battle at Verona:

> oblatum Stilicho violato foedere Martem
> omnibus arripuit votis *ubi Roma periclo
> iam procul et belli medio Padus arbiter ibat.*
>
> (*VI Cons.* 210–12.)

Alaric proceeds to lament that his friends are alienated and
are deserting him:

> nullusne clientum
> permanet? offensi comites, odere propinqui.
>
> (*VI Cons.* 314–15.)

But in Claudian's own narrative this is precisely the position after Verona:

> iamque frequens rarum decerpere transfuga robur
> coeperat inque dies numerus decrescere castris,
> nec iam deditio paucis occulta parari,
> sed cunei totaeque palam discedere turmae.
>
> (*VI Cons.* 250–3 and cf. 253–64.)

Alaric after bewailing these desertions asks whither he may flee to hide the remnants of his shipwrecked forces: this is represented in the narrative by vv. 265–71—Alaric's appealing gaze to the Alps.

The speech ends: Claudian's narrative resumes with the flight of Alaric and the pursuit of Stilicho (*VI Cons.* 320 sqq.). The parallelism between the speech of Alaric *after* Verona, giving a continuous account of his invasion, and Claudian's own narrative in the two poems is complete. The conclusion is to my mind irresistible that the *anni vapor* which oppressed Alaric's troops at Verona (*VI Cons.* 241) was the summer heat of the same year in which on April 6 the Goths had been defeated at Pollentia: the battle of Verona was, indeed, but an incident in Alaric's retreat from Italy A.D. 402.

As soon as Alaric had departed from Italian soil the timorous Honorius determined not to run the risk of a return of the Goths in the spring of 403 and of another investment of Milan. He retired to the remote security of Ravenna. The first constitution issued from Ravenna is dated viii. Id. Dec. 402, and that is concerned with the levying of recruits. It has been objected that if the Battle of Verona had been fought in 402 Honorius would have celebrated the victory by entering on his sixth consulship in 403 and not only, as he did, in 404. Rather Honorius expected a return of the Goths early in 403, and only when his fears proved groundless did he commemorate alike the completion of his Decennalia (Gabotto) and the retreat of Alaric by his sixth consulship. It is thus no wonder that in 404 Claudian felt that the Gothic War as a theme for the court poet had somewhat lost its freshness and preferred to lay most stress on the unusual sight of the arrival of an Emperor of Rome within the walls of the capital (*VI Cons.* 125–6, 331–660).

Y   B.B.S.

We thus obtain an increasing sidelight upon Claudian's literary methods, and we are released from the necessity of inferring a Gothic invasion of Italy of which chroniclers and historians alike have made no mention.

The Policy of Stilicho.

Mommsen in his study of Stilicho's policy accentuated the significance of a passage of Olympiodorus where, referring to Stilicho's designs upon Illyricum in A.D. 405, he writes (fr. 3) Ἀλάριχος ὁ τῶν Γότθων φύλαρχος ὃν Στελίχων μετεκαλέσατο ἐπὶ τῷ φυλάξαι Ὁνωρίῳ τὸ Ἰλλυρικόν (τῇ γὰρ αὐτοῦ ἦν παρὰ Θεοδοσίου τοῦ πατρὸς ἐκνενεμημένον βασιλείᾳ) κ.τ.λ. Mommsen's comment on this is 'Ob Theodosius dies in der That verfügt hat, kann bezweifelt werden, nicht aber, dass Stilicho dies behauptet hat, und wenn gleich erst bei Gelegenheit der letzten Verhandlungen zwischen Alarich und Stilicho dies erwähnt wird, so liegt es doch auf der Hand dass Stilicho nicht erst lange Jahre nach Theodosius Tode diesen Anspruch geltend gemacht haben kann. Meines Erachtens giebt diese wenig beachtete Notiz des gleichzeitigen und vor allen anderen dieser Epoche zuverlässigen Schriftstellers recht eigentlich den Schlüssel für Stilichos Verhalten gegenüber dem Ostreich.'[1] Professor Bury has adopted Mommsen's suggestion (i, pp. 110–11, 120, 169), and has himself stressed the need of the West for the recruiting ground which Illyricum would afford. Thus the question of recovering Illyricum for Honorius is from the first a determining factor in Stilicho's Eastern policy. Mommsen would further appear to have thought that Stilicho's aims, so far as the East was concerned, were confined to the settlement of this question, and that he did not in any way seek to control the fortunes of the realm of Arcadius: 'Die Umgestaltung des constantinopolitanischen Regiments hat Stilicho nicht unternommen; die weitere Entwicklung der Dinge daselbst zeigt bei vollständiger Meisterlosigkeit unter dem unfähigen Kaiser keine Spur des Eingreifens von Seiten Stilichos; und dass ein solches nicht einmal versucht ward,

---

[1] *Gesammelte Schriften*, iv, pp. 517–18. Gratian had surrendered E. Illyricum to Theodosius the Great: Seeck has inferred from *C. Th.*, i, 32, 5, that it was reunited to the West on the revolt of Maximus, and that on the tyrant's defeat the province once more reverted to the praefecture of the East. *Rheinisches Museum*, N.F. lxix (1913), pp. 37–8.

kann wohl nur darauf zurückgeführt werden dass Stilicho die Herrschaft über das Gesammtreich keineswegs angestrebt hat.'[2] This latter question Professor Bury has not considered in any detail, but it may perhaps be doubted whether the policy of Stilicho was not more complex than Mommsen would have us believe. It is not without interest to study the aims of Stilicho so far as they are reflected in the poems of Claudian: he, at least, must have had opportunities for intimate acquaintance with his patron's hopes and fears.

Theodosius the Great on starting for the West to suppress the tyrant Eugenius had left in the East as adviser of Arcadius his highly-trusted minister Rufinus, while he had summoned from Constantinople his son Honorius who was recognized as his presumptive successor in the West of the Empire. Death did not find the great emperor unprepared. As Ambrose writes:[3] 'gloriosus . . . in eo Theodosius qui non communi iure testatus est: de filiis enim nihil habebat novum quod conderet quibus totum dederat, nisi ut eos praesenti commendaret parenti [=Stilicho]; et de subditis sibi et commissis testari debuit, ut legata dimitteret, fidei commissa signaret?' This last sentence is, of course, as Mommsen says, a 'verneinende Frage'.[4] The *filiis* in this passage are, I think, no less clearly Honorius and Arcadius, not Honorius and Galla Placidia;[5] this is shown by the words *quibus totum dederat. Commendaret* cannot, as Mommsen has shown, apply to a legal guardianship of the sons of Theodosius as emperors: Roman constitutional law knew of no such *tutela*. Birt writes on this passage:[6] 'Quodsi de tutela filiorum mandata interpretaberis, celerius ages; nihil enim iis verbis inesse video nisi optasse Theodosium ne tutor Honorii [=Stilicho] hostilia contra Arcadium pararet.' And in this sense Stilicho was for many years loyal to his trust. The importance of the passage in the funeral oration of Ambrose lies in the words *de filiis . . . nihil habebat novum quod conderet.* The bishop who enjoyed the dying emperor's confidence knew that the provision made by him for the government of the East was

---

[2] *Gesammelte Schriften*, iv, p. 521.   [3] *De Obitu Theodosii*, 5.
[4] Mommsen: op. cit, p. 516.
[5] So M. Assunta Nagl, *Galla Placida. Studien zur Geschichte und Kultur des Altertums*, II, Heft iii (Paderborn, 1908), p. 9, n. 5.
[6] Preface to his edition of Claudian's Works. *M.G.H*, p. xxviii.

not changed upon his death-bed: Rufinus was therefore to
remain minister in the East. In the words of Orosius vii. 37,
'Interea cum a Theodosio imperatore seniore singulis potis-
simis infantum cura et disciplina utriusque palatii commissa
esset, hoc est Rufino orientalis aulae, Stiliconi occidentalis
imperii', etc.

The interesting point is that the minister of the West was
not content to adopt this view: he desired to control the fortunes of *both* halves of the Roman world. But since Theodosius
had made no such disposition, how might the claim of Stilicho
be at least colourably supported?—obviously only through
the report of a *secret* conversation between the Emperor and
himself. When this claim was first made we do not know, but
in Claudian's earliest court poem the claim appears (*III Cons.
Honorii*, 142) and this expedient is adopted in its support—
'cunctos discedere tectis dux iubet'—and this explanation once
offered, Claudian, discreetly, never again mentions that momentous interview. In this poem, however, the claim is boldly
stated: Stilicho *alone* is to direct the policy and command the
armed forces of the whole Empire:

> tu pignora *solus*
> nostra fove; geminos dextra tu protege fratres. . . .
> indue mente patrem, crescentes dilige fetus
> ut ducis, ut soceri.
>
> (vv. 152–3, 157–8.)

With this compare *In Rufinum* ii, 4.

> iamque tuis, Stilicho, Romana potentia curis
> et rerum commissus apex, tibi credita fratrum
> utraque majestas, geminaeque exercitus aulae.

This double task of civil and military control recurs *In Ruf.
I Praef.* 17:

> qui stabilem servans Augustis fratribus orbem
> *justitia pacem, viribus arma* regit.

and cf. *IV Cons. Honorii*, 432

> quem fratribus ipse [sc. Theodosius]
> discedens clipeum, defensoremque dedisti

with *Nupt.* 307:

> dignus [sc. Stilicho] cui leges, dignus cui pignora tanti
> principis et rerum commendarentur habenae

(and see further *De Bell. Gild.* 301, *Laudes Stil.* i, 140).

Such is the claim, and to realize that ambition Stilicho
would seek to overthrow any minister of Arcadius who withstood it, would endeavour to have at his command barbarian
forces, who would open a way of escape for Alaric because he
had need of Gothic support against the ministers of the East,
but yet there always remained for Stilicho the fact that both
Honorius and Arcadius were the sons of Theodosius and that
therefore his own pretensions could only be made good *with
the consent of Arcadius.* The overthrow of any hostile minister
of the Eastern court could be justifiably compassed, since that
overthrow but opened a vacancy into which Stilicho himself
might step. But, granted that military forces were necessary
to counter the machinations of his Eastern rivals, those forces
might not be employed in civil war against Arcadius. This is,
I believe, the limitation which causes the policy of Stilicho to
appear contradictory and ambiguous. The most illuminating
summary of a policy based upon a distinction in Stilicho's
thought between Eastern ministers and Eastern emperor is
given by Claudian in a poem addressed to Stilicho, which must
therefore be regarded as mirroring that policy, so far as
Claudian was free to express it:

> fratrem levior nec cura tuetur
> Arcadium; nec, si quid iners atque impia turba
> praetendens proprio nomen regale furori
> audeat, adscribis iuveni. discordia quippe
> cum fremeret, numquam Stilicho sic canduit ira,
> saepe lacessitus probris gladiisque petitus,
> ut bello furias ultum, quas pertulit, iret
> inlicito, causamque daret civilibus armis:
> cuius fulta fide mediis dissensibus aulae
> intemeratorum stabat reverentia fratrum.

The rich treasure of Theodosius is divided equally between his
sons

> ne non augusta supellex
> ornatusque pares geminis heredibus essent.
> mittitur et miles, quamvis certamine partes
> iam tumeant. hostem muniri robore mavis
> quam peccare fidem: permittis iusta petenti
> idque negas solum, cuius mox ipse repulsa
> gaudeat et quidquid fuerat deforme mereri.
> (*In Prim. Cons. Stil.* ii, 78–87, 93–9.)

These lines furnish us with the starting-point from which we may approach an understanding of Stilicho's policy. In 395, on the direct order of the court of Constantinople, the troops of the East are restored (v. 95), though at the same time it can hardly be doubted that a plot was concerted for the assassination of Rufinus. But Eutropius, the successor of Rufinus, pursued the same policy toward the West as had the murdered minister, and no summons came to Stilicho from Arcadius to guide the policy of the eastern half of the Empire. Thus in 397 Stilicho moves the western troops into Greece against Alaric. It is possible that in taking this step he had a double motive: if he could free Greece from the invader, he would prove his power to achieve on behalf of Arcadius that in which the Emperor's own advisers had signally failed; such a success might suggest to Arcadius the wisdom of relying upon Stilicho's aid; at the same time he might renew with the defeated Goths the old federate relation, and strengthen the military forces of the West. Birt is of the opinion that the expedition was undertaken on a direct appeal from the eastern court: 'Tandem eo perventum est ut Stilicho arcesseretur.'[7] This is exactly what Stilicho would have wished: the silence of Claudian is to my mind conclusive that there was no such appeal. Against Birt's view there is not only the *argumentum e silentio*: an important passage of Zosimus has been overlooked; in v, 11, he writes

Εὐτρόπιος τοίνυν ἐν μὲν τῇ Κωνσταντινουπόλει παντάπασιν ἔχων οὐδένα τὸν ἀντιβλέπειν τολμῶντα, μόνον δὲ Στελίχωνα τῶν κατὰ τὴν ἑσπέραν κυριεύοντα πραγμάτων κατὰ νοῦν ἔχων ἀνελεῖν αὐτῷ διενοεῖτο τὴν ἐπὶ Κωνσταντινούπολιν ἄφιξιν. ἀναπείθει δὴ τὸν

---

[7] Birt, op. cit., p. 30, and cf. J. Koch's article, 'Claudian und die Ereignisse der Jahre 395 bis 398', *Rheinisches Museum*, N.F. xliv, pp. 575–612 at pp. 607–8.

βασιλέα, τέως συναγαγόντα τὴν γερουσίαν, κοινῷ δόγματι τῆς βασιλείας αὐτὸν πολέμιον προσειπεῖν (ed. Mendelssohn, p. 228, 15). Eutropius divined aright the policy of Stilicho and was determined to bar Constantinople before his approach: once within the city Stilicho might gain the ear of Arcadius: he anticipates any such catastrophe by wringing from emperor and senate the declaration that the minister of the West was a public enemy. It may be at this time that a European praefecture was created within the territories subject to the eastern sovran:[8] the danger from the West was the sole menace to the authority of Eutropius. Thus Eutropius represented Stilicho's action in Greece as a presumptuous invasion of an Eastern province: his answer was a *diplomatic* invasion of a Western province: the generals of Honorius were apparently encouraged to offer no resistance to Gildo in Africa (cf. Claudian, *Cons. Stil.* i, 275 sqq.), while the Moor's offer to transfer the province to the allegiance of Arcadius was eagerly accepted.

Stilicho's attempt to force the hand of Arcadius had failed, while Alaric was driven into the Eastern camp. For a time Stilicho is occupied with the suppression of the revolt in Africa but, directly that task is achieved, he proclaims his former policy with redoubled energy. This it is which gives its interest to the first book of the unfinished *De Bello Gildonico* of Claudian. The result of that war should be the reconciliation of East and West: the opening words of the poem introduce the theme: *concordia fratrum | plena redit*; its central episode is the address of Theodosius to Arcadius with its expostulation: *in fratres medio discordia Mauro | nascitur et mundus germanaque dissidet aula*—its result: the confession of Arcadius *nec carior alter | cognato Stilichone mihi* (v. 322). The whole poem is an eirenicon between East and West: Arcadius owes to Stilicho his liberation from Rufinus (v. 304): the suggestion is obvious: Stilicho is ready to take the place of Eutropius. (Cf. *In Eutrop.* ii, 543 sqq.). But Arcadius continued to support his chamberlain. Against that minister Stilicho sought to win the aid of Alaric, whose policy was to play off the East against the West. Stilicho, without reference to the Senate, refused to

[8] Cf. O. Seeck in *Rheinisches Museum*, N.F. lxix (1913), p. 38; *Regesten der Kaiser und Päpste*, i, pp. 140, 36–43; 148, 39–42.

recognize a eunuch as consul in 399 'idque negas solum . . . quidquid fuerat deforme mereri', but himself could not hold that office so long as Eutropius was supreme in Constantinople. The fall of Eutropius, which opened the consulship to Stilicho in 400, only gave to Claudian a new opportunity for pressing Stilicho's constant policy: the poet boldly represents the East as yearning for that approach of Stilicho which it had formerly feared, *In Eutrop.*, ii, 501 sqq.—notice that this passage of Claudian supports the account of Zosimus quoted above. The last 100 lines of the poem are devoted to this theme, and its closing words are

> nec te subtrahimus [sc. Orientales] Latio; defensor
>   utrique
> sufficis. armorum liceat splendore tuorum
> in commune frui; clipeus nos protegat idem
> unaque pro gemino desudet cardine virtus.
>
> (vv. 599–602.)

This is far more audacious than anything which Claudian had previously written. The explanation of that audacity is perhaps bound up with one of the most remarkable silences in Claudian's works: nowhere in his poems is the name of Gainas mentioned, yet Gainas had, it would seem, been Stilicho's agent in the assassination of Rufinus, and now Gainas, having overthrown Stilicho's enemy Eutropius, was master in Constantinople. The silence of Claudian is clearly studied: he did not wish to suggest that through the influence of the Goth Stilicho's long-cherished aim might be realized; he therefore paints that consummation as the desire of the whole East Roman people.

But at the moment when Stilicho's hopes were brightest, they were irretrievably ruined. The anti-barbarian fervour of the East after the massacre of the Goths rendered it impossible for a Vandal to control the fortunes of the realm of Arcadius: Stilicho's policy was doomed.

For some years the affairs of the West absorb his energies: 401 Invasion of Raetia, 402 Invasion of Italy by Alaric, 404–5 (see *infra*) Invasion of Italy by Radagaisus. The problem of these years is the problem of man-power: how can recruits be raised for the armies of the West? The Empire is swept for men: troops are drawn from Raetia and Britain, the Rhine frontier is left almost undefended, Huns from the Dobrudscha, Alans, Goths—all are enrolled. The West must gain a new recruiting ground at any cost. On the defeat of Radagaisus there follows Stilicho's attempt to annex Illyricum. Mommsen, as we have seen, and, following him, Professor Bury have considered that this annexation was from the first the aim of Stilicho, and would thus explain the operations of A.D. 397. I believe, however, that we ought not to abandon the chronology of Olympiodorus. In 397 the East thought that Stilicho was aiming at Constantinople: in substance I believe that it was right: now its measures are directed towards improving the defences of the threatened territory: the objective of Stilicho is not the same. If the annexation of Illyricum had been Stilicho's policy throughout, why was no attempt made to occupy that province in A.D. 399, when the domestic difficulties of the East would have hindered any effective resistance? Rather the projected annexation of Illyricum is the result of the repeated invasions of the Western Empire and of Stilicho's despair of gaining influence with Arcadius since the fall of Gainas. The need of the West could not wait upon the pleasure of the East. But even now, as in the case of his claim to control the whole Roman world, Stilicho shelters himself behind the will of the great Theodosius:[9] *he* had determined that Illyricum should belong to the West, in the same way as— if Seeck be right in his inference—it had for a time under Theodosius himself been subject to Valentinian II.

On the death of Arcadius Stilicho at once reverts to his earlier policy and forces upon Honorius the acceptance of the view that he, rather than the Emperor, shall in person go to Constantinople to advise the child sovran.

To sum up: I believe as against Mommsen that Stilicho did wish to guide the fortunes alike of the Eastern and Western halves of the Roman world, but that he refused to employ civil war as a means to that end, and as against Mommsen and Professor Bury I believe that we should interpret strictly the chronological reference of Olympiodorus. I think that Stilicho's actions can in fact be satisfactorily explained on the lines of

[9] Cf. the fragment of Olympiodorus quoted *supra.*

the policy consistently advocated by Claudian.[10] With the criticism of that policy I am not here concerned.

The Invasion of Radagaisus and the Revolt of Constantine.

Professor Bury still maintains (i, p. 160) that it was Radagaisus who invaded Raetia in concert with Alaric in A.D. 401. He does not seek to justify that view, nor does he refer to the appendix in the third volume of his edition of Gibbon where reasons in support of it are given. I very much doubt the inference that is there drawn from a confused passage in Zosimus (v, 26, 3–5).[11] In our sources Radagaisus is a *rex Gothorum*:[12] there would seem no reason to question the title:[13] he, like Alaric,[14] was the leader of a *Gothic* horde,[15] even though his forces were swelled by contingents from other tribes. But the only evidence that we possess for the invasion of Raetia in 401 states that the invaders were *Vandals*.[16] Despite the argument of Gabotto,[17] I should prefer to consider, with Schmidt, that the entry of Prosper s.a. 400 is due rather to a misunderstanding of Orosius, and that the only invasion by Radagaisus of Roman territory was his incursion into Italy.

[10] Koch has suggested that the sources of Zosimus depend in part upon the poems of Claudian; this cannot, I imagine, be proved, but the suggestion raises an interesting question: How far were Claudian's poems designed to provide propaganda *in the East* for Stilicho's policy? This purpose is at least possible in the case of the latter part of *In Eutropium*, ii.

[11] For another explanation of this confusion see Mendelssohn's note on the passage in his edition of Zosimus, p. 249. The ninth fragment of Olympiodorus must have suffered in the epitomized form in which it has been preserved. It has been suggested that it, too, refers to the year A.D. 401 and records an alliance of Stilicho with Radagaisus in that year. To my mind, the silence of Claudian is conclusive against this view. The words 'Ραδαγαίσον προσηταιρίσατο must in their original form have been equivalent to τοὺς τοῦ 'Ραδαγαίσον π. and = the enlistment by Stilicho in the Roman army of survivors after the Battle of Faesulae. They were so understood by Zosimus πλὴν ἐλαχίστους ὅσους αὐτὸς (= Stilicho) τῇ 'Ρωμαίων προσέθηκεν συμμαχίᾳ (loc. cit.). On these passages cf. Stein, *Studien zur Gesch. des byzantinischen Reiches*, etc., p. 127.

[12] Aug., *De Civ. Dei*, v, 23; Orosius, vii, 37, 8 and 15; Mommsen, *Chron. Min.* in *M.G.H.*, i, pp. 299, 652.

[13] So Schmidt, *Gesch. d. deutschen Stämme*, i, p. 121, n. 3. 'König war Radagais so wenig wie Odotheus, nur Führer freiwillig zusammengekommener Scharen'; but cf. Seeck, *Geschichte des Untergangs*, etc., v, 587 s.f.

[14] Cf. Orosius, vii, 37, 8, 'duo tunc Gothorum populi cum duobus potentissimis regibus suis, etc.'

[15] Cf. also Olympiodorus, fr. 9.

[16] Claudian, *De Bello Gothico*, 415, with the apparatus criticus of Birt in *M.G.H.* ad. loc. and his preface pp. xlviii and xlix.

[17] F. Gabotto, *Storia della Italia occidentale*, appendix i and ii.

What is the date of that incursion? It is, I think, to be regretted that Professor Bury has adopted the view of Gothofred who dated the invasion of Radagaisus to the years 405 and 406, since he considered that the constitutions *C. Th.* vii, 13, 16 and 17, issued on 17 April and 19 April, 406, must be referred to this invasion. Of these constitutions addressed to the provincials one orders the enrolment of slaves in the army, the other calls upon the provincials to act in their own defence. 'Provinciales pro imminentibus necessitatibus omnes invitamus edicto quos erigit ad militiam innata libertas. Ingenui igitur qui militiae obtentu arma capiunt amore pacis et patriae' are to receive pay at a rate fixed by the constitution—'nam optimos futuros confidimus quos virtus et utilitas publica necessitatibus obtulit'. But if these constitutions issued in the middle of April 406 are designed to raise forces to meet the Goths of Radagaisus, who had entered Italy in the previous year, this surely implies an incredible delay on the part of the imperial government. Seeck, who also follows Gothofred, feels this difficulty so acutely that he proposes to emend the date of both constitutions, and to read xv and xiii Kal. *Mar.* in place of Kal. *Mai.*[18] Professor Bury has not, however, adopted this improbable expedient.

I think that a different explanation possesses greater plausibility. Freeman long ago[19] accentuated the importance of the twelfth fragment of Olympiodorus in which we read: ἐν ταύταις ταῖς Βρεταννίαις, πρὶν ἢ Ὁνώριον τὸ ἕβδομον ὑπατεῦσαι, εἰς στάσιν ὁρμῆσαν τὸ ἐν αὐταῖς στρατιωτικὸν Μάρκον τινὰ ἀνεῖπον αὐτοκράτορα: that is to say that the revolt of the army in Britain took place in A.D. 406. But Zosimus (vi, 3) when describing the ravages of Vandals, Sueves and Alans in Gaul proceeds καὶ πολὺν ἐργασάμενοι φόνον ἐπίφοβοι καὶ τοῖς ἐν Βρεταννίαις στρατοπέδοις ἐγένοντο, συνηνάγκασαν δὲ δέει τοῦ μὴ κἀπὶ σφᾶς προελθεῖν εἰς τὴν τῶν τυράννων ὁρμῆσαι χειροτονίαν, Μάρκου λέγω καὶ Γρατιανοῦ καὶ ἐπὶ τούτοις Κωνσταντίνου. But before these barbarians could have penetrated to the Gallic coast line —we know that they reached the neighbourhood of Boulogne —a considerable interval must have elapsed since the time

[18] Seeck, *Geschichte des Untergangs*, etc., v, p. 587.
[19] Freeman, *Western Europe in the Fifth Century*, p. 45, n. *.

when they first crossed the Rhine. Thus it would appear that Prosper's entry under the year 406: 'Arcadio vi et Probo Coss. Vandali et Alani traiecto Rheno Gallias pridie Kal. Januarias ingressi' should in substance = 'During the year 406 the Vandals, etc., invaded the provinces of Gaul, having crossed the Rhine on the last day of 405' (when the river was probably frozen). The constitutions addressed 'to the provincials' were issued from Ravenna in the following April, when news of the seriousness of the peril in Gaul had reached the western court. We should retain for the invasion of Radagaisus the date A.D. 404–405: Stilicho's projected annexation of Illyricum in A.D. 405 is the result, as we have seen above, of that invasion, and we should in consequence of the statement of Olympiodorus correct Seeck's date for the outbreak of the rebellion in Britain from A.D. 407 to A.D. 406.

That rebellion is for our island history of special significance; how did it come about? Professor Bury writes: 'We may conjecture that the revolt was due to discontent with the rule of the German Stilicho, just as the revolt of Maximus had been aimed at the German general Merobaudes.' Further, Professor Bury thinks that Constantine in crossing to Gaul 'was following the example of Magnus Maximus, who had in like manner crossed over to the continent to wrest Gaul and Spain from Gratian' (i, pp. 187–8). Frankly these suggested explanations appear to me far fetched: Maximus had crossed to Gaul to meet his death as a defeated 'tyrant'; it was hardly an auspicious augury! What little we know of the revolt of the British troops seems to me to point to a different conclusion. Think of the position in Britain at the time with Pict and Scot on the northern frontier (Claudian, *In Eutrop.*, i, 393), with a High King of Ireland ravaging the South (Bury, *Life of S. Patrick*, p. 331), with Saxon pirates harrying the coasts of the Channel,[20] and to add to it all a wave of invasion in Gaul which threatened to cut off the army in Britain from the rest of the Empire.

The army needed a general of its own—in Professor Bury's words 'a supreme responsible authority on the spot'—they needed such an authority, surely, to justify their escape from

[20] Cf. Ferdinand Lot: 'Les migrations saxonnes en Gaule et en Grande-Bretagne du IIIe. au Ve. Siècle,' *Revue Historique*, cxix (1915), pp. 1–40.

the island. They chose Marcus, apparently a civilian (*municeps*, Orosius), but possessing a good imperial name (Sozomen, ix, 11). Unfortunately for the army Marcus was not prepared to play the part of a general: they removed him ὡς οὐχ ὁμολο-γοῦντα τοῖς αὐτῶν ἤθεσιν (Zos., vi, 2). They looked around for some one bearing another name of good augury: they selected a Gratian; he, too, proved unsatisfactory; after four months they tired of him. If their emperor was to do what they wished, he must be one of themselves, a common soldier. The only man who had been raised to the purple in the island who had proved himself the ever-victorious general was Constantine the Great —British legend attests his popularity—and there chanced to be a common soldier in their midst who with his sons bore the imperial names of the dynasty of Constantine.[21] It was no wonder that they chose him as their third candidate for Empire οἰηθέντες καθότι ταύτην εἶχε προσηγορίαν καὶ βεβαίως αὐτὸν κρατήσειν τῆς βασιλείας (Sozomen); and this man, with the lamentable fate of his predecessors before him as instant warning, knowing, as being himself a common soldier, what the army wanted, led that army straightway out of Britain into S. Gaul, back to the centre of the world's life, away from this threatened northern outpost of the Empire. Here surely was no abstract principle of hostility to a Vandal minister: rather, Stilicho's withdrawal of forces from Britain to Italy may have caused those who remained to contrast their lot with that of their more favoured comrades: they would desire more and not less of Stilicho's policy! It was Constantine who had founded an empire in Gaul and whose name was a household word who inspired that flight from Britain. However unflattering to our national pride the conclusion may be, it certainly looks as though the revolt of the Roman troops sprang from the fact that they had grown tired of life in our much-harassed island, and hankered for the flesh-pots of Provence. And if this be true, it perhaps throws some light upon the Roman evacuation of Britain: one of the reasons for that evacuation may well have been that Roman troops were unwilling to remain as

---

[21] 'The collection of Flavian names in the family of this private soldier is certainly remarkable. Most likely they were popular in Britain.' Freeman, op. cit., p. 57.

a standing garrison in the island. Of Professor Bury's views on the re-occupation of Britain by Rome I am not qualified to judge: on such a point the final judgement rests with the archaeologist; but to the student of the period it must appear improbable that, when men were urgently needed for the operations of Aëtius in Gaul, so strong a force as Professor Bury has suggested should have been allowed to remain in Britain.[22]

[For Stilicho now see S. Mazzarino, *Stilicone* (Rome, 1942), and E. Demougeot, *De l'unité à la division de l'empire romain, 395–410* (Paris, 1951).]

[22] Cf. R. G. Collingwood, *Roman Britain* (Oxford, 1923), pp. 97 sqq.

XXVI

The Imperial Cult

From a review of J. Vogt and E. Kornemann, *Römische Geschichte*, Leipzig, 1933.

[*Journal of Roman Studies*, xxv (1935), pp. 81–7 at pp. 83–4.]

Dr Kornemann states 'dass das römische Kaisertum in seinem durch die Rezeption des hellenistischen Herrscherkultes bedingten Emporstreben zum reinen Gottkönigtum schon vor Diocletian eine theoretische Grundlegung erfahren hat die den mazdaïschen Lehren entnommen ist' (p. 142). This sentence, I confess, puzzles me: for a loyal Zoroastrian no human ruler could be a god, though he might well be the elect of God, chosen to fight in the cause of truth against the Lie. And it is indeed precisely this latter theory of the Divine Right of Kings which, we are told, was that adopted by Aurelian. We learn from a fragment of Petrus Patricius (*FHG* iv, 197) ὅτι Αὐρηλιανὸς πειραθείς ποτε στρατιωτικῆς ἐπαναστάσεως ἔλεγεν ἀπατᾶσθαι τοὺς στρατιώτας εἰ ἐν ταῖς αὐτῶν χερσὶ τὰς μοίρας εἶναι τῶν βασιλέων ὑπολαμβάνουσιν. ἔφασκε γὰρ τὸν θεὸν δωρησάμενον τὴν πορφύραν (καὶ ταύτην ἐπεδείκνυ τῇ δεξιᾷ) πάντως καὶ τὸν χρόνον τῆς βασιλείας ὁρίσαι. Such an asseveration excludes the human 'Gottkönigtum'. The same view of the basis of the imperial power is reflected in the legend *Providentia deorum* on the coinage [cf. A. D. Nock, 'A Diis Electa', *Harvard Theological Review*, xxiii (1930), 266–8]. Note in particular the new type of Providentia Deorum coinage introduced by Aurelian, 'Fides standing right holding two ensigns and facing Sol, who stands left and holds the globe' (Mattingly-Sydenham-Webb, v, i, 268, 281, 286, 294, 297). Very possibly, as Mr Mattingly suggests to me, the sun is commending the emperor to the loyalty of the legions. This we find also on a coin of Severina (ibid. 316). It must be the deliberate expression of Aurelian's belief in the supernatural support of Sol. A. D. Nock (op. cit., pp. 267–8) compares the words of another Sun-worshipper,

Julian the Apostate, who in his *Caesares* writes of Aurelian
Ἥλιος δὲ οὑμὸς δεσπότης αὐτῷ πρός τε τὰ ἄλλα βοηθῶν κ.τ.λ.
(Hertlein, p. 403, 11–12). Further, writes Dr Kornemann, to
the symbols of the imperial power derived from the state of the
Achaemenids 'treten jetzt die offiiziellen Kaisertitel Pius Felix
Invictus unter dem Einfluss des Mithraskultes' (p. 142). Is
there really any evidence for this derivation? The third century adopts *officially* practices and titles which had long been
in general use. 'Pius' and 'Felix' may be united as part of the
imperial titulary in inscriptions for the first time under Cara-
callus (cf. G. Schoener, *Über die Titulaturen der römischen
Kaiser*, Dissertation (Erlangen, 1881), pp. 44–5), but such
attributes of the Princeps were already familiar: thus *pius* and
invictus are so applied from the earliest days of the Empire:
for *pius*, cf. T. Ulrich, 'Pietas (pius) als politischer Begriff im
römischen Staate bis zum Tode des Kaisers Commodus' (*Historische Untersuchungen*, Heft 6, Breslau, 1930); J. Liegle,
'Pietas', *Zeits. f. Numismatik*, xlii (1932), 59–100, and H.
Mattingly's review of this in *Num. Chron.*, 1933, pp. 236–9; for
invictus, cf. F. Sauter, 'Der römische Kaiserkult bei Martial
und Statius' (*Tübinger Beiträge zur Altertumswissenschaft*, Heft
xxi, Stuttgart, 1934, pp. 153–9). 'Die Übertragung des Epi-
thetons Invictus vom Sonnengott (Ἥλιος ἀνίκητος) der mit
Mithras identifiziert wird auf den Erdenherrscher beweist dass
dieser als der fleischgewordene oberste Gestirngott angesehen
wird' (p. 142). 'Wie der religiöse Synkretismus der Zeit in
diesem solaren Monotheismus von der Vielheit zur Einheit des
Gottes sich durchdrang, so stand jetzt auch auf Erden als
Emanation des Sonnengottes der Herrscher aller Schranken
enthoben auf einsamer Höhe dominus et deus zugleich' (p. 96).
It may be doubted whether this represents Aurelian's conception of his own position. Again, Dr Kornemann can speak of
Diocletian (p. 106) as 'der Mensch gewordene oberste Gott der
in dem neuen Monotheismus des Zentralgestirns (Sol) verehrt
wird, im Geiste des religiösen Synkretismus der Zeit zugleich
Juppiter auf Erden: daher Diocletians Beiname Jovius während sein Mitaugustus Maximianus . . . Herculeus heisst, wie
sein Prototyp im Himmel, der Gehilfe des Oberkaisers'. For
any special relation of Diocletian to the Sun-God there is little

evidence: cf. *CIL.*, v, 803; Mattingly and Sydenham, *The Roman Imperial Coinage*, vol. v, part ii, by P. H. Webb, 1933: *Oriens*, no. 60 (p. 226), no. 147 (p. 235), no. 174 (p. 238); *Soli Invicto*, no. 302 (p. 252). The Carnuntum inscription (Kornemann, p. 141) dates, it would seem, from A.D. 307 after Diocletian's abdication (see further G. Costa, *L'imperatore Dalmata*, Rome, 1912, p. 146), and the significant point is that though Diocletian's coins in vast numbers bear the legend 'Jovi', he is precisely not Jupiter but Jov*ius*, just as Maximian is Hercul*ius*—they are not gods, but God's chosen agents for the restoration of the Roman world: cf. *CIL.*, iii, 12326, *Diis auctoribus ad rei publicae amplificandae gloriam procreato pi . . . nostro Jovio maximo*[1], or such a legend on the coinage as *Jovi conser(vatori) Jovii consulis* (Cohen, 185). Panegyrists continuing an earlier tradition can regard Diocletian as a god (cf. *Pan.*, 10 (2), 2–3, ed. Guilielmus Baehrens, Leipzig, 1911; or *CIL.*, iii, 710, *diis genitis et deorum creatoribus*), but this is not the official view. Neither *divinus* nor *divus* is (it would seem) used in epigraphy as an attribute of Diocletian (cf. Costa, op. cit., p. 199).

But, if this be so, the significance is obvious: the theory of the 'Gottkönigtum' was abandoned by Aurelian and the Mazdaean theory of rule by the grace of God was substituted therefor.[2] This theory could be adopted without modification by a Christian ruler: there is here no break between Diocletian and Constantine. The theory remains the same: the Christian God has simply taken the place of Jupiter. In fact the Persian theory was far more fitted to survive: the Hellenistic 'Gottkönigtum' was a mistake.

[1] For 'maximus' as epithet of the Princeps cf. Sauter, op. cit., pp. 96 sqq., at p. 99.

[2] Cf. A. D. Nock, *Harvard Theological Review*, xxiii (1930), p. 263. This idea is found in various forms 'in Egypt, Judaea and Persia: in Greece it goes back to Homer (*Il.*, ii, 205) and is so natural an outcome of the very existence of monarchy that it is precarious to construct a pedigree.' See the bibliographical note of Professor Nock, ad. loc.

XXVII

Julian the Apostate
and Alexander the Great

From a review of OTTO SEECK, *Geschichte des Untergangs der antiken Welt*, vol. iv, Berlin, 1911.

[*English Historical Review*, xxvii (1912), pp. 755–60 at pp. 759–60.]

One of the most interesting questions in Julian's life is that of the ideals which he set before himself. Dr Seeck, while recognizing the influence of Marcus Aurelius, denies[1] that the emperor also took Alexander the Great for his model, and cites in support of his view the unfavourable judgements on Alexander which are found in Julian's works. In this, I think, Dr Seeck has forgotten what he himself has excellently explained in his chapter on rhetoric. Writers of Julian's time do not always express personal views: they are influenced by a tradition, and the rhetorical tradition was in the main hostile to Alexander.[2] Now it has been recognized that Julian drew much material from the works (especially the περὶ βασιλείας) of Dio of Prusa, and it seems at least probable that many of Julian's references unfavourable to Alexander may be traced to the influence of Dio and the rhetoricians.[3] In fact, as philosopher and ruler Marcus Aurelius was Julian's model; his exemplar as general and conqueror was Alexander. Thus the latter's generosity (p. 54, l. 8), his love for Homer (p. 494, l. 9, cf. Am-

---

[1] Seeck, p. 472; contrast J. Geffcken, 'Kaiser Julianus und die Streitschriften seiner Gegner', in *Neue Jahrbücher für das klass. Altertum*, xxi, 164.

[2] Cf. W. Hoffmann, *Das literarische Portrait Alexanders des Grossen im griechischen und römischen Altertum, Leipz. hist. Abhandlungen*, viii (1907), p. 45; and see C. Neumann, *Griechische Geschichtschreiber und Geschichtsquellen im zwölften Jahrhundert* (Leipzig, 1888), pp. 5 sqq.

[3] With Alexander's greed for fame, Jul. 324, l. 23, cf. Dio περὶ βασ., iv, 4; with Alexander's intolerance of his father, Jul. 51, l. 21, cf. Dio περὶ βασ. ii, 15–16, and περὶ τυχ. (2) lxiv, 20; with Julian's taunt as to Alexander's murders, 575, l. 13 (cf. 425, l. 16), compare the last-mentioned passage in Dio, while the τρυφή of Alexander, Jul. 333, l. 3, had long been a rhetorical commonplace. For the judgements of the early rhetoricians cf. Franz Weber, *Alexander der Grosse im Urteil der Griechen und Römer* (Leipzig, 1909), and see J. R. Asmus, *Julian und Dio Chrysostomos, Beilage zum Jahresbericht des Grossherzoglichen Gymnasiums zu Tauberbischofsheim* (1895), 20 sqq.

mianus, 16. 5. 4), his nobility (p. 123, l. 18, p. 263, l. 1), and especially his conquests over Persia (p. 20, l. 20, p. 274, l. 17, and the paeans, p. 137 and p. 417) are all celebrated.[4] In the light of the confession of the intimate letter to Themistius (p. 328, l. 7) καί μοι πάλαι μὲν οἰομένῳ πρός τε τὸν Ἀλέξανδρον καὶ τὸν Μάρκον καὶ εἴ τις ἄλλος γέγονεν ἀρετῇ διαφέρων εἶναι τὴν ἅμιλλαν κ.τ.λ. two passages from the *Vita S. Artemii* to which Dr Seeck does not refer are of particular interest. The first describes Julian's journey in 362 from Constantinople to Antioch:[5] Ἄρας οὖν ἐκ τῆς Κπόλεως σὺν παντὶ τῷ στρατῷ τὴν ἐπὶ τῆς Συρίας ἐποιεῖτο ὁδόν· διελθὼν τοίνυν ἅπασαν τὴν Φρυγίαν καὶ πρὸς τὴν ἐσχάτην αὐτῆς πόλιν τὸ καλούμενον Ἰκόνιον καταν-τήσας, ἐξέκλινε τὴν Ἰσαυρίαν καταλιπὼν καὶ τὸν λεγόμενον Ταῦρον ὑπεραναβάς, ἦλθεν ἐπὶ τὰς πόλεις τῆς Κιλικίας, καὶ τῷ σταθμῷ προσπελάσας τῷ ἐν Ἰσσῷ αὐτοῦ κατασκηνοῖ, τὸν ἐκ Μακεδονίας Ἀλέξανδρον μιμησάμενος· αὐτόθι γὰρ κἀκεῖνος ἐν Ἰσσῷ τὸν πρὸς Δαρεῖον τῶν Περσῶν βασιλέα συνεκρότησε πόλεμον, καὶ τοῦτον νικήσας ἐπίσημον τὸν τόπον εἰργάσατο. Ἐκεῖθεν τὸν Ἰσσικὸν κόλπον διαπεράσας, ἦλθεν ἐν Ταρσοῖ τῇ πόλει, κἀκεῖθεν εἰς Ἀντιό-χειαν κ.τ.λ. Julian went right out of his way to visit the spot where the Hellenic hero had defeated the foe which he himself was now preparing to attack.[6] The other passage is as follows:[7] τὴν Κτησιφῶντα πόλιν καταλαβὼν ἐδόκει μέγα τι διαπραξάμενος ἔργον ἐφ᾽ ἕτερα μεταβαίνειν κρείττονα ... ἔρωτα γὰρ διαβολικὸν τῆς εἰδωλομανίας ἐγκτησάμενος καὶ ἐλπίσας διὰ μὲν τῶν ἀθέων θεῶν αὐτοῦ πολυχρόνιον τὴν βασιλείαν ἕξειν καὶ νέον γενέσθαι Ἀλέξανδρον, περιγενέσθαι δὲ καὶ τῶν Περσῶν, κ.τ.λ. The evidence in fact points, I think, to a conclusion contrary to that of Dr Seeck.

[4] Alexander is under the protection of Heracles, pp. 406, 431, l. 1. Cf. περὶ βασ., iv, 70. Compare Hoffmann's judgement (p. 87): 'Alexander gilt nur etwas wenn's in den Krieg geht; sobald der Januskopf Julians das Philosophenantlitz zeigt, sieht er Alexander nicht mehr.'

[5] P. Batiffol, 'Fragmente der Kirchengeschichte des Philostorgius', *Römische Quartalschrift*, iii (1889), p. 274.

[6] With this compare Julian at Arbela, Libanius, ii, 349, l. 9 sqq., and note Julian's ambition to march to Hyrcania and the rivers of India, ibid., 350, l. 5. See also ii, 213, l. 10, Ἀλεξάνδρου τοῦ φίλου τε αὐτῷ καὶ οὐκ ἐῶντος καθεύδειν κ.τ.λ.

[7] With this compare the remarkable passage in Socrates, *Hist.*, iii, 21, πεπιστευκὼς δὲ μαντείαις τισίν, ἃς αὐτῷ συμπαρὼν ὁ φιλόσοφος Μάξιμος ὑπετίθετο, καὶ ὀνειροπολήσας τὴν Ἀλεξάνδρου τοῦ Μακεδόνος δόξαν λαβεῖν ἢ καὶ μᾶλλον ὑπερβαί-νειν τὰς ἱκεσίας Περσῶν ἀπεκρούσατο· καὶ ἐνόμιζε κατὰ τὴν Πυθαγόρου καὶ Πλάτωνος δόξαν ἐκ μετενσωματώσεως τὴν Ἀλεξάνδρου ἔχειν ψυχήν, μᾶλλον δὲ αὐτὸς εἶναι Ἀλέξανδρος ἐν ἑτέρῳ σώματι. Αὕτη ἡ οἴησις αὐτὸν ἐξηπάτησε καὶ παρεσκεύασε τότε τὴν ἱκεσίαν τοῦ Πέρσου μὴ παραδέξασθαι.

XXVIII

1. Lactantius, the *Divine Institutes*
2. St Ambrose

From a review of K. M. SETTON, *Christian Attitude towards the Emperor in the Fourth Century*, New York, 1941.

[*Journal of Roman Studies*, xxxiv (1944), at pp. 136–8, 139–40.]

1. LACTANTIUS

In Mr Setton's book, in my judgement, less than justice is done to Lactantius. 'Whatever the norm of comparison,' Mr Setton writes, 'whether religious, philosophical, or literary, certainly the works of Aristides, Justin Martyr and Athenagoras are superior to the productions of Arnobius, Lactantius, and Firmicus Maternus' (p. 33). So far as concerns the work of 'the Christian Cicero' this is a judgement which it might not prove easy to defend. Again, Mr Setton speaks of Lactantius as 'fighting windmills' in his apologetic (p. 63): he was merely repeating arguments which had lost their relevance in the decline of pagan faith. This view has often been expressed, but is it really tenable? Take Brandt's index to his edition of Lactantius and note which pagan deities are most frequently attacked and ridiculed: they would appear to be Jupiter and Hercules, and these are precisely the patron deities of the Jovian and Herculian rulers of the pagan Empire. Can these attacks be regarded as a tilting at windmills? Are they not rather of immediate contemporary significance? Take the references to the demons in the same Index and compare with the passages noted there the later writings of Porphyry: are not the religious pagan and the Christian both alike united in a crusade against the peril to true religion presented by the popular beliefs of the Roman world? I believe that in his apologetic Lactantius was very far from an unintelligent repetition of themes which had lost their urgency and relevance. That may be a small point, but Mr Setton's treatment of the *De Mortibus Persecutorum* is more important. On that work his comment is that in his judge-

ments on the imperial misfortunes 'Lactantius' hatred vies
with his incontinence'. Beyond this we have only the apparently ironic remark: 'Lactantius is singularly well-informed
in all the details of God's relations with the emperors, but
after the marvelous triumph of the Christian cause under
Constantine hesitancy to press his interpretation to its
logical conclusion must have seemed to Lactantius little
short of criminal scepticism.' This does not seem to me a
happy approach to the study of the *De Mortibus Persecutorum*:
the starting-point for such a study must surely be the
Divine Institutes which provides the only complete contemporary statement known to me of the attitude of the Christian
Church towards the emperors and the imperial power during
the Galerian persecution. It may be of service to outline that
statement.

The background is Apocalypse. Apocalyptic literature was
born of persecution, and under the stress of the Galerian persecution Apocalyptic is reborn. The Book of Revelation, at
least according to one interpretation, exults in the overthrow
of Rome, the great whore: the same conclusion—the coming
overthrow of Rome—is reached by the Christian of the fourth
century, but the 'Romanism' of Lactantius can no longer
regard with exultation the fall of the Empire: it is with a
shudder of horror ('horret animus dicere', *Div. Inst.*, vii, 15,
11, Brandt i, p. 632, l. 17), that he is compelled by the authority of scripture to contemplate the passing of a 'regnum tanta
mole fundatum ac tamdiu per tot et tales viros auctum, tantis
denique opibus confirmatum'. Alas! 'mortalia sunt opera mor-
talium'. And with this background of 'Romanism' the Christian Church under the strain of bitter persecution still refuses
to meet violence with violence, still remains loyal to its inherited principles: 'nam cum isti defensores falsorum deorum'
—the pagan emperors—'adversus verum deum rebelles nomen
eius in nobis persecuntur, nec re nec verbo repugnamus, sed
mites et taciti et patientes perferimus omnia quaecumque adversus nos potest crudelitas machinari' (*Epit. Div. Inst.*, c. 48,
4); 'et ideo cum nefanda patimur, ne verbo quidem reluctamur
sed deo remittimus ultionem' (*Div. Inst.*, v, 20, 10). And when
that tradition of non-resistance is abandoned, the fourth-

century Christian disapproves the act (cf. Lactantius, *De Mort. Pers.*, 13, § 2, 'etsi non recte').

And if it be asked: Why does God permit His worshippers to suffer thus?—Lactantius has his answer to that question: Suffering (*pati*) is necessary to bring to full effect the difficult virtue of *patientia*—'quomodo enim patientia vim suam nomenque retineret si nihil esset quod pati cogeremur'? (*Div. Inst.*, v, 7, 6)—for virtue 'nisi agitetur, nisi vexatione adsidua roboretur, non potest esse perfecta, siquidem virtus est perferendorum malorum fortis atque invicta patientia. ex quo fit ut virtus nulla sit, si adversarius desit' (ibid., 111, 29, 16). 'ergo iustus et sapiens quia virtutem capit, habet in se patientiam: qua carebit omnino, si nihil patietur adversi' (ibid., v, 22, 4). It is for this purpose that God permits 'quidquid adversus nos mali principes moliuntur'. But this will not give to the emperors an excuse for their action when in their inhuman cruelty they overstep the limits of their divine charge. Then they can no longer claim that they are the *ministri dei*. 'Punientur enim iudicio dei qui accepta potestate supra humanum modum fuerint abusi et insultaverint etiam deo superbius eiusque nomen aeternum vestigiis suis subiecerint impie nefarieque calcandum' (*Div. Inst.*, v, 23, 2). The prophecy of the divine vengeance is thus stated in the *Divine Institutes*, its realization is proclaimed in the *De Mortibus Persecutorum*: the *Divine Institutes* is to the *De Mortibus Persecutorum* as Isaiah, ch. x, is to the proclamation of Assyria's fall in the triumph song of Nahum.

And for the understanding of the work of Lactantius it may be suggested that the idea of *ultio*—of divine vengeance—is of the highest significance. God 'quamvis populi sui vexationes et hic in praesenti soleat vindicare, tamen iubet nos expectare patienter illum caelestis iudicii diem, quo ipse pro suis quemque meritis aut honoret aut puniat . . . demus operam totis viribus ut mereamur a deo simul et ultionem passionis et praemium' (*Div. Inst.*, v, 23, 3–5). When Lactantius is considering the effect of the persecutions on the pagans he points out that very many desert the worship of the gods through their hatred of the cruelty practised on the Christians, others suspect that there must be something evil in the pagan cult when so many are

prepared to die rather than worship: the crowd hears the
martyr in the midst of torment refusing to sacrifice to stones
carved by the hands of men—he will worship only God in
Heaven—and many realize that here is truth and accept the
faith (cf. *Div. Inst.*, v, 13, 11); and, besides this, 'ultio con-
secuta, sicut semper accidit, ad credendum vehementer impellit' (*Div. Inst.*, v, 22, 23). Further note *Epitome*, 48, 4–5,
'habemus enim fiduciam in deo a quo expectamus secuturam
protinus ultionem. nec est inanis ista fiducia siquidem eorum
omnium qui hoc facinus ausi sunt miserabiles exitus partim
cognovimus partim vidimus'. This is, of course, the theme of
the *De Mortibus Persecutorum*—that divine *ultio* which 'ad
credendum vehementer impellit'. The *De Mortibus Persecutorum*—after Galerius' palinode—must have formed a striking
reinforcement of the argument of the *Divine Institutes*. 'Sicut
semper accidit': it was a bold statement. Melito in his apology
presented to Marcus Aurelius could point to Nero and Domitian who μόνοι πάντων—alone among Roman emperors—
ἀναπεισθέντες ὑπό τινων βασκάνων ἀνθρώπων τὸν καθ' ἡμᾶς ἐν
διαβολῇ καταστῆσαι λόγον ἠθέλησαν (Eusebius, *Hist. eccles.*, iv,
26, 9); Tertullian, as Professor Last reminds me, had said that
to be condemned by a Nero could be regarded only as 'grande
aliquod bonum', while Domitian in cruelty had been a 'demi-
Néron' (Waltzing's translation of 'portio Neronis'): 'tales
semper nobis insecutores, iniusti, impii, turpes, quos et ipsi
damnare consuestis, a quibus damnatos restituere soliti estis'
(*Apologeticum*, v, 3–4). The scope of Lactantius' 'semper' is
revealed not in the *Divine Institutes*, but in the *De Mortibus
Persecutorum*: here the line of emperor-persecutors is continued
through Decius perishing in battle, through Aurelian assassinated at the moment when he was planning an attack upon
the Christian Church, down to Lactantius' own day—the contemporary imperial defeat puts its amazing seal upon the
demonstration.

There have been those who have complained of the violence
of the *De Mortibus*: the philosopher who composed the *Divine
Institutes*, it has been urged, could not have written thus:
'bestia' and 'belua' used of a Roman Emperor, the exultation
over the death of Galerius 'eaten of worms', etc. But in the

study of the works of Christian writers of the fourth century one must never forget the biblical background of their thought: Lactantius knew that the persecutors, those 'qui deorum suorum moribus congruunt', who 'eandem inpietatem suam qua in ceteris rebus utuntur adversus iustos violenter exercent', deservedly 'a prophetis bestiae nominantur' (*Div. Inst.*, v, 11, 1). Therefore God 'vindicaturum se in eos celeriter pollicetur et exterminaturum bestias malas de terra' (ibid., v, 23, 3). He is citing in support of his argument Leviticus xxvi. 6, Ezekiel xxxiv. 25. And the death of Galerius recalls to mind another ruler who 'stretched forth his hands to vex certain of the church' and who was smitten by the angel of the Lord, Acts xii. 1, 23. In the description of Galerius' malady we must see no mere *Schadenfreude*, but once more, as in the past, so now God's *ultio*. We may not accept Lactantius' argument, but before we give play to irony we are at least in duty bound to seek to comprehend the philosophy of history which is its basis. For Lactantius the history of man acquires dignity through being seen as the exemplification of the unchanging justice of God.

Mr Setton has not referred to the two addresses to Constantine the Great, contained in some MSS. of the *Divine Institutes*. These addresses, it will be remembered, Brandt regarded as later interpolations into Lactantius' work.[1] It is generally assumed that the second address implies that the persecution of the Christians has ceased throughout the Empire, while the first address states that 'mali adhuc adversus iustos in aliis terrarum partibus saeviunt'. Thus they cannot both of them have been written at the same time. The *Divine Institutes* must have been written while Galerius was still alive and before the publication of the palinode which preceded his death (cf. the present tenses in *Div. Inst.*, v, 11, 5–6, and see Brandt's index under Maximianus—'Galerius "sine dubio, non Diocletianus"'). Is it necessary to assume that the second address does indeed imply a complete cessation of the persecution throughout the

[1] *Div. Inst.*, i, 1, 13–16; vii, 27; Samuel Brandt, 'Über die dualistischen Zusätze und die Kaiseranreden bei Lactantius, nebst einer Untersuchung über das Leben des Lactantius und die Entstehungsverhältnisse seiner Prosaschriften.' *Sitzungsberichte der phil.-hist. Klasse der Kaiserl. Akad. der Wiss.*, Wien, vols. cxviii, no. 8, cxix, no. 1 (1889), cxx, no. 5 (1890).

Empire? The passage reads: 'illi enim qui ut impias religiones defenderent, caelestis et singularis dei cultum tollere voluerunt, profligati iacent . . . illi poenas sceleris sui et pendunt et pependerunt': some have already paid the penalty, some are paying it now. It would seem to me that if this address were written at the time of Licinius' attack on Maximin there is no need to assume an interval between the writing of the two addresses: persecution still continues in the Eastern provinces of the Empire, but already for Maximin and his supporters the end is near. It might be suggested that Lactantius wrote the *Divine Institutes* in Gaul, completing the work before 311. Constantine, although he had granted toleration to the Christians, had not yet declared himself a Christian. Successively Maximian and Maxentius are overthrown. Constantine has triumphed over the persecutors with the aid of the Christian God: *profligati iacent*. After the meeting of Constantine and Licinius at Milan, when the first successes of Licinius against Maximin are announced, Lactantius dedicates his work to Constantine—presents to the convert the apologia which before his victory had predicted his success, the *ultio* which God had promised. There was no need to alter the text, no need to turn the persecution of Galerius into the past tense. The book could be left to speak for itself in its prophetic confidence. Brandt thought that these addresses were inserted into Lactantius' work *c.* 370 by a Gallic rhetor: the theory seems to me to be quite incredible, and I do not think that we are forced to adopt it. The addresses themselves, short as they are, would appear to take their place naturally in the suggested setting: the language should be compared with that of the so-called 'Edict of Milan', while the passage on the Roman Emperors is of considerable interest (*Div. Inst.*, vii, 27): 'nec immerito rerum dominus ac rector te potissimum delegit per quem sanctam religionem suam restauraret, quoniam unus ex omnibus extitisti qui praecipua virtutis et sanctitatis exempla praeberes, quibus antiquorum principum gloriam, quos tamen fama inter bonos numerat, non modo aequares, sed etiam quod est maximum praeterires. illi quidem natura fortasse tantum similes iustis fuerunt: qui enim moderatorem universitatis deum ignorat, similitudinem iustitiae assequi potest, ipsam vero non potest.' Lactantius with his 'Romanism' cannot condemn all those emperors reputed generally to be 'good', but something unprecedented has now come into being—a Christian Emperor—and to meet this fact Lactantius distinguishes between a natural goodness which is inadequate and goodness which finds its support in a Christian God. Can it be that in these 'rejected addresses' we have the first recognition preserved to us in Christian literature of the change which had been wrought by the victory at the Milvian Bridge?

2. ST AMBROSE

When shortly before his death Duchesne was asked why he had not published the fourth volume of his history of the early Church he replied: 'Je n'ose pas' [G. P. Gooch in *English Historical Review*, lviii (1943), 483]. The aureole of a saint may at times haunt and daunt the student of history. Dr Homes Dudden's picture of St Ambrose could easily be transferred to a stained-glass window. It is not often that we can follow the attitude toward the Emperor of a high Roman imperial official turned bishop. It is this which gives a special interest to the career of Ambrose, and which at the same time presents us with a special difficulty: in the school of the imperial service Ambrose had learned diplomacy and what he says in his letters and speeches may be of less significance than that on which he maintains a discreet silence. Mr Setton has realized that Ambrose 'could play the courtier', but that admission does not go far enough; Ambrose, the imperious ex-governor and the astute diplomat, has been inadequately represented by Mr Setton. The point may be briefly illustrated.

When the Christians of Milan had acclaimed Ambrose as their bishop, the imperial governor prudently withdrew into retirement for a season and awaited the emperor's response to the appeal of the Church of Milan. When a favourable reply had been received he was sure of his ground and could accept consecration (*Epist.*, 21, § 7). In 378 Gratian met Ambrose in Sirmium, and was much impressed by the bishop. In that year Gratian sequestered a church in Milan for the use of the Arians. In his *De Fide*, i and ii, Ambrose attacked the Arians and sent his work to Gratian. Probably in the spring of 379

Gratian wrote to Ambrose with his own hand asking that the treatise on Faith might be enlarged to include an exposition of the doctrine of the Holy Spirit, and while engaged in operations against the Goths the emperor urged Ambrose to hasten to his side. To that letter Ambrose sent no reply; he remained in Milan preparing to write on the Holy Spirit and preaching sermons on that theme. Gratian guessed the reason for that diplomatic silence, and while on his way to Italy spontaneously cancelled the sequestration (cf. *De Spiritu*, i, §§ 19–20). The act is a striking tribute to the influence of Ambrose.

Early in 381 Theodosius summoned to Constantinople the Eastern bishops and at this Council Nectarius was chosen as bishop of the Eastern capital and Flavian as bishop of Antioch. Of both consecrations Ambrose disapproved: the work of the Eastern Council must be undone. If a diplomatic silence could achieve so much in 379, surely Ambrose could carry Gratian with him in an attack on Theodosius; he would exploit Gratian's promise of a general council. Ambrose was playing for high stakes—the control of the Church throughout the Empire by the West. Completely ignoring the Council of Constantinople and all its doings, he appealed to Gratian to summon the promised council to meet at Alexandria, the one Eastern see which had consistently stood as an outpost of the West. But Gratian refused to play the part for which he had been cast by Ambrose: he replied that he must first confer with Theodosius. Ambrose, foiled in his diplomacy, can only suggest that the council should meet at Rome. Meanwhile he took matters into his own hands and purported to hold a general council in Aquileia, to which he summoned for judgement and condemnation the Balkan bishops Palladius and Secundianus, who were charged with Arianism. At that Council Ambrose controlled the proceedings: it was not for nothing that he had been an imperial governor. No freedom of discussion was allowed, all objections were brutally brushed aside and, at length, through physical violence the cause of orthodoxy triumphed, and a subtly distorted account of the proceedings of the Council was despatched for the information of the emperor. The supporters of the condemned bishops complained, not without reason, that this was no council: it was a cabal of the haughty bishop of Milan and the bishop of Aquileia. Ambrose was a courageous but very bellicose saint.

And if one would study the diplomatic skill of Ambrose, one has but to read the speech *De Obitu Valentiniani*. It is now clear that Theodosius had withdrawn from his Western colleague both Italy and Africa: only the European provinces in the West of the Empire were left to Valentinian II. When Valentinian appealed to Ambrose to join him in Gaul Ambrose remained in Italy: would Theodosius approve of a journey to Gaul undertaken by a bishop from Italy? At the time of his death Valentinian was planning a visit to Italy—to assert his rights to the territory of which he had been deprived by Theodosius? Might it not be that his assassination—coming just then—was not unwelcome to Theodosius? The body was brought to Milan, but what should be done with it? Theodosius must decide. Thus through the summer, with a putrefying corpse still unburied, the sisters of Valentinian awaited the message from the East, and when at last it came it was not easy to know what—or how much—could be said with safety. In his funeral oration Ambrose is walking on a rhetorical tightrope. This explains § 33: 'Ecce in primo vitae occidit cursu. De celeritate mortis, non de genere loquor; non enim accusationis voce utor, sed doloris.' It is a masterly performance.

Indeed, the relations between the Theodosian house and Valentinian II are shrouded in mystery. When Ambrose delivers his funeral oration on Theodosius the Great he can picture the emperor's reunion with his first wife Flaccilla, with Gratian, and with Pulcheria, but there is no mention of Valentinian and, what is stranger still, no mention of Theodosius' second wife Galla, the sister of Valentinian, who had died in childbirth only a year before. Heaven had no room for the house of Valentinian. What were the circumstances which imposed upon Ambrose this diplomatic silence we may never know, but the silence does serve to show with what discretion a court bishop had to frame his speeches when an emperor—in this case Honorius—was one of his hearers. In writing a biography of Ambrose one must refuse to be daunted by the aureole of the saint.

XXIX

1. On the *Historia Augusta* as a Historical Source
2. Diocletian and Mithraism

From a review of W. Seston, *Dioclétien et la Tétrarchie*, vol. i, Paris, 1946.

[*Journal of Roman Studies*, xxxviii (1948), pp. 109–13 at pp. 110–11, 111–12.]

1. The 'Historia Augusta'

In M. Seston's book we find ourselves faced once more with the problem of the use of the *Historia Augusta* as a historical source. The more closely one studies the later biographies, and especially the *Nebenviten*, the more sceptical one becomes. M. Seston endeavours to date the work of Claudius Eusthenius (*Carinus*, 18, 5)—but did such a writer ever exist? Is not the author of the *Vita Carini* simply manufacturing for himself an excuse for ending his work where he did? This question of the use of the *Historia Augusta* may cause a reader to hesitate before adopting M. Seston's view of the *Vita Firmi*: Scythianus, the Manichean missionary, learned his faith on the borders of Palestine and Africa; he was a rich merchant engaged in the Indian trade (Epiphanius, *Panarion*, 66, 1). The additions made by Epiphanius to the account of Scythianus given by the *Acta Archelai*, it is urged, must have some basis in fact; they are too precise to be pure invention. Epiphanius must have had a source which for us is lost: can it be recovered? We turn to a consideration of the *Vita Firmi*. In Zosimus, i, 61, 1, we read that Aurelian suppressed the Alexandrians στασιά-σαντας καὶ πρὸς ἀπόστασιν ἰδόντας: the name of their leader is not given. In the *Vita Aureliani*, 32—at least a better source than the *Vita Firmi*—the rebel leader is named: 'Firmus quidam'. In the deplorable *Vita Firmi* it is said that the rebel was born in Seleucia—which Seleucia the reader is not told—

'though many of the Greeks give him a different *patria*'. Presumably the writer, being completely ignorant on the point, plays for safety. Firmus was a rich merchant in the Indian trade, had close relations with Blemmyes and Saracens and after his revolt cut off the grain-supply from Egypt. So far as facts are concerned that is all; the rest of the *Vita* is obviously the fabrication of the writer following the customary anecdotal lines. It may be suspected that the author had no real knowledge of this obscure disturbance; he may well have strung together the traditional elements in an Egyptian revolt. Why this meagre account should not refer to the rebel of Aurelian's reign, as it purports to do, I fail to understand. In M. Seston's view the Firmus of the *Vita* cannot be the 'usurpateur banal' of Zosimus; the *Vita* must be describing the revolt of 296 under Diocletian—the revolution of Achilleus. The *Vita Firmi* thus provides us with a new source for the history of that 'tyranny'. Not only is Firmus modelled on Achilleus, but, surprisingly, it is suggested that in this *Vita* we also recover the lost source of Epiphanius. M. Seston asks: is Scythianus the same man as Firmus-Achilleus?—although, so far as we know, Scythianus did not revolt. But to talk of a 'récit de l'insurrection égyptienne perdu *et retrouvé dans l'Histoire Auguste*' (the italics are mine) would certainly suggest that a student of the *Vita Firmi* is easily satisfied. The significant question remains: What use as historical sources can we make of the subsidiary biographies of the *Historia Augusta*? I cannot share M. Seston's confidence.

2. DIOCLETIAN AND MITHRAISM

On the influence of Mithraism upon Diocletian, M. Seston writes: 'En distinguant dans l'empereur, de l'être de chair que la raison répugne à faire dieu, le souverain qui porte la grâce divine, Dioclétien est revenu à une conception plus romaine du monde'—it is well said. He proceeds: 'D'où lui vient en effet l'idée d'une épiphanie tardive aussi strictement liée à l'exercice de la fonction impériale? Ne craignons pas de répondre: du mithriacisme' (p. 225). Similarly Mithraism sets its mark upon the type of government: it was Diocletian's devotion to Mithras which 'a donné une marque particulière à un type de gouvernement qui a survécu à l'invasion d'idées religieuses la plus grave que l'État romain ait subie, car l'Empire devenu chrétien devait garder le bénéfice de cette consécration' (p. 230). It may be doubted whether the Christian Empire needed for its consecration the support of a Persian deity. But for this paramount influence of Mithras upon Diocletian what is the evidence? It does not appear that we know of a single dedication to Mithras made by the rulers of the tetrarchy save the famous inscription at Carnuntum which was probably erected after Diocletian's abdication (*ILS.*, 659). M. Seston cites in support of Diocletian's devotion to Mithras the *lux aeterna* which Constantius brought to Britain by his victory over Allectus (p. 226. 'Redditor lucis aeternae' on the medallion of the treasure of Arras). But this has no necessary connexion with Mithraism; one remembers that sun-worship of the Balkan lands which was hereditary in the family of Constantius (cf. Julian, *Or.*, iv. ed. Hertlein, p. 170, πρὸ τριγονίας ἀπὸ πολλῶν πάνυ προπατόρων), and perhaps with greater relevance one may recall the Gallic sun-worship; the Celtic god Taranis combines the attributes of Jupiter and Apollo (cf. P. Lambrechts, *Contributions à l'étude des divinités celtiques* (Bruges, 1942), 95–6, and see the Index s.v. Taranis). M. Seston further quotes from a panegyrist: 'tota Italia clarior lux effusa' (*Pan.* 11, 10, 4), but this light is shed by the emperors: 'ut primum ex utrisque Alpium iugis vestrum numen effulsit',[1] and so with the other passages from the same speech which M. Seston adduces: 'ut vero lucem gentibus extulistis, exinde salutares spiritus iugiter manant' (15, 3). Indeed with these quotations should be compared the passages collected by André Grabar (*L'empereur dans l'art byzantin* (Paris, Les Belles Lettres, 1936), 104): 'nous savons, en effet, que depuis Horace [*Odes*, 4, 5, 5, 'Lucem redde tuae, dux bone, patriae' of Augustus] les panégyristes des empereurs comparaient les souverains romains à la lumière qui éclaire l'Univers et les peuples soumis à leur pouvoir. Cette lumière, pour les orateurs palatins des IIIe et IVe siècles, est "romaine"

---

[1] [I quote the passages from the panegyric according to the numeration of the edition of Guilielmus Baehrens, (Leipzig, 1911). The recent edition by E. Galletier (1949-52) returns to the numeration of the edition of Aemilius Baehrens (Leipzig), 1874].

et les empereurs en sont les porteurs. *Romana lux coepit* avec l'avènement de Théodose [Pacatus, ed. Baehrens, 1911, p. 91, 23]. Si telle province est séparée de Rome c'est un *a Romana luce discidium* [*Pan.*, 8, 10, 1]; telle autre, ramenée sous le sceptre des empereurs, *liberata ad conspectum Romanae lucis emersit* [*Pan.*, 9, 18, 3].' It may be doubted whether there is any adequate evidence to support M. Seston's view. After all one may hesitate to believe that an emperor who attacked Manicheism as a pestilential Persian faith would have chosen for his personal devotion a Persian deity.

XXX

Symmachus

From a review of J. A. McGeachy, Jr., *Quintus Aurelius Symmachus and the Senatorial Aristocracy of the West*. Dissertation of the University of Chicago, 1942.

[*Journal of Roman Studies*, xxxvi (1946), pp. 173–7 at pp. 175–7.]

The most questionable part of Dr McGeachy's dissertation is his treatment of the action of the aristocracy of Rome in defence of the altar of Victory in the senate-house. His contention is that 'the economic aspects of the rights of paganism were more important than such symbolical questions as the status of the altar of Victory'. 'Control of the priesthoods meant control of landed estates and in the late Empire land was the basis of wealth. The landed property of the priesthoods could be maintained and increased only so long as the pagan religion of Rome was the official religion of the Roman Empire. . . . The select group of pagans who had so much power in Rome felt that the victory of Christianity over paganism presaged for them a severe economic loss.' The aristocracy clung to the formal worship of the gods, 'one is forced to believe, not so much because these gods actually commanded the respect of their worshippers as because it seemed to the Roman nobles a part of their way of life'. 'The withdrawal of State support from the ancient cults meant that one more excuse for the continued dominance of the senatorial aristocracy had been removed.' This is but to carry a little further the argument of Malunowicz (Leocadia Malunowicz, 'De Ara Victoriae in curia Romana quo modo certatum sit'. *Rozprawy i Materiały Wydziału i Towarzystwa Przyjaciot Nauk w Wilnie* Tom ix, Zeszyt 2 (Wilno, 1937); see especially Caput III, 'Certamen de Ara Victoriae quid valuerit quoque spectaverit', pp. 108 sqq.), who contended that it was primarily the sequestration of pagan religious property and not the removal of the altar of Victory to which objection was raised. The question is crucial for the understanding of paganism in the western capital during the fourth century, and in particular for the understanding of the correspondence of Symmachus.

It may be suggested that the most potent factor in the senatorial resistance was the passionate adherence to tradition— to the legacy bequeathed by *vetustas*. The words with which Furius begins his speech in Macrobius (*Sat.*, iii, 14, 2, Eyssenhardt, p. 199, 18) set the keynote of the age: *Vetustas quidem nobis semper, si sapimus, adoranda est*. A pagan when he begins to state his creed prefaces his confession with the words: *Verum quid traditum sancte atque antiquitus teneam atque custodiam ut potuero paucis edicam* (Longinianus to Augustine, *Ep.*, 234, § 2). The maxim *Recte enim facta mutari nisi iniuste non possunt* had a wider application than that given to it by Volusianus (Augustine, *Ep.*, 136, § 2). Christianity had come to the Roman world as a revolutionary force: it was not only in the sphere of constitutional precedent that Constantine had shown himself a 'novator turbatorque priscarum legum et moris antiquitus recepti' (Ammianus Marcellinus, xxi, 10, 8, summarizing the letter of Julian the Apostate to the senate of Rome). Of this legacy of antiquity religious observance formed the most significant part; it was precisely on its strict performance of the rites of religion that the Roman State based its pre-eminence over other nations and peoples: 'pietate et religione, atque hac una sapientia, quod deorum numine omnia regi gubernarique perspeximus, omnes gentes nationesque superavimus' (Cicero, *De Haruspicum Responsis*, 19). 'Si conferre volumus nostra cum externis, ceteris rebus aut pares aut etiam inferiores reperiemur, religione, id est cultu deorum, multo superiores' (Cicero, *De Natura Deorum*, 2, 8). 'Roman religion was far more an observance than a creed. . . . In the eyes of men of letters . . . this public religion'—the ritual of the Roman State—'was the outward representation of the belief that a Providence governed the progress of the Roman Empire' (Henry Nettleship, *Lectures and Essays on Subjects connected with Latin Literature and Scholarship* (Oxford, 1885), p. 133). One thinks of Warde Fowler's classical exposition of the mission of the Roman State to maintain the Pax Deorum; the maintenance of that Peace did not primarily depend upon the efforts of individuals, but on the faithful performance of its religious duties by the community, and traditionally 'the senate's position as guardian of the constitution really rests on the idea that it is the great Council of State and as such must be the ultimate arbiter when any religious questions arise. The fundamental principles of the constitution are not purely secular matters. They and indeed the whole of Roman public life were conceived as having divine sanction and any departure from established custom might call down divine wrath' (H. F. Jolowicz, *Historical Introduction to the Study of Roman Law* (Cambridge, 1932), 31, n. 2).

'Consuetudinis amor', writes Symmachus, 'magnus est' (*Rel.*, iii, 4); 'illud maluimus cuius usus antiquior' (*Rel.*, iv, 3), and part of that *consuetudo* and that *usus* was the State worship of the gods: 'convenit inter publicos sacerdotes ut in custodiam civium publico obsequio traderemus curam deorum. benignitas enim superioris, nisi cultu teneatur, amittitur' (*Ep.*, i, 46, § 2).

Nor is that all: Wytzes in an unobtrusive note (*Der Streit um den Altar der Viktoria* (Amsterdam, 1936), 120) has referred to (but has not quoted the text of) Zosimus, iv, 59, § 3. That text is of great significance, for Zosimus as a pagan should reproduce faithfully pagan sentiment. Of the representatives sent by the Senate to plead the cause of traditional religious observance before Theodosius Zosimus writes: τῶν δὲ ἀπὸ τῆς γερουσίας μὴ κατὰ θεσμὸν εἰπόντων πράττεσθαι τὰ τελούμενα μὴ δημοσίου τοῦ δαπανήματος ὄντος, διὰ τοῦτο τότε τοῦ θυηπολικοῦ θεσμοῦ λήξαντος καὶ τῶν ἄλλων ὅσα τῆς πατρίου παραδόσεως ἦν ἐν ἀμελείᾳ κειμένων, ἡ Ῥωμαίων ἐπικράτεια κατὰ μέρος ἐλαττωθεῖσα βαρβάρων οἰκητήριον γέγονεν κ.τ.λ.

We tend to foreshorten the religious struggle of the fourth century because we know its issue. To the pagans their cause could not have appeared finally lost: that is proved by the insurrection of Eugenius. There is a curiously modern ring about the pagan oracles which while exculpating Jesus made Peter responsible for the introduction, by magic arts, of the worship of Christ as God. That worship should utterly cease in 365 years from Pentecost (Augustine, *De Civitate Dei*, xviii, 53–4). When Symmachus wrote, the fated date has not been reached, the Battle of the Frigidus, that deadly blow to the paganism of the West, had not been fought. We know that the famine of 383, the year before the Senate's appeal, had been attributed to the confiscation of the property of the gods; some years later Augustine would not have begun the writing of the *De Civitate Dei* if a similar conviction had not been widely held. At times we fail to realize that the pagans could defend by argument their conviction that the new faith was contrary to the *mores* which had made Rome great. Celsus had feared for the Empire because of the danger of Christian pacifism; Volusianus, probably the son of that Publius Caeionius Caecina Albinus who appears in the *Saturnalia* of Macrobius, objected to Christianity 'quod eius praedicatio atque doctrina reipublicae moribus nulla ex parte conveniat'. Romans xii. 17, Matthew v. 39–41, are all 'reipublicae moribus contraria. Nam quis tolli sibi ab hoste aliquid patiatur, vel Romanae provinciae depraedatori non mala velit belli iure reponere?' Marcellinus in his letter asks Augustine to answer the objections of Volusianus and adds another objection which needs a reply—a point which Volusianus had not raised—that it was clear that 'per christianos principes christianam religionem maxima ex parte servantes tanta . . . reipublicae mala evenisse' (Augustine, *Ep.*, 136, § 2).

The religion of Symmachus was a *Roman* paganism: other Roman aristocrats might in their inscriptions record the priesthoods which they had held in eastern cults (G. Wissowa, *Religion und Kultus der Römer*, 2nd edn. (Munich, 1912), 98, n. 5); but in the inscription by which his son commemorated Symmachus no such priesthood is mentioned, only the fact that his father had been *pontifex maior* (*ILS.*, 2946, cf. Wytzes, op. cit., 31). In the works of Symmachus, as we possess them, it would seem that there is no reference to any oriental deity. Thus when famine threatened Rome it was to the gods of his own country that he appealed: 'dii patrii, facite gratiam neglectorum sacrorum! miseram famem pellite!' (*Ep.*, ii, 7, § 3). It was the festival of Minerva, *dea sobria*, that was remembered from his school-days (*Ep.*, v, 85, § 3). He took his duties as Pontifex very seriously: 'me impedit pontificalis officii cura' (*Ep.*, i, 47, § 1). He had intended to stay away from Rome, but he feels that when so many are neglecting their duties, he must not act by delegation: 'ad hoc sacri pontificalis administratio curam de me et officium stati mensis exigit. Neque enim fert animus in tanta sacerdotum negligentia sufficere collegam. fuerit haec olim simplex divinae rei delegatio: nunc aris deesse Romanos genus est ambiendi' (*Ep.*, i, 51)—a very interesting reference to those who found it profitable to disavow their faith. When his brother reminded him of a coming religious festival Symmachus protested: 'desine memorem commovere. notae nobis sunt caerimoniae deorum et festa divinitatis imperata' (*Ep.*, ii, 53)—'as if I should forget!' 'Nunc Vestalis festi gratia domum repeto', he writes to his brother (*Ep.*, ii, 59, § 1). He was anxious to be assured that the virgins dedicated to Vesta—*pudicum numen* (*Ep.*, ix, 148)—were keeping their vows, and when one Vestal had confessed her unchastity he pressed for the infliction of the supreme penalty. To this guardianship of tradition 'officio pontificis, fide senatoris admoneor' (*Ep.*, ix, 108, cf. viii, 6): 'restat ut in eos qui caerimonias publicas abominando scelere polluerunt legum severitas exeratur' (*Ep.*, ix, 147; cf. *Ep.*, ix, 148)—note *caerimonias publicas*—the defence of the State religion. He was distressed that prodigies had not been duly expiated by rites performed in the name of the State: 'angor animi quod . . . necdum publico nomine Spoletinum piatur ostentum' (*Ep.*, i, 49). The evidence is throughout consistent: it should be noted how when Symmachus is writing in praise of the citizens of Beneventum there slip in quite naturally the words 'deos magna pars veneratur' (*Ep.*, i, 3, § 4). 'Symmaque est un dévot' (Boissier in his review of Seeck's edition, *Journal des Savants*, (1888), 402–10, 597–609, 712–26, at p. 718); 'ein Hauch von Frömmigkeit durchzieht die ganze Briefsammlung' (Wytzes, op. cit., 29). Symmachus could with full conviction plead for the retention of the worship of the gods of Rome by the Roman State.

Thus it may be suggested that neither economic sacrifice nor class consciousness was the primary motive for the action of the Senate. It was natural for Ambrose to urge that Christian senators should not be compelled to be present at pagan sacrifices, but it was also natural that the aristocracy, which at that time was cultivating a wider interest in Roman history and Roman literature, should plead for the retention of rites which were deeply rooted in the Roman past. A worshipper of Mithras might boast that he needed no monies from the Roman State (*ILS.*, 4269, 'sumptusque tuos nec, Roma, requirit'), but Mithras was not a Roman god and therein lay the difference. The future, it is true, lay with Ambrose proclaiming a doctrine of progress through change (Johannes Geffcken, *Der Ausgang des griechisch-römischen Heidentums* (Heidelberg, 1920), 151–2), but as against ecclesiastical intolerance there was a catholic width of view in the plea of Symmachus: 'uno itinere non potest perveniri ad tam grande secretum' (*Rel.*, iii, § 10). And with that may be compared the profession of faith in a God, 'unus et universus, incomprehensibilis et ineffabilis', the 'infatigabilis Creator', made by another pagan: 'Via est in Deum melior qua vir bonus piis, puris, iustis, castis, veris dictis factisque sine ulla temporum mutatorum captata iactatione probatus et deorum comitatu vallatus . . . ire festinat. via est, inquam, qua purgati antiquorum sacrorum piis praeceptis, expiationibusque purissimis . . . anima et corpore constantes deproperant' (Augustine, *Ep.*, 234, § 2).[1]

---

[1] It would seem that no modern student has called attention to Symmachus' strange—and beautiful—use of the traditional 'pax deorum': 'quando Paulinae nostrae valetudinem rursus locavit in solido pax deorum' (*Ep.*, i, 48, and cf. *Ep.*, vii, 21).

XXXI

Athanasius

From a review of F. L. CROSS, *The Study of St Athanasius.*
Oxford, 1945.

[*Journal of Roman Studies*, xxxv (1945), pp. 121–4 at pp. 123–4.]

Dr Cross recognizes the need for a new biography of Athanasius, and with that view students of the history of the Empire
in the fourth century will agree. But if that new biography is
to serve its purpose truly it must fulfil certain conditions. It
must not be composed merely *in pios usus*: it is the 'hagiographical' character of much work on Athanasius which has by
reaction therefrom influenced modern work. Thus for Otto
Seeck Athanasius was primarily the accomplished forger of
documents: he began the practice in early years, it grew upon
him in middle life, until in old age it became second nature. If
the saint wanted to prove a point he sat down and created the
necessary document, just as Coke, if he could find no authority
wherewith to support his opinion, is said to have straightway
invented a Latin maxim on which to base his judgement. This
view is quite unjust to Athanasius: he was far too astute a controversialist to do anything so risky.[1] To Schwartz Athanasius
was always and in all circumstances the unbending hierarch;
ambition, a ruthless will, and a passion for power are his constant characteristics. But a papyrus has shown us a very different Athanasius debating with himself in hesitation and despondency whether he dare disobey the Emperor's summons to
a Council. No, this time he dare not: his luggage is put on board
ship; then he gains fresh heart—the luggage is brought ashore
—only in the end to obey the Emperor's behest. It is a very
human glimpse.[2] A modern essayist has passed judgement on
Athanasius: 'not one single generous action by him is re-

---

[1] For a discussion of one of these Athanasian 'forgeries' see *Journal of
Egyptian Archaeology*, xi (1925), pp. 61–5; reprinted, *supra* pp. 282–7.
[2] H. I. Bell, *Jews and Christians in Egypt* (British Museum, 1924), Pap. 1914,
53 sqq.

corded',[3] but Dr Bell has urged in extenuation that with old age Athanasius mellowed: after the fall of Pope Liberius and of Hosius he could still treat them with respect. When this new biography comes to be written it will be remembered that it is not easy for the modern reader to be attracted by Athanasius; presumably he was a Greek, say the books, but still one wonders: he had all the passionate intransigence of the Copt with whom he could always find a secure hiding-place. He was a persecutor and a man of violence who was always complaining of the violence of others. That the creed presented by Arius after his condemnation by the Council of Nicaea was orthodox Athanasius might be constrained to admit, but he refused to accept him into communion; the rigorously orthodox Melitians ὁπωσδήποτε—Heaven alone knew how!—were reconciled at Nicaea, but Athanasius always regretted that reconciliation, and it was only on an appeal to the Emperor that the Melitians were given the right to meet in peace. If we only possessed an account of the tempestuous Odyssey of Athanasius when he returned from his first exile it would be a remarkable story: by what authority did he eject bishops from their sees? Is there any reason to think that a provincial council was summoned before action was taken? And, further, this new biography will not do Athanasius the injustice of treating his 'apologies' as though they were intended to be works of history. They are, of course, the briefs of one who might have been an ornament of the Roman bar, and in common fairness to their author they should be treated as such. And then we can make allowances for the ecclesiastical Billingsgate, the bitter vituperation, which it might otherwise be difficult to excuse. This is in the tradition of ancient advocacy: Demosthenes and Cicero would have comprehended Athanasius better than have many modern commentators.

And if Athanasius is to be put in the setting of his age this new biography cannot begin with Athanasius; it must reach back into the third century and show how a policy of conciliation was drawing together into alliance Christian Church and pagan State. That process of unification was rudely inter-

[3] E. M. Forster, *Pharos and Pharillon*, 3rd edn. (London, Hogarth Press, 1926), p. 49.

rupted by the persecution set on foot by Galerius. But, the persecution ended, the same process was resumed forthwith, but this time under a Christian emperor. Constantine in the West had looked to Rome as the representative centre of the Catholic Church: Miltiades was called upon to act as judge in the schism caused by the Donatists. Arrived in the East the Emperor looked to Alexandria as the source of a unified faith, and found instead the Arian controversy. An oecumenical council should put its seal upon a unified empire. There has been much debate concerning the origin of the Homoousion: whence came it? Eusebius of Nicomedia had written, according to Ambrose, De Fide, iii, 15, § 125, 'Si verum Dei Filium et increatum dicimus ὁμοούσιον cum Patre incipimus confiteri'. A Greek bishop had brought the word into the debate.[4] What was Constantine's policy? Why did he press upon the bishops assembled at Nicaea the acceptance of the Homoousion? It might be suggested that the ὁμοούσιον was chosen because not only would it satisfy the orthodox vanguard, but it could also, *if its meaning were not further defined*, be accepted by subordinationists of the school of Origen: cf. Origen, *Selecta in Psalm.* (Lomm., xiii, p. 134), ὁ σωτὴρ οὐ κατὰ μετουσίαν ἀλλά κατ' οὐσίαν ἐστὶ θεός. 'Hieraus folgt dass er das Wesen Gottes, also des Vaters mitbesitzt und demnach ὁμοούσιος τῷ πατρί ist' (Harnack, *Dogmengeschichte*, 4th edn., i, 671; Matthias Weis, *Die Stellung des Eusebius von Cäsarea im arianischen Streit*, Dissertation, Freiburg im Breisgau (no year, but preface dated November 1919) p. 64). This is surely the significance of the passage quoted from Eustathius of Antioch by Theodoret: 'Some at the Council craftily (ἐκ συσκευῆς) under the pretext of establishing peace silenced all those who were accustomed to speak to the best purpose' (Theodoret, i, 8, 3, ed. Parmentier, 34). The word had gone round from the Emperor, and the orthodox refrained from setting forth their case so that the Origenists could give their assent to the creed of the Council, trusting the Emperor that he would allow them a liberal interpretation of the crucial word. The bishops thus continued the policy of co-operation with the State which had marked the

[4] Cf. G. Bardy, *Recherches sur Saint Lucien d'Antioche et son École* (Paris, Beauchesne, 1936), pp. 305–6.

period before the persecution, the policy which received its theological justification in the writings of Eusebius of Caesarea. It is in opposition to that policy that Athanasius takes his stand: he is the first great Egyptian non-co-operator, the man who initiated the tradition of the opposition of the church of St Mark to the upstart see of Constantinople. Constantine, when his policy had carried the day at Nicaea, loyally observed the tacit understanding: it was only in Egypt that Athanasius continued to create disturbances until the Emperor, losing patience with the refractory bishop, banished him to Trier while showing his magnanimity and statesmanship by leaving the patriarchal see vacant until such time as Athanasius should have repented of his intransigence. It is important to realize the contrast between Egypt and the rest of the Empire.[5]

And for this biography Dr Bell has already provided the model in an admirable sketch of the life of Athanasius[6] which, it may be feared, is not so well known as it should be. And if Athanasius is painted, warts and all, then it will be easy to bring into high relief his historical significance. It was he who challenged the policy of inclusion which was the aim of Constantine and of Eusebius of Nicomedia: it was he who more than any other man imposed *one* interpretation only upon the Homoousion: it was he who through his splendid masterpiece —the *Life of Antony*—first gave literary expression to the ideals of monasticism, while it was a Latin translation of that masterpiece which inspired the West with a passion for the life of asceticism. Though Athanasius will hardly awake the affection of the modern student, yet to his iron resolution, to the confidence and courage which rarely failed him, we can at least pay the tribute of our admiration and respect.

[5] Cf. K. F. Hagel, *Kirche und Kaisertum in Lehre und Leben des Athanasius.* Dissertation (Tübingen, 1933).
[6] 'Athanasius: A Chapter in Church History', *Congregational Quarterly* (1925), no. 2, pp. 158–76.

APPENDIX

The Custody of a Tradition

[A Foundation Address delivered to the members of University College, London, at Bangor on 13 March 1942. Privately printed.]

MISS ORR, fellow-students, this is for me a proud occasion. To the students of University College, London, gathered here in Bangor, would I first of all express my very sincere gratitude for their invitation to deliver this Foundation Address. Never in my most exalted moments had I dreamed of such a distinction, for speakers at your Foundation celebrations have been men whose noise had gone forth into the world, while of my name the world still remains in an ignorance which could not well be more complete. And for this generosity, this daring breach with customary observance, I am especially grateful since this address is also my swan song: within a few months my academic career comes to its close: the axe falls. *Moriturus vos saluto.* And if you will allow me, I should like to take this opportunity of re-assuring my colleagues on the staff of University College: they need have no fears. When I retire, in September of this year, from academic life, I shall retire not in word only but in physical corporeal fact. I shall not continue to haunt the College like a wan ghost, unhouselled and unaneled. I am firmly convinced that retirement should mean what it says, and that meaning should not be circumvented by any specious subterfuges. We academic folk should never for a moment be encouraged in the facile persuasion that we are indispensable. So here I stand on the brink of my academic demise, and if I seem to hesitate, if on close inspection you notice a slight convulsive shudder despite my rigorous determination to face my passing without a lapse in muscular control, you will, I feel confident, temper your scorn with pity and allow me—it is asking a great deal I know —allow me a parenthetical moment of self-disclosure. If the mouths of the academically dead are doomed to an unbroken silence, the tongue of the academically moribund may perhaps be permitted to wag in a garrulity which recognizes the now-or never-ness of its opportunity. As I look back on my life there is, I must confess, little to give me any cause for satisfaction, but when everything else fails me I shall still hold firmly to my confidence that on three occasions I made the right choice, though at the time it was no easy matter to decide between the alternatives set before me. In the first place when a Liberal Party whip asked me if I would contest one of two seats in the London area I had to make my choice between politics and education, for I believe that either education or politics is a whole-time job and that the 24-hour day, when one has sub-tracted the hours claimed by the body for sleep—which in my case meant six hours, an effort to reduce the period to five hav-ing proved unsuccessful—the 24-hour day is not long enough for one effectively to play one's part both in the House of Commons and in the University. That, I may say, is still my belief. On that occasion I turned my back on politics and made up my mind that if I could do anything at all it must be in teaching that my work would lie. Yet I believe that to take part in a political campaign, to learn to present your argu-ments in different forms to different audiences, to keep the thread of an argument firmly in your hand despite raucous and unflagging intervention from your audience—all this is excel-lent training for the academic life. It is not in the university alone that the young academic teacher should serve his appren-ticeship. If I may speak from personal experience, it is on the upturned tea-chest at the street corner in front of his local public-house—the *local* public-house, mark you, where natur-ally he will be well known—that the young academic teacher will be given some of his most valuable lessons. And then dur-ing the last Great War I made my second choice: I determined to abandon the teaching and the practice of the law and to devote myself to the teaching of history. I came to the Evening School of History at University College—my salary £40 a year. I think friends regarded me with grave concern: was it war-strain or bomb-shock?—the ceiling of the chambers where I worked in Lincoln's Inn had come down, though I was absent at the time. It was after all only natural that they should have such doubts; but for me it was the right decision, and the responsibility for the consequent sufferings of students does not rest with me: it lies on the shoulders of those who appointed me. And then, when the War was over, my own college asked me to go back to Oxford as a teacher of history: after considerable hesitation I declined that invitation and decided to stay and work in Gower Street: and once again I was right in my decision. And that is why by your courtesy and kindness I am singing this swan-song—so improbably—in Bangor this evening. I would assure you that it is no little comfort to be able to throw those three choices into the scale which is so heavily counterbalanced by the mistakes and follies which have made up so much of my life.

That is why, too, I thought of giving to my remarks as alliterative title 'The Valediction of a Victorian, or the Indiscretions of an Individualist'. Ultimately I concluded that that would be too tell-tale a heading—it would give too much away; for indeed I remain to-day a child of the nineteenth century: at times I feel rather like a stranded jellyfish left high and dry by a receding wave: and the wonder is that during my years at University College some students have in their largeness of heart accepted me just as I was—a period piece—and have given to an anachronism their friendship. And if you ever try yourselves to do that you will find how difficult it is—what calls upon your forbearance the task entails. But University College students have done that thing on my behalf: and that fact I do not forget. At least as a child of the nineteenth century, I am not so far away from the understanding of what University College has stood for as I might otherwise have been, and since I do profoundly sympathize with much of that which has been representative of the spirit of the College in the past I preferred to suggest to Miss Orr that I should speak on 'The Custody of a Tradition'. And my remarks shall be brief: they have been put together in the midst of an attempt to produce a terse account of the local government of Germany—and that you will realize is no light task. Continually when I tried to concentrate my thoughts on University College the Prussian *Landrat* would poke his head round the door and enquire in tones of exasperation whether I had by now discovered

his precise relation to the *Regierungspräsident*, only to be met
by a querulous confession of failure. It is to the persistence of
the Prussian *Landrat* that you in your generosity will attribute
some at least of the inconsequences of this address.

'The Custody of a Tradition': That may perhaps provide an
answer to a problem: a problem which you see arises in this
way: Why is it that you as students of the University of London are here on the coasts of Cambria at this time? Of course
you thereby escape the perils of life in London: when the project of establishing a University in London was being discussed
in the twenties of the last century it was objected that 'to
educate youth in the metropolis was to court their physical
decline and their moral ruin'. Set amidst the innocency of
Wales you certainly avoid that danger. But it was not of that
escape that I was thinking: The problem of which I was thinking was rather: in a country at war, when an effort is being
made to mobilize all the available resources of the kingdom,
why is it that while you pursue your studies here you are immune from the general compulsion? And to that question one
answer at least would be that you are in training for the preservation of a tradition, you are being prepared to play your
part as the custodians of that tradition. This college, housed
in partibus by the courtesy of your Cambrian hosts, is indeed
your spiritual O.C.T.U. You are already mobilized for future
battle. And if there is any truth in this answer it cannot be out
of place to consider for a few minutes some aspects of that
tradition which it will be your task in the future to defend.

And if you cast your minds back to the years when the University of London was coming into being you will recall that
its foundation was a response to a social challenge. The Indus-
trial Revolution had brought into existence new types of men
with fresh needs for which the older universities made no provision. 'The history of the foundation of the University of
London', Professor Bellot has said, 'is but a paragraph in the
story of that change in the intellectual, social, political and
economic structure of public life which came about between
the American Revolution and the Reform Bill.' As Professor
Hearnshaw has written in his History of King's College: 'In
the reign of George IV the only two universities in England

were on the one hand the close preserves of the Anglican Church and on the other hand were capable of providing little education that was of any use to anyone except a prospective clergyman who wished to give his congregation the benefit of original translations of the Greek Testament, or a budding member of Parliament who wished (as was then expected) to sprinkle his orations with gems from the Latin poets.' Existing universities as finishing schools for the upper classes did not meet the needs of newly-created classes, did not supply the teaching of the rapidly developing scientific subjects. Men felt that 'a different and a better furniture of mind was requisite to be brought into the business of life'. A schooling for the life of action—a new realism—this was the demand and the challenge of a new age, and it was the founders of the University of London who took up the gage. They did not seek to plant their foundation in the sequestered peace of the countryside: the Cockney University should be set within the reach of Cockneys. In the Statement issued before the University was opened to the public it was said: 'By the formation of an University in this metropolis the useful intercourse of theory with active life will be facilitated.' Our founders were the Lord Nuffields of their day.

What the situation will be when this war shall have come to an end none can say: what reactions that situation may have upon our university life is equally obscure; but one thing is certain: the universities of this country will best meet that situation and the challenge of a post-war world if they are animated by the same courage as that with which our founders looked their new problems in the face and did not seek to run away from them. For university life may not infrequently encourage a spirit of escapism, an absorption in familiar studies, which can absolve the teacher and the researcher from considering awkward facts and unwelcome demands—until his peace is disturbed from without by a Royal Commission. It is the clear-eyed recognition of needs which were nowhere receiving an adequate response and the determined resolution to fill that vacuum which our founders have left to us as their legacy; there was no escapism in their outlook on their world.

And one may regard their choice of site—a melancholy and obscene morass—as a symbol of their resolute realism. On the confirmation of the purchase of that site the paper *John Bull* wrote: 'what were called the minutes were then read which occupied more than an hour: in which the Committee stated that having by a careful study of Mercator's chart and other authentic documents, together with a series of lunar observations, discovered a large space of mud and nastiness lying near the end of Gower Street bounded on the north by the New Road, on the south by St Giles's, on the west by Carmarthen Street and on the east by a stagnant pond, they had purchased the said 'unknown tract of dirt for thirty thousand pounds.' And on that unknown tract of dirt was in time raised one of the finest fronts to a building which can be found anywhere in London. The sting was thereby drawn from Barham's poem 'Stinkomalee Triumphans'. If the present generation can transform its spaces of mud and nastiness in like fashion it will have learned to some purpose the lesson taught by the founders of our College.

And of course the outstanding characteristic of the new foundation was to be intellectual liberty, its freedom from religious tests. That basis on which the new University was to be founded was in the first quarter of the nineteenth century a really revolutionary standpoint, and the outstanding characteristic of the England of the nineteenth century was perhaps the triumph of this conception of the freedom of thought as the necessary condition of that progress which to the men and women of that day seemed to be assured. That was the thought-world into which I was born. As against the claims of authority, whether that authority were a State or a Church, the individual possessed an inalienable right to self-expression, a right which was but reflected in the freedom of the Press. It must be impossible for you to realize how natural, how inevitable, that right appeared to the ordinary Englishman of the eighteen-nineties. The recognition of that right had been won at the cost of long struggle, but won it had been, and the victory was now unquestioned and secure. The right was gained: the only question which remained open was whether men would have the courage to make full use of the right, whether, despite their right, they might not prefer the easy path of conformity with general opinion. There was a Victorian hymn, of which probably none of you has ever heard, of which the refrain was:

> Dare to be a Daniel,
> Dare to stand alone,
> Dare to have a purpose true
> And dare to make it known.

It was my own favourite when as a child I chose my hymn after tea on Sundays. It is a clear statement not only of a Christian's purpose, but also of the purpose of the Victorian individualist. And yet, as it seems to me, the folk of the generation into which I was born made two serious mistakes. For in the first place the right of intellectual freedom inevitably carries with it an obligation—the corollary of the right is the duty of self-determination, the burden of making your own choices, the heavy responsibility of taking charge of your own actions: and people forgot that when once the ordered progress, which then seemed so assured, was menaced, and much more when that ordered progress had given place to a world of disorder, that responsibility might become too heavy to be borne and men would seek refuge from an intolerable burden. They would jettison rights in order to lighten the foundering ship of their storm-tossed lives. Some of you may have read a recent book *I Was a Nazi Flier* by Gottfried Leske, written by him when a prisoner of war in Canada. In that book a letter is quoted which he sent to a friend and in it he said: 'I think everything you write about democracy is just phrases. What is liberty anyhow? I for one have always found that it is much easier if someone tells you what you have to do. Then you know what you have got to do. I don't know whether I make myself clear. The point is: where would we be if everybody in the world were to make his own life? We don't know what's good for us. The Führer [cut by censor]. Don't misunderstand me. I don't only mean that it's better for the whole nation when one man decides. It's also better for each of us. It's easier to do a job if you are told what to do than to figure it out for yourself.' Just because that letter is expressed so simply, with such sincerity, it seems to me a very illuminating document. You don't want human *Grundrechte*, fundamental rights of the individual, such as were formulated in Republican Germany by the Weimar Constitution—they are too expensive, too burdensome a luxury in the modern world. The folk of my generation never, I fancy, contemplated such a refusal. And what of modern England? How far has an ever-expanding bureaucracy already undermined the sturdy individualism of the ordinary Englishman? Graham Wallas, wishing to illustrate the difference in outlook between the England of the nineteenth and the England of the twentieth century, put it thus: faced by some obvious abuse, the reaction of the nineteenth-century Englishman was: 'This is intolerable: *I* must see that it is stopped': the reaction of the twentieth-century Englishman: 'This is intolerable: really *they* ought to put a stop to this.' Are the rights claimed by the Englishman of the nineteenth century too heavy to be borne? That question nineteenth-century England never thought to ask itself. And its second mistake surely was that it thought that a victory once won was secure for all time: that it needed no continuous, no passionate defence. 'There is no such thing as a gained cause,' says Aldous Huxley in one of his essays: I quote from memory, for I cannot recall where the remark occurs: 'for every cause must be fought for again and again.' We are beginning to realize afresh that each victory of the human spirit must be appropriated, must be made distinctively its own, by every succeeding generation if it is not to slip through the hands and be lost. And every victory must be re-asserted in the language of each succeeding generation: a platitude is generally a truth clad in the fashions of yesterday: the platitude has but to go to a good tailor and to procure modern raiment and it becomes what it was at the outset—a truth, and then its life and its cogency are renewed. The academic mind, as Hitler, the master propagandist, has said, is mortally afraid of becoming platitudinous: the politician and the advertiser must both comprehend the force of relentless repetition. The value of the victory won, the peril of ineffective guardianship of that victory, must be constantly kept before the mind.

And in Europe of to-day what remains of that nineteenth-century liberty of self-expression? It has not only been inadvertently mislaid, it has been passionately repudiated. I am

simply a teacher, and as a teacher I am baffled by this acceptance of dictation. For the one thing of real worth which a
teacher can bring to his self-chosen task is any little gift of
personality which may have been given him—or her. And if
what we are to say and *how* it must be said are completely and
finally determined for us from above, by the State, by the
Powers that be, then the justification for our existence is taken
from us: we are but parasites on the body politic, and a
gramophone would be much less expensive. And thus to me,
Fascist, National Socialist and Communist, all alike, appear as
hostile forces if it is sought to introduce them into this England
of ours so long as they claim that one *Weltanschauung* and one
Weltanschauung alone can be allowed expression. All three of
them appear to me to be alien to the spirit of England; have I
not confessed that I am an anachronism? But if there be any
truth in what I have been trying to express, it is surely even
more true of the world of the University. A prominent National
Socialist has said: 'I do not mind freedom of thought in the
least provided I can control what facts go into the mind—a
logical mind must then draw the right conclusions, the conclusions I want, and its workings need not be feared.' The authoritative statement of the attitude of the Third Reich toward
'Wissenschaft'—knowledge, science, is to be found in the
speeches of Rust, the Minister for Education, and of Krieck,
the principal educational theorist of National Socialist Germany,
delivered at the celebration of the 550th anniversary of the
founding of the University of Heidelberg: Rust dismissed the
whole conception of the absence of presuppositions in research,
all objectivity, as false, and Krieck affirmed: 'we recognize no
truth for truth's sake, no "Wissenschaft" for "Wissenschaft's"
sake.' It needed a formal official pronouncement by Rosenberg,
published under the heading 'Freedom of Research' (*Freiheit
der Forschung*) in the *Nationalsozialistische Monatschrifte* in
1938, to assure scholars that in 'Kosmophysics', experimental
chemistry and prehistoric geology the Party had no 'weltan-
schauliche dogmatische Haltung'—in its view of the universe
the Party had adopted no dogmatic position on these subjects.
In these spheres the way was clear. Could one have done better
had one desired to parody the National Socialist attitude? Here

in this sphere of *Wissenschaft* University College, London, derives from its founders a clear tradition, and that tradition has, so far as I know, remained unbroken. You are now receiving that legacy and enjoying the liberty of that tradition: it may well be that in the near future that tradition may be seriously, vitally challenged. Your time within that atmosphere of liberty whose home has been in Gower Street should constrain you hereafter, if the challenge is launched, to abandon neutrality in a matter of such primary significance. You may, of course, support the challenge: I may for my part, however, be allowed to hope that you will not do so, that on the contrary you will prefer to stand forth as custodians of the tradition which is the legacy of our founders. A University set in England, which in this our day should do otherwise, would at least be a denial of a remarkable past. 'You must fuse your wills with mine': that is Hitler's claim: as students of the University of London will you be content humbly and submissively to bow to that demand if it comes from an English Government? Will you yourselves make such a demand of your Professors? In Marburg Professor Manigk, Professor of Law, holding since 1927 the chair once occupied by Savigny, one of Germany's greatest jurists, when comparing Roman law with the present law of Germany, had said: 'one of the roots of the political idea which dominates us to-day comes from outside Germany— there is *eine ausserdeutsche Wurzel.*' This denial of the complete originality of the National Socialist conception led to a demonstration by the students at the Professor's lecture when Professor Manigk 'sought to defend himself'. Choruses of students then gave a performance outside the Professor's house and outside the University. The Student-Leader delivered a speech in the market-place of Marburg, and the students sent to the Minister for Education a demand for the instant dismissal of Professor Manigk. This report, which I have translated from the *Frankfurter Zeitung,* was published without comment: *Freiheit der Forschung*? Freedom of Research?

When in 1933 the National Socialists organized all students in German universities in *Studentenschaften,* it was stated that an important function of the new bodies would be the boycotting of professors whose political orthodoxy was suspect. As

students you may feel that this leaves you with withers un-
wrung. But at the same time it was declared to be the duty of
the newly-formed *Studentenschaften* to exclude from their
membership any student who did not wholeheartedly profess
belief in the *Weltanschauung* of the National Socialist Party,
and exclusion from the *Studentenschaft* carried with it exclusion from the University. Is that the kind of freedom which
you as students desire? At the heart of the tradition of University College there has been in fact the spirit of the pioneer, and
the originality of the pioneer can be measured by the reaction
initiated by his action. It was the foundation of the 'godless'
University in Gower Street which led to the creation of King's
College. *John Bull* believed that 'by the institution of King's
College the finishing blow has been given to the style of in-
fidelity now building at the end of Gower Street. Public indig-
nation has at length been roused and the greatest and best
amongst us have rallied round the altar and the throne in
order to protect them from the destructive influence of an
infidel rabble who are to be educated according to the rules of
modern philosophy in perfect darkness as to the duties they
owe to their God and their King'. That violence of the High
Tory journal is itself a tribute to the courage of the initiative
of our founders. The hostility between the two colleges is now
largely a matter of ancient history: its reflection in the tradition is the historic feud between the students of the two
colleges. That feud cannot be successfully waged between
Bristol and Bangor, but when I was in Bristol recently I
learned that the students of King's College still preserve the
spirit of that time-honoured rivalry: it is ready to spring into
active life so soon as the two Cockney colleges shall have
returned to the metropolis. The Battle of the Mascots must
await that day for its renewal.

And the most revolutionary of the decisions reached by the
pioneering spirit in our history was the opening of the College
to women in 1878. But even a pioneer may have his battle with
prepossessions: there are hesitations which must first be overcome. Before that revolutionary step was taken caution had
been the order of the day. For some years previously the lecturers of the College had been allowed to use the College

premises for lectures delivered under the control of the London Ladies' Educational Association. For those lectures the College was not responsible, but of their danger they were profoundly conscious: for the tender morals of their male students they were intensely anxious: the women's classes met and separated at the half-hours so that the men might be safely occupied both at the coming and at the departure of the fair, while the women were admitted by a side door to avoid the risks of crossing the front quadrangle. But in the end the adventurous daring of the pioneer triumphed over discretion. And still to-day it is not every English university which has admitted women students on an equality with men. Women students are still presumably carriers of emotional and spiritual dynamite. In London at University College I presume that the women students have come to stay, and are thus part of the tradition. Some may even now wish them away: one of my own students told me, if I remember aright, that only once during his three years at College had he spoken to a woman student, and that was when the audacious hussy had first addressed him. His view was that men and women students could attend the same college, provided that in social intercourse a complete segregation was rigidly enforced. I do not know to what extent his opinion is still represented in the student body. Of course, you run risks: it would appear that at times Eros leaves his airy post in Piccadilly Circus and visits Gower Street: and if that visit should happen to occur in the second or third term of a student's third year in College it may on occasion be responsible for regrettable consequences in the Final Examination: but the victims are rarely heard to complain. And I for one would here, too, cast my vote in favour of safeguarding the tradition.

And University College has from the first been catholic: it has opened its doors to all creeds and to all races. Orthodox Jew, Jesuit, or infidel: Christian or sceptic, they have sat side by side in the same lecture-room. And to us this seems only a matter of course: yet there is but little territory in Europe where that rule holds to-day. And once again I feel that we need from time to time consciously to re-affirm that principle of catholicity. We look out upon the Anti-Semitism of other lands and we comfort ourselves with the soothing thought:

'That could never happen here.' But have we any right to be so sure of that? There are British Fascists who are prepared to inflame hostility against the Jews, and there will be many who will listen. Have you read the reports of the situation in the East End of London published in the papers of the Society of Jews and Christians? One feels there is a lot of gunpowder lying about. And the conduct of alien Jews in this country—if Oxford provides a fair sample—does not help: there are many in Oxford to-day who will tell you that Hitler in his Anti-Semitic policy has provided a model for others to follow. I have an uncomfortable feeling that a wave of Anti-Semitism in this country might be called up at short notice, without insuperable difficulty. And then the question will arise: are we in earnest about our protestations that racialism is no part of our creed? Unless we are consciously prepared beforehand to take our stand and immediately to make our opinion known—students and staff—we may find that an animosity encouraged by able propaganda has outstripped us and that we have come too late to the defence of our tradition. I hope my vision of what *may* happen is an idle fear, but it will do us no harm to be forearmed.

I desire, however, to play the game fairly with you and not to burke uncomfortable facts: there is another aspect of the tradition of the College: the system of teaching was based from the first on lectures—an importation, I believe, from Scotland. Indeed the *Edinburgh Review*—I quote Professor Bellot once again—drew attention to the zeal of the professors at the new University and to the prospect that at the University you would get more lectures for your money than at any other establishment. It is recorded that W. B. Carpenter, when a student, attended thirty-five lectures a week, while Cambridge dubbed the University a lecture bazaar. You remember doubtless Dr Johnson's opinion of lectures: 'People have nowadays (said he) got a strange opinion that everything should be taught by lectures. Now I cannot see that lectures can do so much good as reading the books from which the lectures are taken. I know nothing that can be best taught by lectures except where experiments are to be shewn.' I gather that many students would support Dr Johnson's view. They would, if I understand them aright, desire to have in their hands brief printed analyses or précis which might relieve them from the necessity of attending the lectures. But I wonder if they are right. I am quite prepared to admit that many a learned don has failed to realize that lecturing is an art: that it is not enough to hurl material, however good that material may be, in undigested and indigestible lumps at the heads of students; but if a don has learned that half at least of the time spent on the preparation of a lecture may well be devoted to the problem of presentation, then the personality of the lecturer, his living interest in his theme, will give to the student something which no bald printed summary could ever supply. Long after the facts have passed from the memory, the lecturer's individuality may remain as an enrichment of one's own experience—it may even be as an inspiration. And as to reading the books from which the lectures are taken, what if those books are in German—not at all times the most pellucid of languages—may not an interpreter perform a useful function? Some discrimination is needed, I feel, before you reject a time-honoured tradition root and branch. Two modifications of the tradition I should like to see introduced: in the first place that on appointment greater weight should be attached to the capacity of the candidate as a teacher and lecturer—that might carry with it the corollary that there should be further endowments for pure research with no teaching duties attached to such endowments: this would create the needed economic basis for researchers: the nation would not lose the benefits to be derived from a man's original genius, while students would no longer be afflicted by those who regard them merely as a necessary but disagreeable adjunct to an appointment which interests its holder only as providing the means for pursuing his own studies. And in the second place, it is clear that there are those who positively enjoy lecturing: this may well be regarded as merely an amiable eccentricity, provided only that no one is constrained against his will to listen to them. I, for my part, would put no check upon their activity, but I would completely abolish the present system of the 'signing up' of students and of attendance registers. All attendance at lectures throughout a student's career should be voluntary, and the effect of this liberation of the student upon the lecturer himself would in my judgement be only salutary: deprived of artificial support by his lectures he would stand or fall, and the better the lecturer the more readily would he accept the challenge. And at the same time some lecturers might learn more rapidly than under the present system that they had in fact mistaken their vocation. Thus modified, I believe the system would commend itself to students so that in the future they might be prepared to act as custodians of even this part of the College tradition.

And I have left to the last one aspect of the tradition which at this time would appear to me to be of special significance, and that is the community life as it is lived in a University. For the last two years and more I have been engaged on a study of National Socialist Germany and on a translation of extracts from Hitler's speeches, and it is in the light of that experience that I want to say a few words this evening. The opportunity must not be missed.

I have naturally been forced to consider conditions in Germany at the close of the last Great War and particularly in Bavaria before Hitler's 'Putsch' of 1923. And one cannot but be struck by the contrast between the sweet reasonableness of the Weimar Constitution with its extreme liberalism and its elaborate safeguards for the individual, and on the other hand the violence and despair of the demobilized soldiers, so many of whom had served but one apprenticeship, had learned but a single trade—the apprenticeship to war, the trade of fighting. They were launched on a world which had no use for them —and that is man's supreme tragedy—human flotsam and jetsam tossed hither and thither by circumstance which they were powerless to control. In the war they had been members of a community which was at times something more than a community of suffering. But with demobilization that community had been shattered: men were but particles lonely and unattached. That community of the trenches where differences of class, of religion and of party had disappeared since all alike were subject to one iron compulsion—that background must always be kept in mind if one would seek to understand with any sympathy the early days of the National Socialist Movement. For Hitler himself knew what the loss of that *Gemein-schaft*, of that community, meant. Leaning in utter exhaustion against the doorpost of the Gasthaus in Munich, he had been found there by Dietrich Eckart and taken home and given food and drink. Perhaps there is only one personal tie to which Hitler has been consistently loyal, the memory of the homo-sexual, drug-obsessed poet, Dietrich Eckart, who one even-ing in Munich befriended the 'nameless soldier'. And for men whose world had crumbled beneath their feet where was there room for that confidence in human reasonableness which in-spires the Weimar Constitution? Reason, thought—that way lay madness and despair: they sought relief in emotion, in violence, in passionate activity. What could liberty mean to them?—except perhaps the liberty to commit suicide. What they craved was the sense that they belonged, they sought some association with their fellows, even if it were only an association in fighting—the one trade which they had really mastered. And that *Gemeinschaft*—that sense of belonging, of comradeship, they found in the National Socialist Movement. In those early days Hitler declared that what the Party was seeking was to transfer into the period of peace that *Gemein-schaft* of the war which had known no distinctions of party, creed or class. That vision of a new community which might in time grow into a *Volksgemeinschaft*—a community of the whole German people, was, I am persuaded, in those days in Munich before the 'Putsch' a very genuine emotion, there was in it a true idealism.

And in England the end of the four years of warfare was to have seen such great changes, the world was to have been made safe for democracy: yet when the end of the war came change was so slow, things went on so much as they had gone on before ever the war came, that youth's hope was mocked and dis-illusionment and bitterness took its place. You know that bitterness and disillusionment from the post-war literature. For change is so difficult a thing to compass in the face of powerful interests which have good reason to be quite content with things as they are, and patience is so hard a virtue: it needs to be sustained by so resolute a passion, by so unfaltering a will, it makes such great demands on human persistence that men's hearts fail them and they cease their striving.

And you ask me why on a festal occasion like the present I have brought this mournful picture to your remembrance: I would answer that I do so only because it is so desperately important that it should not happen again. Priestley, borrowing the National Socialist terminology, has spoken of the new community which shall arise in England after the war. When he speaks, the establishment of that community seems a natural, almost inevitable result of the present conflict. But that is an illusion: it will be a matter of immense difficulty, I cannot help thinking. And as it was in the years after 1918, discouragement and bitterness may lurk in the doorway and force their entry. It will be only those who know something of the meaning of a community, of a life shared in common, who are profoundly convinced of its fundamental worth, who will be able to persist in their resolution, able to master disappointment and to remind themselves that disillusionment and bitterness never constructed anything which could permanently benefit the life of man. Only a passionate conviction that there must not be another failure such as the last will avail before the vastness of the task which will be the war's legacy.

In the life of a University, students are initiated into a community and can learn the meaning of intimate contact with their fellows. The don may do something for the student, at least when I am in a mood of unreasoning optimism that is my hope—but it is very certain, I can vouch for it by my own experience, that most of the benefit comes from a student's intercourse with fellow-students. That is a University's best gift. And that tradition of Life in community you are preserving; it will be ready for those who are now on military service when they return; but more than that: it should have convinced you yourselves of the value of the sense of belonging, of being knit together with others. And that consciousness should steel your resolution not to surrender to disillusionment and dismay when in the period of reconstruction things obstinately refuse to go aright. Your task will be to carry into the peace the lessons which you have learned in the University during the war. Then indeed in the fullest sense you will be playing the part of the custodians of a tradition. Where my generation failed you may succeed: and for that most splendid of adventures I wish you God-speed.

And perhaps you may be able to do something more even than that. There is a problem which haunts me—the problem of that German youth whose only faith is National Socialism: when National Socialism is overthrown, what of German youth? Will it be able to find its way into a *Gemeinschaft* which it will share with the youth of other nations from contact with which it has been so sedulously excluded?—It is idle to attempt to disguise the magnitude of the problems which will cry aloud for solution: for a solution in which you will have your part to play.

I said at the outset of these remarks that your presence here *in partibus* on the coasts of Cambria raised a problem: how could your presence be justified? And my answer to that question is unhesitating: it is essential that the succession of those who can appreciate that tradition which is our England should be unbroken, and a not unimportant part of that tradition is bound up with the freedom of our modern university life, that freedom in which University College was a pioneer. It is when our possessions are menaced that we realize most fully their value. May you enjoy to the full, appropriate, make in a very true sense your own this your life in College: a Cockney student who is about to be discharged from service salutes his Cockney fellow-students and would wish each and all *Bon Voyage*. It is with very real gratitude that I recall all that students have given to me through the years: quite simply: Thank you.

INDEX